THE COGNITIVE
PSYCHOLOGY
OF SCHOOL
LEARNING

THE COGNITIVE PSYCHOLOGY OF SCHOOL LEARNING

Ellen D. Gagné

THE UNIVERSITY OF TEXAS AT AUSTIN

Little, Brown and Company

BOSTON   TORONTO

This book is dedicated to my husband, William Davis,
and my parents, Robert and Harriet Gagné

Library of Congress Cataloging in Publication Data

Gagné, Ellen D.
  The cognitive psychology of school learning.

  Bibliography: p.
  Includes index.
  1. Learning.   2. Cognition in children.   3. Learning,
Psychology of.   I. Title.
LB1060.G34   1985   370.15′2   84–20083
ISBN 0–316–30165–5

Copyright © 1985 by Ellen D. Gagné

Library of Congress Catalog Card Number 84–20083

ISBN 0–316–30165–5

9 8 7 6 5 4 3

MV

Published simultaneously in Canada
by Little, Brown & Company (Canada) Limited

Printed in the United States of America

Acknowledgments

Figure 2–1. From Robert M. Gagne, *Essentials of Learning for Instruction.* Copyright © 1974 by The Dryden Press. Reprinted by permission of The Dryden Press, CBS College Publishing.

Figure 2–2. From Roberta L. Klatzky, *Human Memory: Structures and Processes,* first edition. Copyright © 1975 by W. H. Freeman and Company. Reprinted by permission.

Table 2–2. From W. K. Estes, ''Is Human Memory Obsolete?'' *American Scientist,* 1980, vol. 68. Reprinted by permission.

Figure 2–4. Adapted from D. E. Rumelhart and D. A. Norman, ''Analogical Processes in Learning'' *Cognitive Skills and their Acquisition,* edited by J. R. Anderson (Lawrence Erlbaum Associates, Hillsdale, NJ). Reprinted by permission of the publisher and author.

Figure 2–5. From Bruce K. Britton, A. Piha, J. Davis, and E. Wehausen, ''Reading and Cognitive Capacity Usage: Adjunct Question Effects'' *Memory and Cognition, 3.* Reprinted by permission of The Psychonomic Society, Inc.

Figure 2–7 and 2–8. From R. E. Snow, ''Aptitude Processes'' *Aptitude, Learning, and Instruction,* Vol. 1, edited by R. E. Snow, P–A Federico, and W. E. Montague (Lawrence Erlbaum Associates, Hillsdale, NJ). Reprinted by permission of the publisher and author.

Figure 2–14 and Table 2–3. Adapted from W. Kintsch, ''On Modeling Comprehension'' *Educational Psychologist,* vol. 14. Copyright 1979 by Division 15 of the American Psychological Association. Reprinted by the permission.

Figure 2–15. Adapted from P. A. Carpenter and M. A. Just, ''Sentence Comprehension: A Psycholinguistic Processing Model of Verification'' *Psychological Review,* vol. 82. Copyright 1975 by the American Psychological Association. Adapted by permission of the author.

Figure 3–2. Adapted from H. E. Wanner, *On Remembering, Forgetting, and Understanding Sentences: A Study of the Deep Structure Hypothesis.* Unpublished doctoral dissertation, Harvard University, Cambridge, MA. Reprinted by permission of the author.

Figure 3–5. Adapted from B. Hayes-Roth and P. W. Thorndyke, ''Integration of knowledge from text'' *Journal of Verbal Learning and Verbal Behavior,* 18. Reprinted by permission of the author and Academic Press, Inc.

Writers'' *New Inquiries in Reading Research and Instruction,* edited by J. Niles. 31st National Reading Conference Yearbook, Washington, D.C., National Reading Conference, 1982. Reprinted by permission of National Council of Teachers of English.

Table 8–7. Adapted from M. Scardamalia and C. Bereiter, *The Psychology of Written Language: A Developmental Approach,* edited by M. Martlew. Reprinted by permission of John Wiley & Sons Ltd.

Table 8–8. Adapted from E. J. Bartlett, ''Learing to Revise; Some Component Processes'' *What Writers Know: The Language, Process, and Structure of Written Discourse,* edited by M. Nystrand. Reprinted by permission of Academic Press, Inc.

Figure 8–7. From Jacqueline Tetroe, ''Information Processing Demand of Plot Construction in Story Writing.'' Reprinted by permission of the author.

Table 8–9. Adapted from J. Voss et al., ''Text Generation and Recall by High-knowledge and Low-knowledge Individuals'' *Journal of Verbal Learning and Verbal Behavior,* 19. Reprinted by permission of Academic Press, Inc. and the author.

Pages 223–225. From S. Freedman and D. Swanson-Owens, ''Metacognitive Awareness and the Writing Process.'' Paper presented at the American Educational Research Association, Montreal, Canada, April, 1983. Reprinted by permission of the author.

Tables 8–10, 8–11, and 8–12. Adapted from E. Cohen and M. Scardamalia, ''The Effects of Instructional Intervention in the Revision of Essays by Grade Six Children.'' Paper presented at the American Educational Research Association, Montreal, April, 1983. Reprinted by permission of the author.

Table 9–4 and Figure 9–1. From J. Brown and R. Burton, ''Diagnostic Models for Procedural Bugs in Basic Mathematical Skills'' *Cognitive Science,* 1978, 2. Reprinted by permission of Ablex Publishing Corporation.

Tables 9–5, 9–6, and 9–7, Figures 9–2 and 9–7. From R. Gagne and N. Paradise, ''Abilities and Learning Sets in Knowledge Acquisition'' *Psychological Monographs: General and Applied,* 75. Copyright © 1961 by the American Psychological Association. Reprinted by permission of the author and publisher.

Figure 9–3. From G. J. Groen and J. M. Parkman, ''A Chronometric Analysis of Simple Addition'' *Psychological Review,* 79, 1972. Copyright © 1972 by the American Psychological Association. Reprinted by permission of the author.

Table 9–9. Adapted from D. Houlihan and H. Ginsberg, ''The Addition Methods of First- and Second-grade Children'' *Journal for Research in Mathematics Education,* 12. Reprinted by permission of National Council of Teachers of Mathematics.

Figure 9–7, Table 9–11. From W. Geeslin and R. Shavelson, ''An Exploratory Analysis of the Representation of a Mathematical Structure in Student's Cognitive Structures'' *American Educational Research Journal,* 12. Copyright 1975 by American Educational Research Association, Washington, D.C. Reprinted by permission of American Educational Research Association.

Table 9–12. Adapted from E. Silver, ''Recall of Mathematical Problem Information: Some Related Problems'' *Journal for Research in Mathematics Education,* 12. Reprinted by permission of National Council of Teachers of Mathematics.

Tables 9–13 and 9–14. From C. Robinson, and J. Hayes, ''Making Inferences About Relevance in Understanding Problems'' *Human Reasoning,* edited by R. Revlin and R. E. Mayer, Washington, D.C., V. H. Winston and Sons. Reprinted by permission of the author.

Table 9–15. From R. E. Mayer, ''Memory for Algebra Story Problems'' *Journal of Educational Psychology,* 1982, 72. Copyright 1982 by the American Psychological Association. Reprinted by permission of the publisher and author.

Tables 9–16 and 9–17, Figures 9–8, 9–9. From B. Adelson, ''Problem-solving and the development of abstract categories in programming languages'' *Memory and Cognition,* 5. Reprinted by permission of The Psychonomic Society, Inc.

Figures 10–1, 10–2. Adapted from R. Siegler and D. Richards, ''The Development of Two Concepts,'' *Recent Advances in Cognitive Developmental Theory,* edited by C. Brainerd. Reprinted by the publisher, Springer-Verlag, Inc., New York.

Figures 10–3, 10–4. From A. Champagne et al., ''Structural representations of students' knowledge before or after science instruction'' *Journal of Research in Science Teaching,* 18. Copyright © 1981 by John Wiley & Sons, Inc. Reprinted by permission of John Wiley & Sons, Inc.

Figures 10–5, 10–6. From J. Okey and R. Gagné, ''Revision of a science topic using evidence of performance on subordinate skills'' *Journal of Research in Science Teaching,* 7. Copyright © 1970 by John Wiley & Sons, Inc. Reprinted by permission of the publisher.

Figures 10–7, 10–8, Table 10–2. Adapted from R. Siegler, ''Three Aspects of Cognitive Development'' *Cognitive*

Figures 12–3, 12–4 and Table 12–14. From A. Brown et al., ''The effects of experience on selection of suitable retrieval cues for studying text'' *Child Development*, 49. Reprinted by permission of the author and The Society for Research in Child Development, Inc.

Tables 12–16 and 12–18. From E. Gagné, C. Weideman, M. Bell and T. Anders, ''Training Thirteen Year Olds to Elaborate While Studying Text,'' *Journal of Human Learning*. Reprinted by permission of John Wiley & Sons, Chichester, England.

Preface

TO THE STUDENT

Cognitive psychology is currently one of the most rapidly growing branches of psychology, and it is a field of study that has much to offer education. At a general level, it conceives of learning as an active process and suggests that teaching involves facilitating active mental processing by students. This notion contrasts sharply with the behavioristic view of students as passive receptacles of information.

In addition to positing the view that the learner is an active participant in the learning process, recent research in such areas as reading, writing, mathematics, and science reveals how more skilled individuals differ mentally from their less skilled peers. These findings have implications for determining *what* should be taught in order to effect maximum development of the learner's competence. Also, recent research on learning reveals the mental processes that underlie cognitive change. These ideas have implications for *how* teaching can most effectively influence the development of competence.

There is, therefore, a need for a book addressed to educators that describes these new developments in cognitive psychology and explores their implications for teaching and learning. Accordingly, this book is intended for advanced undergraduate and graduate students in education or fields related to education. Practitioners should find some useful principles in this book. Those who are involved in or plan to be involved in educational research should find this book helpful as an introduction to the current state of knowledge of the cognitive psychology of school learning.

If you have an interest in conducting cognitive psychological research on school learning, you should be aware that this book does not provide a comprehensive overview of the research. Rather, it provides a theoretical integration of current work and allows for identifying important areas in need of research. The studies that I have described in detail exemplify the type of work being done and they illustrate particular theoretical points. This is especially evident in Chapters 1–6 and 11–12. The summaries of research provided in Chapters 7–10 are somewhat more comprehensive, though still far from exhaustive. The references provided at the end of each chapter will point to a wealth of additional research.

Because of the revolutionary quality of current cognitive psychology, many theoretical frameworks are presently used for thinking about mental representations and processes. "Schemas," "propositional networks," "logits," and "cognitive maps" are but a few of the terms used to describe mental representations. "Schema restructuring," "inheritance of generalizations," "composition," and "spread of activation" are only a few terms used to label mental processes. Also because of the nature of cognitive psychology it is not always clear whether each term refers to a separate structure or process, or different terms refer to the same process.

This jungle of terminology posed a problem for me as a textbook writer. Should I introduce the entire jungle in an effort to reflect the state of the field, and risk alienating some of my readers? Or should I choose one framework within which to view cognitive psychology and thus provide a more coherent book, but risk imparting a less-than-comprehensive view of the field? My choice was to work within one framework, yet to introduce from time to time competing ideas and alternate frameworks when it seemed appropriate. I believe that using one framework enhances the memorability of the material and provides explanatory principles that can be used by teachers in solving classroom problems. I trust that by introducing alternatives, I will help you become aware of the fact that there are indeed various conceptions being actively explored in current research.

The framework that I have adopted relies a great deal on the theoretical work of John R. Anderson (1976, 1983). Anderson's theory is useful for educators for two main reasons. First, he distinguishes between declarative and procedural knowledge. This conception of knowledge was pioneered by R. M. Gagne (1965, 1974) two decades ago. He contended that there are major differences in the conditions for learning declarative and procedural knowledge, which he called verbal information and intellectual skills respectively. Since then, this notion has become accepted in education and has continued to be validated in psychological experimentation.

A second reason that Anderson's theory is of use to us is because it deals with learning processes. Although learning theory is a relatively weak area within contemporary cognitive psychology, Anderson's theory is exceptional in its attempt to explain learning within a cognitive framework. Ausubel (1968) and R. M. Gagné (1977) also explain learning within a cognitive framework. However, the bulk of cognitive psychological theory centers on issues of performance rather than issues of learning.

Despite my reliance on J. R. Anderson's theory, you should not expect to understand his thinking fully after reading this text. Because instruction is our focal point in this book, I have presented only a few of the assumptions of Anderson's theory and have glossed over points that are significant for the theory itself but not for instructional implications. I also put forward some ideas that are not explicitly stated in Anderson's work and are probably not even implied. For example, I distinguish between "pattern-recognition" and "action-sequence" forms of procedural knowledge, because I believe this is a useful distinction for instructional psychologists and educators. Anderson does not make this distinction.

Some of you may be discouraged by the chapter titles if you do not see your own field of expertise represented. For example, there are no chapters on art, history, or "adult education." This is because research from a cognitive psychological perspective in these fields is not as prevalent as research in the "basic skills." However, Chapters 1–6 and 11–12 are quite general in their applications. Furthermore, the middle chapters on basic skills are important for several reasons even if one is not specializing in these areas. First, all teachers must deal with students who have deficiencies in basic skills when those deficiencies interfere with the learning of other content. If teachers have a better understanding of the causes of problems in basic skills, they may be able to remediate some of these problems with relatively simple interventions. A second use of these middle chapters is as analogs for other areas of instruction: creative writing provides an analog for creative production in art or music, and mathematical competence provides an analog for

other areas of technical competence such as engineering. Each chapter describing a basic skill demonstrates the application of the theoretical ideas presented in Chapters 1–6. By seeing how ideas apply in a variety of domains, you will gain a deeper understanding of the theory. This should lead to greater proficiency of application in your own area of expertise.

TO THE INSTRUCTOR

As a faculty member in Departments of Educational Psychology first at the University of Georgia and now at the University of Texas, I have spent a good deal of time in teaching students in education about cognition, learning, and instruction. Because of the recent enormous growth in knowledge in these areas, I have been frustrated in finding just the right books for my courses. Books written for an education audience do not, by and large, contain much about recent work in cognitive psychology. Books written for psychology students cover topics that are far removed from classroom concerns. Thus, as many a frustrated professor has done in similar situations, I determined to write my own text.

One of my goals for the text was to describe much of the recent work that has been done on school tasks such as reading and solving algebra word problems and on classroom processes and student learning strategies. That is, I wished to describe the parts of cognitive psychology that I judged to be most relevant for instruction.

A second goal was to make the information contained in this text both memorable and usable. Research has demonstrated that memorability and usability are both enhanced by an emphasis on models and explanatory principles (Mayer, 1975, 1980).

Therefore I have attempted to use models and causal principles throughout the book.

These two goals have resulted in a book that is different in several ways from currently available textbooks in cognitive psychology. The major differences are:

1. Emphasis on skills and subject matter domains

Most cognitive psychology texts do not delve deeply into the nature of basic skills such as reading, writing, and math skills, nor do they describe the nature of expertise in subjects such as physics. This text has a chapter each devoted to reading, writing, math, and science because these are areas of great importance for school learning.

2. Emphasis on experiments that have classroom analogs

Most cognitive psychology texts report research on tasks that are far removed from those students perform in school. This research is usually of a very high quality, and it is useful for proving theoretical points. However, experiments of equally high quality have been done on school tasks or on tasks with obvious school analogs. To support points in this book, experiments on school-like tasks are reported even when an experiment on a contrived task might show more dramatic findings. My belief is that readers exposed to experiments on school tasks are more likely to transfer their knowledge to classroom settings than are readers exposed to experiments on laboratory tasks.

I have described some experiments in more detail than in most texts. This is done in part because some students may not have had much experience in reading research and so brief descriptions may not communicate adequately. Also, for an experiment to provide a model for analogical reasoning, it needs to be described in some detail.

3. Emphasis on one knowledge-representation system

Most cognitive psychology texts are somewhat more eclectic in their approach to knowledge representation than is this one. Here I have selected one system for thinking about knowledge representation (which has for basic units propositions and productions) and used this system throughout the book in explaining results of various studies. My purpose is to give readers a model for thinking in a rather detailed manner about cognitive processes. To prevent readers from forming the belief that propositions and productions are the *only* model they might use to think about mental processes, alternatives are discussed at various junctures.

4. Emphasis on learning

The cognitive psychology of learning is truly in its infancy. Therefore, it is not surprising that most cognitive psychology texts do not cover this topic. However, the topic is of central importance to education, so this textbook provides a cognitive view of learning processes.

Although the book is intended mainly for graduate students in education, it could also be used in some psychology courses. Specifically, it might be used in instructional psychology courses or applications-oriented cognitive psychology courses at both undergraduate and graduate levels. Students with strong backgrounds in psychology and little or no teaching experience might find the style of this text to be different from the style to which they are accustomed. However, if they are interested in getting an overview of the parts of cognitive psychology that appear to be most relevant to instruction, this book should be useful.

As a source for educational researchers, this book can provide (1) an introduction to the methods and theoretical constructs used in cognitively oriented educational research, (2) an overview of what is known about cognition in reading, writing, math, and science, and (3) some suggestions of where more research is needed. However, researchers should be aware that I expect many of my readers to be more interested in obtaining valid and usable knowledge than in obtaining detailed knowledge of the many gaps in our current understanding of cognitive processes.

Many people have given me useful feedback on all or part of this book. John Glover, The University of Nebraska, Lincoln; Richard Mayer, University of California, Santa Barbara; John Surber, The University of Wisconsin, Milwaukee; and Frank Yekovich, The Catholic University of America, read an early draft in its entirety and gave me many helpful comments. Stanford University, where I was a Visiting Scholar for a year, provided a congenial environment for writing the first draft of this book. People who commented on parts of the book include John R. Anderson, Charles Bethel-Fox, Bruce Britton, Joseph Burns, Patricia Carpenter, Russell Durst, Linnea Ehri, Sarah Freedman, Shawn Glynn, Jill Larkin, Ellen Mandinach, and John Rickards. My editor, Mylan Jaixen, raised perceptive questions at crucial times. Finally, my husband, William Davis, provided much needed encouragement.

Brief Contents

Contents

THE COGNITIVE PSYCHOLOGY OF SCHOOL LEARNING

The Human Information-Processing System

Chapter

1

Introduction

SUMMARY

1. Cognitive psychology is the scientific study of mental processes.

2. Experimental psychology started out in 1879 with a cognitive orientation, but behaviorism soon became the dominant framework in American psychology. After World War II there was a rebirth of interest in cognitive psychology, stimulated by both pressure from applied settings and developments in information science.

3. This book provides an information-processing framework for learning, memory, and problem solving and then uses this framework to analyze the learning of school subjects.

LEARNING

Human learning is a perpetually fascinating topic. Children seem to learn so much in the first few years of life. They learn to walk, to defer gratification, and to comprehend and use language. By the time they reach school age, they have mastered many of the skills of daily living. During the school years humans learn to read, write, and compute, and, sometimes, to think and solve problems. They also acquire masses of information about the world as it was and as it is today. In adulthood people continue to learn. They learn job-related skills and acquire more information. They may refine their reading, writing, and thinking skills. When they switch careers, they may learn new job-related skills, and when they retire, they will learn skills and information related to leisure-time activities.

The great adaptability of our species seems to be one characteristic that sets us apart from other species. We are more able than other animals to live in a variety of environments ranging from the Arctic to the tropics to space. And we live in a variety of cultures from the simple agrarian to the complex technological. Because of these impressive feats of human learning, most people have an intrinsic interest in the topic.

There are also impressive failures of human learning. People labeled retarded or learning disabled seem to learn slowly, if at all. Older people feel that they have a more difficult time learning new information than do younger people, although the truth of this remains to be seen. Finally, "unmotivated" students seem unwilling to learn. Knowledge about human learning processes is interesting not only because it explains successes in learning, but because it may help us alleviate or prevent failures.

This book is about human learning. Although it emphasizes skills and knowledge that typically are learned in school settings, the learning *processes* described are thought to be universal. They should apply whether the learner is two years old or one hundred and whether the situation is an informal parent–child interaction or a more formal teacher–student interaction.

COGNITIVE PSYCHOLOGY

Cognitive psychology is the scientific study of mental events. The cognitive psychology of school learning is that which studies mental events in learners and teachers during schooling. It is a science that sheds light on such questions as why two similar students react differently to the same lesson, what is behind the blank stare of one student or another's flash of insight, and what methods should be used to teach a given topic.

Although cognitive psychology sheds light on these questions, it cannot provide definitive answers to them. Just as physiology and anatomy guide a doctor's thinking about medical problems, but do not tell him or her exactly what dosage of what drug to prescribe, so psychology guides a teacher's thinking about learning problems. It provides a theoretical basis for teachers' decision making rather than absolute answers.

All psychologists share the goal of understanding the behavior of individuals. However, they differ in (1) their commitment to a particular level of analysis, and (2) the areas of behavior they study.

Figure 1.1 shows a matrix that results from crossing three levels of analysis (behavioral, physiological, and cognitive) with three areas of behavior (social, emotional, and intellectual). The behavioral level of analysis focuses on identifying relationships between externally observable stimuli and responses. On the physiological level one tries to explain aspects of behavior in terms of physiological causes such as neural pathways or chemical

| LEVELS OF | TYPES OF BEHAVIOR | | |
ANALYSIS	SOCIAL	EMOTIONAL	INTELLECTUAL
Behavioral			
Physiological			
Cognitive			

Figure 1.1. Areas of study within psychology are defined by the type of behavior involved (social, emotional, intellectual) and the level of analysis (behavioral, physiological, cognitive). This book focuses on cognitive analyses of intellectual behavior.

changes. On the cognitive level one tries to explain behavior in terms of mental constructs. Psychologists who study social behavior are interested in such topics as how individuals present themselves to others and how people interact. Those who study emotional behavior are interested in such topics as why different individuals react to the same situation with different feelings or what parental behaviors affect the emotional development of the young. Finally, those who study intellectual behavior are interested in such topics as how people solve problems and how they learn.

Of course, any event has social, emotional, and intellectual aspects that can be usefully analyzed at behavioral, physiological, and cognitive levels, but psychologists, like other scientists, find it helpful to divide up the work so that each scientist focuses on only one or two cells of the matrix. Educators do not have the luxury of dividing up their students but rather must deal with students' social, emotional, and intellectual states all at once, using behavioral, physiological, and cognitive levels of analysis to understand the situation.

In this book the focus is on the interaction of cognitive analysis with intellectual behavior (although in Chapter 11 we will explore a cognitive view of some emotional aspects of behavior). Thus, the questions raised in this book mainly have to do with the mental processes that underlie intellectual performance. What is going on in one's head, for example, when one is learning a new scientific principle, a new mathematical concept, or new information about nutrition?

A BRIEF HISTORY OF COGNITIVE PSYCHOLOGY

Psychology started as an empirical science in 1879, and many of the psychologists of the late 1800s were cognitive psychologists in the sense that they were interested in understanding mental events. Wundt studied the elements of consciousness whereas Freud tried to understand the unconscious. William James (1890) defined psychology as ''the Science of Mental Life.'' The method used by many psychologists during this era was introspection (self-observation).

Early in the twentieth century, American psychologist John B. Watson launched an attack on the view that psychology was the science of mental life and instead proposed that it was the science of behavior (Watson, 1914). He argued that introspective data could never be independently verified (as science demanded) because they were private. Mental life, in other words, could never be studied objectively. Hence, we should focus our attention on behavior, which could be studied objectively and about which there was much to be discovered.

From the time of Watson's attack through World War II, American psychology was predominantly behavioral. It produced the laws of effect and practice (Thorndike, 1913) and the principles of reinforcement (Skinner, 1938). Although these principles were shown to be quite powerful, they did little to explain important intellectual achievements such as learning to read, discovering a theorem, composing a song, or making good decisions under stress. Because behaviorism eschewed references to mental events, complex human performance, which begged for references to mental events, was rarely studied.

During World War II some psychologists were called into the military to do research on the selection and training of skilled military personnel. They looked at complex tasks—such as flying an airplane—which they made some progress in understanding. Perhaps because of their success many of these psychologists continued to study complex tasks after the war when they returned to university settings. The study of complex human performance led rapidly to theorizing about mental structures and processes (e.g. Ausubel, 1968; Bruner, Goodnow, and Austin, 1956; R. Gagné, 1962). These events marked the rebirth of cognitive psychology.

Concurrently a great deal was happening in other fields that facilitated the growth of cognitive psychology. Information science was developing, starting with a formal definition of a ''bit'' of information (Shannon, 1962) and with the publication in 1948 of N. Weiner's highly influential book called *Cybernetics*. Linguistics was also developing as a formal science, and the linguist Chomsky (1959) challenged Skinner's behavioristic explanation of language development as being woefully inadequate. Both information theory and linguistics provided psychologists

with models of formal analysis and suggested to some that formal analysis of mental events and structures might be attempted.

Another event that led to the rebirth of cognitive psychology, one that was spurred by the growth of information science, was the development of the computer. As we shall see in the next chapter, the computer provides a methodological tool that allows for objective measurement of mental process indicators. The behaviorist argument that there are no objective ways to study mental events may have been valid in 1914, but it is more difficult to make today.

OVERVIEW OF THE BOOK

This book is divided into four major sections. The first section introduces some of the major concepts of an information-processing view of human cognition. After this introductory chapter, Chapter 2 describes an information-processing model and some of the methods used by cognitive psychologists to study mental processes. Chapter 3 introduces ideas about mental structures that are used to represent knowledge.

The second major section of the book describes some principles of learning, memory, and problem solving. These principles will be used throughout the book. In Chapter 4, principles of learning and remembering information are described; and in Chapter 5 principles of learning intellectual skills are described. This section concludes with Chapter 6 on problem-solving processes.

The third and fourth sections of the book apply the framework developed in the first two sections to specific areas. In the third section the areas are literacy skills and subject domains (reading, writing, math, and science, respectively, in Chapters 7, 8, 9, and 10). In the fourth section, the areas are classroom processes: motivation in Chapter 11 and teacher and student strategies in Chapter 12.

SUMMARY AND PREVIEW

This book is about human learning processes. It describes an information processing framework for viewing human learning in the first six chapters. It then applies this framework to school subjects and classroom dynamics in the final six chapters.

The information-processing view clarifies the incredible complexity of human performance, on the one hand, and the relative simplicity of the principles underlying performance, on the other. Often, the better one understands a phenomenon, the more amazing it seems. This is certainly true of human learning.

ADDITIONAL READINGS

For further information about the history of psychology and the history of information science, consult the following:

Boring, E. G. (1950). *A history of experimental psychology*, 2nd ed. New York: Appleton-Century-Crofts.

Leahey, T. H. (1980). *A history of psychology*. Englewood Cliffs, N.J.: Prentice-Hall.

McCorduck, P. (1979). *Machines who think*. San Francisco: W. H. Freeman.

Chapter 2

Models and Methods in Cognitive Psychology

SUMMARY

1. Information-processing psychologists describe psychological events in terms of transformations of information from input to output.

2. Information is initially received by *receptors* and is registered centrally in the *sensory register*. A portion of all information that is in the sensory register is transferred to *working memory*, but the rest is lost.

3. Working memory is limited in capacity and, if information in it is neither rehearsed nor coded, it will be lost. Coded information goes into *long-term memory*, which has a very large capacity.

4. Stored information may be retrieved. It is then organized by the *response generator* into a performance pattern that guides the *effectors* into a sequence of actions.

5. Several types of data observed by cognitive psychologists provide indirect evidence of mental processes. These include response latencies, eye fixations, and verbal reports.

6. Several types of theory development are used by cognitive psychologists to construct models of mental processes. These include the subtractive technique, information-processing analyses, and computer simulation.

INFORMATION-PROCESSING MODELS

The majority of cognitive psychologists in America today espouse a theoretical framework known as *information processing*. In this framework mental events are described in terms of transformations of information from input (stimulus) to output (response).

An Information-Processing Model

Information-processing models may be represented graphically by sets of boxes and lines interconnecting them. Sometimes the boxes represent functions or states of the system and the lines represent transformations of information as it moves from one state to another. An information-processing model represented this way is shown in Figure 2.1.

In this model information, in the form of some physical energy (light for print, sound for speech, pressure for touch, etc.) is received by *receptors* that are sensitive to that particular form of energy (rods and cones, middle ear bones, proprioceptor cells, etc.). These receptors send signals, in the form of electrochemical impulses, to the brain. Thus, the first transformation of information is from

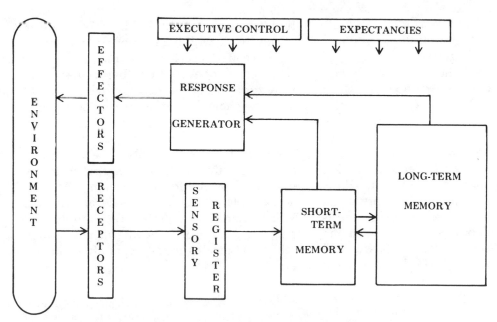

Figure 2.1. An information-processing model. (From R. M. Gagné, 1974.)

one of several forms of energy to a common form.

From the receptors the nerve impulse goes to a *sensory register* in the central nervous system. There appear to be different sensory registers for each sense, but all hold a fairly veridical representation of sensory information in the central nervous system for an extremely brief time (one-fourth of a second according to Sperling, 1960). From this complete representation of sensory information, a small fraction is kept for continued representation in *short-term memory* while the rest is lost from the system. This reduction process is called *selective perception*.

Short-term memory (STM) corresponds roughly to awareness. That is, what you are aware of at any given moment is said to be in your short-term memory. This memory store is called "short term" because information passes out of it within about ten seconds (cf. Murdock, 1961) unless it is rehearsed. When you look up a telephone number, for example, the number goes into your short-term memory. If you do not mentally rehearse this number as you walk from the telephone book to the telephone, you may find that you have forgotten it.

Besides having limited duration, short-term memory has a limited capacity. Miller (1956) claims that short-term memory holds seven (±2) units of information, whereas Simon (1974) claims that it holds only about five units. The exact number of units of information that STM holds may depend on one's operational definition of information. However, the important point for educators is that it is small. Therefore short-term memory is often called the "bottleneck" of the human information-processing system. As we shall see, the small capacity of STM has important implications for instruction.

More and more psychologists are using the term *working memory* (WM) for short-term memory. The two terms emphasize different aspects of the concept: "short term" emphasizes the duration of information, whereas "working" emphasizes its function. Working memory is the "place" where conscious mental work is done.[1] For example, if you are solving the problem 26 × 32 mentally, you would hold the intermediate products 52 and 78 in working memory and add them together there. Or, if you are imagining the consequences of an action, the scenario that you imagine is in your working memory. Figure 2.2 shows Klatzky's (1975) notion of working memory as a workbench. As you can see, some items are falling off the workbench, illustrating the limited capacity of working memory. In this book, I will use the term working memory rather than short-term memory because I believe the functional aspect of this store is the most important for education.

Information in working memory may be *coded*; it is then stored in *long-term memory* (LTM). Coding is a transformation process in which new information is integrated in various ways with known information. Long-term memory stores information for later use. In contrast to working memory, it may last as long as a lifetime. There is a controversy over whether or not everything that we have ever stored in LTM stays there permanently, but most psychologists agree that much of what we have stored stays with us for quite a long time. The feeling of not being able to remember something is thought to be due more often to a failure to find a good retrieval cue than to a loss of information from LTM. (For an example of the role of retrieval cues, see Williams and Hollan's [1981] description of people's success at retrieving names of high school classmates many years after graduation.)

---

[1]"Place" here does not necessarily imply a distinct anatomical location in the brain. It simply means a distinct function of the information-processing system.

Figure 2.2. Working memory serves as a "workbench" in the human information-processing system. (From Klatzky, 1975.)

Once information is stored in LTM, to be used again it must be *retrieved*. Retrieved information forms the basis of *response generation*. In conscious thought information is said to flow from LTM to STM and thence to the *response generator*. For an automatic response, however, information is said to flow directly from LTM to the response generator during retrieval.

The response generator organizes the response sequence and guides the *effectors*. The effectors include all of our muscles and glands, but, for school tasks, the main effectors are the arms and hands for writing and the voice apparatus for speaking.

The flow of information in the human system appears to be purposeful and organized (at least sometimes), as shown by the boxes labeled *expectancy* and *executive control.* Specifically, expectations about the outcome of mental activities influence information processing, as do control procedures and strategies for reaching goals.

An Example of Information Processing

Suppose that a second-grade teacher wants Joe to learn the fact that the capital of Texas is Austin. The teacher asks Joe, "What is the capital of Texas?" and Joe says, "I don't know." At the same time Joe may set up an expectancy that he is about to learn the capital of Texas, which will cause him to pay attention. The teacher then says, "The capital of Texas is Austin." Joe's ears receive this message along with other sounds such as the other pupils' speech and traffic outside the school.

All of the sounds that Joe hears are translated into electrochemical impulses and sent to the sensory register. The pattern that the capital of Texas is Austin is selected for entry into working memory, but other sound patterns are not entered.

Joe may then code the fact that the capital of Texas is Austin by associating it with other facts that he already knows about Austin (e.g., that it is a big city and that he once visited it). This coding process causes the new fact to be entered into long-term memory. If Joe has already developed special memory strategies (which is somewhat unlikely for a second grader), his executive control processes would direct the coding process to use these special strategies.

The next day Joe's teacher might ask him, "What is the capital of Texas?" This question would be received and selected for entry into WM. There it would provide cues for retrieving the answer from LTM. A copy of the answer would be used by the response generator to organize the speech acts that

produce the sounds, "Austin is the capital of Texas." At this point Joe's expectancy that he would learn the capital of Texas has been confirmed.

A Comparison with Computers

Any system in which information undergoes a series of transformations from input to output can be analyzed from an information-processing perspective. Telephone systems, television systems, and computer systems are all information-processing systems. Computer systems are an especially seductive source of analogies for cognitive psychologists because the behavior of computers is sometimes nearly as complex as that of humans.

Some people think that it is ridiculous to compare humans and computers because they are so different; after all, computers can't "feel" and can't "be creative." Other people think that the similarities between humans and computers are so great that computers may wrest control from humans. It is important to understand just how computers and humans are alike and different as information-processing systems in order to assess these claims. But first let us look briefly at a simple computer system.

A Computer System. Most computer systems contain at least these parts: (1) an input device, (2) a central processing unit (CPU), (3) a long-term storage medium, (4) a device for putting information into long-term storage and retrieving it from storage, and (5) an output device. The most common input device for a computer is the terminal. A human sits at a terminal, which has a keyboard, and types information that is transmitted to the central processing unit—where the work of a computer is done. The CPU consists of many elements, each of which is on or off at any given time. The patterns of on and off are used to represent information, and these patterns change as work is done.

To save products of the computer's work, one directs the computer to transfer them to a storage device, usually either a tape or disc on which information is coded electromagnetically. To see the products of the work, one directs the computer to output this information, usually by printing it on paper or on a cathode ray screen at a terminal.

The Comparison. The parts of a computer system are functionally similar to the parts of the human information-processing system. Humans, like computers, have various ways of receiving input. After receiving input, they do some mental work in working memory, just as computers do work in the CPU. After working with information, humans store it in long-term memory, just as computers store information on tape or disc. Finally, humans output information through effectors, whereas computers output information on paper or screen.

Thus humans and computers have similar functional units within their systems. However, the two systems differ a great deal in detail. Estes (1980) has compared the size and speed of the two systems' corresponding parts, using experimental data for the human system and engineering data for the computer system. The results of this comparison are shown in Table 2.1.

Human working memory (five bits of information) is much smaller than a computer's central processing unit (estimated by Kemeny, 1955, to be 10 million bits). Earlier we saw that the small capacity of WM is an extremely important aspect of the human system; now we see that it clearly distinguishes humans from computers. Humans and computers also differ in their storage capacity. Human long-term memory is quite large (one billion bits according to Kemeny). However, a computer's storage capacity is theoretically unlimited, depending only on the number of available tapes and discs. Although human storage capacity is finite and computer storage capacity is theoretically infinite, humans never use up their storage, so this difference between humans and computers is not a crucial one.

Computers' access times are faster than are those of humans. Access time in the CPU refers to the speed with which electricity moves from one area to another. Computers are very rapid in this regard; one microsecond (.000001 seconds) is a typical access time. Humans, as has been determined in experiments done by S. Sternberg (1966), take about 25 milliseconds (.025 second) to shift attention from one part of working memory to another. Access time to storage devices that

Table 2.1. A comparison of human and computer memories in terms of size and speed of access. CPU = central processing unit, WM = working memory, and LTM = long-term memory. (As described in Estes, 1980.)

	SIZE	SPEED OF ACCESS
Computer CPU	10,000,000 bits	0.000001 seconds
Human WM	5 bits	0.025 seconds
Computer storage	unlimited	0.001 seconds
Human LTM	1,000,000,000 bits	0.200 seconds

are loaded on a computer are in the range of one millisecond (.001 second), whereas access time to human long-term memory is about 200 milliseconds (.200 second).

Computers thus appear to be more capacious and faster as information-processing systems than humans. They often have a workspace that is a millionfold larger than human workspace (WM); their speed of access to information in the workspace is about 20,000 times faster than ours; and their speed of access to information in storage (if the storage device is loaded) is 200 times faster than ours. Clearly, computers have the advantage over humans in the amount of information they can work with and the speed with which they work. This is what makes computers so useful for "number-crunching" problems in which large amounts of data are manipulated in complex ways.

However, computers and humans differ in another way that seems to give an advantage to humans. As Estes has suggested (see Table 2.2), the structure of memory in humans differs from that in computers. Human memory is not all-or-none; that is, we remember partial information. By contrast, in computers, a set of information is either available in its entirety or not at all. Human memory capacity and retrieval depend on the context—in familiar contexts, we seem to be able to deal with much more information. Computer memory capacity and retrieval,

however, are context independent. Human dependency on context allows for learning and adaptation, and our tendency for partial memory allows us to think of novel solutions to problems. In short, the human system has evolved to be adaptive. One adaptation of the human system has been to create fast, capacious machines that perform some routine problem-solving tasks.

METHODS USED IN COGNITIVE PSYCHOLOGY

The comparison of humans and computers is only one way in which computer science has influenced cognitive psychology. Other ways will be described in this section, which illustrates the methods used by cognitive psychologists to validate ideas about the mental processes that underlie learning and performance.

First, however, consider the question of whether or not practice improves the ability to generate geometry proofs (see Figure 2.3). A typical experiment designed to answer this question might ask one group of subjects to solve twenty proofs such as the one shown in Figure 2.3 and another group only ten. The group that had more practice would probably perform faster and with fewer errors on new proof problems. In fact, improvement of intellectual skills with practice is often found (Newell and Rosenbloom, 1981). Although it

Table 2.2. A comparison of human and computer memory. (From Estes, 1980.)

	HUMAN MEMORY	COMPUTER MEMORY
Preferred storage mode	analog; time-oriented	digital; list-oriented
Retention of information	graded	all-or-none
Efficiency (bits/sec.)	low	high
Capacity	dependent on experience	independent of experience
Retrieval		
relative to context	strongly dependent	independent
relative to previous retrievals	dependent	independent
Purpose	general purpose; open set of functions	special or general purpose; closed set of functions

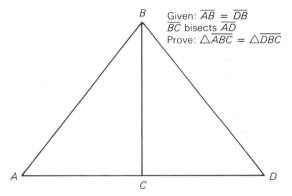

Given: $\overline{AB} = \overline{DB}$
$\overline{BC}$ bisects $\overline{AD}$
Prove: $\triangle \overline{ABC} = \triangle \overline{DBC}$

Figure 2.3. A sample geometry problem.

is interesting to know that skills improve with practice, it would be even more interesting to know *why* they improve. In the past it was difficult to answer such questions, because the tools available to most psychologists were not sensitive enough to detect the mental processes that occurred during learning. Now, however, tools for studying cognitive processes are widely available.

Recent methodological improvements in cognitive psychology may turn out to be analogous in their effects to those which occurred in genetics in the 1950s. Before the 1950s geneticists were stuck at a fairly global level of description. They knew that certain characteristics of organisms were passed on to offspring in predictable proportions. They called the cause of this predictable event a "factor" or gene, but they did not know how genes exerted their influence. Then there was a major breakthrough in the methods used to study genes: x-ray crystallography was perfected, allowing geneticists to discover the structure of the genetic material DNA. Other techniques such as protein synthesis and radioactive tracing made it possible to crack the genetic code. As many experiments using these new or improved technologies were completed, it became clear that a "factor," or gene, is a segment of a DNA molecule that controls the production of a certain enzyme

or other protein and this enzyme or other protein in turn determines whether a characteristic occurs or not.

Cognitive psychology may be at a point in its development now similar to the point that genetics was at in the 1950s, when dramatic methodological improvements led to dramatic increases in understanding. If so, we may expect our understanding of cognitive processes to increase substantially over the next few decades.

Advances in methodology have come from many sources, but a major source is improvements in computers. Now that microcomputers are relatively inexpensive, many cognitive psychologists and educational researchers use them to conduct experiments. A typical experimental setup is shown in Figure 2.4. The computer is programmed to display stimuli on a screen, to record a subject's response and the response's latency, and to summarize and analyze the data. Subjects in different conditions of the experiment see different stimuli on the screen. Sometimes the experimenter may sit by the subject and ask her or him questions at various times during task performance. The experimenter's questions and subject's answers are tape recorded for subsequent analysis.

In the rest of this chapter I will describe six methods that are often used by cognitive psychologists—three empirical and three theoretical. These are not the only methods used by cognitive psychologists, but they are ones that have experienced significant improvements in recent years.

Empirical Methods

Latency Data. Psychologists have always been interested in the speed, or *latency*, of responses. However, until recently such data have been more useful for studying motor skills than for cognitive skills. This is because

Subject: reads screen. Responds on keyboard.

Experimenter: Watches, asks subject questions

Response Program: Collects speed and accuracy data

Analysis Program: Reduces and analyzes data

Stimulus Program: Displays task

Ready?

Computer software that guides stimulus presentation, response collection, and response analysis.

Computer Terminal

Tape recorder

Figure 2.4. A typical cognitive psychology experimental setup using a computer. (Adapted from Rumelhart and Norman, 1981.)

cognitive operations occur very fast—anywhere from one to 250 milliseconds—and only recently has it become convenient to time responses with millisecond accuracy. Now psychologists typically measure latencies with 15 millisecond accuracy, and an even greater accuracy can be achieved if needed.

One use of latency data is in conjunction with the "secondary task" technique in which a subject is asked to perform a main task, but also to give some attention to a less important (secondary) task. For example, Britton and his students (Britton, Piha, Davis, and Wehausen, 1978) gave subjects the main task of reading textbook-like passages in order to answer test questions. The subjects also had a secondary task of responding to occasional clicks by releasing a button. The time that elapsed between the presentation of the

click and the release of the button was automatically recorded. This time was usually in the range of a few hundred milliseconds. Britton took these latency data as evidence of the amount of cognitive capacity that was being devoted to the main task. The more slowly the subject responded to the click, the more capacity was being devoted to the main task and, therefore, the less was left over for the secondary task.

Figure 2.5 shows the latency data collected in the Britton et al. experiment. In this study subjects read a twenty-five-page passage about ecology. After reading the first fourteen pages, half of the subjects received "inserted questions" while reading the rest of the passage and half did not. (Inserted questions are questions embedded in the text that ask about material just read). Previous studies have shown that inserted questions

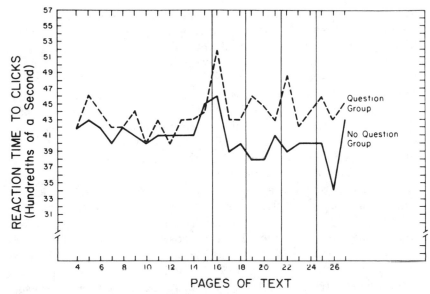

Figure 2.5. An example of the use of latency data. Here the reaction times of two groups of subjects to clicks diverged once inserted questions were introduced into the text for the Question Group. (From Britton, Piha, Davis, and Wehausen, 1978.)

increase learning (Rothkopf and Bisbicos, 1967). The question addressed by Britton et al. was *why* do they increase learning?

As can be seen in Figure 2.5, after page 14, when the first question was inserted, the reaction times for the two groups diverged; the group receiving questions took longer to respond to the clicks than the group not receiving questions. According to Britton et al. this indicates that the group receiving questions was using more cognitive capacity for the primary task of learning the text material and less for the secondary task of responding to clicks. Thus, inserted questions lead us to try harder to learn. This is just one of many examples of the use of latency data in understanding human intelligence. We will see other examples throughout this book.

Eye Fixations. Eye fixations are data about where in a stimulus array a subject fixes his or her gaze at a given time. Eye fixations have been used as data since the beginnings of experimental psychology as have latencies. However, eye fixations are a dense type of data, providing many data points during a subject's performance of even a brief task. Thus, in the past, the formidable task of data reduction discouraged many psychologists from using eye fixations. Now, however, computers can perform the data-reduction task quickly and reliably, so now more and more psychologists are using eye-fixation data.

The principle behind tracking eye fixations is that a small but detectable percentage of light hitting the eye is reflected back from various surfaces of the eye such as the cornea and the front surface of the lens. Therefore, to measure eye fixations a light (usually a nondistracting infrared light) is beamed to the subject's eyes, and then the reflections from various surfaces of the eyes are recorded. A subject's moving his or her head potentially can generate "noise" in the data. However, head movements can be distinguished from eye-fixation changes by different reflectance patterns from various surfaces of the eyes.

Figure 2.6 shows a typical eye-fixation laboratory. In it a subject sits in a chair gazing at a cathode ray screen hooked up to a computer. To one side of the screen is the eye-fixation equipment that beams a light into the subject's eyes. The subject reads or examines the stimulus presented on the screen, and the duration and course of his or her eye fixations on different parts of the stimulus are determined from reflectance patterns.

Snow and his students (reported in Snow, 1980) used eye-fixation data to study how people solve items on tests of spatial ability. Figure 2.7 shows a typical test item from a "paper-folding" test. The subject is told that the stem of the item shows a paper being folded and then punched through all of the layers. The alternatives show various ways the paper could look when it is then unfolded. The subject's task is to decide on the correct alternative.

Snow compared the eye-fixation patterns of high-scoring subjects with those of low scorers. Figure 2.8 shows the eye-fixation patterns of a typical high-scoring subject and a typical low-scoring subject. The patterns are dramatically different. The high-scoring subject spent 10 seconds examining the stem of the test item before ever looking at the alternatives (top left of Figure 2.8). In particular, she spent 7.2 seconds looking at the final part of the stem. The low-scoring subject spent only .2 second looking at the stem initially before looking at one of the alternatives (bottom of Figure 2.8). The low-scoring subject shows a pattern of bouncing back and forth between stem and alternatives whereas the high-scoring subject, once finished looking at the stem, does not look back at it before she responds.

Snow concluded from these data and

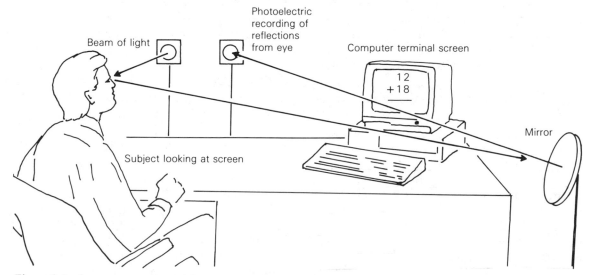

Figure 2.6. An eye-movement laboratory. A beam of light is directed at the subject's eyes as the subject is performing a task. Reflections of this light from the subject's eyes are deflected by a mirror to a photoelectric recording device.

Item stem:

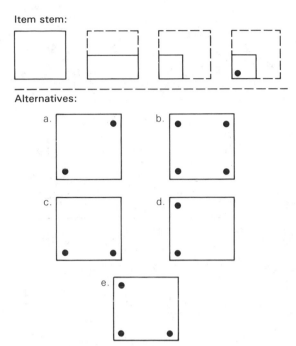

Alternatives:

Figure 2.7. A sample test item from a spatial aptitude test. Subjects are told to assume that the sequence from left to right in the item stem represents a sequence of folds in a piece of paper. Dots represent punches in all the layers of paper that are under the dot. The goal is to choose the alternative that shows what the punched paper would look like after it is unfolded. In this example, *b* is the correct alternative.

from subjects' verbal reports that high scorers use a strategy in which they mentally unfold the paper and then search the alternatives for a match to their mental image. This explains why high scorers spend so much time gazing at the final part of the stem: it is at this point that they are forming a mental image of the unfolded piece of paper. Low scorers, on the other hand, do not form a mental image. Rather, they focus on a perceptual attribute of the stem, such as the placement of a hole, and look for alternatives that somehow match that perceptual attrib-

ute. If one perceptual attribute does not work, they return to the stem to find another. This, then, explains the low scorers' tendency to bounce back and forth between the stem and the alternatives.

As this example illustrates, the interpretation of eye-fixation data is greatly facilitated by comparing them with some other processing data such as verbal reports. Psychologists who use eye-fixation data generally assume that there is some relationship between where the subject is looking and what he or she is thinking. Since this assumption may not always be correct, it is useful to have some other measure that validates it.

Verbal Reports. Verbal reports may be made before, during, or after performing a task. Such reports were the main type of data used by introspectionist psychologists at the turn of the century. Because different psychologists got different results, this method fell into disrepute and for over half a century most American psychologists were unwilling to take seriously any reports made by subjects.

Recently, Ericsson and Simon (1980) proposed a theory of verbal reports that distinguishes the conditions under which reliable and valid subject reports can be obtained from those under which verbal reports may not be valid. Their theory states that the giving of verbal reports is like any other cognitive task in that it can make demands on limited-capacity working memory, long-term memory, and reasoning processes. What demands are made depend on the exact nature of the report requested.

For example, if one is asked to report what one is doing while doing it, this places a great burden on working memory because one has to attend to two complex tasks at once: the task of interest, and the task of reporting what one is doing to perform the task of interest (see Figure 2.9). This heavy de-

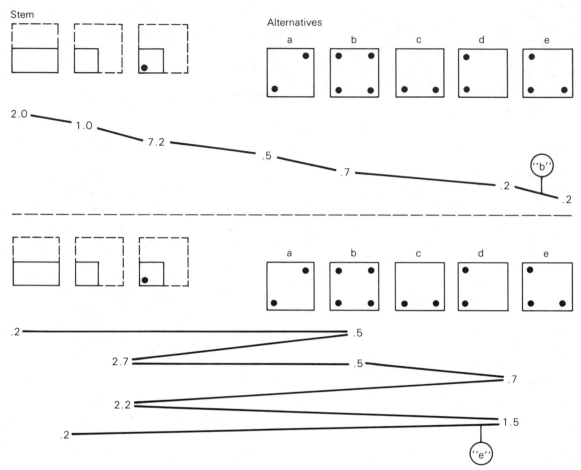

Figure 2.8. Duration and sequence of eye fixations of a typical "good" subject (top) and a typical "poor" subject (bottom) while solving a paper-folding problem. The balloon shows where the subject made a choice. Notice that the subject with high spatial aptitude spends a great deal of time gazing at the last part of the stem and never returns to the stem once she looks at the alternatives. The subject with low spatial aptitude jumps back and forth between stem and alternatives. (Adapted from Snow, 1980.)

mand on attention may lead a subject to use different strategies than would be used when there was no such a demand. Thus, it is not usually very useful to ask people to reflect on what they are doing while they are doing it.

However, as Ericsson and Simon (1980) demonstrate, there is a valid type of verbal report that can be given while performing a task. This type has become known as "thinking aloud." In thinking aloud, subjects do not report *how* they are thinking; rather, they report *what* they are thinking. That is, they report whatever thoughts pass through working memory while performing a task. For example, try this: report whatever goes through your mind as you try to solve the fol-

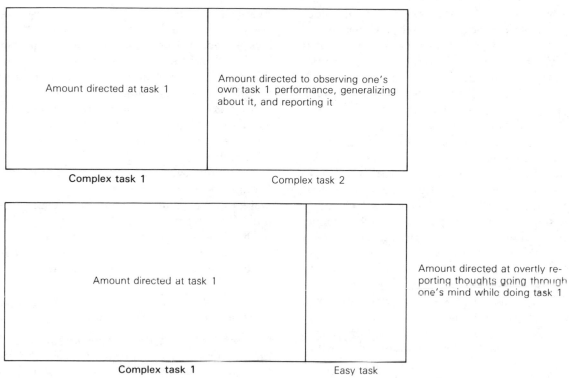

Amount directed at task 1	Amount directed to observing one's own task 1 performance, generalizing about it, and reporting it
Complex task 1	Complex task 2

Amount directed at task 1	Amount directed at overtly reporting thoughts going through one's mind while doing task 1
Complex task 1	Easy task

Figure 2.9. The relative amount of attention directed at two complex tasks versus one complex task and one easy task. When one's attention to complex task 1 is severely limited, one may use different strategies to complete the task than when one's attention is less limited.

lowing analogy. (Start by reading the analogy out loud and then just continue talking out loud):

Washington is to Lincoln as 1 is to ____.

    a. 5 b. 12 c. 13 d. 22

Your thoughts may have gone something like this:

"Washington is to Lincoln as 1 is to __

. . . presidents . . . first, . . . 5, no . . .

22, no . . . 13."

That would have been a good thinking-aloud protocol. However, if you said something like:

"First, I am comparing Washington and Lincoln and asking how they are similar . . ."

you did not state *what* was going through your mind; rather you tried to state *how* you were thinking. Examining how you are thinking while you are thinking detracts from the main task. It takes time for subjects to learn not to reflect but simply to report the contents of working memory. Once they are good at it, thinking aloud demands very little capacity and, therefore, does not disrupt the main task (as is shown in the bottom part of Figure 2.9).

Just as latency and eye movement data

provide clues, the data from thinking aloud protocols provide clues about thinking processes. In the protocol for solving the analogy, it looks as though the person first recognizes that both Washington and Lincoln are presidents ("presidents"), then realizes that Washington was the first president ("first"), and then scans the possible numbers for the number corresponding to Lincoln's presidency ("5, no . . . 22, no . . . 13"). He eliminates 5 and 22 and settles on 13. By the way, Lincoln was the sixteenth president, which was not one of the choices. The correct answer to this analogy is 5. Think of money and you will probably figure out why 5 is correct. (You can verify your answer by turning to the end of this chapter).

Besides overloading working memory during a task, there are other sources of invalidity for verbal reports. Specifically, a subject who is asked a *general* question such as "How do you go about studying your history text?" can generate the answer in many ways, and the way it is generated affects its validity. For example, a student may try to decide what answer you want and tell you this even if it has nothing to do with what he really does. Another student may try to remember two or three past occurrences of studying history texts and generalize across them. If her memory is poor or her sample of occasions somehow biased, the report will not be valid.

Ericsson and Simon (1980) argue that one kind of retrospective report (given after a task is completed) can be valid. It is a report that is given *immediately* after the task is completed, so that memory losses are minimal, and it is tied to a specific instance of task performance so that generalization does not come into play. In the example of studying history texts, a good procedure would be to assign a student a chapter in his history text and then, when he indicates that he has finished studying, immediately ask, "Can you tell me what you did just now to study?" An-

swers can be checked against other observations. For example, if the subject says, "First I skimmed through the chapter to get an overview and then I read carefully" and you did not observe him flipping through the chapter at the beginning of the study period you would have good reason to be suspicious of this subject's reports. Usually, however, retrospective reports about specific tasks have high validity.

In summary, latency, eye-movement, and verbal-report data are frequently used to make inferences about mental processes. Although in the past such data have been difficult to obtain in reliable and valid forms, with current technological and theoretical advances they can yield valuable information.

Methods of Theory Development

Concomitant with the improvement in empirical measures of cognitive process indicators has been the development of logical analysis techniques that facilitate theorizing about cognitive processes. These include the subtractive technique, information processing analysis, and computer simulation.

The Subtractive Technique. The subtractive technique uses latencies as its data source. It is a logical technique used to isolate elementary cognitive processes. The typical experiment involves having subjects perform two slightly different tasks. One of these tasks is thought to involve just one more cognitive operation than the other; all the other cognitive operations involved in performance on the two tasks are thought to be the same. The average time to perform each task is then measured and the time to perform one task is subtracted from the time to perform the other. The result is an estimate of the time needed to perform the one cognitive operation that is different in the two tasks. The logic of the subtractive technique is shown in Figure 2.10.

An example of this technique is provided in a study of sentence comprehension con-ducted by Clark and Chase (1972). In this study subjects saw pictures and sentences such as those shown in Figure 2.11. Subjects might see the sentence "Star above plus" and

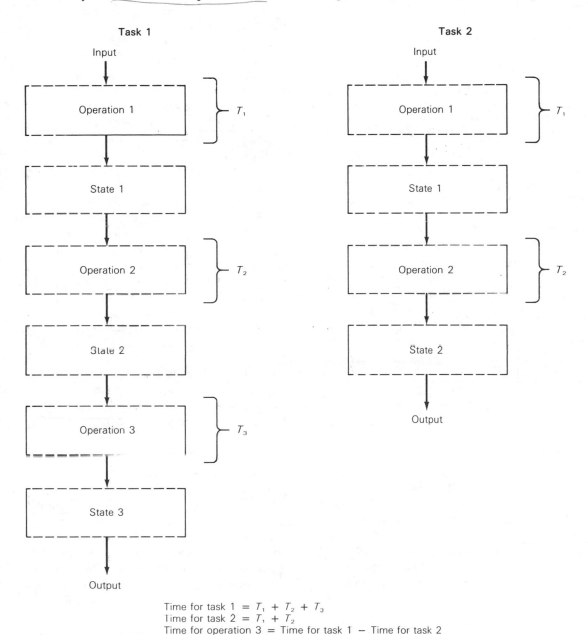

Time for task 1 $= T_1 + T_2 + T_3$
Time for task 2 $= T_1 + T_2$
Time for operation 3 = Time for task 1 − Time for task 2

Figure 2.10. A schematic representation of the logic of the subtractive technique.

Figure 2.11. Two of the stimuli seen by subjects in the Clark and Chase (1972) study of sentence verification.

the picture $\overset{*}{+}$, or they might see the same picture but read "Plus above star." Each subject should indicate by pressing a button whether or not the sentence correctly described the picture. On 50 percent of the trials, the correct answer was yes. Clark and Chase hypothesized that recognizing that the sentence matched the picture would take less time than recognizing that the sentence did *not* match the picture, and, therefore, that latencies for mismatches would be reliably longer than those for matches. Their data confirmed this prediction. We will see exactly how the subtractive technique was used by Clark and Chase shortly, but first it is necessary to describe another theoretical tool they used, called "information-processing analysis."

Information-Processing Analysis. In this type of performance analysis the product is a map of the flow of information. That is, the mental representations and operations that occur during performance and the order of their occurrence are described. Figure 2.12 shows an information-processing analysis for the Clark and Chase (1972) sentence-verification task. The first event that occurs is the subject's assumption that the sentence and the picture will match (signified by setting the

"truth index" at true). Next, the subject observes a sentence on the screen and constructs a meaning representation for the sentence. Then, he or she constructs a meaning representation for the picture. Finally, the subject asks whether or not the representations for the sentence and the picture match. If they do, then he or she reports the value of the truth index (which was set at true). If they do not match, the value of the truth index is changed to false before being reported. Thus, when there is a mismatch, an additional operation—changing the truth index—takes place.

For the subtractive technique described in the last section, Clark and Chase (1972) reasoned that since there was one more mental operation involved in responding to a mismatch than in responding to a match between sentences and pictures, subjects should reliably take longer to respond to mismatches than to matches. Their data supported this prediction. Thus they had some support for the mental model they proposed.

Information-processing analyses generally are written like computer program flow charts. Diamond-shaped boxes are used to indicate choice points, rectangular boxes indicate mental operations, and arrows indicate the direction in which information flows. Flow charts are useful for displaying many ideas compactly. Because cognitive theories tend to be complex, flow charts are helpful in abstracting their important outlines.

Information-processing analyses do not necessarily reflect what a person is aware of thinking. In fact, sometimes the mental operations proposed take place too rapidly for a person to be aware of each step. This is because they are so practiced that they have become highly automatic. Just as many people drive a car without awareness of the motor operations in which they are engaging (turning the wheel, looking in the mirror, putting on the brakes, etc.), so too people perform

INPUT

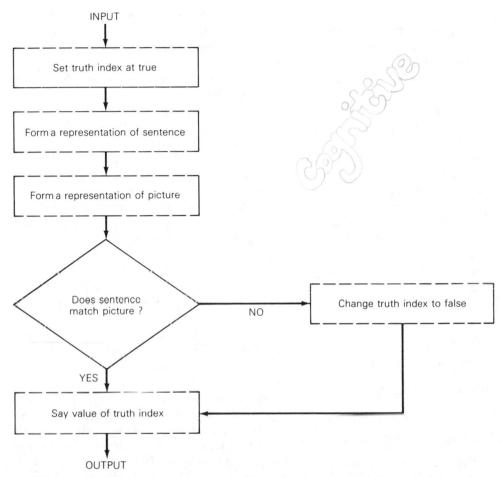

Figure 2.12. An information-processing analysis of the Clark and Chase (1972) sentence-verification task.

many cognitive tasks automatically. In the sentence-verification task, most of us are not aware of laboriously forming meaning representations, setting truth indexes, and comparing meaning representations. We simply "know" whether a sentence and picture match or not. This lack of awareness does not invalidate the model.

Computer Simulation. Computer simulation is information-processing analysis pushed to its limits. In computer simulation

a theory of cognitive operations is translated into a computer language and run as a computer program. (This task is similar to a computer programmer's translation of a flow chart into a program). If the program runs, the theorist knows that the theory is logically consistent—that there are no undefined or circular terms. More important, if the performance of the computer matches human performance on the same task, then the theory that underlies the computer's performance is a plausible one for human performance.

One interesting example of computer simulation comes from the work of Kintsch and van Dijk (1978) on language comprehension. A part of their theory has to do with how humans, with their limited-capacity working memory, manage to integrate language inputs. If our working memory were large, we could wait until we had heard many sentences and then inspect them for interrelationships. However, its capacity is limited, so we need some rules for deciding what parts of previously heard sentences to keep in working memory as we listen to new sentences. Naturally we want to keep those parts which are most likely to be integrated with the new sentences. Kintsch and van Dijk proposed that the most *central* and most *recently stated* parts of sentences are most likely to be integrated with new sentences. For example, in the sentences:

(1) The Swazi tribe was at war with a

neighboring tribe because of a dispute

over some cattle. (2) Among the war-

riors were two unmarried men named

Kakra and his younger brother Gum.

the central part of the first sentence is that the Swazi tribe was at war with a neighboring tribe. This central part connects with the idea of *warrior* in the next sentence.

Or, for example, in the sentences:

(2) Among the warriors were two un-

married men named Kakra and his

younger brother Gum. (3) Kakra was

killed in a battle.

Kakra is the idea that unifies the two sentences. It is also an idea that is from the latter part of the first sentence and hence from the most recently stated part.

Once the problem of what to keep active

in working memory is solved, there is still the problem of integrating one's memory of ideas in prior sentences with the ideas in the current sentence. Kintsch and van Dijk proposed two mechanisms for integration. The first is to use any common concept labels to tie the two sentences together. *Kakra* is a common concept label in sentences 2 and 3. The second mechanism comes into play only if the first does not succeed. It is to infer a relationship between the two sentences based on prior knowledge. There are no common concept labels between sentences 1 and 2, so readers must use their prior knowledge about wars and about syntax to infer that the warriors mentioned in sentence 2 were members of the Swazi tribe mentioned in sentence 1. Figure 2.13 is a flow chart of the processes of selection and integration that I have just described.

Kintsch (1979) translated his and van Dijk's ideas into a computer program. The program was then loaded into the computer and sentences 1, 2, and 3 were read into the computer for processing. The processing of each sentence was said to take place on one "cycle." The events during each cycle are shown in Figure 2.14. During the first cycle the program selected [the Swazi tribe], [was at war with], and [a neighboring tribe] to keep active.[2] It let [because of] and [a dispute over some cattle] become inactive. During the second cycle, the program tried to find a common concept label between the three ideas kept active from the first sentence and the ideas in the second sentence. No common concept label was found, so the program drew the inference that the idea of [the Swazi tribe] is connected to the idea of [warriors] and marked this connection. (This is symbolized in Figure 2.14 by the line from [the

[2]Throughout the book, brackets signify ideas. They are distinct from quotation marks which signify verbal phrases used to communicate ideas.

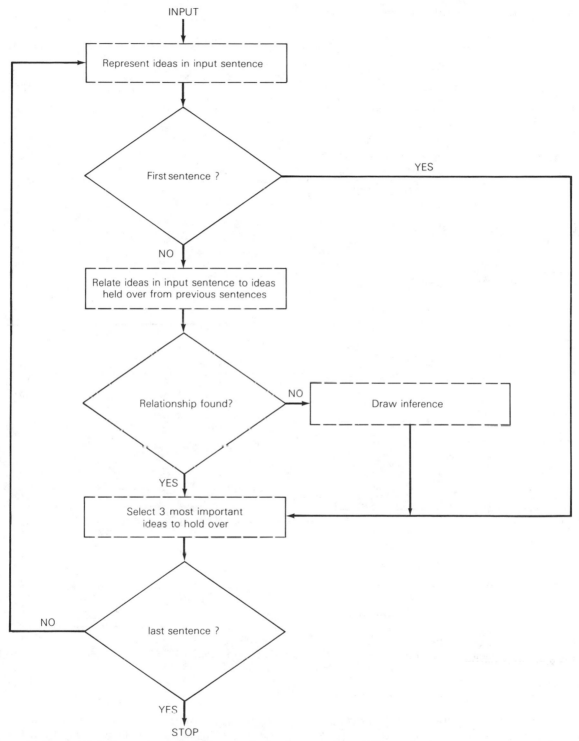

Figure 2.13. An information-processing analysis of some stages in language comprehension.

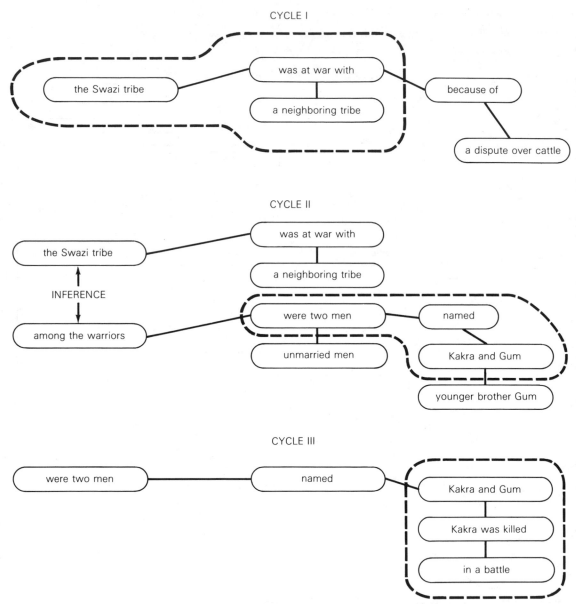

Figure 2.14. The events in a computer simulation of comprehension. The broken lines surround ideas selected for further processing. (Adapted from Kintsch, 1979.)

Swazi tribe] to [among the warriors]). Next, three ideas were selected to keep active. They were: [were two men], [named], and [Kakra and Gum]. During the third cycle, the pro-

gram looked for a common concept label between these three ideas and the new ideas from the third sentence. This time it found a common concept label. Finally, the connection between the second and third sentences was noted (symbolized by the line between [Kakra and Gum] and [Kakra was killed]).

Does this program's output somehow correspond to human behavior on this same task? If it does, the theory proposed may be a good theory of human comprehension. If it does not, it cannot explain comprehension. Kintsch reasoned that if humans use a process similar to that used by the computer program, then they should show better memory for the ideas that the computer worked with on more than one cycle than for the ideas that it worked with on only one cycle. This is because the more operations an idea is involved in in working memory, the more memorable that idea will be. The computer analog to the number of operations on an idea is the number of cycles in which an idea appears.

Table 2.3 shows the results from a study of 100 college students' recall protocols for the passage shown earlier and compares the recall frequency for each idea to the number of cycles this idea occurred on in the computer.

Idea 2 [was at war with], which was recalled by eighty subjects, occurred on two computer cycles, whereas idea 4 [because of], which was recalled by only forty-six subjects, occurred on only one cycle. The data from almost all the ideas showed this same pattern: ideas used on two cycles were recalled by more subjects than were ideas used on only one cycle. (The exceptions are ideas 1 and 13). In general, then, the data are consistent with Kintsch and van Dijk's theory.

Unlike Kintsch and van Dijk's theory, some psychological theories are vague or circular or both. Such theories may have intuitive appeal, but they really do not forward the generation of knowledge because they can be bent and molded to account for almost anything and, therefore, can never be refuted. Scientific knowledge is built on the overturning or refinement of theories and educational practice benefits from the development of new psychological knowledge. Thus the development of clear, consistent theories is an important goal for cognitive psychology. An

Table 2.3. Recall of the passage ideas and the number of computer cycles on which the idea occurred. Notice the positive correlation between the number of subjects recalling an idea and the number of cycles in which the idea occurred. (From Kintsch, 1979.)

IDEA NUMBER		NUMBER SUBJECTS (OUT OF 100) RECALLING IDEAS	NUMBER OF CYCLES IN WHICH IDEA OCCURRED
1	The Swazi tribe	45	2
2	was at war with	80	2
3	a neighboring tribe	78	2
4	because	46	1
5	a dispute over some cattle	39	1
6	Among the warriors	42	1
7	were two men	82	2
8	unmarried men	47	1
9	named	79	2
10	Kakra and Gum	81	2
11	younger brother Gum	45	1
12	Kakra was killed	84	2
13	in a battle	17	2

advantage of testing a cognitive model as a computer simulation is that the model must be clear and consistent if the program is to run.

THE PROBLEM OF NONIDENTIFIABILITY

Running computer programs that simulate some aspect of human performance provide *plausible* theories about that performance. Unfortunately, they do not provide *unique* theories. In fact, it is generally true in cognitive psychology, whether theories are implemented on a computer or not, that more than one theory can be proposed to account for the same performance. J. R. Anderson (1976) calls this the problem of "nonidentifiability."

Recall the sentence-verification task that was discussed on pages 23–25. The flow chart in Figure 2.12 is one plausible model of the cognitive operations involved in verification of sentences. It is plausible because it is consistent with the latency data showing that it takes longer on the average for subjects to recognize mismatches of sentences and pictures than it takes to recognize matches.

Figure 2.15 shows another model (from Carpenter and Just, 1975) that is equally consistent with the data from Clark and Chase (1972). This model starts out the same as the Clark and Chase model (by setting a truth index at "true" and forming a representation of the sentence and the picture). After that, however, the two models differ. In the model shown in Figure 2.15, the next step is to set a "constituent index" at one. A constituent is an idea in the representations of sentences and pictures. For example, the representation of the sentence "star above plus" has three constituents: star, above, and plus. The pictorial representation also has three constituents.

The next step is to find and compare the first constituents (star and star in the above

example). If they match, and if all the constituents have not been compared, the constituent index is incremented by one and the second constituents are compared (above and below). This time the constituents do not match, so the pair is tagged and the truth index is changed to false. Then the constituent index is reset to one and the process of comparing constituents starts again. This time, however, when the second pair of constituents is encountered they are treated as a match (even though they are not) because they are tagged. So the comparison proceeds to the third constituents (cross and cross). Since these match and since there are no more constituents, the value of the truth index is stated. This value is "false" because of the mismatch of the second pair of constituents and because no later comparisons changed the truth index back to true.

The main difference between the two models is in what adds time to the decision-making process. In the Chase and Clark (1972) model it is assumed that changing the truth index and making comparisons both take time, but it is the changing of the truth index that makes mismatches take longer than matches. In the Carpenter and Just (1975) model, it is assumed that the only process that takes time is making comparisons. It takes longer to identify mismatches than matches because the comparison process starts over each time a mismatch is found.

Both models predict a longer reaction time for mismatches, but they do so for different reasons. This is an example of the problem of nonidentifiability because both theories account equally well for some data. Other examples of this problem are scattered throughout this text. One hotly debated issue is whether or not knowledge is stored in long-term memory in one abstract code or in both an abstract code and a visual imagery code. To some extent both theories account equally

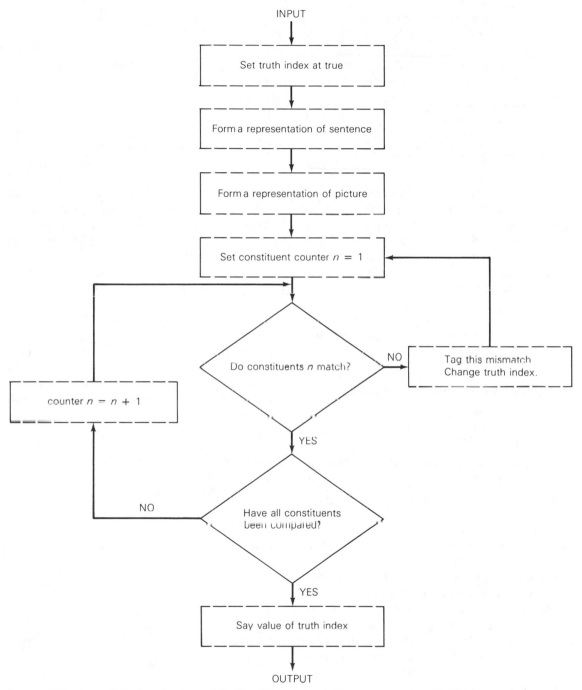

INPUT

Set truth index at true

Form a representation of sentence

Form a representation of picture

Set constituent counter $n = 1$

Do constituents n match?

NO

Tag this mismatch
Change truth index.

YES

counter $n = n + 1$

Have all constituents been compared?

NO

YES

Say value of truth index

OUTPUT

Figure 2.15. A model of sentence verification. This information-processing analysis provides an alternative to the one shown in Figure 2.10. (Adapted from Carpenter and Just, 1975.)

well for data from studies of memory. We will return to this controversy in the next chapter.

If we can never be sure what model is true, can a model be useful? Yes, for two reasons. First, even though two models may account equally well for one set of data, one of them may account for another set better and so have the advantage of breadth. Second, and perhaps more important for educators, a model may be useful in solving practical problems. Different teachers will find different models to be useful depending on what specific learning problems they are trying to understand. However, all teachers should find some cognitive model to be helpful. It is not as important to learn specific models from this text as it is to learn to think about mental representations and processes. Perhaps after you have learned to think this way more explicitly than you do now you will be able to come up with new and better models than the ones described here.

EDUCATIONAL IMPLICATIONS

Classroom Analogs of Cognitive Psychology Methods

Teachers have always been interested in the minds of their students and have, therefore, been using analogs of cognitive psychology methods ever since there have been students. For example, a teacher who observes that one student is consistently faster than another at solving algebra word problems may conclude that the strategy used by the faster student has fewer mental operations than that used by the slower student. This is a form of subtractive technique theorizing. Or a fourth-grade teacher who watches a student's eye fixations during "silent reading," and sees that the student spends lots of time looking at the pictures, may guess that this student is forming a mental representation of the story based on pictures rather than on words.

This is making use of eye-fixation data to hypothesize about a student's mental processes.

Perhaps the most common educational analog to methods used by cognitive psychologists is "showing one's work" in solving math problems (see Figure 2.16). Showing work is like thinking aloud except that one writes rather than states one's thoughts. Arithmetic and math teachers who use this procedure realize that a student may get the wrong numerical answer to a problem yet be performing the correct mental operations. (The wrong answer might be due to misremembering an addition fact). Also, showing one's work reveals certain incorrect mental operations. For example, Rachel, the student whose work is shown in Figure 2.16, can borrow correctly except when she runs into a zero. When she runs into a zero, as can be seen from her notes, she borrows a ten from it, instead of going to the next column to borrow. A teacher who understands a student's mental operations can point out an incorrect operation and describe the correct operation.

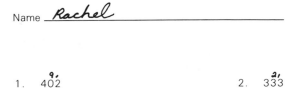

Name *Rachel*

1. $\begin{array}{r} \overset{9.}{40}2 \\ -137 \\ \hline 365 \end{array}$ 2. $\begin{array}{r} \overset{2.}{33}3 \\ -126 \\ \hline 207 \end{array}$

3. $\begin{array}{r} \overset{9.}{50}4 \\ -325 \\ \hline 279 \end{array}$ 4. $\begin{array}{r} \overset{5.13.}{64}3 \\ -255 \\ \hline 388 \end{array}$

Figure 2.16. An arithmetic worksheet on which the student has shown her work. Notice that 1 and 3 are wrong. A teacher can quickly figure out that Rachel has an incorrect rule that borrowing from zero leaves nine.

This brief procedure sometimes clears up the problem immediately.

One contribution of cognitive psychology to observational techniques in the classroom is simply to encourage teachers to use these techniques more. Although showing one's work is a well-known method in math education, it is used less often in other subject areas. Just as psychologists have hesitated to use verbal reports because of threats to validity, so have teachers hesitated to rely on student's verbal reports. Yet, when the right question is asked at the right time, verbal reports can be quite revealing. For example, in teaching writing, students could be asked to hand in notes, outlines, and drafts as well as their finished products. Teachers could then try to identify effective and ineffective strategies revealed by these notes. Or, in a discussion during a history class, a teacher could ask students not only to answer a question, but to describe the steps in their reasoning that led to the answer. This description could reveal faulty mental operations such as overgeneralization, false deductions, or failure to recognize multiple causes for a given event. These are just a few ways verbal reports can be used to find out about students' cognitive processes.

Cognitive psychology can also make teachers more aware of sources of invalidity. In particular, asking students general questions about how they solve problems or how they study does not seem to produce informative answers. The students may try to give an answer that they think will please or they may invent an answer. Just as it is best for psychologists to collect retrospective reports immediately after a specific event, so too it is best for teachers to ask students about a specific performance soon after that performance occurred.

Finally, with the advent of microcomputers in the classroom, many laboratory techniques may become available to teachers for use in diagnostic testing. Computers can be programmed to detect common error patterns in students' responses and then to branch to a variety of instructional procedures depending on the error pattern discerned.

Greater Emphasis on the Teaching of Strategies

Strategies are goal-directed sequences of cognitive operations that lead from the student's comprehension of a question or instructions to the answer or other requested performance. Because strategies are mental they have been difficult to observe using the traditional method of examining the number correct on some task. Therefore, little precise knowledge of strategies has been available until recently.

With our increasing ability to observe and model cognitive processes as they take place, we can describe the cognitive strategy differences between skilled and less skilled performance. Once the strategies used by skilled individuals are known, we should be able to teach them directly to less skilled individuals. For example, Snow's research on spatial ability tests shows that a good strategy to use on such tests is to look at the known shape, imagine the shape going through specified changes, and finally focus attention on the end result, holding that image in working memory while scanning alternatives for a match. These steps might be taught to students who do not use them naturally. Egan (1983) has trained people to use a strategy similar to the one described by Snow.

ADDITIONAL READINGS

Many of the methods described in this chapter have rather technical justifications. If you plan to conduct research using one of these methods, it would be well worth your while to read further before using the method.

Subtractive Technique

Chase, W. G. (1978). Elementary information processes. In W. K. Estes (ed.), *Handbook of learning and cognitive processes*, Vol. 5. Hillsdale, N.J.: Lawrence Erlbaum Associates.

Donders, F. C. (1969). On the speed of mental processes. *Acta Psychologica*, 30, 412–31. (Translated by W. G. Koster from the original in *Onderzoekingen gedaan in het Physiologisch Laboratorium der Utrechtsche Hoogeschool*, 1868, *Tweede reeks*, II, 92–120).

Sternberg, S. (1969). The discovery of processing stages: Extensions of Donder's method. In W. G. Koster (ed.), *Attention and performance II. Acta Psychologica*, 30, 276–315.

Eye Fixations

Monty, R. A. and J. W. Senders, eds. (1976). *Eye movements and psychological processes*. Hillsdale, N.J.: Lawrence Erlbaum Associates.

Verbal Reports

Egan, D. E., and D. Grimes-Farrow (1982). Differences in mental representations spontaneously adopted for reasoning. *Memory and Cognition*, 10, 297–307.

Ericsson, K. A., and H. A. Simon (1980). Verbal reports as data. *Psychological Review*, 87, 215–51.

Computer Simulation

Bower, G. H., and E. R. Hilgard (1981). Information-processing theories of behavior. In G. H. Bower and E. R. Hilgard, *Theories of learning*, 5th ed. Englewood Cliffs, N.J.: Prentice-Hall.

The following articles provide examples of the use of cognitive psychology in instructional design:

Gagné, E. D., and M. S. Bell (1981). The use of cognitive psychology in the development and evaluation of textbooks. *Educational Psychologist*, 16, 83–100.

Greeno, J. G. (1980). Some examples of cognitive task analysis with instructional implications. In R. E. Snow, P. Federico, and W. E. Montague (eds.), *Aptitude, learning, and instruction*, Vol. 2. Hillsdale, N.J.: Lawrence Erlbaum Associates.

Posner, G. (1982). A cognitive science conception of curriculum and instruction. *Journal of Curriculum Studies*, 14, 343–51.

Resnick, L. B. (1976). Task analysis in instructional design: Some cases from mathematics. In D. Klahr (ed.), *Cognition and instruction*. Hillsdale, N.J.: Lawrence Erlbaum Associates.

These books are excellent introductions to the field of cognitive psychology:

Anderson, J. R. (1980a). *Cognitive psychology and its implications*. San Francisco: W. H. Freeman.

Wood, G. (1983). *Cognitive psychology: A skills approach*. Belmont, CA: Wadsworth.

ANSWER TO ANALOGY

Five is correct because Lincoln's picture is on a five-dollar bill; Washington's is on a one-dollar bill. (This example comes from R. Sternberg, 1979.)

Chapter 3

Representation of Knowledge

SUMMARY

1. Knowledge is represented mentally in a variety of forms including propositions, productions, and images.

2. A proposition is a basic unit of information, corresponding roughly to one idea.

3. Propositions are linked in memory as propositional networks; propositions sharing topics are more closely associated than those not sharing topics.

4. Declarative knowledge, represented by propositions, is knowing *that* something is the case, whereas procedural knowledge is knowing *how* to do something. Procedural knowledge is faster to activate and more reactive to the environment than is declarative knowledge.

5. Productions represent procedural knowledge. They are condition-action rules that perform specified actions under specified conditions.

6. Productions are linked into production systems whenever the action taken by one production creates the conditions of another production.

7. Images represent information continuously, rather than discretely. They are used in working memory to reason about entities that have a spatial dimension.

In the previous chapter we discussed the basic architecture of the human information-processing system (receptors, sensory register, working memory, etc.). This architecture constrains the manner in which knowledge can be represented, just as certain building designs constrain the types of furnishings that will go inside.

As we have seen, a major difference between the architecture of humans and that of computers is in the size of their workspace. Even a small personal computer has many thousands of times the space in its central processing unit that humans have in their working memories. Computer programming languages are compatible with the computer's large workspace: they are clear, logical languages that allow for unambiguous identification of various areas in the workspace. However, since there is plenty of room to move around in, they are not particularly economical languages.

What form should knowledge take to be compatible with human architecture? One very important aspect is economy. This is necessary because of the severe limitations on human working memory. Somehow knowledge must be packaged to minimize the burden on working memory. As we shall see in this chapter, each form of knowledge representation that humans use has its own economy. Each does something different to minimize the load on working memory.

Three forms of representation will be discussed in this chapter: (1) propositions, (2) productions, and (3) images. Although most people have some idea about what images are, propositions and productions may seem nonintuitive at first. Because of this, several practice exercises that require you to interpret information in propositional and production form are given throughout the chapter. Plan to read this chapter at a slow pace, giving yourself time to complete the exercises.

You may wonder why it is important to learn to do what is required in the exercises. By doing them you should improve on your ability to think in terms of mental representations and this should help you in several ways. Most immediately it will help you understand the rest of the book. Later it may help you read further in cognitive psychology, where propositions, productions, and images are commonly used. Finally and perhaps most important, it may help structure your future thinking about practical educational problems such as designing a lesson or figuring out what is going on in the mind of a particular student. You may realize this final benefit as you are reading this book, or you may not realize it for several months or even years to come.

PROPOSITIONS

A basic unit of information in the human information-processing system is the proposition. It corresponds roughly to an idea. For example, which of the following two phrases seems to be a complete idea?

the man

the man fixed the tire

Clearly the second phrase is more complete.

Although the sentence "The man fixed the tire" contains only one proposition, many sentences contain more than one. For example, "The man fixed the tire and left" contains two ideas (propositions): one is that the man fixed the tire and the other is that he left.

A proposition always contains two elements: a *relation* and a *set of arguments*. The arguments are the topics of the proposition, so they tend to be nouns and pronouns (although they can also be verbs and adjectives). The relation of a proposition *constrains* the topics, so relations tend to be verbs, adjectives, and adverbs. For example, in the idea represented by "Joe walked," *Joe* is the topic (argument) and *walked* is what constrains the topic (relation). *Walked* constrains the topic of *Joe* in that it tells us that of all the information we have about Joe, we are attending only to information about Joe walking. Figure 3.1 is a Venn diagram for the argument *Joe* and the relation *walked*. In general, relations narrow focus; *walked* narrows the focus of a topic considerably. This aspect of relations makes them the most informative part of the proposition.

Table 3.1 shows some other ideas and their arguments and relations. All of these

Knowledge of Joe (argument)

Knowledge of Joe walking (relation)

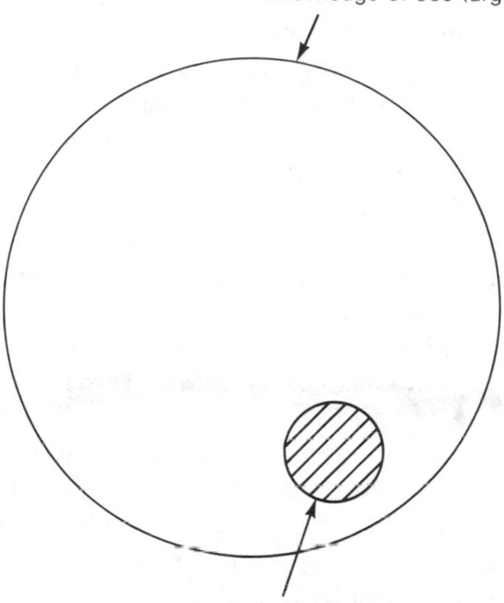

Figure 3.1. The relationship between the relation and argument of a proposition is shown here for the proposition [walked, Joe]. Arguments establish general areas of information and relations narrow the focus within the general areas established by arguments.

ideas have verbs as relations (*walked, read, swam,* and *gave* for ideas 1, 2, 3, and 4, respectively) because in all of these ideas it is a verb that constrains the topics. Ideas 2 and 3 have not one, but two arguments. That is, they have two topics. Idea 2, that Sandra read a book, has both *Sandra* and *book* for topics. *Read* constrains these topics, telling us that what is happening between Sandra and the

Table 3.1. Some examples of propositions, showing their relations and arguments. In these examples all the relations are verbs and all the arguments are nouns.

IDEA	RELATION	ARGUMENT(S)
1. [Joe walked.]	walked	Joe
2. [Sandra read a book.]	read	Sandra, book
3. [Jane swam to shore.]	swam	Jane, shore
4. [Bill gave the car to Ellen.]	gave	Bill, car, Ellen

book is reading, as opposed, say, to stealing or burning. Idea 3 has the topics (arguments) *Jane* and *shore*, and *swam* tells us that what is going on between Jane and the shore is swimming. Finally, idea 4 has three arguments—*Bill, car,* and *Ellen. Gave* tells us that the relationship among these three arguments has to do with giving, as opposed to, say, running over (as in "Bill ran over Ellen with the car").

As these examples illustrate, whereas propositions always have only one relation, they may have more than one argument. This is especially true when the relation is a verb, because verbs often set up expectations for more than one argument. For example, the verb *give* leads us to expect information about the giver, the recipient, and the object that was given. The verb *go* leads us to expect information about who did the going, and where he or she went (the goal). Some verbs lead us to expect information about an instrument of action. For example, *cut:* if we hear the sentence "Ralph cut his finger," we anticipate finding out the instrument responsible for the cutting (a razor? a pair of scissors? a knife?).

Because a proposition may have more than one argument, arguments are given different names depending on their role in the proposition. Arguments may be *subjects, objects, goals* (destinations), *instruments* (means), and *recipients*. Table 3.2 shows some ideas with their arguments labeled according to the role that each plays within the idea.

Consider now the sentence "The tall woman played basketball." How many ideas do you think are expressed by this sentence? Clearly, one idea has *played* as its relation. The arguments of *played* include the subject (woman) and the object (basketball). But what about the idea of *tall? Tall* constrains the topic of *woman* because it narrows the focus within the topic to a tall woman. Since *tall* constrains the topic of *woman,* it is a relation and *woman* is its argument. Thus, the sentence "The tall woman played basketball" is said to express two ideas (propositions): (1) that the woman played basketball and (2) that the woman was tall.

In general, adjectives in sentences form the basis for separate propositions. Unlike verb-based propositions, adjective-based propositions take only one argument—that which is being modified. Thus, *tall woman* expresses a proposition with the relation *tall* and the argument *woman.* The arguments of adjective-based propositions are always nouns.

Now consider the sentence "The tall woman played basketball vigorously." How many ideas does this sentence express? The answer is three. The adverb *vigorously* constrains the verb *played,* narrowing the focus within the concept of play to play that has a vigorous quality. Thus *vigorous* is a relation and its topic, or argument, is *play.* As with adjective-based propositions, adverb-based propositions also have only one argument, which is the subject. Unlike adjective-based propositions, however, the subject of adverb-

Table 3.2. Some examples of propositions that have more than one argument. The arguments are labeled according to their role in the idea being represented.

IDEA	RELATION	ARGUMENTS
[Manuel gave Harry a pencil.]	gave	Manuel (subject), Harry (recipient), pencil (object)
[Carol is going to New York.]	is going	Carol (subject), New York (goal)
[Ralph cut his finger with a paper.]	cut	Ralph (subject), finger (object), paper (instrument)

[handwritten annotation, top left:]
subj: Arg. / Relation
wind → blew
obj, subj: tree ← tall
subj: teacher ← eager
obj: microcomp ← selected
subj, intr: selected ← carefully

based propositions is a verb or adjective, rather than a noun or pronoun.

Now it is your turn to try identifying the propositions represented in sentences. For each of the following sentences, list the propositions—relation plus argument(s):

3.1. The wind <u>blew</u> the <u>tall</u> trees.

[handwritten: wind blew trees / 2 props - trees tall]

3.2. The <u>eager</u> teacher <u>selected</u> a microcomputer <u>carefully</u>.

[handwritten: 3 props - teacher eager / teacher selected micro / teacher selected carefully]

A good way to start is to underline each verb, adjective, and adverb. This will tell you how many propositions the sentence has, because only verbs, adjectives, and adverbs can be relations and there is only one relation per proposition. After you have identified each relation, list its argument(s). The answers to this exercise are given at the end of the chapter.

Abstractness of Propositions

It is important to distinguish between words, phrases, and sentences, on the one hand, and propositions, on the other. Words, phrases, and sentences represent ways of communicating ideas, whereas propositions represent the ideas themselves.

Research suggests that we store information as propositions, rather than sentences. That is, we generally remember ideas but not necessarily the exact words used to communicate the ideas. Wanner (1968) demonstrated this in a study that used the following sentences:

1. When you score your results, do nothing to correct your answers but mark carefully those answers which are wrong.

2. When you score your results, do nothing to correct your answers but carefully mark those answers which are wrong.

3. When you score your results, do nothing to your correct answers but mark carefully those answers which are wrong.

4. When you score your results, do nothing to your correct answers but carefully mark those answers which are wrong.

Notice that although there are slight wording differences between sentences 1 and 2 ("mark carefully" versus "carefully mark"), the meaning of these two sentences is the same. There are also slight wording differences between sentences 1 and 3 ("correct your" versus "your correct"). However, in this case the wording change drastically alters the meaning. Sentences 3 and 4 are like 1 and 2 in that they differ in wording but not meaning and 2 and 4 are like 1 and 3 in that they differ in both wording and meaning.

The subjects in this study heard one of the four sentences as part of the directions they received at the beginning of the study. Half of the subjects had been warned that they would be asked to recall the wording of the directions and half were not so warned. After hearing one of the sentences, the subjects were told to turn to the next page in their test booklet and mark which of the sentences shown was identical to the last sentence they had heard in their directions. Two sentences were shown. One was the sentence they had heard and the other was one of the other sentences—one that varied in words only or one that varied in both words and meaning.

If people are as sensitive to wording changes as they are to meaning changes, then they should be as good at identifying the correct sentence when the distractor sentence had only a word change as when it had both a word and meaning change. However, the results did not show such an equality, as can be seen in Figure 3.2. Subjects made more errors when the distractor sentence had only a

[handwritten, bottom: Why confound with a double diff?]

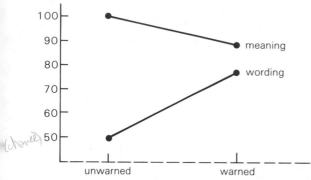

Figure 3.2. Percentage of correct responses when distractor sentence changed the meaning or only the wording of the correct sentence as a function of whether the subjects were warned or not that they should pay attention to wording. (Adapted from Wanner, 1968 as cited in J. R. Anderson, 1980.)

word change than when it had both a word and meaning change. In fact, when they were unwarned about being tested on wording, subjects chose the wrong sentence 50 percent of the time, that is, at a chance level. Thus, it appears that people attend to and store the *meanings* of sentences (propositions) rather than the particular words used.

Propositions in Node-Link Form

Instead of listing a proposition as a relation and one or more arguments, one can draw them in node-link form. For some purposes, such as when one is describing the relationships among several propositions, a node-link structure is more useful than a listing. Figure 3.3 shows some propositions in node-link form. The nodes, or circles, represent the entire proposition. The links, or arrows, point to each of the elements of the proposition. Each link is labeled to identify the role of the element within a particular proposition. So, for example, in the first proposition *Rachel*, *mowed*, and *lawn* serve as subject, relation, and object, respectively. In the second prop-

osition, *mowed* has a different role than in the first proposition. Whereas *mowed* was the relation in the first proposition, in the second it functions as the subject.

3.3. Return now to the propositions you listed for the sentence "The eager teacher selected a microcomputer carefully." Try drawing a node-link structure for each of your propositions. Check your drawings with those shown at the end of the chapter.

Propositional Networks

One of the most important characteristics of any given unit of information is its relationship to other units. Our knowledge of such relationships underlies our ability to make analogies and to see other types of connections. Such abilities are important in novel problem-solving situations.

Because the relationships among sets of information are a crucial aspect of intelligence, it is important to have a way of representing them. One way is in the form of *propositional networks*, which are sets of interrelated propositions. Any two propositions that share an element are interrelated through this element. Figure 3.4 shows two networks for some of the propositions that you have already studied. As you can see, all that was done to generate the networks in Figure 3.4 from the propositions in Figure 3.3 was to identify common elements and then represent these elements only once rather than twice. This brings related propositions closer together than unrelated propositions. For example, *mowed* is a common element in the first two propositions. In Figure 3.3 *mowed* is shown twice, whereas in Figure 3.4 it shows up only once, as a bridge between the two propositions.

A propositional network is a hypothetical construct and should be kept distinct from the notion of neural network, which is poten-

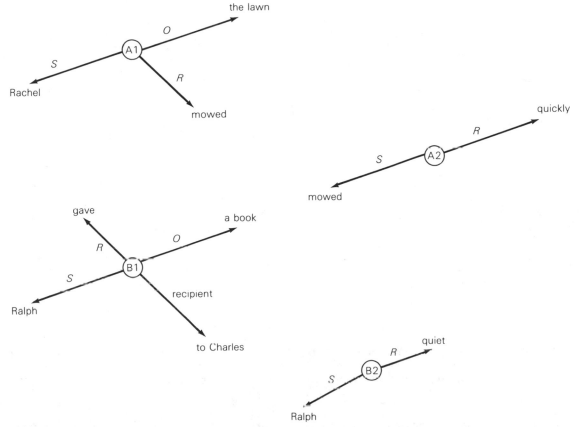

Figure 3.3. Propositions drawn as node-link figures. The nodes (or circles) represent propositions. The links (or lines) point to the elements of the proposition and label them. (S = subject, O = object, R = relation.)

tially observable. At present we do not know in a detailed way how information is represented in a physiological sense. It may be represented in neural network patterns or it may be represented in chemical sequences within protein molecules or it may be represented some other way. Even when a physiological substrate is found, however, propositional networks should continue to be convenient constructs for helping us think about cognitive processes.

One area in which the notion of propositional networks has been particularly useful is in thinking about memory storage and re-

trieval. This topic will be discussed at greater length in the next chapter, but to introduce it here, I will describe two studies of how people store and retrieve information using propositional networks.

The first study (B. Hayes-Roth and Thorndyke, 1979) examined networks among just a few propositions. Figure 3.5 shows some of these propositions. At the top of the figure are two sentences on which the networks are based. The middle of the figure shows the networks that can be generated for each sentence separately. As you can see, the networks for the two sentences are almost

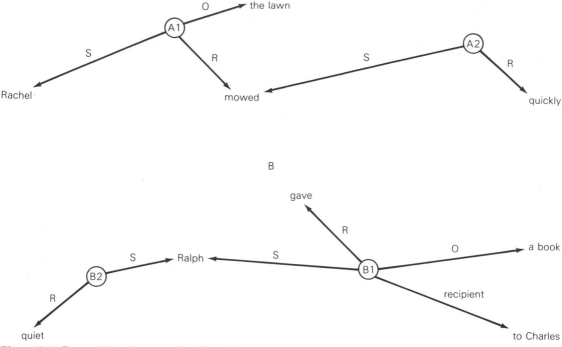

Figure 3.4. Propositional networks show the interrelationships between propositions that share ideas. Network *A* is composed of two propositions that share the element *mowed*. Network *B* is composed of two propositions that share the element *Ralph*.

identical except that for the first sentence it is the Domestic Welfare Agency that distributes information, whereas for the second sentence it is computer terminals. Since the information from the two sentences is partially redundant, it can be combined and represented as shown in Figure 3.5c. Here the network represents the idea that the Domestic Welfare Agency uses computer terminals to distribute information about professional options.

B. Hayes-Roth and Thorndyke were interested in the conditions under which people were likely to create two separate propositional networks for the two sentences (as shown in Figure 3.5*b*) versus those under which they were likely to create just one network (as shown in part *c*). One condition that they thought would be important was the sequence in which the two sentences were encountered. Specifically, students might be

more likely to interrelate two networks if the sentences from which the networks were derived were presented one right after the other than if they were separated by the presentation of several other sentences.

B. Hayes-Roth and Thorndyke view information acquisition as a process in which new propositions are created in working memory and then shipped off to long-term memory. (Their view is not unlike the view held by Kintsch and van Dijk which was described in the computer simulation section of Chapter 2). When new information is presented, a continuous cycle is generated in which a unit of new information is perceived, a proposition is created for it, another unit of information is perceived, a proposition is created for it, and so on. As working memory fills up with new information, propositions that have recently been created are stored in

a. The Domestic Welfare Agency distributes information about professional options.

  Information about professional options is distributed by means of computer terminals.

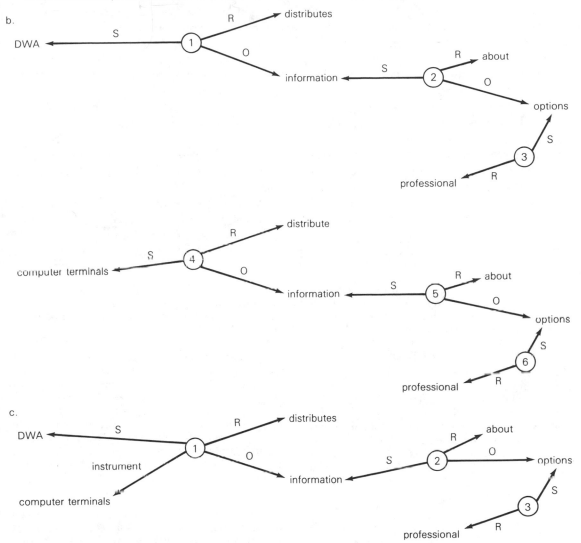

Figure 3.5. Part a shows two sentences that form the basis of the networks shown in part b. In part c the two propositional networks with redundant information are merged into one. (Adapted from B. Hayes-Roth and Thorndyke, 1979.)

long-term memory to make room for the new information. Given this view, one would predict that two sets of propositions that share an idea will be interrelated into a larger network only if they are both active in working memory at the same time. Otherwise the in-

terrelationship will not be noticed and the two sets will be stored separately in long-term memory.

To test this prediction, B. Hayes-Roth and Thorndyke had two groups of students read different versions of the same set of information about a fictional country called Brownland. In one set (version *A*), as shown in Table 3.3, certain crucial pairs of sentences (such as the pair I have already described) were separated by several sentences and by two paragraph boundaries. In the other set (version *B*), the crucial sentences occurred one right after the other within the same paragraph. Each crucial pair contained a common idea (such as career counseling). Thus, the materials were constructed so that for the group that read version *B* the two propositions related to a common idea would be active in working memory at the same time, whereas for the group that read version *A* these two propositions would not be active at the same time.

One way to measure how close together information is in long-term memory is to see if one part of the information cues the other part. In this study if the propositions "the Domestic Welfare Agency distributes information about professional options" and "computer terminals distribute information about professional options" are stored close together, then the cue words *Domestic Welfare Agency* should lead the student to think of computer terminals. If, on the other hand, the propositions are stored separately, then the cue words *Domestic Welfare Agency* should not lead the student to think of computer terminals.

The results showed that when the subjects had read the two crucial sentences one right after the other (version *B*), a cue from one of the sentences led them to select a re-

Table 3.3. Version *A* of a set of three passages about Brownland. There are two italicized sentences that refer to professional options and are separated by sentences and by passage boundaries. In Version *B* (not shown), sentences in the passages were rearranged so that sentences in crucial pairs occurred together. (Adapted from Hayes-Roth and Thorndyke, 1979)

BROWNLAND 1

In Brownland, the work of the government is divided among several different bureaucratic agencies. Some of the agencies and their responsibilities are given below. The National Intelligence Group collects data regarding the international superpowers. The Navy attacks enemies of Brownland. The Broad of Banking studies supply and demand fluctuations in order to prevent fiscal crises. The Royal Knowledge Society monitors scientific investigations in universities. The Internal Guard uses negotiations to deal with civil riots. *The Domestic Welfare Agency distributes information about professional options to all citizens.*

BROWNLAND 2

Government activities in Brownland are undertaken with particular purposes in mind. A representative sample of activities and purposes is given below. The movement of citizens within Brownland is reported to the Statistics Department in order to minimize census-taking difficulties. Spying operations are undertaken primarily to evaluate the likelihood that Brownland will be invaded. The government collects data regarding the international superpowers in an effort to anticipate major disruptions. Scientific investigations in universities are monitored so that important findings can be made available to the government. The state keeps track of the wealth of individual citizens in order to facilitate economic planning. County agents maintain permanent files of all violations of the law so that repeat offenders can be punished.

BROWNLAND 3

The Brownland government makes use of various kinds of equipment and personnel in carrying out its functions. Some of these are described below. Social workers are used to insure that children are given adequate home environments in order to promote an egalitarian society. The vice squad uses electronic surveillance equipment to detect crime in the streets at night. Long range missiles are used to attack enemies. Spying operations utilize paratroopers. *Information about professional options is distributed by means of computer terminals.* The state keeps track of the wealth of individual citizens by means of ID cards.

lated idea from the other sentence 45 percent of the time. When they were read separately (version *A*), they cued one another only 35 percent of the time. Thus, the extent to which information is integrated into networks depends partly on whether the information was presented close together in time.

The B. Hayes-Roth and Thorndyke study shows humans behaving as if they stored information in propositional networks. It suggests that how well information is integrated in memory depends on whether or not two related bits of information are active in working memory at the same time. This principle is a very important one for teaching. Review, thoughtful organization of material, and reminding students of ideas they know but are not thinking of at the time all help them have related information active in working memory when it can be used to integrate new information. Figure 3.6 shows a teacher who is presenting information in a manner that supports knowledge integration.

A classic study that supports the notion that information is stored in long-term memory as propositional networks was done by Collins and Quillian (1969). They examined larger networks of information than did B. Hayes-Roth and Thorndyke. Figure 3.7 shows one of these networks. It has a hierarchical structure in which facts about certain animals are stored at different levels of generality. For example, the fact that birds have feathers is stored at the level of birds. The fact that birds have skin is not actually stored, but rather is inferred from the fact that animals have skin. In other words, facts are stored at the level of generality where they are used to distinguish among classes of objects. All animals have skin but no rocks have skin so the idea of skin is useful for distinguishing animals from minerals. On the other hand, only some animals have feathers, so the possession of feathers is not a useful guide to classifying animals versus minerals. Feathers *are* a useful guide to classifying birds versus other

Figure 3.6. This teacher is promoting the integration of knowledge about different ways to identify themes. If he had not reminded the students of what they did yesterday and explicitly related it to what they were about to learn, some students might not have integrated the information learned yesterday with that learned today.

Figure 3.7. A hypothetical memory network for information that is hierarchically organized. (From Collins and Quillian, 1969.)

small creatures, so the fact that birds have feathers is stored at the level of birds in the knowledge hierarchy.

Collins and Quillian proposed that we store classificatory knowledge in hierarchical networks such as the one shown in Figure 3.7. Further they proposed a mechanism for verification of facts based on this structure. They argued that when a person is asked to verify a statement such as "Fish have skin," a search starts at the level of fish and looks for the property of skin. If *skin* is not found at this level, the search moves up a level and again looks for the property of skin. This time *skin* is found. Because of the structure of the hierarchy, all things that are true at the higher levels are also true at lower levels, so once *skin* is found at a higher level the subject responds "true."

To test their notion of hierarchical storage of facts, Collins and Quillian predicted that time to verify facts would depend on the distance between the two concepts (e.g., animal and property) in the hierarchy. Thus, it should take longer to verify "Canaries have skin" than to verify "Canaries are yellow,"

because the search from *canaries* to *skin* includes two levels whereas the search from *canaries* to *yellow* takes place on the same level.

The researchers had subjects sit at a computer terminal and watch the screen. A subject who read a fact such as "Fish have skin" on the screen decided as quickly as possible if the fact was true or false. If it was true, the subject pressed one key on the keyboard and if it was false, another key. The times it took subjects to verify facts with concepts of varying distances from each other in the proposed hierarchy were recorded by the computer.

Figure 3.8 shows the average reaction times to verify true sentences whose concepts spanned 0, 1, or 2 levels in the proposed memory structure. The researchers looked separately at sentences that identified properties and sentences that identified supersets. In both cases the reaction time increased with the distance between the concepts, thus verifying the predictions.

These results suggest that people organize knowledge into efficient packages. We could store every fact at every level of generality. For example, we could store the fact

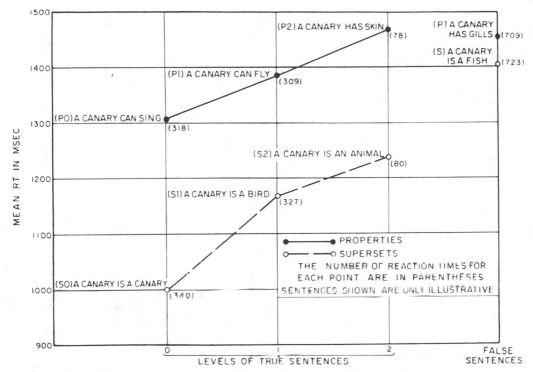

Figure 3.8. Reaction time to verify sentences as a function of distance between concepts in the hierarchical memory structure. (From Collins and Quillian, 1969.)

that birds have skin. Instead, we store the fact that animals have skin and use this to infer that birds have skin when we need such knowledge. In other words, we use our understanding of superordinate-subordinate relationships to reduce the amount of knowledge we need to store directly.

Although these results are consistent with the view that some of our knowledge is organized hierachically, an interpretation that does not assume hierarchical storage has also been proposed (Landauer and Meyer, 1972), and the issue has not been resolved. The important point for the moment is that knowledge is represented mentally in organized ways. Further research is needed before we can specify the exact nature of organization.

Summary

One form of representing information is the proposition, which is roughly equivalent to one idea. Propositions are not the same as sentences but are more abstract.

Propositions that share elements are related in networks. Networks underlie our ability to think of related information at appropriate times. Unlike most computer systems, which store information in arbitrary locations in the central processing unit, propositional networks store related bits of information closer together than unrelated bits. This is important in a system with a limited-capacity working memory because it means that related information that is not active in working memory will be easy to activate because it is closer to what is active than is unrelated information.

By now you should be able to identify the propositions in simple sentences and to identify the relation and argument(s) in any given proposition. Also, you should be able to draw a propositional network structure for sets of related propositions. If you can do these things, you should be able to generate a propositional network for each of the following sentences:

3.4. The very hungry child devoured the hamburger.

3.5 A triangle is a three-sided, closed figure.

To do this, start out by listing each proposition in the sentence. Then draw each proposition as a node-link structure. Finally, look for common elements among the propositions and merge the propositions at the juncture of common elements. Answers are given at the end of the chapter.

DECLARATIVE VERSUS PROCEDURAL KNOWLEDGE

Propositions are used to represent *declarative knowledge. Procedural knowledge* is represented by productions. In the next section, we will look at productions; here we will discuss the differences between declarative and procedural knowledge.

Declarative knowledge is knowledge *that* something is the case, whereas procedural knowledge is knowledge of *how* to do something. A child who says, "To divide fractions, invert the divisor and multiply" knows *that* something is true for dividing fractions yet may not know *how* to divide fractions. This can only be determined by his performance on a test of dividing fractions. Similarly, a child who knows *that* she lives at 2309 Macon Street may not know *how* to get there from school. This can only be determined by

telling her to go home and seeing whether or not she gets there.

Declarative knowledge varies tremendously in topic and scope. One can know facts such as [The capital of Nigeria is Lagos] and generalizations such as [Caterpillars turn into butterflies]. One can know personal events such as [We went to the movies yesterday] and one can know personal attitudes such as [I don't like science fiction]. Furthermore, facts can be organized into sets, generalizations can be organized into theories, and personal events can be organized into life histories. Thus declarative knowledge varies a great deal.

All declarative knowledge, however, is relatively static. Procedural knowledge is more dynamic. When it is activated, the result is not simple recall of information but a *transformation* of information. For example, the result of doing the problem 286/2 is 143. The input information (286/2) has been transformed to produce an output (143) that looks different from the input. Or, for example, the product of procedural knowledge about the teaching of reading might be a lesson plan. The input information ("I need to get a lesson ready for tomorrow's reading class. The students are having trouble with the *ch* sound.") has been transformed to produce an output—a lesson—that looks quite different from the input. Thus procedural knowledge is used to operate on information to transform it.

Declarative and procedural knowledge also differ in the speed with which they are activated. Once it is well learned, procedural knowledge operates in a fast, automatic fashion. For example, skilled readers decode print quickly and with little awareness of the decoding process. The decoding of print is procedural in that it transforms print into either a phonemic or a meaning representation or both. Declarative knowledge activation is slower and more conscious. For example, to answer the question "What events led up to World War II?" a student might retrieve these events by consciously thinking of cues such as "economic events," "political events," or "Chapter 10 in my textbook." If one event is retrieved, it then might be used to cue the retrieval of other events. This process is clearly much more deliberate than decoding print. This is because the facts about World War II have been stored as declarative knowledge, not procedural knowledge.

Table 3.4 shows some test items that em-

Table 3.4. Test items measuring declarative knowledge, procedural knowledge, or a mixture of declarative and procedural knowledge.

DECLARATIVE KNOWLEDGE

1. True or false? The legal drinking age in this state is 18.
2. *Moby Dick* was written by _____.
   a. Hawthorne   c. Melville
   b. Thoreau   d. Hemingway
3. State the definition of a circle.
4. Describe the events leading up to World War I.

PROCEDURAL KNOWLEDGE

5. Which of the following is a pentagon?

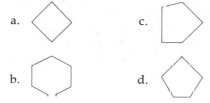

a.   c.

b.   d.

6. Identify the symbol of peace used in the attached passage.
7. Balance this equation: 2 H+ + 2 OH− = _____.
8. Change the following verbs to the present tense, first person singular: écriver, entrer, convoyer

COMBINATION OF PROCEDURAL AND DECLARATIVE KNOWLEDGE

9. Write an essay that tells what you think was the major cause of the Civil War. In this essay you should attempt to be as persuasive as possible.

phasize either declarative or procedural knowledge. As you can see, tests emphasizing declarative knowledge require recognition or recall. Tests emphasizing procedural knowledge require learners to do something other than recognize or recall, such as identify a geometric figure or balance a chemical equation. At the bottom of Table 3.4 is a question that taps both declarative and procedural knowledge (as essay questions often do). A student who is asked to write an essay about the most important cause of the Civil War must recall facts about the Civil War (declarative knowledge) and must also know how to write persuasively (procedural knowledge).

The distinction between procedural and declarative knowledge was made by the philosopher Ryle (1949) and is a fundamental distinction in R. Gagné's learning theory (1977). It is also a distinction made in J. R. Anderson's cognitive theory (1976). Psychologists who make this distinction believe that although the two types of knowledge are interdependent, they are distinct. Physiological psychologists are also beginning to distinguish two forms of knowledge along similar dimensions (Mishkin and Petri, 1984). Other psychologists do not find the procedural/declarative distinction to be useful (cf. Rumelhart and Norman, 1978).

From the standpoint of education, the distinction seems to be quite useful because the conditions for learning declarative and procedural knowledge are different, as will be described in Chapters 4 and 5. A teacher who can determine that a given learning problem is largely due to a deficit in one of these two forms of knowledge will be much more likely to remediate the problem than will a teacher who cannot determine the type of knowledge involved.

In summary, procedural knowledge transforms information. In a well-learned state, the transformations take place fast and automatically. Declarative knowledge is held in long-term memory ready to be activated when related information is in working memory. In comparison to the procedural knowledge activation, declarative knowledge activation is slow and deliberate.

INTERACTIONS OF DECLARATIVE AND PROCEDURAL KNOWLEDGE

Declarative and procedural knowledge interact both in learning and in performance. The precise nature of their interactions is not well known and, in fact, describing the interactions is on the current research agenda in cognitive psychology. Nonetheless, we can say at a general level how they interact.

Interactions during Performance

For some tasks declarative knowledge provides the data needed to perform some procedures. For example, a potter may be heating up a kiln to fire some pots. He will stop the heating process when the temperature is appropriate for the glaze with which he is working. The knowledge of the appropriate temperature for a particular glaze may be stored as declarative knowledge, so the potter must stop heating up the kiln while he retrieves this relevant bit of declarative knowledge. Once retrieved it is used in setting the stopping point for the heating procedure.

For other tasks the role of declarative knowledge is less mundane. Many creative discoveries call on declarative knowledge. A process for making stabilized whipped cream (as in Redi Whip) was discovered by a man who had been a cook in a restaurant and was later trained as a food chemist. As a cook he had often wished that there was some way to keep fresh whipped cream from rapidly going flat. As a chemist, he learned about the stabilizing force of certain chemicals. As he was learning about stabilization processes he re-

called his previous experiences as a cook and wondered whether or not certain stabilizing chemicals might be added to whipped cream. After having this insight, which was mediated by declarative knowledge, he used his procedural knowledge of how to combine chemicals and test the results, to try various chemicals in combination with whipped cream until he found an appropriate combination. As in this example, the seeing of connections between two seemingly disparate areas is the essence of many creative acts, and it appears to be mediated by declarative knowledge.

Thus declarative knowledge interacts with procedures in everyday problem solving by providing data needed for procedures. It also interacts with procedures during creative problem solving, providing new insights about where some known procedures might be carried out.

Interaction during Learning

Procedural and declarative knowledge interact during learning as well as during performance. For example, while learning new procedures, learners sometimes represent the procedure to themselves in declarative form. This declarative representation may be used to cue the steps in a procedure until the procedure becomes automatic. One example of this occurs when one is learning a new programming language. At first one does a lot of talking to oneself, which indicates that one is using a declarative representation to guide the procedures. Later one becomes much faster at programming because the declarative representation is no longer needed and the procedural representation operates automatically.

Learning a new procedure is one way in which declarative knowledge facilitates the acquisition of new procedural knowledge. The reverse—procedural knowledge facilitating the acquisition of declarative knowledge—also occurs. Some people have well-developed procedures for learning declarative knowledge. For example, a teacher may have procedures for learning names such as associating a student's name with something unique about that student. This teacher will probably learn the names of students faster than someone who does not use a name-learning procedure. Thus a specific type of procedural knowledge—knowledge of learning procedures—helps in the acquisition of new declarative knowledge.

In summary, declarative and procedural knowledge interact in a variety of ways in both learning and performance. Procedural knowledge appears to be especially important for competent functioning in familiar situations, whereas declarative knowledge seems to be useful in figuring out what procedures to bring to bear in novel situations. Both seem important to teach in school.

REPRESENTATION OF PROCEDURAL KNOWLEDGE AS PRODUCTIONS

At the beginning of this chapter you learned how to represent knowledge in the form of propositions and propositional networks. Propositional networks are static forms of representation and hence are used to represent declarative knowledge. Procedural knowledge is represented in a more active type of representation called *productions.*

Productions are condition-action rules. That is, they program certain actions to take place when specified conditions exist. Table 3.5 shows two sample productions, one for administering reinforcement and one for classifying triangles.[1] A production has two clauses, an IF clause and a THEN clause. The IF clause specifies the condition or conditions that must exist for a given set of actions to take place. The THEN clause lists the actions that take place when the conditions of the IF clause are met. For example, in the first production (P_1) two conditions must exist: (1) someone must want to make a child pay more attention and (2) the child in question must have just shown an above-average amount of attending behavior. If both of these conditions exist at the same time, then the action that takes place is that the person praises the child.

The conditions of a production can be either external to the individual or they can be internal, mental conditions. In the reinforcement production in Table 3.5, the first

---

[1] Throughout the text "informal" productions will be used. By informal is meant the productions may not be well specified enough to be implemented on a computer.

Table 3.5. Procedural knowledge represented in production form. Each line in the IF clause specifies a condition that must exist. Each line in the THEN clause specifies an action that will take place when all of the conditions in the IF clause are met.

P_1 REINFORCEMENT

IF Goal is to increase child's attending behavior
    And child has paid attention slightly longer than is typical for this child
THEN Praise child.

P_2 TRIANGLE

IF Figure is two-dimensional
    And figure is three-sided
    And figure is closed
THEN Classify figure as triangle
    And say "triangle."

---

condition is a personal goal, internal to the individual. It is not necessarily something that others can observe and agree on. By contrast, the second condition exists outside of the individual and a group of observers (who knew the child's typical attention span) could agree on it.

Just as the conditions of a production can be external or internal, so, too, can the actions. In the triangle production (P_2), for example, the first action is a mental one. The individual involved has made a mental note (classify) that a triangle is being observed. The second action—say "triangle"—is external because the individual has put some information out into the environment.

A Comparison of Propositions and Productions

Figure 3.9 shows a propositional network representing the idea "Triangles are two-dimensional, three-sided, closed figures." This is knowledge *that* a triangle has certain attributes. In Table 3.5, the second production represents the action of classifying a figure as a triangle if the figure has certain attributes. This is knowledge of *how* to classify a figure as a triangle.

These two forms of representation illustrate the differences between declarative and procedural knowledge discussed in the pre-

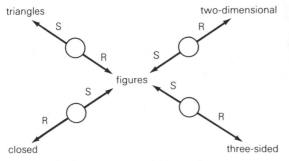

Figure 3.9. A propositional network representation for "Triangles are two-dimensional, three-sided, closed figures."

vious section. Someone who has the proposition about the triangle in long-term memory could answer the question "What is a triangle?" Someone who has the production about the triangle in long-term memory could correctly classify new examples of triangles. However, someone who has the proposition may not be able to classify triangles and someone who has the production may not be able to give a definition for triangle. In other words, knowledge in propositional form underlies the ability to reproduce information and knowledge in production form underlies the ability to operate on information.

Another difference illustrated by the two types of knowledge representation is their closeness to the environment. Propositions seem to be less closely tied to the environment. They are, it seems, just sitting there in one's mind. In contrast, productions seem to be very reactive to the environment (both the internal, or mental, and the external environments). The IF clause recognizes certain patterns and the THEN clause reacts to these patterns. The distance and nonreactivity of propositions make them a good representational form for thinking and problem solving. We can use propositions, for example, to imagine possible scenes and their consequences without actually having to live through them.

Thus, two ways in which propositions and productions differ are (1) the type of performance that they underlie, and (2) their reactivity to the environment. Presently we will see that they also differ in their automaticity.

Interpreting Productions

Throughout the rest of the book you will see knowledge represented in production form. Therefore, it is worthwhile to practice interpreting productions. Table 3.6 lists three productions that might underlie the skill of paragraph comprehension. Try answering the

Table 3.6. Some productions that underlie the skill of paragraph comprehension.

P_1

IF Goal is to comprehend paragraph
And words are known
THEN Find topic sentence
And check to see if other sentences support topic sentence.

P_2

IF Goal is to comprehend paragraph
And one or more words are not known
THEN Look up unknown words in dictionary
And find topic sentence
And check to see if other sentences support topic sentence.

P_3

IF Goal is to comprehend paragraph
And other sentences support topic sentence
THEN Find topic sentence ← not necessary
And state topic sentence.

following questions about these productions and then check your answers with those given at the end of the chapter.

3.6. Remember that the action of a production takes place only if *all* of the conditions specified in its IF clause are met. Suppose that Barry has the goal of comprehending a paragraph and does not know the meaning of the word "egregious" encountered in the paragraph. Which (if any) of the three productions will take place under these conditions?

3.7. Suppose that Barry understands all the words in a paragraph, but does not have the goal of comprehending the paragraph. Which (if any) of the three productions will take place under these conditions?

3.8. In the THEN clause of P_3, which action is most clearly an observable (external) action?

Production Systems

You may have noticed in the examples of productions that have been given, that they tend to represent fairly small pieces of performance such as identifying a triangle or praising a child. Yet humans engage in much more complex performance in systematic ways. Identifying a triangle might enter into the more complex activity of solving a geometry problem. Praising a child might enter into a whole sequence of events designed to modify that child's behavior. Thus, just as something was needed to represent interrelationships among propositions, so too something is needed to represent interrelationships among productions. Propositions are related through common ideas. Productions, on the other hand, are related through the *flow of control.*

Flow of control passes from one production to another when the actions of one production create the conditions needed for another production to take place. This idea is exemplified by the production system shown in Table 3.7, one that a teacher might possess for dealing with inattentive students. If the conditions of the first production are met—that is, if the goal is to make a particular child pay attention but it is not known what reinforces the child—the action taken is a mental one, setting the subgoals of finding out what reinforces the child and of reinforcing the child's behavior. This action creates the condition necessary for production P_2 to take place. The action of P_2 is to set the subgoal of observing, which is one of the conditions for

Table 3.7. A production system that underlies the skill of dealing with an inattentive student.

P_1	IF	Goal is to get child to pay attention and don't know what reinforces child
	THEN	Set Subgoal of determining what reinforces child and set subgoal of reinforcing child for attending.
P_2	IF	Subgoal is to determine what reinforces child
	THEN	Set subgoal to observe conditions under which child misbehaves.
P_3	IF	Subgoal is to observe the conditions under which child misbehaves
		and child misbehaves when I pay attention to him/her
		and child doesn't misbehave when I ignore him/her
	THEN	Create proposition that child is reinforced by my attention.
P_4	IF	Subgoal is to observe the conditions under which child misbehaves
		and child misbehaves when other children pay attention to her/him
		and child does not misbehave when other children ignore her/him
	THEN	Create proposition that child is reinforced by peer attention
P_5	IF	Subgoal is to reinforce child for attending
		and child is reinforced by my attention
		and child has paid attention for longer than average
	THEN	Give child my attention.
P_6	IF	Subgoal is to reinforce child for attending
		and child is reinforced by peer attention
		and child has paid attention longer than average
	THEN	Allow child to be with preferred peer.

P_3 and P_4. If the child misbehaves when the teacher pays attention to the misbehavior, but not when the teacher ignores it, then the conditions of P_3 are met and its action is mentally to classify the child as one who is reinforced by teacher attention. On the other hand, if the child's behavior varies as a function of peer attention, then the conditions of P_4 are met and the child is classified as one who is reinforced by peer attention.

The knowledge of what reinforces the child allows control to pass to either P_5 or P_6, depending on whether teacher or peer attention reinforces the child. In addition to knowing what reinforces the child, the conditions needed for either of these two productions are that a goal of reinforcing the child for paying attention (a goal set by P_1) exists and that the child has paid attention for longer than av-

erage. Under these conditions the action is appropriately to reinforce the child.

You may object that this description of a teaching skill implies that a teacher consciously thinks through each of these steps, just as we have consciously thought them through here. However, just because we have articulated the conditions and actions underlying a skill here does not mean that people who possess these skills articulate them. In fact, this is patently false. One hallmark of expert performance is that it is fast and automatic. Skilled chess players do not consciously think through every step; skilled writers do not say to themselves the rules of grammar underlying their well-formed sentences. And skilled teachers are not aware of all of the details of decision making described here.

In fact, this simple production system demonstrates the idea of automaticity, which is an important characteristic of productions. A production system is like a set of thermostats that switch on automatically under certain conditions. When knowledge is represented in production form, decision making occurs without much conscious work. Of course, a person must be aware of conditions, such as having the goal of making a child pay attention, but the slow thinking process involved in deciding what is to be done is short-circuited because actions automatically take place when certain conditions are noted. Much of the content of Section III of this book is about what skills must become automatic in the acquisition of reading, writing, and mathematics competence and how they become that way. Productions provide a way of talking about competence analytically.

For now, the most important idea to note about production systems is how control flows automatically from one production to another. Table 3.8 shows another production system, having to do with designing an experiment. The productions in this system have been intentionally mixed up. Try to answer the following questions about this system and then check your answers with those given at the end of the chapter:

3.9. Assume that the starting conditions are having the goal of designing an experiment and knowing the hypothesis but not knowing explicitly the independent or dependent variables. Which production will apply under these conditions?

3.10. Starting with the production you identified in 3.9 trace the flow of control from one production to the next until no more productions are available. List the productions in the order in which they take place.

Summary

Productions and production systems are ways of representing procedural knowledge. Each production contains an IF, or condition,

Table 3.8. A mixed-up set of productions that form a production system for the skill of designing experiments.

P_1	IF	Subgoal is to determine dependent variable
	THEN	Find the result in the hypothesis
		And classify the result as the dependent variable.
P_2	IF	Subgoal is to determine independent variable
	THEN	Find the cause in the hypothesis
		And classify the cause as the independent variable
		And set subgoal to determine dependent variable.
P_3	IF	Goal is to design experiment
		And hypothesis is known
		And independent variable is known
		And dependent variable is known
	THEN	Plan a way to manipulate independent variable
		And plan a way to manipulate dependent variable.
P_4	IF	Goal is to design experiment
		And hypothesis is known
	THEN	Subgoal is to determine independent variable.

clause and a THEN, or action, clause. The IF clause specifies the internal and external conditions that must exist for the action(s) of the production to take place. The THEN clause specifies the internal and external actions that take place when all the conditions listed in the IF clause exist. The result of the application of a production is a transformation of information.

In production systems, which are sets of related productions, the information transformation that results from the application of one production provides the conditions needed for another production in the system to apply. Thus, a sequence of related actions takes place automatically. This automaticity is an asset in the human information-processing system because it means that procedural knowledge takes up very little space in working memory and thus individuals may use this limited resource in other ways. It is difficult for humans to pay conscious attention to two things at once—say reading a paragraph for comprehension while mentally computing the product of 24 × 37. However, if one activity can be performed automatically, then another can be performed consciously at the same time. A specialist such as a doctor, for example, can carry on a dialogue with a patient while automatically diagnosing the patient's problem.

SCHEMAS: AN ALTERNATIVE TO PROPOSITIONS AND PRODUCTIONS

Another form of knowledge representation that is described in current psychological literature is the *schema*. It is much more difficult to find an agreed-on definition for schema than for proposition and production. However, what is common to all uses of the term schema is some reference to organized knowledge structures. Also, schemas seem to have both static qualities (such as their structures) and active qualities (such as leading us to expect certain information). Also, they sometimes seem to be used consciously (for example, in guiding retrieval) and sometimes seem to operate automatically (for example, in recognition of a new instance of a concept or in drawing an obvious inference).

Because schemas can have both static and dynamic qualities and are sometimes deliberate and sometimes automatic, they probably consist of both declarative and procedural knowledge. It makes sense that procedural and declarative knowledge relevant to a given situation should be packaged together in memory and the idea of schemas captures this sensible notion. To find out more about this alternative framework, see the references at the end of this chapter.

IMAGERY

Imagery is a form of knowledge representation that preserves as continuous dimensions some of the physical attributes of that which it represents. This is something that propositions (and productions) do not do. Look, for example, at Figure 3.10. This figure shows two alternative ways of representing the ideas contained in the sentence ''The book is on the table''. Part *a* is an image. It implicitly represents information about the three-dimensionality of books and tables and about the relative sizes of each. Part *b* is a propositional network. It does not represent information about spatial relationships or size. Images are analog representations. Propositions are discrete representations. Thus images are an economical way of representing spatial or continuous information. Although the picture in Figure 3.10 is fairly concrete, images are not necessarily concrete. What is crucial to images is that they are continuous.

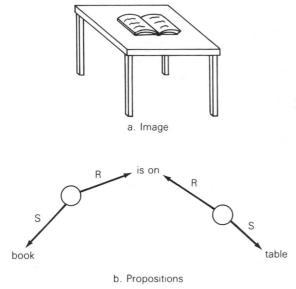

a. Image

b. Propositions

Figure 3.10. Two forms of mental representation of the idea that the book is on the table. Much spatial information implicit in the mental image is lost in the propositional network representation.

Imagery in Working Memory

Because of the limited capacity of working memory, images seem to be particularly useful in working memory representations of spatial information. Recall, for example, the work of Snow that was described in Chapter 2. Snow studied how students solved "paper folding" test items and concluded that successful students unfold in their minds an image of the punched paper. Suppose for the moment that a particular student could not generate mental images. Instead, he or she had to represent all the relevant information as propositions. Table 3.9 shows my guess as to all the propositions that would be needed to solve the paper-folding item shown in Figure 2.7 without using mental imagery. Clearly, these twenty-one propositions go far beyond the limits of working memory's ca-

pacity. The mental image of the paper being unfolded does not exceed the limits of working memory, however, because it is a functional unit.

A great deal of evidence suggests that people use mental imagery in tasks for which spatial or visual information is crucial. One task for demonstrating mental imagery is counting the window panes in one's living room. Meudell (1971) asked sixty-two people to tell him how many window panes they had in their living rooms and recorded the time that it took for them to respond. Figure 3.11 shows the relationship between the speed of response and the number of panes. If people are simply retrieving a proposition from long-term memory, there should be no relationship between speed and number of panes. However, if people are visualizing their living rooms and counting the panes in their mental image, then they should take longer if there are many panes than if there are few panes. As can be seen, people did take longer to respond if there were many panes in their living room than if there were only a few. In addition, most of the participants in the study reported that they did create an image of their living rooms and then count the panes in the windows.

Kosslyn, Ball, and Reiser (1978) demonstrated the analog nature of mental imagery. Figure 3.12 shows the line drawings of faces that they used in their study. Notice that the top three faces have dark eyes and the bottom three have light eyes. Also, notice that in moving from left to right, the distance between the mouth and the eyes on the faces decreases.

The subjects in this experiment were told to study a given face very carefully. The face was then removed and the subject was told to image the face at either half size, full size, or overflow size. Full size was said to mean the face was seen in the mind's eye as large

Table 3.9. Propositions needed to solve the paper-folding item shown in Figure 2.7.

[The paper is square.]	[The paper is folded.]
[The paper is folded.]	[It is folded again.]
[It is folded once.]	[The fold is vertical.]
[The fold is horizontal.]	[The fold creates layers.]
[Now there are layers.]	[The layers are four.]
[The layers are of paper.]	[One corner is open.]
[The layers are open.]	[It is the bottom corner.]
[They are open on the bottom.]	[It is the left corner.]
[The layers are closed.]	[A punch goes through corner.]
[They are closed on the top.]	[It is the bottom corner.]
	[It is the left corner.]

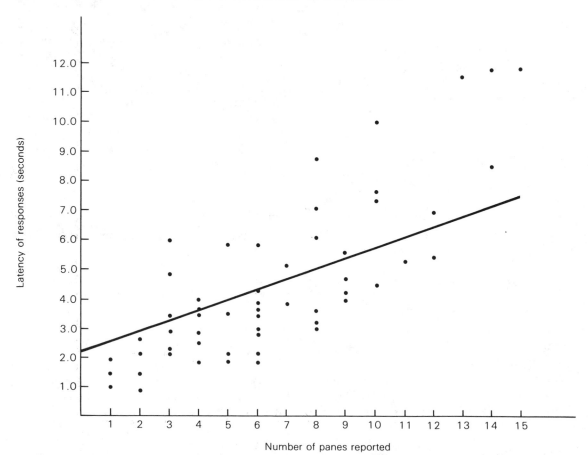

Figure 3.11. Time to respond to the question "How many window panes are in your living room?" as a function of the number of panes. (From Meudell, 1971.)

Figure 3.12. Faces that have either dark or light eyes and different distances from the mouth to the eyes. (From Kosslyn, Ball, and Reiser, 1978.)

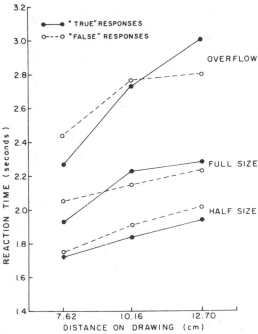

Figure 3.13. Reaction time to focus on eyes when starting at the mouth in an image. Reaction time is longer for larger images and for longer distances between mouth and eyes. (From Kosslyn, Ball, and Reiser, 1978.)

as possible without losing part of the face from the image. Half size was said to be half of full size. Overflow size was said to mean making the image so large that only the mouth could be seen.

After a subject visualized a face at a given size, he or she was then told to focus on the mouth. When the subject indicated readiness, the word "light" or "dark" was presented. The experimenter then told the subject to "glance up" the image and decide if the color of the eyes agreed or disagreed with the presented color. One or another button was pressed to indicate agreement or disagreement and the reaction time was recorded.

The results are shown in Figure 3.13. As you can see, reaction time increased as a function of the size of the image and also as a function of the distance between the mouth and the eyes in the drawing. These results are in keeping with the notion that mental images preserve distance information in an analog form. Subjects act as if they are scanning an internal image and not as if they are

searching a set of propositions formed to describe the pictures that they saw.

One objection to the Kosslyn et al. (1978) study might be that the subjects guessed what the experimenters' hypotheses were because of the directions to "glance up." Wishing to please, they then took longer to respond when they had been shown a picture with a greater distance between the mouth and eyes. However, there are many studies of the use of imagery in working memory in which subjects appear to use an analog representation even when they receive no instruction to use imagery.

A classic example of the spontaneous use of mental imagery is in mental rotation. Subjects are shown stimuli (often letters) that are rotated away from their normal upright position. Some of the stimuli are in their normal orientation and some are mirror images of their normal orientation. The subject's task is to decide if the stimulus is normal or a mirror image, which can be done by first mentally rotating an image of the stimulus to an upright position and then comparing it with an image of the normal orientation. If the two images are identical, then the stimulus is said to be normal. If the two images are the reverse of one another, then the test stimulus is said to be a mirror image.

Cooper and Shepard (1973) studied mental rotation of letters such as those shown in Figure 3.14. As you can see, the letters varied in their angle of rotation from the upright and in whether they were normal or mirror image. Subjects' reaction times to decide if the stimulus letter was normal or mirror image were recorded. Then they were plotted as a function of the angle of rotation of the letter (Figure 3.15).

Reaction time increased from 0 to 180 degrees and then decreased from 180 to 360 (0) degrees. This pattern of results is what one would expect if subjects are mentally rotating

the test letter and then seeing if it matches the letter in its normal orientation. The farther the test letter is from the upright, the longer the mental rotation should take, and this is exactly what was found.

Note that in this study, subjects were not told to form a mental image, yet they still behaved as if they had formed one. Thus many people spontaneously use mental imagery when a task requires the spatial manipulation of information.

These studies suggest that for tasks that involve thinking about spatial relationships among concrete objects people construct images of these objects in working memory. If this were the only role that imagery had to play, it would be a highly useful one. People are required to think about spatial relationships among concrete objects almost every day. Spatial relationships are important in parallel parking, in judging distance in sports, in planning how to furnish a room, and in finding one's way around in unfamiliar territory. Thus, our ability to use imagery in working memory is an important one.

However, imagery's importance may be even greater than its role in everyday tasks. People may use imagery in thinking about abstract relationships. There are many anecdotal reports of creative artists and scientists who use mental imagery to solve problems. For example, Faraday, one of the most creative physicists of all time, tended to image the abstract concepts with which he worked. As described by Koestler (1964), he:

> saw the stresses surrounding magnets and electric currents as curves in space, for which he coined the name "lines of forces," and which, in his imagination, were as real as if they consisted of solid matter. He visualized the universe patterned by these lines—or rather by narrow tubes through which all forms of "ray-vibrations" or energy-radiations are propagated. This vision of curved tubes which "rose up before him like things"

THE SIX ORIENTATIONS

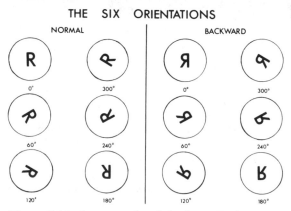

Figure 3.14. An example of the letter R shown in different orientations from upright and sometimes forward and sometimes in mirror image position. (From Cooper and Shepard, 1973.)

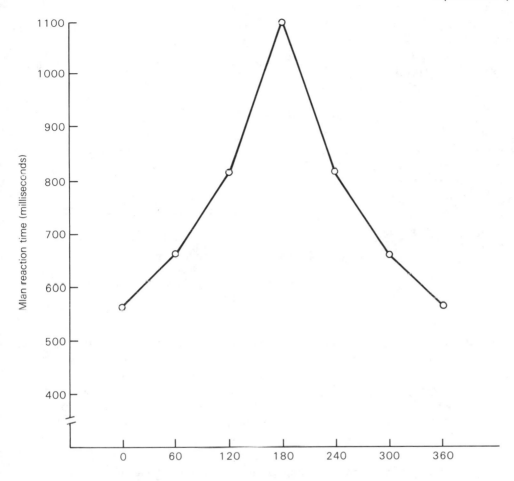

Orientation of test stimulus (degrees, clockwise from upright)

Figure 3.15. Reaction time as a function of angle of rotation of the test letter. (Adapted from Cooper and Shepard, 1973.)

proved of almost incredible fertility: it gave birth to the dynamo and the electric motor; it led Faraday to discard the ether, and to postulate that light was electro-magnetic radiation. (p. 170)

Since spatial and distance metrics seem to be useful analogs for thinking about continuous variables and their interactions mental imagery seems to be useful in abstract reasoning because of its implicit preservation of spatial relationships.

Some studies of mental comparisons suggest that people use imagery to think about abstract dimensions just as they do to think about concrete dimensions. Kerst and Howard (1977), for example, asked students to compare pairs of animals, countries, and cars on the concrete dimension of size and on an appropriate abstract dimension: ferocity for animals, military power for countries, and cost for cars. In a preliminary study, a different group of students rated examples of animals, countries, and cars on size and the appropriate abstract dimension. Table 3.10 shows the results of that study.

The students in the comparison study were shown various pairs of stimuli (e.g., mouse-cow, Mexico-Israel, Toyota-Cadillac) and asked to indicate which one had more of a particular dimension (size, power, cost, or ferocity). Their reaction times to make these comparisons were recorded and later plotted as a function of the distance between stimuli as determined in the preliminary study.

Figure 3.16 shows the findings. The reaction time became slower as the two items being compared became closer. This result makes sense if people are forming mental images. For example, if one images a sheep and a cow, it is more difficult to decide which image is larger than if one images a mouse and a cow, because the sheep and the cow are more similar in size. This difficulty in discrimination is reflected in slower reaction times.

The same pattern of results was observed for the abstract dimensions as for the concrete ones. Since it is not clear what an image

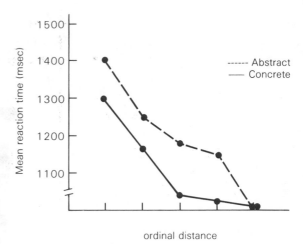

Figure 3.16. Time to compare two stimuli as a function of how close the items are on a particular concrete or abstract dimension. (From Kerst and Howard, 1977.)

of cost or power or ferocity would be, subjects may be using a spatial analogy to represent continuous variation in abstract quantities. Items are arranged in mental space according to how close they are to one another on the abstract dimension. If this is

Table 3.10. Animals, countries, and cars rated on various dimensions. (From Kerst and Howard, 1977.)

		MEAN	SD		MEAN	SD		MEAN	SD
	Animals (size)			Countries (size)			Cars (size)		
Concrete	Mouse	1.22	.85	Israel	1.47	.61	MG	1.09	.30
	Fox	2.41	.53	Japan	2.25	.83	VW	1.91	.57
	Dog	2.66	.51	England	2.53	.71	Toyota	2.31	.54
	Sheep	3.00	.44	Mexico	3.13	.57	Ford	3.41	.46
	Cow	4.25	.62	America	4.25	.57	Pontiac	3.78	.49
	Bear	4.81	.41	Russia	4.97	.14	Cadillac	4.75	.44
	Animals (ferociousness)			Countries (military power)			Cars (cost)		
Abstract	Mouse	1.44	.79	Mexico	1.81	.69	VW	1.47	.56
	Sheep	1.72	.71	Japan	2.81	.85	Toyota	2.06	.71
	Cow	1.91	.75	Israel	3.16	.82	Ford	2.88	.58
	Dog	3.16	.85	England	3.28	.72	Pontiac	3.34	.56
	Fox	3.69	.66	Russia	4.78	.49	MG	3.59	.94
	Bear	4.94	.20	America	4.94	.20	Cadillac	4.69	.44

done, then once again it would take longer to discriminate items that are close together than those that are far apart.

Although these results appear to support the idea that humans use imagery representation in abstract thought, they can also be interpreted by assuming a propositional representation. For two similar animals one must search through more facts to decide which is more ferocious than one would have to search through for two dissimilar animals. For example, to compare a sheep and a cow on ferocity one might think: "they both are herbivores. They both are eaten by wolves. They both are raised by humans for meat. I remember seeing a mad cow once, but I never have seen a mad sheep. So I'll say that a cow is more ferocious." On the other hand, to compare a mouse and a bear on ferocity one might think: "Mice run away. Bears attack. Therefore, bears are more ferocious." Thus, it takes longer to decide between two items that are similar, whether one compares the items by means of images or by means of propositions.

The problem of nonidentifiability, discussed in Chapter 2, must be invoked here. The problem is that for almost any performance, more than one set of representation–process assumptions can be made that produce the same outcome. Until further research is conducted, it will be difficult to say how much mental imagery is used in abstract thought, or how it is used.

Is Mental Imagery a Long-Term Memory Code?

Mental representations serve different functions in working and long-term memory. In working memory representations are manipulated and transformed, whereas in long-term memory representations are preserved. Working memory is like a desk where new compositions are produced (some good, some not so good). Long-term memory is like a library where printed information is stored. While writing a composition, pencil and paper are useful for transforming information. A pencil is better than a pen because pencil marks can be changed. But for storage, pencil marks are unstable and tend to smudge and fade over time. Similarly, imagery may be useful for compact manipulation of spatial information in working memory, but it may not be useful for long-term storage.

Although there is general agreement that mental imagery is used in working memory, there is little agreement on whether or not it is also used in long-term memory. Two contrasting proposals have received attention over the past decade: the dual-code hypothesis and the common code hypothesis. The dual-code hypothesis (Paivio, 1971; 1979) assumes that information is stored in two ways: (1) as a verbal, articulatory string, and (2) as a visual image. The common code hypothesis (e.g., J. R. Anderson and Bower, 1973) assumes that information is stored in one common format—a proposition or some other entity.

A large body of research appears to support the dual-code hypothesis. This research shows that words, sentences, and paragraphs that are highly imageable (concrete) are recalled better than those which are less imageable (abstract). It also shows that when people are instructed to image the information they are learning, they often remember it better than when they are not so instructed. According to the dual-code hypothesis such results occur because the concrete or imaged materials have two representations in long-term memory, (a verbal string and a visual image), whereas the abstract or nonimaged materials have only one representation in long-term memory (a verbal string).

In a prototypical experiment in this area, subjects are randomly assigned to one of two groups. One group learns a list of ten pairs of concrete words (e.g., fork-mountain) whereas the other group learns ten pairs of abstract words (e.g., truth-distance). The concrete and abstract words are carefully matched on number of syllables, grammatical class, and frequency of occurrence in natural language so that any differences in recall cannot be attributed to these extraneous factors.

During a study period subjects see each of the ten word pairs displayed on a screen for a few seconds. Then, during a recall period, only the first word in the pair is shown and the subject is asked to state the other word in the pair. The number of words correctly recalled as a function of word type (concrete or abstract) is the datum of interest. The consistent finding is that more words are correctly recalled by subjects who studied the concrete word pairs than by those who studied the abstract pairs.

Dual-code theorists believe this result occurs because a dual memory code (visual and verbal) is created for the concrete words and only a single code (verbal) is created for the abstract words. The advantage of a dual code is that if one memory trace is lost another is still available; hence memory is better than if only one memory code is used.

Although the data lend themselves to a dual-code interpretation, a common code interpretation can also account for them. It can be argued that the concrete words stimulate the formation of more propositions than do the abstract words. The concrete words are then more memorable because there are more alternative links to these words in a propositional network. This idea is illustrated in Figure 3.17. There, a person who studies the word pair *fork-mountain* may think of ideas about forks (such as that they are used on picnics) and ideas about mountains (such as that picnics happen in the mountains) and these thoughts will be encoded into long-term memory along with the experience of studying fork-mountain. When this person is asked

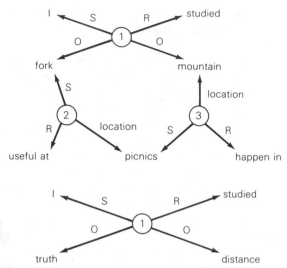

Figure 3.17. The hypothetical memory structures that result from the study of concrete (top) versus abstract (bottom) word pairs. The structure for the concrete pair provides more alternative retrieval pathways to *mountain* than the structure for the abstract pair provides to *distance*.

to recall what word went with fork, he or she can either directly recall mountain by retrieving proposition 1 or retrieve propositions 2 and 3, which will lead to the memory of proposition 1. A person who studies the word pair *truth-distance* is less likely to have elaborative thoughts that tie the two words together. Thus, when this person is asked to recall what word went with truth, if he or she cannot directly retrieve proposition 1, there are no alternative retrieval pathways, and the recall attempt fails.

The debate about whether or not images form a long-term memory code is far from being settled. Fortunately, it is far enough removed from educational applications that its resolution is not crucial for everyday decision making in education. There is ample evidence that the use of concrete materials and/or instructions to image enhances memory so teachers can use this knowledge to augment their lesson materials whatever the explanation of these findings turns out to be.

Summary

Mental images are analog representations. They are used to manipulate spatial information in working memory. They may also be used to think about abstract dimensions. The use of imagery during encoding of new information appears to help in remembering that information.

ECONOMY OF REPRESENTATION

In this chapter we have seen some forms of knowledge representation that fit with the architectural constraints of the human information-processing system. Figure 3.18 shows the system with propositions, images, and productions positioned where they are thought to play a role.

The most important point in this chapter is that knowledge is represented in forms that reduce the burden on working memory. Propositional networks reduce the burden by keeping related knowledge accessible. The result is that when we are thinking about a particular idea, related ideas come easily to mind. Production systems reduce the burden on working memory by allowing control to flow automatically from one step in a sequence of mental operations to another. When a process is automatic, it takes up little space in working memory. Images reduce the burden by implicitly representing spatial information. In comparison to propositions, images can pack more spatial information into working memory without exceeding its capacity.

Computers, with their large central processing units, do not have as great a need for economy of representation as do humans, so it should not be surprising that there are no obvious analogs in computer languages to the propositional networks and images used by the human information-processing system. However, there are computer language ana-

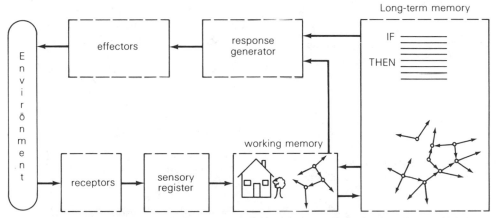

Figure 3.18. An information-processing model showing various forms of knowledge representations and their locations within the system. Both propositions (shown in node-link form) and images are used to represent and manipulate knowledge in working memory. Long-term memory houses both propositions and productions (shown in IF-THEN form). Activation of propositions occurs by way of working memory, whereas activation of productions automatically sends information to the response generator.

logs to production systems. For example, the structure of IF statements in FORTRAN and BASIC is very similar to that of productions. That is, they execute certain actions under specified conditions. Actually, it should not be surprising that for representation of procedural knowledge humans and computers are somewhat similar. Computers are most useful in executing routine procedures and it is the production system language that underlies routine (though important) competence in humans. Propositional and image-based languages are needed for more creative problem solving, and so far computers are not particularly good at creative problem solving. No doubt when they do become good at it, it will be because some human has invented a computer language that has qualities in common with propositional networks and images.

ADDITIONAL READINGS

General

Gagné, R. M. (1984). Learning outcomes and their effects. *American Psychologist, 39,* 377–85.

Propositions

Anderson, J. R. (1980b). Concepts, propositions, and schemata: What are the cognitive units? In J. H. Flowers (ed.), *Nebraska symposium on motivation* (pp. 121–62). Hillsdale, N.J.: Lawrence Erlbaum Associates.

Anderson, J. R. (1976). *Language, memory, and thought.* Hillsdale, N.J.: Lawrence Erlbaum Associates.

Kintsch, W. (1974). *The representation of meaning in memory.* Hillsdale, N.J.: Lawrence Erlbaum Associates.

Productions

Anderson, J. R., Kline, P. J., and Lewis, C. H. (1977). A production system model of language processing. In M. A. Just and P. A. Carpenter (eds.), *Cognitive processes in comprehension* (pp. 271–311). Hillsdale, N.J.: Lawrence Erlbaum Associates.

Newell, A. (1973). Production systems: Models of control structures. In W. G. Chase (ed.), *Visual information processing,* (pp. 463–526). New York: Academic Press.

Newell, A., and H. A. Simon (1972). *Human problem-solving.* Englewood Cliffs, N.J.: Prentice-Hall.

Images

Kosslyn, S. M. (1980). *Image and mind.* Cambridge, Mass.: Harvard University Press.

Paivio, A. (1971). *Imagery and verbal processes.* New York: Holt, Rinehart and Winston.

Richardson, J. T. E. (1980). *Mental imagery and human memory.* London: Macmillan.

Schemas

Anderson, R. C. (1977). The notion of schemata and the educational enterprise. In R. C. Anderson, R. J. Spiro, and W. E. Montague (eds.), *Schooling and the acquisition of knowledge.* Hillsdale, N.J.: Lawrence Erlbaum Associates.

Minsky, M. A. (1975). A framework for representing knowledge. In P. H. Winston (ed.), *The psychology of computer vision,* (pp. 211–80). New York: NcGraw-Hill.

Rumelhart, D. E., and A. Ortony (1977). The representation of knowledge in memory. In R. C. Anderson, R. J. Spiro, and W. E. Montague (eds.), *Schooling and the acquisition of knowledge,* (pp. 37–53). Hillsdale, N.J.: Lawrence Erlbaum Associates.

Shank, R. C., and R. P. Abelson (1977). *Scripts, plans, goals and understanding.* Hillsdale, N.J.: Lawrence Erlbaum Associates.

ANSWERS TO EXERCISES

3.1. [blew (relation), wind (subject), trees (object)]
[tall (relation), trees (subject)]

3.2 [selected (relation), teacher (sub.), microcomputer (obj.)]
[eager (relation), teacher (subject)]
[carefully (relation), selected (subject)]

3.3.

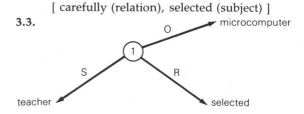

(handwritten margin note: How does figure limit triangle? It just re-names or describes it.)

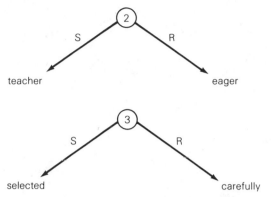

3.4. The very hungry child devoured the hamburger.

1. [The child devoured the hamburger]
2. [The child was hungry]
3. [The hunger was very (extreme)]

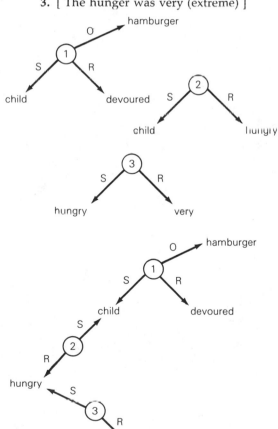

3.5. A triangle is a three-sided, closed figure.

1. [A triangle is a figure]
2. [The figure is three-sided]
3. [The figure is closed]

(handwritten margin note: IS, R, O figure, & why not triangle)

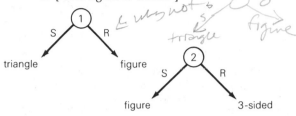

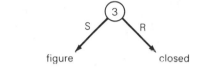

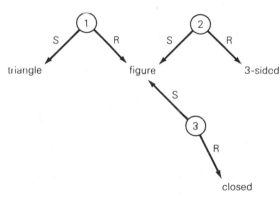

3.6. P_2 will take place because, of the three productions, this is the only one that specifies that one or more words are unknown.

3.7. None of the productions will take place because having the goal of comprehension is a necessary condition for all three of the productions.

3.8. *Stating* the topic sentence. Stating involves producing sounds that others can hear. Finding may or may not involve observable events. If the person underlines the topic sentence, then finding is observable, but if he or she mentally identifies the topic sentence, then finding is not observable. Actions of productions can be internal or external or both.

3.9. P_4

3.10. P_4, P_2, P_1, P_3

Knowledge Acquisition and Problem Solving

Learning and Remembering Declarative Knowledge

SUMMARY

1. All of a person's declarative knowledge can be conceptualized as a large network of interrelated propositions. A person's procedural knowledge can be conceptualized as productions that are pointed to by related propositions.

2. A few propositions in the propositional network are active in working memory at any given time. *Spread of activation* is the process whereby activation spreads from an active proposition to the propositions that are closest to it. As activation spreads, the initially active proposition becomes inactive.

3. Acquisition of new declarative knowledge takes place when new knowledge is linked to prior knowledge in the propositional network.

4. Elaboration is the process of generating new ideas related to the ideas being received from external sources.

5. In retrieval, the internal representation of the question activates propositions that share concepts with the question that started the retrieval process. Activation spreads from these propositions to related propositions until the answer to the question is found.

6. If an answer cannot be retrieved, it can be constructed by bringing logical processes to bear on activated propositions so that a plausible answer is generated.

7. Elaborations generated at the time of learning new information can facilitate retrieval by providing alternative pathways for spread of activation. Elaborations can facilitate constructions by providing more information for logical reasoning processes to use in constructing an answer.

8. Organization of declarative knowledge involves generating propositions that represent relationships between subsets of knowledge. Organization during learning aids in later retrieval of information by providing effective retrieval cues.

As we saw in the previous chapter, our declarative knowledge is all the facts, generalizations, and theories that we have ever stored in long-term memory. In addition, it is all the personal events that we have experienced and our personal likes and dislikes. Declarative knowledge is knowledge that something is the case and it is measured by the ability to verify or recall information.

Students sometimes seem to resist acquiring new declarative knowledge. They may claim that it is too "theoretical," that it will not help them get jobs, that it is "irrelevant," or that it is just plain boring. This resistance seems to slow down the learning process or give it a cynical quality in the sense that students memorize information for tests and make no attempt to assimilate it meaningfully.

In addition to the obstacle of the *initial* learning of information, an even greater obstacle seems to be the later *retrieval* of information. For example, of all the information you learned in tenth-grade history, how much do you think you could recall now? The

ability to recall previously learned information becomes increasingly difficult over time.

Thus, both the acquisition and the retrieval of information pose challenges for educators. Near the end of this chapter I will discuss two processes—*elaboration* (adding to information) and *organization* (structuring information)—that have been found to aid both acquisition and retrieval. However, first we must look at some theoretical assumptions about the structure and dynamics of memory and about acquisition and retrieval processes. These assumptions provide a basis for understanding how elaboration and organization processes work.

THE STRUCTURE AND DYNAMICS OF MEMORY

Memory Structure

There are many possible views of how long-term memory is structured. Klatzky (1980) or Loftus and Loftus (1976) describe a variety of views. The point of view presented here is consistent with a great deal of evidence, and it is at a level of detail that is useful for educators.

In this point of view one assumes that all of an individual's declarative knowledge is represented in a propositional network (J. R. Anderson, 1976). In Chapter 3 the concept of propositional network was introduced and exemplified for coherent sets of knowledge such as knowledge of facts about living things. Here this idea will be extended to include all of one's declarative knowledge in one large network structure. Figure 4.1 is a schematic representation of a propositional network. As this figure suggests, all ideas are ultimately associated with all other ideas, although the bridges between them may be quite long and complex. For example, the idea that "in the fall, the leaves turn color," shown at the bottom right of the network, is ultimately related to the idea that "igneous rock is very hard because it has been subjected to high temperature and pressure," shown at the top left of the network. However, to get from the former idea to the latter, many others ideas, shown in between the two ideas in the network, would have to be traversed (though not necessarily with awareness).

Another set of structures in long-term memory includes all productions that represent an individual's procedural knowledge. Some procedural knowledge, such as the discriminations of motion and brightness or the actions of grasping and sucking, are no doubt "wired in" as a part of the brain's "hardware." The rest of procedural knowledge, from color and letter discriminations to logical reasoning procedures, are "programmed in" (learned) later as part of the brain's "software."

Because of the intimate interactions between declarative and procedural knowledge during learning and transfer, memory is structured in a way that facilitates interaction. My image of all of long-term memory is the propositional network, as shown in Figure 4.1, with procedural units embedded throughout this network, close to declarative knowledge to which they are related. This image is shown in Figure 4.2 with a specific example of a procedure connected to the declarative knowledge that "igneous rocks are hard because they have been subjected to high temperature and pressure." The procedure shown allows someone to classify new examples of igneous rock. If a rock is too hard to break with a hammer tap, then it is classified as igneous. It is very useful to store this procedure close to declarative knowledge about igneous rocks so that the procedural knowledge can give operational meaning (e.g., *break with a hammer tap*) to the concepts represented declaratively (e.g., *igneous*).

Remember that these images are conceptual conveniences. The anatomical basis of memory probably will be found to look quite different from what I have presented here. However, some functional properties of the anatomical system will probably match the functional properties of the conceptual system.

Activity Levels in the Propositional Network

Propositions have varying levels of activity (J. R. Anderson, 1983*b*). At any given time the vast majority of propositions are inactive. This inactive portion of the propositional network corresponds to the long-term memory store discussed in Chapter 2. The few propositions that are active at any specific time are, phenomenally, a portion of what you are thinking about at that moment. They are your old rather than new knowledge. For example, if I read the sentence:

There are tornado warnings

in Ohio today.

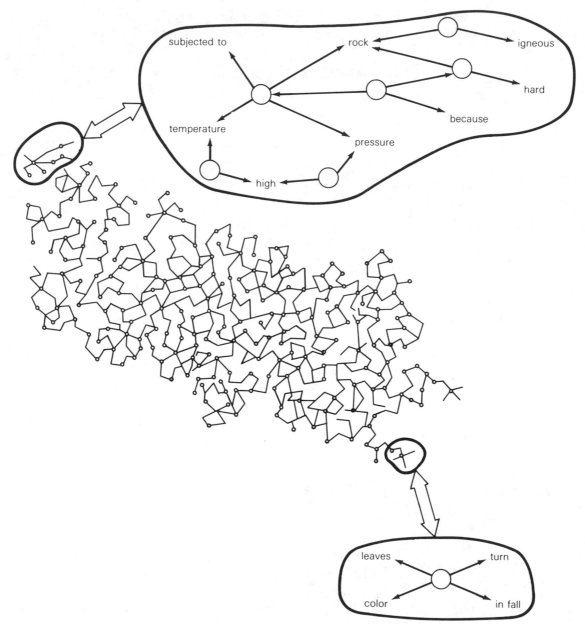

Figure 4.1. The propositional network. Each proposition, indicated by a node-link structure, is linked to other propositions through common ideas. Thus, all of declarative knowledge is interrelated in a vast network of propositions.

the information in this sentence is new. However, it makes me think of the meanings of the words in the sentence and of other related information such as that my uncle lives

in Ohio. These word meanings and related thoughts are old knowledge. They are the active portion of the propositional network in this example.

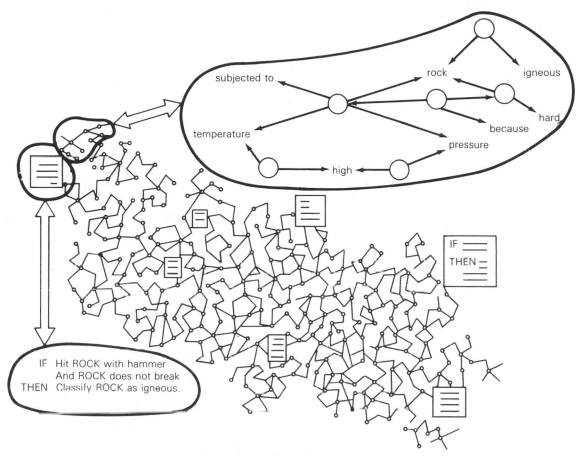

Figure 4.2. Long-term memory includes (1) a network of interrelated propositions and (2) productions interspersed throughout the network in areas where there is related declarative knowledge. Productions are shown here as boxes interspersed throughout the network.

Working memory is the crucible in which new knowledge is added to old knowledge. Thus one part of working memory (the old proposition part) is comprised of that small part of the propositional network that is active. Another part is new propositions that are currently being constructed.

Spread of Activation

How is the activity level of propositions determined? Before considering a general answer to this question, let us first consider the specific example shown in Figure 4.3. Suppose that at time T_1 you are thinking "I like chocolate pies." That is, the propositions [I like pies] and [the pies are chocolate] are active at T_1 (activity is signified by squiggly lines). Activation spreads along all the links of these propositions to related propositions, such as [pies are made with cream] and [the cream is whipping cream]. Since working memory can hold only a few active propositions at once, the propositions that were active at T_1 are no longer active at T_2, but some of the propositions that were inactive at T_1

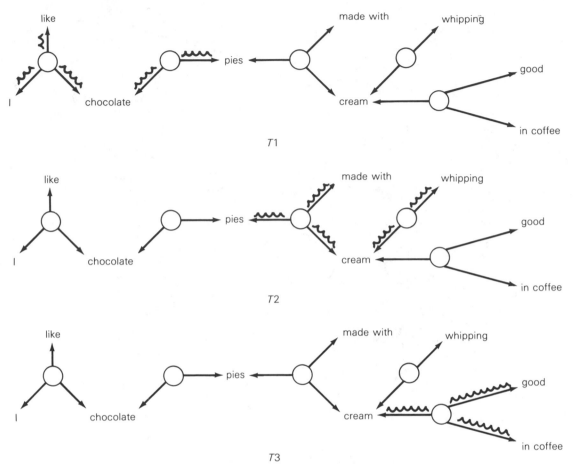

Figure 4.3. The spread of activation in the propositional network. Active propositions are indicated by squiggly lines along links. At time T_1, the propositions [I like pies] and [pies are chocolate] are active. Activation spreads to related propositions such that at time T_2, the propositions [pies are made with cream] and [cream is whipping cream] are active, and at T_3, [cream is good in coffee] is active. Previously activated propositions become inactive due to limited-capacity working memory.

are now active. Activation once again spreads along all the links in the active propositions and moves to related propositions such as [cream is good in coffee]. At T_3 it is this proposition that is active; the propositions that were active at T_2 have become inactive.

To generalize, spread of activation is the process whereby a given active proposition passes activation along to related propositions. We are most aware of a spread-of-ac-

tivation process in free association. However, spread of activation underlies many other thought processes as well.

ACQUISITION OF NEW DECLARATIVE KNOWLEDGE

New declarative knowledge is acquired when a new proposition is stored with related propositions in the propositional network. Figure

4.4 shows a typical sequence of events during acquisition. In panel a the teacher states, "In vitro experiments show that Vitamin C increases the formation of white blood cells." In panel b the student has translated (in working memory) the sounds of the teacher's words into a proposition. This proposition is shown with dashed lines to signify that it is new for the student. The concepts in the proposition (e.g., white blood cells, Vitamin C, etc.) cue the retrieval of related information. That is, activation spreads from *Vitamin C* to the idea that Vitamin C fights colds and from *white blood cells* to the idea that white blood cells destroy viruses. This state is shown in panel c in which the student has a new proposition and two old propositions active in working memory. In panel d spread of activation from *colds* and *viruses* leads to the activation of the proposition that viruses cause colds. With this particular set of propositions active in working memory, the student's inference-making processes (stored as productions) may draw the inference that Vitamin C fights colds because it increases the formation of white blood cells. This inference, shown in panel e, is another new proposition.

This final idea was not an idea from long-term memory or an idea presented by an external stimulus. Rather it resulted from thinking processes. This type of new proposition is called an elaboration because it adds information to the incoming information. The elaboration learning process results in the generation of elaborative propositions.

This example illustrates some important principles about knowledge acquisition:

1. New propositions cue the retrieval of related prior knowledge through the spread of activation.

2. The new propositions and the prior knowledge may stimulate the student's generation of other new prop-

ositions. (This process is called *elaboration*).

3. All the new propositions (both those presented by the environment and those generated by the learner) are stored close to the related prior knowledge that was activated during learning.

Meaningfulness

Notice that the steps in acquisition make no provision for learning totally meaningless information. This is because a requisite for learning is that some connection (some meaning) be established between new and prior knowledge. In Figure 4.4, the term "in vitro" did not activate any related knowledge in the learner's propositional network. It also was never encoded into long-term memory. That is, its failure to generate a connection led to its being lost from the system.

Yet it is easy to think of cases in which students learn information for which they have few connections. In such cases they are probably connecting the new sequence of sounds they are hearing to known sounds. Thus the propositions they form relate only to sounds, not to conceptual meanings. For example, Figure 4.5 shows a proposition that might be created for "in vitro." It is simply a record of the fact that a certain sequence of sounds was heard. This proposition is stored close to the procedures for producing those sounds, rather than close to conceptual knowledge about "in vitro." As we shall see presently, it is difficult to retrieve information that is stored in this manner.

If all learning of declarative knowledge is meaningful (requires connecting new and old knowledge), how does an infant store its first proposition? Just as adults store conceptually meaningless ideas by connecting them to sounds, so infants store their earliest propo-

sitions by connecting them to perceptual and motor procedures. The procedures then cue the retrieval of these early propositions. When more than one proposition sharing an idea are generated, they will be interconnected, starting the formation of a proposi-

tional network. From then on, although sensations and actions will still cue the retrieval of propositions, related propositions will also begin to cue one another.

In summary, meaning is inherent in connections between parts of the knowledge

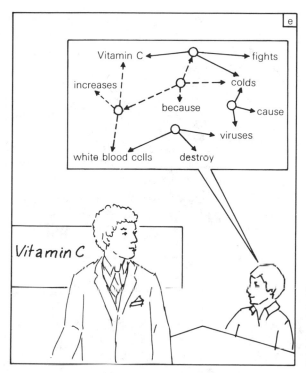

Figure 4.4 The steps in acquisition of new declarative knowledge: (a) New knowledge is presented. (b) It is translated into propositions. (c–d) Related propositions in long term memory are activated. (e) Elaborations are added. (New propositions are signified by broken lines, and old propositions are signified by unbroken lines.)

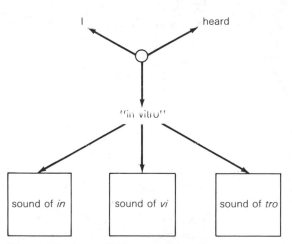

Figure 4.5. A possible propositional representation for information that is conceptually meaningless. The learner records the event of hearing certain sounds in a proposition. This proposition is then connected to productions for each of the sounds.

structure—either proposition-to-proposition connections or procedure-to-proposition connections. Learning of declarative knowledge is synonomous with the creation of meaning. When no meaning (no connections) can be created, nothing is learned.

As we shall see later in this chapter, there are many degrees of meaningfulness depending on both the number and type of connections that are formed between new and prior knowledge. And it is true, as most educators well know, that more meaningful information is better learned and better retained.

Knowledge Acquisition and Limited-Capacity Working Memory

The knowledge acquisition process described earlier, in which new information is connected to old information, takes up space in working memory. It also takes up time. H.

Simon (1974) has estimated that each new bit of information takes ten seconds to encode. These facts have some interesting implications, including a partial explanation of why even the most conscientious of students seem to forget information that they have just been told.

Consider, in information-processing terms, all that is going on during a lecture. A typical speech rate for lectures is 150 words per minute. Let as assume that an average proposition is formed from five words. Therefore, students are being bombarded with thirty propositions per minute. Of course, some of these propositions are not crucial, because they are either already known to the learner or simply providing a context for the main ideas in the lecture. So let us assume that only half of the thirty propositions are new and important. Therefore, the hope is that students will encode fifteen new propositions per minute. But H. Simon's work suggests that the new student will encode only six new propositions per minute. Furthermore, if students are actively elaborating on new propositions, this may slow them down to a rate of one proposition per minute! Thus it is no wonder that students sometimes seem to forget what a teacher has just stated. In fact, they never encoded it to begin with. Sometimes the most thoughtful and creative of students seem to forget the most. This may be because their working memories are filled with elaborations to one idea that was presented and hence ideas that follow this one in the lecture are never even represented in their working memories.

RETRIEVAL AND CONSTRUCTION OF DECLARATIVE KNOWLEDGE

Figure 4.6 shows in flow diagram form how retrieval proceeds in the human information-processing system. An episode of retrieval often starts when someone asks us a question

or when we read a question (for example, in a test booklet). However, another initiator of retrieval is an internally produced query to ourselves, such as when we are solving a problem and need some previously stored information. If the question comes from an external source, it must first be translated into propositions—the medium of internal representation. Once this has been done, the concepts in the proposition will activate that portion of the propositional network to which they belong. Activations will spread to related concepts until an entire proposition is activated. Then the activated proposition will be examined to see if it answers the question. If it does, it will be translated into speech (or into motor patterns if the answer is written) and is output to the environment. If the proposition does not answer the question and if there is more time available to search for the answer, then the search will continue by letting activation spread further until another proposition is activated for consideration as a possible answer. If, on the other hand, there is no time for further search, then the individual may make an "educated" guess that is consistent with the available knowledge.

The majority of steps in this process occur unconsciously. The main point at which awareness is involved is when the activated proposition is judged to see if it answers the question.

The learning episode shown in Figure 4.4 can be used to illustrate the retrieval process. Panel e in that figure shows the learner's knowledge structure at the end of the episode. Suppose that the day after this episode, the teacher asks, "What effect has Vitamin C on white blood cells?" Retrieval will start as the learner translates the sounds in the question into propositions. The concepts of *white blood cells* and *Vitamin C* will then be activated in the propositional network, and activation will spread from these concepts to related ones. As can be seen in Figure 4.7, the first proposition that will be activated is [Vitamin

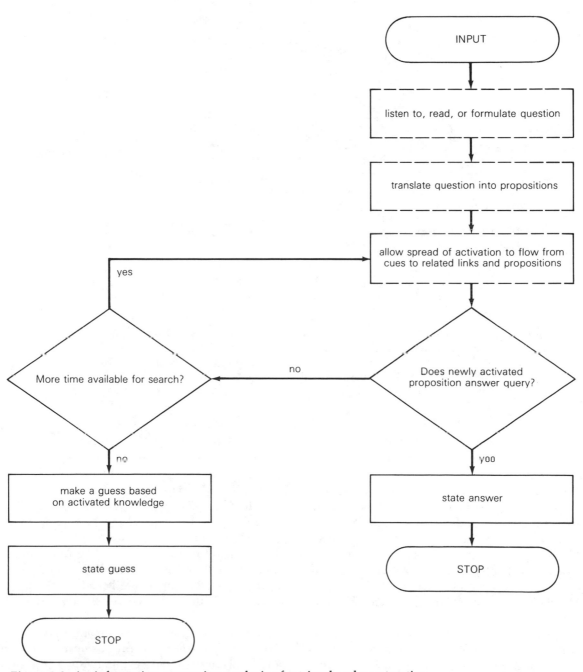

Figure 4.6. An information-processing analysis of retrieval and construction.

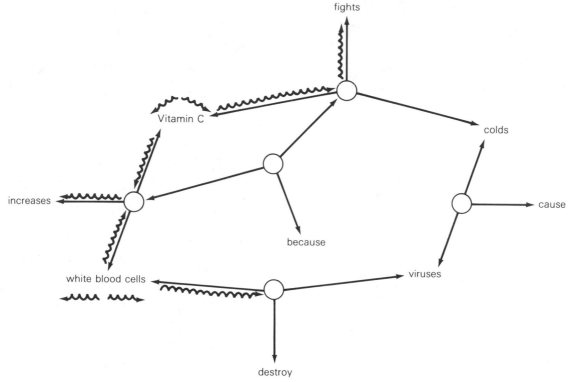

Figure 4.7. Spread of activation during retrieval. With the question, "What effect has Vitamin C on white blood cells?" *Vitamin C* and *white blood cells* are activated. Activation spreads down all links associated with these concepts, as is indicated by squiggly lines. The first proposition to become fully activated (because activation is spreading to it from two directions) is the proposition that Vitamin C increases white blood cells.

C increases white blood cells]. It will be first because activation is spreading from two sides of the proposition and when it meets in the middle, the entire proposition is active. For other propositions, activation is spreading from only one side; hence it must go twice as far and will take twice as long to activate the entire proposition. Since [Vitamin C increases white blood cells] is activated first, it will be the first proposition to be judged for its adequacy in answering the question. It does in fact answer the question of how Vitamin C affects white blood cells, so it will be translated into speech sounds and stated.

What happens when a learner either fails to encode the fact that is being queried or has difficulty finding it? Quite often he or she can *construct* the necessary information from knowledge that was encoded (F. C. Bartlett, 1932; Reder, 1979; Spiro, 1977). Suppose, for example, that a learner failed to encode the proposition that Vitamin C increases white blood cells. She did, however, encode her elaboration that Vitamin C cures colds because of its effect on white blood cells, as is shown in Figure 4.8. When asked what Vitamin C's effect is on white blood cells, spread of activation will lead from *Vitamin C* and *white blood cells* to the propositions: [white blood cells destroy viruses], [Vitamin C fights

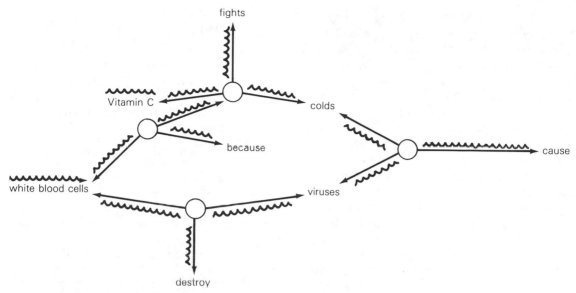

Figure 4.8. Construction of declarative knowledge from partial knowledge. This learner did not store the fact that Vitamin C increases white blood cells. However, when asked "What is the effect of Vitamin C on white blood cells?" the learner can deduce the answer from related knowledge that is activated. Premise 1: white blood cells destroy viruses that cause colds. Premise 2: Vitamin C fights colds by affecting white blood cells. Conclusion: Vitamin C increases white blood cells.

colds because of its effect on white blood cells], and [colds are caused by viruses]. With this information active in working memory, the learner can use logical procedures to deduce that Vitamin C must increase white blood cells.

In summary, retrieval and construction of declarative knowledge both depend on spread of activation. In retrieval, activation spreads from the cues to the to-be-recalled proposition. In construction, activation spreads from the cues to related information and logical processes operate on this information to generate an answer.

ELABORATION

Elaboration is the process of adding to the information being learned. The addition could be a logical inference, a continuation, an ex-

ample, a detail, or anything else that serves to connect information. Suppose that you were reading a story containing the following sentences:

Tim wanted a new model airplane. He

saw the change lying on his father's

dresser.

Try to observe your thoughts as you read these sentences. Are you elaborating? Reder's elaborations to those sentences (1976, p. 394) were "Tim is about 8 to 12, has a crew cut; the father's dresser is just at Tim's eye level; the model airplane is silver with chevron decals; the father is the absent-minded type who would not notice the change missing but who would be furious if he found out his son took it."

There is a great deal of evidence that people often generate elaborations for new information that they are learning. One type of evidence is the time it takes to comprehend material that stimulates different amounts of elaboration. For example, these two sentences—"We checked the picnic supplies. The beer was warm"—stimulate the inference (elaboration) that the beer was among the picnic supplies. By contrast, the two sentences "We got some beer out of the car. The beer was warm," do not stimulate an inference because the repetition of "beer" in the two sentences makes an explicit connection. Since the formation of elaborations takes time, it should take longer for people to comprehend a pair of sentences that require an elaboration to put them together than to comprehend a pair that doesn't have this requirement.

Haviland and Clark (1974) tested this hypothesis by presenting to subjects pairs of sentences (including those given in the preceding paragraph) that did or did not require "bridging inferences." The subjects' task was to press a button when they felt that comprehension of the two sentences was complete. Average comprehension time for pairs of sentences requiring inferences was 1016 milliseconds, whereas that for pairs not requiring inferences was 835 milliseconds. These data suggest that learners elaborate when certain assumptions are left implicit in a text or lecture.

Another type of evidence for elaboration comes from subjects' free recall protocols following the presentation of some new information. Such protocols often include some information that was *not* presented along with information that was presented. For example, Bower, Black, and Turner (1979) had students read short stories such as the one shown in Table 4.1 about a visit to a doctor. All of the stories were about familiar events that clearly are a part of almost everyone's

Table 4.1. A story with a familiar event sequence. (From Bower, Black, and Turner, 1979.)

THE DOCTOR

John was feeling bad today so he decided to go see the family doctor. He checked in with the doctor's receptionist, and then looked through several medical magazines that were on the table by his chair. Finally the nurse came and asked him to take off his clothes. The doctor was very nice to him. He eventually prescribed some pills for John. Then John left the doctor's office and headed home.

---

prior knowledge and hence available for use in elaboration when new related knowledge is encountered. If subjects elaborate on the stories as they read them, they may recall these elaborations when asked to recall the story.

When students in the Bower et al. (1979) study recalled the stories, about 20 percent of what was recalled were elaborations rather than information explicitly stated in the stories. For example, the "Doctor" story did not state that John entered the doctor's office, nor did it state that the nurse checked John's blood pressure and weight. Yet some subjects wrote these ideas down in their recall protocols. These data suggest that subjects elaborated on the stories as they were reading them. They used their knowledge of what typically happens in everyday events to generate elaborations.

The Role of Elaborations in Retrieval and Construction

Elaboration facilitates retrieval in two ways. First, it provides alternate retrieval pathways along which activation can spread (J. R. Anderson, 1976). So if one pathway is somehow blocked, others are available. Second, it provides extra information from which answers can be constructed (Reder, 1982b), as was seen in the "Vitamin C and colds" example described earlier.

Contrast, for example, the memory structures of Student 1 and Student 2 following their reading of the sentence: "Political Action Committees (PACs) influence Congress with money." (See Figure 4.9.) Student 1 was watching TV while "studying." Thus, there was no room in her working memory for elaborating on the new information. She did, however, succeed in encoding the new idea by connecting it with her prior knowledge of what a political action committee is: [a PAC is a group whose goal is to influence policy]. Student 2 was not watching TV. Thus, she had more working memory space available for elaboration. While she read, she activated her prior knowledge of what a political action committee is and, in addition, elaborated on the new information by thinking [The National Organization for Women (NOW) is forming a PAC.]. Thus, Student 2's knowledge structure surrounding the new idea in memory is more elaborate than is Student 1's.

Now suppose that the following day the teacher of these students asks, "What do political action committees do?" and is expecting the answer: "PACs influence Congress with money." Both students use *PAC* as a retrieval cue to start spread of activation. For Student 1 there are two pathways by which activation can reach the desired answer: one goes directly to the proposition that PACs influence Congress with money and the other goes first through the proposition that PACs are groups whose goal is to influence policy. Once the concept *influence* is activated, activation spreads to the proposition that PACs influence Congress with money.

Student 2 has these same two pathways and also a third one moving from *PAC* to the left to the propositions that NOW is forming a PAC, NOW is a group, the group has the goal of influencing policy, and thence to

PACs influence Congress with money. Thus Student 2 has three ways to retrieve the desired information whereas Student 1 has only two.

Student 2 has a further advantage over Student 1 in that even if she cannot retrieve the desired answer, she might be able to infer what a PAC does from her elaboration that NOW is forming a PAC. To do this, she might activate other knowledge about NOW such as NOW's explanation for why the Equal Rights Amendment did not pass—that not enough political pressure was exerted. She then might use this knowledge to infer that the reason NOW is forming a PAC is to exert more political pressure. This would lead her to guess that PACs exert political pressure, which might be an acceptable answer to the question "What do political action committees do?"

Student 1 has less to go on in trying to guess an answer. She might guess that PACs influence policy, but a teacher might well consider this an unacceptable answer because it does not specify *how* PACs influence policy. Because Student 1 did not elaborate as much she has less information to use in constructing an adequate answer.

In summary, Student 2's elaboration helped her in two ways: (1) it provided an alternate retrieval path and (2) it provided useful information for constructing an answer.

A large body of research can be interpreted as demonstrating the value of elaborative processing in the acquisition and recall of declarative knowledge (for a review see E. Gagné, 1978). Another framework that has been applied to the same body of research is called the "depth of processing" framework, a recent discussion of which can be found in Cermak and Craik (1979). J. R. Anderson and Reder (1979) argue that an elaboration account of the learning of declarative knowl-

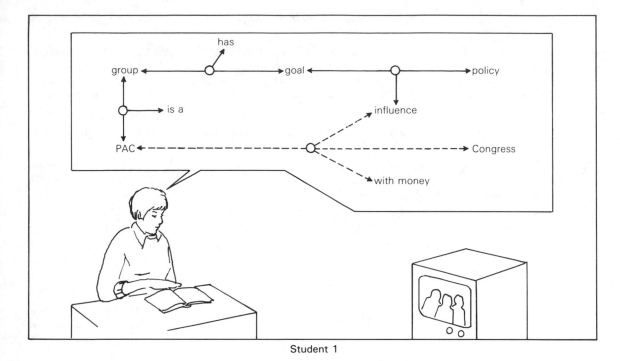

Student 1

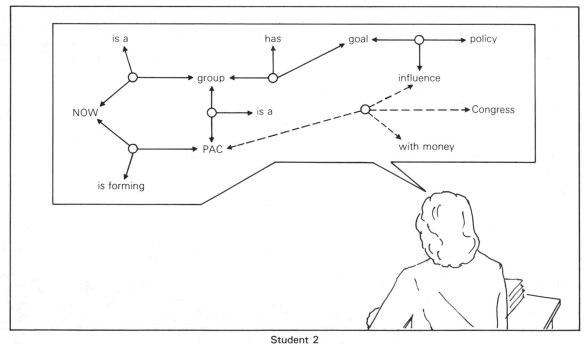

Student 2

Figure 4.9. Encoding of the new proposition that PACs influence Congress with money. (New propositions are indicated by broken lines, old ones by solid lines.) Student 1 attaches the new proposition to relevant prior knowledge, but does not elaborate. Student 2 attaches the new proposition to relevant prior knowledge and also elaborates on it.

edge is more quantifiable and predictive than is a depth-of-processing account.

Types of Elaboration

Although almost any elaborative processing is better than none, elaborations vary, and some are more effective as retrieval cues than are others. Effective elaborations tie together parts of the propositions that one wants to remember or stimulate adequate recall of the learning context. Less effective elaborations do not tie the parts of the to-be-remembered propositions together and do not stimulate recall of the learning context (Reder, 1982a).

This idea was first demonstrated in studies of learning lists of "paired associates" (e.g., Rohwer and Levin, 1968). Paired associates are pairs of verbal stimuli—either words or nonsense syllables—that are rather arbitrarily paired (e.g., cow-shoe). The subject's task is to learn the pairs so that given the first item in the pair (*cow*) as a cue, he or she can retrieve the second item (*shoe*).

In one such study (A. Wang, 1983), college students learned lists of twelve noun pairs to the point where they could recall all twelve second items when given the first item in each pair as a cue. Subjects were encouraged to think of an association between items in a pair and to produce "one word that is related to the picture, story, sentence, rhyme, or relationship" used to associate the items.

The words generated were then used by the experimenters to infer the types of elaborations subjects were forming. For example, for the noun pair doctor-stone, the word "gallstone" is related to both the first and second item because it may cause one to think of both a doctor and a stone. The word "Mr." is related to the first item because it may cause one to think of doctor, while the word "Flintstones" is related to the second item because it may cause one to think of stones. The word "movie" is an idiosyncratic elaboration whose relationship to *doctor* and *stone* is not obvious.

According to the number of trials subjects took to reach criterion, they were classified as fast, medium, or slow learners. The elaborations produced by the fast and slow groups were then compared. Figure 4.10 shows the results. Both early and late in learning, the fast learners produced more elaborations that related either to the first item or to both items than did the slow learners, whereas the slow learners produced more elaborations related to the second item, and, late in learning, produced more idiosyncratic elaborations.

The results suggest that some types of elaborations are more effective than others. Specifically, elaborations that either relate the cue word (first item) to the word to be recalled (second item) or relate to the cue word are better than elaborations that relate only to the to-be-recalled word. If an elaboration relates only to the to-be-recalled word, there is no way to get to it from the cue word. Levin, Pressley, McCormick, Miller, and Shriberg (1979) have used these ideas to develop successful programs for learning foreign language vocabulary.

Although elaborations that relate to both a cue and the to-be-remembered item may be effective in learning arbitrary word pairs, this may not be true of more meaningful types of material. Bransford and his colleagues have studied the effect of different types of elaborations on recalling sentences. In one of their studies (Stein, Bransford, Franks, Owings, Vye, and McGraw, 1982) fifth graders were divided into three groups according to success in school (based on teacher ratings and achievement test scores). These groups were called "successful," "average," and "less successful." All of the students were given a list of sentences such as "The tall man used the paintbrush" or "The hungry man got into the car." They were told that each sentence

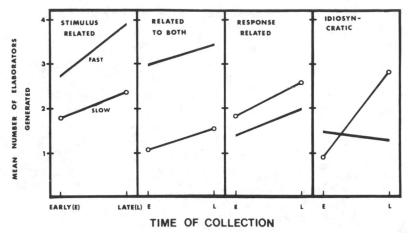

Figure 4.10. The frequency of production of various types of elaborations by fast and slow learners, early and late in learning. (From Wang, 1983.)

referred to a different type of man (e.g., strong, hungry, etc.). Then the children were asked to provide phrases that would help them remember each sentence.

The phrases that the children provided were categorized as being "precise" if they suggested a connection between the action the man was taking and the quality that the man possessed. Thus if a child read the sentence "The tall man used the paintbrush" and provided the phrase "to paint the ceiling," this phrase was judged to be precise because it connected height (he had to be tall to reach the ceiling) to paintbrush (he needed a paintbrush to paint). Phrases that did not connect the man's quality and action (e.g., "to paint the room") were categorized as imprecise.

The results showed that for any group a student who gave a precise phrase was more likely to correctly recall the sentence than one who gave an imprecise phrase. This suggests that, just as with paired associate learning there are better and worse elaborations. The better elaborations are those which interconnect parts of the to-be-recalled information.

Another interesting finding in the Stein et al. (1982) study was that more successful

students were more likely to generate precise elaborations than were less successful students. The successful, average and less successful students generated, respectively, 70 percent, 46 percent and 30 percent precise phrases. Perhaps successful students do well in school partly because they are more likely to provide good elaborations to new material.

To better understand why precise elaborations are more effective than imprecise ones, let us return to the learning episode involving information about political action committees. Recall that there were two students, one of whom connected the idea that PACs influence Congress with money to the idea that PACs are groups whose goal is to influence policy. The other student added an elaboration that NOW is forming a PAC.

The elaborations generated by a third student are shown in Figure 4.11. This student thinks [Oil companies have PACs], [Oil companies have money], and [Oil companies influence Congress with money]. The structure of Student 3's knowledge is qualitatively different from that of Student 2's, even though both students elaborated on the new information. Student 3's knowledge is more tightly organized around the new idea than

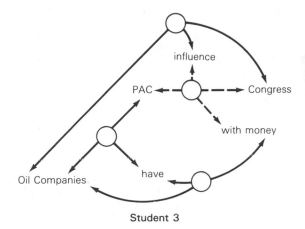

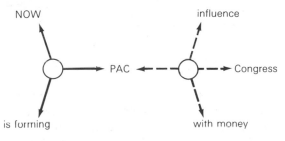

Figure 4.11. The elaborations of two students to the new proposition that PACs influence Congress with money. (Elaborations are indicated by solid lines, new propositions by broken lines). Student 3's elaborations interconnect parts of the new proposition (e.g., *Congress* and *PAC*). Student 2's elaboration does not interconnect parts of the new proposition.

is Student 2's. The important effect of this organization is that spread of activation keeps looping back around to the new information for Student 3, whereas for Student 2 spread of activation may just as easily lead away from the new idea as lead toward it. Thus, Student 3 will be more likely to recall the new idea than will Student 2.

Thus, the principle of spread of activation provides an explanation for why precise elaborations are better for recall than are imprecise elaborations. Precise elaborations do not provide as many opportunities for spread of activation to lead away from the to-be-remembered information. This is not to say that imprecise elaborations always have negative effects. For something other than recall of information, such as divergent thinking, imprecise elaborations may be more effective than precise ones. There has not been too much research on the effect of different types of elaborations in divergent thinking situations, although some of Mayer's work (e.g., 1980) can be interpreted as bearing on this question.

ORGANIZATION

Ideal students, given a reading assignment, would elaborate on the information as they read it. That is, they would think of related ideas, examples, images, or details. They would also *organize* the new information. Organization is the process of dividing an information set into subsets and indicating the relationship among the subsets. In the example of reading about political action committees, one might put the information about PACs in a subset of information about political pressure. Other members of this subset might be voting, demonstrating, and trading votes, since each of these is a distinct way of exerting political pressure. The subset of information about political pressure might be part of a larger set of information about American Government (see Figure 4.12). Other subsets might include: the structure of American government, the Constitution and Bill of Rights, and the role of each branch of government.

This example may seem far removed from elementary school, but young children use organizational processes also. For example, a fourth grader may organize her study of American Indians into geographical groups. Or a second grader might design a bulletin board display about the seasons so that in-

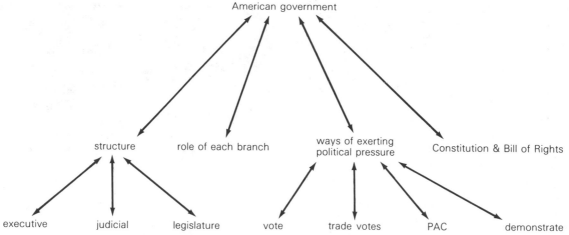

Figure 4.12. A partial knowledge structure for information about American government. Information is divided into subsets, and relationships between subsets are indicated. This structure organizes information.

formation about each season is grouped in one location of the display.

People seem to organize information spontaneously. J. Reitman and Rueter (1980), for example, gave introductory psychology students sixteen words to memorize on their first day of class. They used technical words from psychology with which students were not familiar. The next day the students, using free recall, spoke into a tape recorder the words they had memorized. The experimenters used both the order and the pauses in recall to induce the subsets being used by individual students. They assumed that a pause in output usually indicated a break in the organization of the words in the student's memory structure.

Despite the fact that the words were unfamiliar, the students attempted to organize them. Figures 4.13 and 4.14 show two recall organizations that were found. Figure 4.13 shows an alphabetical organization, and Figure 4.14 shows an attempt to organize by meaning. For example, *hue* and *saturation* occur in sequence in Figure 4.14, and these are both concepts that have to do with color per-

ception. Also, *feature, demon,* and *Pandemonium* are grouped together and these three concepts relate to a particular model in psychology. The student who attempted to organize by meaning clearly had more prior knowledge of psychology than did the student who organized alphabetically. However, the important point is that almost all the students tried to organize the words somehow.

The Effect of Organization on Recall

Organization enhances the memorability of material tremendously. Whether the material is lists of nouns (Bousfield, 1953), narratives (Thorndyke, 1977), or expository text (Frase, 1973; Meyer, 1977), the data show great benefits of organization.

Elementary school students increasingly take advantage of organization to improve their memories over the years of school. The task that has been used most frequently to study this trend is showing children a set of about fifteen pictures of objects and asking them to study the pictures and then recall as

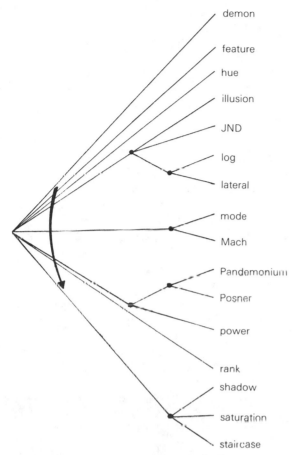

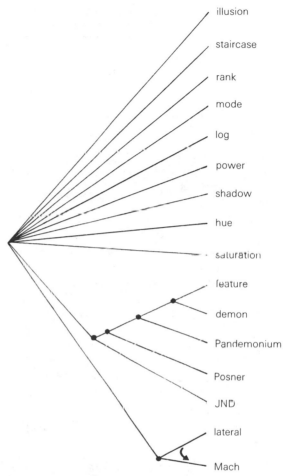

Figure 4.13. A student's alphabetical organization of psychology terms. The branch structure indicates pauses in output. For example, there was a shorter pause between *Pandemonium* and *Posner* than between *Posner* and *power*. (From Reitman and Ructer, 1980.)

Figure 4.14. A psychology student's attempt at meaningful organization of psychology terms. (From Reitman and Rueter, 1980.)

many as they can. The set is comprised of subsets such as furniture (e.g., chair, table, lamp), vehicles (bus, truck, car), and animals (cat, dog, cow).

Table 4.2 shows the typical findings in such studies. These particular results are from a study done by Yussen, E. Gagné, Gargiulo, and Kunen (1974). As you can see, the amount recalled increases with the child's grade level. In addition, the amount of clustering in recall increases with grade level.

Clustering is measured as two or more items from the same subset being recalled consecutively. For example, a child who says, "car, bus, chair, table, cow, dog, cat" gets a higher clustering score than one who says "car, cat, table, bus, cow, chair, dog." Clustering scores range from about 0 to 1.

These data suggest that the older children recall more because they cluster more. Somehow, organizing response output into categories seems to allow for greater recall.

Organization processes improve recall in

Table 4.2. Increase in recall and clustering across elementary school grade level. (Adapted from Yussen, Gagné, Garguilo, and Kunen, 1974.)

	SCHOOL GRADE				
	1	2	3	4	5
Recall of items	7.13	8.38	9.47	9.41	11.28
Clustering	.16	.21	.28	.22	.38

adults as well as in children. Thorndyke (1977) conducted a study in which he made it increasingly difficult for subjects (college students) to use organizational processes. He postulated that decreased organization would lead to decreased recall. The materials used for this study were two short stories, one of which is shown in Table 4.3.

Well-structured stories (narratives) typically have four main subsets of information (Rumelhart, 1975): *setting, theme, plot,* and *resolution.* Narratives usually begin with a setting of the stage (e.g., ''Once upon a time in Northern England . . .''). Then they introduce some characters to whom something has happened and who therefore have some goal. This information is the theme of the narrative and motivates the action or plot. That is, the characters do some things to reach their goal. Finally, there is a resolution in which the goal is reached or the characters adjust to failure to reach the goal.

Figure 4.15 shows the structure of the Circle Island story shown in Table 4.3. As you can see, the top level of the structure has the typical subsets of setting, theme, plot, and resolution. The ideas in the narrative that fit into each of these subsets are indicated by numbers. For example, ideas 13 and 14—that the farmers wanted to build a canal across the island—fit into the theme subset. More specifically, they belong to the *goal* part of the theme, rather than the *event* part.

Thorndyke progressively degraded the organization of this story by (1) putting the theme statements at the end of the story

Table 4.3. A story used to study the role of story organization in recall. The numbers indicate the idea units that are shown in Figure 4.15. (From Thorndyke, 1977.)

CIRCLE ISLAND

(1) Circle Island is located in the middle of the Atlantic Ocean, (2) north of Ronald Island. (3) The main occupations on the island are farming and ranching. (4) Circle Island has good soil, (5) but few rivers and (6) hence a shortage of water. (7) The island is run democratically. (8) All issues are decided by a majority vote of the islanders. (9) The governing body is a senate, (10) whose job is to carry out the will of the majority. (11) Recently, an island scientist discovered a cheap method (12) of converting salt water into fresh water. (13) As a result, the island farmers wanted (14) to build a canal across the island, (15) so that they could use water from the canal (16) to cultivate the island's central region. (17) Therefore, the farmers formed a procanal association (18) and persuaded a few senators (19) to join. (20) The procanal association brought the construction idea to a vote. (21) All the islanders voted. (22) The majority voted in favor of construction. (23) The senate, however, decided that (24) the farmers' proposed canal was ecologically unsound. (25) The senators agreed (26) to build a smaller canal (27) that was 2 feet wide and 1 foot deep. (28) After starting construction on the smaller canal, (29) the islanders discovered that (30) no water would flow into it. (31) Thus the project was abandoned. (32) The farmers were angry (33) because of the failure of the canal project. (34) Civil war appeared inevitable.

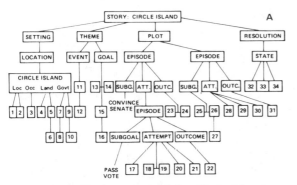

Figure 4.15. The structure of the Circle Island story. The numbers indicate idea units that are numbered in the text of the story shown in Table 4.3. (Adapted from Thorndyke, 1977.)

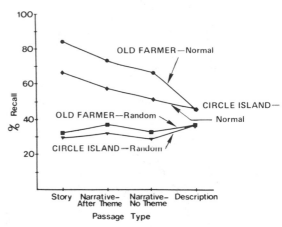

Figure 4.16. Recall of passage ideas as a function of passage organization. (Adapted from Thorndyke, 1977.)

rather than in their normal position toward the beginning of the story, (2) eliminating the theme statements altogether, and (3) deleting causal connectives in the story so that what was left was a simple description rather than a narrative. He presented four groups of subjects with the normal story, the story with the theme after, the story with the theme deleted, or the description. In addition, he presented another four groups with randomizations of each of these versions in which the order of sentences varied.

Following presentation of the story, the subjects wrote down what they could remember and their recall protocols were scored for the number of ideas recalled. Figure 4.16 shows the percentage recalled by each group. As the stories became less well organized, recall was less good. The recall difference between the well-structured stories and the random presentation was about 40 percent. However, the difference between the description and the random condition was only about 10 percent. These data show the large effect of organization on recall. When the normal cues for organization, such as a theme statement or causal linkages, are absent, it is difficult for people to organize in-

formation and this in turn affects their ability to recall it later on.

The Mechanisms of Organization

It seems clear that organization greatly enhances recall, but the question remains: How does it enhance recall? There is more than one answer to this question and it is still an area that is being investigated actively (cf. Yekovich and Thorndyke, 1981).

One possibility is that organization operates in the same way as precise elaborations. It provides tight connections to the to-be-recalled information so that spread of activation will remain in the relevant area of long-term memory rather than spreading away from it.

The other ways that organization may help have to do with the small capacity of working memory. This small capacity causes problems because after retrieving a few items of information, one runs out of space. It would not be a problem in and of itself if to-be-remembered items formed a queue in which as one item became output and left working memory, the next popped up auto-

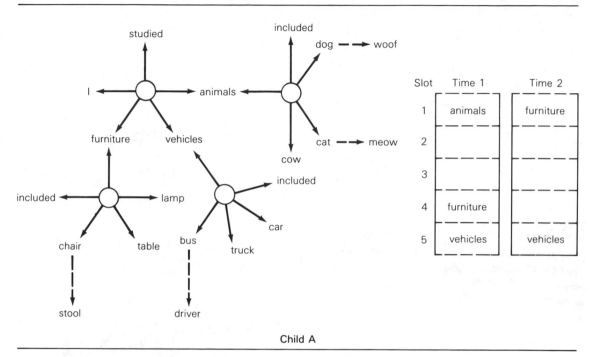

Child A

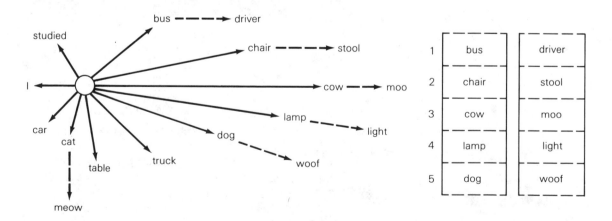

Child B

Figure 4.17. The contents of long-term memory and working memory of two children attempting to retrieve studied items. Organization helps Child A by leaving more space in working memory and by guiding the search.

matically. However, spread of activation is not very selective about what is represented in working memory: it is just as likely to put an irrelevant item into working memory as a relevant one. Thus, it is the combination of limited-capacity working memory and the nature of spread of activation that creates problems for retrieving information greater than a few bits.

People can use organization strategically to overcome this problem. When information is divided into subsets, the subsets, being fewer than the individual items, provide a way of keeping track of all the information without actually having it all in working memory at once. Computer scientists use the term *pointer* to refer to a tag that points to a given address in a storage device. Subsets serve as pointers in the human system. For example, Figure 4.17 shows the hypothetical long-term and working memories of two children. Here working memory has five slots. Information can be held in these slots or work can be done in them. Child A, who has organized her memory, uses three slots to keep track of three subsets (vehicles, animals, and furniture) and has two slots in which to do mental work (which consists of generating instances of a category and deciding whether or not that instance was in the list just studied). Child B, who has not organized her memory, fills each slot with an individual item from the set of studied items. Because there are no subsets, she has no way of pointing to other items to keep them in mind. Also, there is no space for doing mental work.

In addition to providing pointers to subsets of information, organization can provide a source of internally produced retrieval cues that guide the spread of activation. For example, the idea of *animals* suggests *cat, mouse,* and *dog.* Child A, who has slots available for doing mental work, can consider each of these specific animals as they come to mind. If activation from the specific animal and from

memory for the study episode intersect (as they would for *cat*) then the child knows that the item was studied. If activation from the animal and the memory of the study episode does not intersect, then the child knows the item was not studied. After Child A has exhausted her knowledge of animals, she can consider furniture, because she still has in working memory a pointer to the furniture subset.

Child B cannot guide the search process by generating her own retrieval cues, because she has not used subsets to organize her memory. For this child, activation will continue spreading in a variety of directions and the probability of recalling more items than were originally represented in working memory is low.

In summary, organization may influence recall in a variety of ways. It may keep spread of activation in the relevant area of long-term memory, it may provide pointers in working memory to the relevant areas of long-term memory, and it may provide a source of retrieval cues for searching further in memory.

INSTRUCTIONAL SUPPORT OF ELABORATION AND ORGANIZATION

Since elaboration and organization facilitate learning and recall, it would be useful during instruction somehow to increase the probability that these processes occur. As we have seen, individuals differ in the extent to which they spontaneously elaborate on and organize information. Also, some materials stimulate more elaboration or organization than do others. What then, can be done to encourage students who do not always use these processes spontaneously or to improve on materials that do not stimulate these processes?

A great deal can be done through instructions or supplementary materials to increase students' use of elaboration and organization processes. I will sample here just a few studies that demonstrate what can be done. In some of these studies just a few words were needed to stimulate more elaboration. A few carefully chosen and well-timed words can have powerful effects.

Imagery Instructions

Asking students to think of images of what they are studying enhances recall. For example, Kulhavy and Swenson (1975) had 128 fifth and sixth graders read a twenty-paragraph passage called "The Island of Ako and Its People." The passage included a question after each paragraph that required the student to use information in the paragraph just read. These questions were either verbatim from the passage or paraphrases of passage words. For example, for a paragraph about how the people made clothes, the questions were:

Verbatim: The islanders made their

clothes from_____.

(palm leaves)

Paraphrase: Garments worn by the

natives are made

with_____.

(palm leaves)

Fifty of the students were directed to form mental images of the activities in the paragraph before trying to answer the question. Forty-eight students were simply directed to study the passage and questions for a test. Half of the students in each group took a test immediately following their reading of the passage and all of the students took the same test a week later. The test consisted of forty items—twenty verbatim and twenty paraphrase—so each subject had answered twenty of these items during the reading session.

The average number correct on the delayed test, as a function of imagery instructions and of whether the immediate test had been taken, are shown in Table 4.4. The students who received imagery instructions performed better, especially on the paraphrase items. The paraphrase items provided no superficial wording cues to the correct answer. Rather, they had to be answered on the basis of a meaning representation for the passage. Thus it appears that the imagery instructions helped students form a more meaningful representation.

Imagery instructions may not be helpful for all materials or for all students. However, since they are so easy to give, you may want to try them to see what happens.

Presentation of Analogies

Imagery instructions may be particularly helpful with fairly familiar material that suggests images. However, some material that we ask students to learn is so unfamiliar or abstract that it does not evoke images. In situations in which material is fairly unfamiliar, analogies are useful.

D. Hayes and Tierney (1982) demonstrated the effectiveness of analogies in one domain that is fairly unfamiliar to American high school students—the game of cricket. Cricket has many points in common with baseball, so it might be useful to teach the new information about cricket by comparing it to baseball. The comparison could be explicit (specific points about cricket would be compared to specific points about baseball) or implicit (the rules of the game of baseball would be reviewed just before introducing the game of cricket with the hope that students would make comparisons between the two games).

D. Hayes and Tierney (1982) compared both implicit and explicit comparison with no comparison of baseball and cricket. The im-

Table 4.4. Average number of questions correctly answered on a one week retention test as a function of type of instructions and whether or not an immediate test was taken. (Adapted from Kulhavy and Swenson, 1975.)

| | INSTRUCTIONS | | | |
| | NO IMAGE | | IMAGE | |
	VER-BATIM	PARA-PHRASE	VER-BATIM	PARA-PHRASE
Received immediate test	11.06	10.89	12.95	14.23
No immediate test	8.94	8.04	8.01	10.93

plicit group read a passage about baseball before reading a passage about cricket. The explicit group also read a passage about baseball before reading one about cricket, but the cricket passage made explicit comparisons between baseball and cricket (see Table 4.5). The no-comparison group read an irrelevant passage before reading the passage about cricket. After reading, all subjects wrote down everything they could remember from the cricket passage. The subjects were eleventh and twelfth graders who participated in the experiment during school.

Table 4.6 shows the amounts (number of idea units) recalled by the three groups. The researchers counted the idea units in recall that directly matched text units and also the reasonable inferences that were inserted in recall protocols. The explicit-comparison group remembered more from the text itself

Table 4.5. Parts of two versions of a passage about cricket. In the version on the left, cricket is explicitly compared with baseball. The version on the right contains no explicit references to baseball. The comparisons and the corresponding sentences in the no-comparison version are in italics here but not in the version the subjects read. (Adapted from Hayes and Tierney, 1982.)

PORTION OF TEXT WITH EXPLICIT COMPARISONS	CORRESPONDING PORTION OF TEXT WITH NO COMPARISONS
Cricket is a bat and ball game played between two teams of 11 players each on a large grassy field. *It is from cricket that the American game of baseball developed.* In a cricket match, the teams take turns at bat. While one team bats the other team defends the field. The object of the batting team is to score runs, while the object of the fielding team is to dismiss batsmen. *Unlike baseball,* there are always two batsmen in play at the same time. Batsmen score runs by exchanging positions on the field.	Cricket is a bat and ball game played between two teams of 11 players each on a large grassy field. *It is one of the most popular games in England and several other British Commonwealth countries.* In a cricket match, the teams take turns at bat. While one team bats the other team defends the field. The object of the batting team is to score runs, while the object of the fielding team is to dismiss batsmen. *In cricket* there are always two batsmen in play at the same time. Batsmen score by exchanging positions on the field.
The center of activity is an area in the middle of the field called the pitch, *which corresponds to the infield in baseball.* At both ends of the pitch stands a wicket consisting of three vertical sticks, called stumps, with two horizontal sticks, called bails, resting across the top. Wickets *are a bit like home plate in baseball.*	The center of activity is an area in the middle of the field called the pitch, *which measures 10 feet wide by 66 feet long.* At both ends of the pitch stand a wicket consisting of three vertical sticks, called stumps, with two horizontal sticks, called bails, resting across the top. Wickets *are 28 inches high and nine inches wide.* They provide a target for . . .

Table 4.6. The amount of information recalled about cricket as a function of whether or not cricket was compared to baseball and, if so, whether or not the comparison was explicit. (Adapted from Hayes and Tierney, 1982.)

	TYPE OF RECALL	
	TEXT STATEMENTS	INFERENCES
Implicit comparison	24.05	6.15
Explicit comparison	27.19	3.43
No comparison	24.90	3.79

than did the other two groups, but the implicit group produced the most inferences. This latter result may be due to the fact that readers in the implicit group were drawing comparisons (inferences) between baseball and cricket while reading the cricket passage.

If drawing inferences helps recall, why didn't the implicit-comparison group recall any more than the no-comparison group? Since all groups were given the same amount of time to read, and since making comparisons takes time, the implicit group may not have had as much time to encode passage information. The group that was given the comparisons explicitly did have almost as much time as the no-comparison group to encode passage information, and this group showed enhanced recall. If a delayed-retention test had been given, one would predict from elaboration theory that the implicit comparison group would recall more from the text than the no-comparison group because elaborations become more and more helpful over time.

Of course, for analogies to be effective, the students must be familiar with the analogous domain. Bell (1980) demonstrated this with paragraphs that used a metaphor in their summary sentences. For example, in a paragraph about Beethoven's eccentricity and paranoia, the summary statement was ''Beethoven was the Howard Hughes of early 19th-century Vienna.'' Students read such passages and then answered fill-in-the-blank

questions about them. They also were asked a question to assess whether or not the metaphor was understood. The results showed significantly better recall among students who understood the metaphor than among those who did not understand it. In other words, students who do not understand a metaphor cannot use it to elaborate on passage information.

Despite the warning that learner's must understand the analogous domain for analogies and metaphors to be effective, the effectiveness of analogies has been demonstrated in several studies (Mayer, 1975; Shustack and Anderson, 1979).

Instructions to Elaborate

One way to get around the problem of selecting an analogy or metaphor that is familiar to all of one's students, is to have them generate their own analogies or metaphors. This is exactly what Linden and Wittrock (1981) asked children to do during three days of reading instruction. The children involved were lower-middle-class Hispanic children in the fifth grade.

These researchers compared four methods of instruction for three stories from grade-school reading books. In all methods each story was read and discussed for forty-five minutes before a fifteen-minute test period. The test included multiple-choice items over facts specifically stated in the stories and fill-in-the-blank comprehension items that required the children to draw inferences about the stories. One story was read each day for three consecutive school days.

Two groups of children were instructed to elaborate. The first group, called *imaginal to verbal*, received instructions on day 1 to draw pictures about the story they had read, on day 2 to write one- or two-sentence summaries for different sections of the story that they had read, and on day 3 to write down analogies or metaphors about the story they had read. In other words, this group's instructions proceeded from imaginal elaboration to verbal elaboration. The second group, called *verbal to imaginal* received the same instructions over the three days, but in the reverse order: day 1—metaphors, day 2—verbal summaries, and day 3—pictures.

Two other groups of children did not receive instructions to elaborate. The *no instruction* group, had the same teacher as did the two groups that elaborated. Instead of elaborating they answered standard (main idea and phonetic analysis) questions during their reading of the stories. The classroom teacher group received instruction from the regular classroom teacher. Her instruction varied a great deal across days: one day she gave the students the test questions ahead of time and told them to read the story with the test questions in mind, another day students read aloud, and a third day they tried to anticipate at different points in the story what would happen next.

Table 4.7 shows the summaries of the tests over the three stories. The most striking difference is on the comprehension questions, which the groups who elaborated were much better at answering. They averaged about 30 correct on the comprehension test, whereas the two groups that did not do much elaborating averaged about 19 correct.

The experimenters examined the students' elaborations to make sure that they were relevant to the stories (precise). All the elaborations were found to be relevant. The experimenters also correlated the number of elaborations generated by an individual student and that student's score on the comprehension test for the two groups that were instructed to elaborate. The correlations were .57 and .24, respectively, for the imaginal to verbal and the verbal to imaginal groups. These correlations are consistent with the notion that elaborations improve recall.

Organization

So far, the instructional manipulations described here have all encouraged elaboration. However, many things can be done to stimulate organization as well. One is to give students an outline before they listen to or read information that fits into the outline. The outline should encourage students to organize their memories.

Glynn and DiVesta (1977) tried this technique with college students who were studying a fifteen-paragraph passage about the

Table 4.7. Number of correct answers following story reading as a function of what students were asked to do during reading. (Adapted from Linden and Wittrock, 1981.)

	NUMBER OF GENERATIONS	FACT RECALL	COMPRE-HENSION
Imaginal to verbal	13.0	27.63	28.63
Verbal to imaginal	10.7	23.29	31.28
Traditional	0.0	25.14	17.71
Classroom teacher	1.2	21.57	21.57

Table 4.8. The topics discussed in a passage about stones. (From Glynn and DiVesta, 1977.)

MINERALS

I. Metals
   A. Rare metals
      –Silver
      –Gold
   B. Alloys
      –Steel
      –Brass
II. Stones
   A. Gem stones
      –Diamond
      –Ruby
   B. Masonry stones
      –Granite
      –Marble

attributes of various kinds of rocks. The hierarchical structure of this passage is reflected in the topical outline shown in Table 4.8. The most general topics discussed were metals and stones. Under metals were two subtopics (rare metals and alloys), and stones also had two subtopics (gemstones and masonry stones). Finally, within each subtopic were two sub-subtopics. For example, within rare metals, silver and gold were discussed.

Some of the students studied the outline of topics before they read the passage. Others simply read the passage. All students read at their own rate. When they were finished, they all were asked to write down what they could remember from the passage.

Table 4.9 shows the results. For general ideas from the passage both groups recalled about the same proportion (10 percent). However, the group that studied the outline recalled 8 percent more specific details than the group that did not study the outline. This is what one would expect if the outline helps the students search memory.

More recent work on "networking" (Holley, Dansereau, McDonald, and Collins, 1979) and "mapping" (Armbruster and Anderson, 1980) has shown that methods of organizing information, besides traditional outlines, also enhance recall.

SUMMARY AND CONCLUSIONS

Acquisition of declarative knowledge occurs when new knowledge stimulates the activation of relevant prior knowledge, which leads to storing the new knowledge with relevant prior knowledge in the propositional network. Retrieval of declarative knowledge occurs when a retrieval cue activates a particular area of the propositional network and activation thence spreads to related areas until the desired information is activated. Construction of knowledge occurs when a particular fact cannot be retrieved and so the activated knowledge is used to infer the desired information.

Elaboration is the process of adding related knowledge to the new knowledge. These additions (elaborations) provide alternate pathways for retrieval and extra information for construction. Elaborations that relate to more than one part of the new knowledge are more effective in enhancing retrieval than are elaborations that relate to only one part of the new information.

Organization is the process of putting

Table 4.9. The proportion of ideas recalled from the passage about stones as a function of whether or not an outline was studied. (Adapted from Glynn and DiVesta, 1977.)

	PROPORTION OF IDEAS RECALLED FROM PASSAGE	
	GENERAL IDEAS	SPECIFIC IDEAS
Studied outline	.08	.32
Did not study outline	.10	.24

declarative knowledge into subsets and indicating the relationships among subsets. It enhances management of limited-capacity working memory during retrieval.

Some procedures that can be used by teachers to encourage elaboration include the use of analogies, instructions to the learners to form images, or instructions to generate elaborations. One procedure that encourages organization is the provision of an outline. Other procedures that should facilitate elaboration and organization include asking students to give examples of new concepts, asking them to fill in a partially completed outline, or using words that cue organization. The list of procedures and questions that stimulate declarative learning processes is limited only by the imagination of the teacher or designer of instruction.

With so many possibilities, it may be more important to focus on what *not* to do rather than on what to do to encourage the acquisition of declarative knowledge. Clearly, one should not present new material in a way that reduces its meaningfulness and organization. This is not necessarily an easy task since many instructional materials do not attempt to make new information particularly meaningful and do not organize information in the most effective way. A teacher who takes materials off the shelf and hands them to the student is therefore failing to enhance elaboration and organization. A few words or questions at the start of a lesson that show the student how the new materials relate to something already known can increase learning and recall substantially. A few words or questions throughout a lesson that indicate an organization for the new information can also help substantially.

This chapter started with a problem that is familiar to many teachers—students who appear to resist learning new declarative knowledge. The term "motivation" was used to label the problem, implying an affective cause, but resistance to learning may have a cognitive cause. Students naturally seek to elaborate on and organize new information. If they cannot, because the new information does not remind them of anything, then they may become "unmotivated." One solution to this problem is to find out what the students know that can be related to the new information and, as frequently as is needed, to remind them of these connections. Another solution is to encourage students to use elaboration and organization habitually. In Chapter 12 we will look at a program that trained students to elaborate.

ADDITIONAL READINGS

The Structure of Memory

Anderson, J. R. (1976). *Language, memory, and thought*. Hillsdale, N.J.: Lawrence Erlbaum Associates.

Klatzky, R. L. (1980). *Human memory: Structures and processes* (2nd ed.). San Francisco: W. H. Freeman.

Loftus, G. R., and E. T. Loftus (1976). *Human memory: The processing of information*. Hillsdale, N.J.: Lawrence Erlbaum Associates.

Tulving, E., and W. Donaldson (eds.). *Organization of memory*. New York: Academic Press, 1972.

The Acquisition of Declarative Knowledge

Ausubel, D. P. (1968). *Educational psychology: A cognitive view*. New York: Holt, Rinehart and Winston.

Bransford, J. D. (1979). *Human cognition: Learning, understanding, and remembering*. Belmont, Calif.: Wadsworth.

Cermak, L. S., and F. I. M. Craik, eds. (1979). *Levels of processing in human memory*. Hillsdale, N.J.: Lawrence Erlbaum Associates.

Gagné, R. M. (1977). *The conditions of learning* (3rd ed.). New York: Holt, Rinehart and Winston.

Rohwer, W. D., Jr. (1980). An elaborative conception of learner differences. In R. E. Snow, P. Federico, and W. E. Montague (eds.), *Aptitude, learning, and instruction* (Vol. 2). Hillsdale, N.J.: Lawrence Erlbaum Associates.

Wittrock, M. C. (1974). Learning as a generative process. *Educational Psychologist*, 11, 87–95.

Chapter 5

Acquisition of Procedural Knowledge

SUMMARY

1. There are two main types of procedural knowledge: pattern-recognition and action-sequence. The former underlie classification skills, whereas the latter underlie the ability to carry out sequences of symbolic operations.

2. Generalization and discrimination are learning processes associated with developing pattern-recognition procedures. The result of generalization is a procedure that applies to a broader class of entities. The result of discrimination is a procedure that applies to a narrower class.

3. Generalization is supported by presenting, close together in time, examples that vary widely on irrelevant attributes. Discrimination is supported by presenting, close together in time, examples and matched nonexamples of the concept to be learned.

4. Proceduralization and composition are learning processes associated with developing action sequence procedures. Proceduralization translates a declarative representation of an operation into a procedural one. Composition changes several small procedural steps into a unit that takes place automatically as a whole.

5. External prompts for steps in a sequence can support proceduralization. Practice and feedback can support both proceduralization and composition.

A major difference between experts and nonexperts in any field is that the experts have far more procedural knowledge of that field. They know how to classify and they have specialized rules for manipulating information. For example, a chess master recognizes significant patterns of players on the chess board and can decide on correct moves quickly (Chase and Simon, 1973a; 1973b). An electronics expert recognizes patterns in circuit diagrams that help him or her to diagnose problems (Egan and Schwartz, 1979). A physicist rapidly solves physics problems by recognizing what special formulas (e.g., mass × acceleration = force) apply (Larkin, McDermott, Simon, and Simon, 1980a). No matter what the domain, procedural knowledge is necessary for expertise.

The goal of public school education is not to produce chess masters or electricians or physicists, but to produce experts in the basic skills. Expertise in basic skills, just like expertise in specific disciplines, is largely a matter of having the right procedural knowledge. Thus, it is extremely important to know how procedural knowledge is acquired and what can be done to facilitate its acquisition.

As a first step in understanding the acquisition of procedural knowledge, it is important to distinguish between two types of procedure because the learning processes associated with each differ somewhat. *Pattern-recognition* procedures underlie the ability to recognize and classify patterns of internal and external stimulation. *Action-sequence* procedures underlie the ability to carry out sequences of operations on symbols. In performance, pattern-recognition and action-sequence procedures become linked, but in the early stages of learning it is useful to separate them.

PATTERN-RECOGNITION VERSUS ACTION-SEQUENCE PROCEDURES

Table 5.1 shows some test items from various subject areas. The items on the left require students to classify or recognize something (for example, a frog). The knowledge representation underlying performance on such items is called a pattern-recognition procedure because it looks for a particular stimulus pattern. New instances of concepts are identified by pattern-recognition procedures.

The items on the right require that an individual not only recognize the pattern specified by the conditions, but also carry out a sequence of actions—either covert ("mental") actions or both covert and overt ("physical") actions. To get these items right the individual must carry out a series of steps in their correct sequence. For example, to combine two contrasting sentences one must first remove the period from the end of the first sentence, then put a comma between the first and second sentence, and finally add the

Table 5.1. Test items for pattern-recognition and action-sequence procedures.

PATTERN RECOGNITION	ACTION SEQUENCE

1. Which of the following is a frog?
 	
  a. (picture of a water snake)
  b. (picture of a toad)
  c. (picture of a frog)
  d. (picture of a slug)
	4. Take care of the animal (frog) you found on a field trip so that it doesn't die.

2. Which of the following pairs of ideas form a contrast?
 	
  a. Joe is short. Joe is fat.
  b. Joe is short. Jim is tall.
  c. Joe likes fishing.
     Joe likes hiking.
  d. Jim walked to school.
     Jim walked to the store.
	5. Use conjunctions and punctuation to combine the following sentences:
	I liked the movie.
	John didn't like the movie.

3. $y = 3x + 5$ describes a _____.
  a. circle
  b. straight line
  c. hyperbola
  d. parabola
	6. Draw a figure corresponding to $y = 3x + 5$.
	
	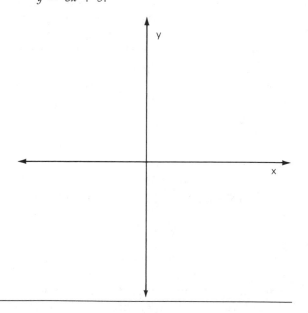

word "but" after the comma. The knowledge representation underlying performance on such items is called an action-sequence procedure because it implements a series of actions.

Table 5.2 shows production representa- tions for procedures needed to answer the items in Table 5.1. Notice that whereas the pattern-recognition procedures each involve only one action (to classify), the action-se- quence procedures all involve more than one action. Notice also that the conditions of the

Table 5.2. Production representations for knowledge underlying the ability to answer the test items shown in Table 5.1.

PATTERN RECOGNITION	ACTION SEQUENCE

1.   IF   ANIMAL has four legs
      and ANIMAL is green
      and ANIMAL is slimy
      and ANIMAL is size of fist
 	
    THEN   Classify ANIMAL as a frog.
	4. IF GOAL is to keep ANIMAL alive
	      and ANIMAL has four legs
	      and ANIMAL is green
	      and ANIMAL is slimy
	      and ANIMAL is size of fist
	
	    THEN Put ANIMAL near water
	      and catch flies
	      and feed ANIMAL flies.

2.   IF   There are two IDEAS
      and one IDEA is different from other
      IDEA on one DIMENSION
 	
    THEN   Classify pair of IDEAS as a contrast.
	5. IF GOAL is to combine 2 SENTENCES
	      and there are 2 IDEAS in the
	      SENTENCES
	      and the IDEA in one SENTENCE is
	      different from the IDEA in the other
	      SENTENCE on one dimension.
	
	    THEN Remove period from end of first
	      SENTENCE
	      and put comma at end of first
	      SENTENCE
	      and write "but" after comma
	      and write second SENTENCE after
	      "but."

3.   IF   EQUATION has the form
      $y = mx + b$
 	
    THEN   Classify EQUATION as one that
      describes a straight line
	6. IF EQUATION has the form $y = mx + b$
	      and GOAL is to draw line
	
	    THEN Put POINT1 at b on y-axis
	      and count m to the right from POINT1
	      and count 1 up
	      and put POINT2 here
	      and draw LINE through POINT1 and
	      POINT2.

pattern-recognition productions show up in the conditions of the action-sequence productions. For example, both item 3, which classifies straight lines, and item 6, which draws straight lines, contain the condition that the equation have the form $y = mx + b$. For action sequences to be useful, they should only take place under certain conditions. Thus action-sequence procedures are sequences of actions *coupled with* pattern-recognition procedures.

The relationship between pattern-recognition procedures and action-sequence procedures is similar to the relationship between concepts and rules in R. M. Gagné's (1977) learning theory. Specifically, in the present framework, based largely on J. R. Anderson's theory, and in R. M. Gagné's theory recognition of patterns is a necessary condition for correct application of rules. In both views patterns are *prerequisite* to actions.

Despite the fact that pattern-recognition

and action-sequence procedures are intimately related in performance, the learning processes involved in learning to recognize patterns and in learning to carry out sequences of actions are distinct. Because they are learned differently, they will be discussed separately here.

ACQUIRING PATTERN-RECOGNITION PROCEDURES

Many patterns are learned through experience, without direct instruction. A dramatic example of experiential learning is young children's acquisition of vocabulary. Much of vocabulary consists of agreed-on labels for patterns. For example, in English we agree that a large, four-legged animal with an udder is called "cow" and a large, four-legged animal with a mane is called "horse."

Most children start elementary school with about 7500 words that they can comprehend (Carroll, 1964). How do they master this large vocabulary without any direct schooling? The main processes involved are *generalization* and *discrimination*.

Generalization

When an individual responds in a similar manner to stimuli that differ, he or she is said to be generalizing. For example, a toddler who sees a new cat and calls it "cat" is generalizing from old examples of cats to a new one.

One way of conceptualizing generalization, which has been proposed by J. R. Anderson and his colleagues (Anderson, Kline, and Beasley, 1980), is as the process of changing a production so that its action applies to more cases. Look, for example, at the productions shown in Table 5.3. Productions P_1 and P_2 apply to a single animal—"Toby" in the case of P_1 and "Max" in the case of P_2. The action of both of these productions is to

Table 5.3. An example of generalization. Production P_3 is more general than either P_1 or P_2. It was created by keeping the common conditions and actions and deleting the unique conditions of P_1 and P_2.

P_1	IF I see THING THAT MOVES and THING THAT MOVES is small and THING THAT MOVES is furry and THING THAT MOVES says "meow" and THING THAT MOVES is Toby THEN Say "cat" and classify THING THAT MOVES as a cat.
P_2	IF I see THING THAT MOVES and THING THAT MOVES is small and THING THAT MOVES is furry and THING THAT MOVES says "meow" and THING THAT MOVES is Max THEN Say "cat" and classify THING THAT MOVES as a cat.
P_3	IF I see THING THAT MOVES and THING THAT MOVES is small and THING THAT MOVES is furry and THING THAT MOVES says "meow" THEN Say "cat" and classify THING THAT MOVES as a cat.

classify the creature as a cat. A child who hears a parent say "Toby is a cat" in the presence of the family cat on several occasions might well create the production P_1. If she hears the parent say "Max is a cat" on several occasions in the presence of the neighbor's cat, then she might create production P_2. At this point, the child would gleefully say "cat" upon seeing either Toby or Max, but might not generalize this response to other cats.

Once these two productions have been

created, the stage is set for generalization. In this example the result of generalization is P_3. Production P_3 recognizes any small furry thing that says "meow" as a cat. It will do so even if a totally unfamiliar cat is seen by the child.

Notice that in these productions the words THING THAT MOVES are written in all capital letters. This is to signify that THING THAT MOVES is a variable that can take on many different values (e.g., dogs, frogs, people, and cars are all things that move).

According to J. R. Anderson's theory (Anderson, Kline, and Beasley, 1980), generalization takes place automatically whenever two productions that have the same action are in working memory at the same time. The generalization mechanism looks for common conditions and then creates a new production that retains the common conditions and deletes any unique conditions. In the cat example the common conditions were a small, furry, thing that moves and says "meow." The unique conditions were the names of the specific cats.

Another example of generalization is shown in Table 5.4. Here, a student is learning the concept of polygon. Suppose that the teacher's early examples of polygons all have less than eight sides. After seeing these examples, the student might construct P_1, which has three conditions: (1) that there is a two-dimensional figure, (2) that the figure has all equal sides, and (3) that the number of sides is small (less than eight). Suppose that the teacher later gives several more examples of polygons all with eight or more sides. Then the student might create a second production (P_2) for classification of polygons when there are many sides. Like P_1, this production has three conditions: (1) that there is a two-dimensional figure, (2) that the figure has all equal sides, and (3) that the number of sides is greater than or equal to eight. The

Table 5.4. An example of generalization. P_3 keeps the action that was present in P_1 and P_2 (classify FIGURE as polygon) and also keeps the common conditions. P_3 is the result of automatic generalization across P_1 and P_2.

P_1	IF	FIGURE is two dimensional and SIDES are all equal and number of SIDES is less than eight
	THEN	Classify FIGURE as polygon.
P_2	IF	FIGURE is two dimensional and SIDES are all equal and number of SIDES is eight or more
	THEN	Classify FIGURE as polygon.
P_3	IF	FIGURE is two dimensional and SIDES are all equal
	THEN	Classify FIGURE as polygon.

two productions are alike in their first two conditions and in their actions, but different in their third conditions.

At this point the student has the raw material for generalization. That is, he or she has two productions that have the same action. If these two productions become activated at the same time, the automatic generalization mechanism will notice that they have the same action and will inspect their conditions for common elements. The common elements in this example are the first two conditions. A new production (P_3) is created that contains just these conditions and the action of classifying figures as polygons.

Thus, the main result of generalization is deletion of conditions. Deletion of conditions is achieved by inspecting the condition clauses of productions that have common actions. The effect of deleting conditions is to allow a production to apply to more situations.

At this point it would be helpful for you to try creating a generalized production from two specific productions. As we shall see shortly, one of the best ways to learn procedural knowledge is through practice and feedback, not through simply reading about a procedure.

5.1. Write a production that would result from generalization across these two productions:

$$P_1$$

IF There is a two-dimensional FIGURE

and the FIGURE is closed

and all points on the line of the FIGURE are equidistant from an imaginary center

and the FIGURE is drawn in red

THEN Classify the FIGURE as a circle.

$$P_2$$

IF There is a two-dimensional FIGURE

and the FIGURE is closed

and all points on the line of the FIGURE are equidistant from an imaginary center

and the FIGURE is drawn in blue

THEN Classify the FIGURE as a circle.

5.2. Write a production that would result from generalization across these two productions:

$$P_1$$

IF MUSIC has harpsichords

and MUSIC is by Bach

and MUSIC has trio form

THEN Classify MUSIC as baroque.

$$P_2$$

IF MUSIC has harpsichords

and MUSIC is by Vivaldi

and MUSIC has trio form

THEN Classify MUSIC as baroque.

Evidence for Generalization

Generalization explains how people can classify concept examples they have never seen before. An alternative explanation, called *instance matching*, proposes that people classify new examples by matching them to the closest known example stored in long-term memory. New examples do not match known examples completely, but they do match some known examples better than others. The best-matching known example is used to select the category to which the new example belongs. That is, if the best-matching known example was associated with the category label ''A'' in memory, then the new example is labeled ''A'' also. The idea of instance matching certainly has intuitive appeal because it fits with introspections about how we sometimes classify new entities. For example, on meeting someone new, one may be reminded of a friend who is athletic, and therefore classify the new person as athletic too.

Some recent research has been conducted to determine which of these two mechanisms—generalization or instance matching—accounts for the ability to recognize new instances of patterns. The results of some of these studies support the notion that people form generalizations (also called "schemas" or "prototypes") and then use these to classify new instances (e.g., Reed, 1972). The results of other studies support the notion that people use old instances to classify new instances (e.g., Medin and Schaffer, 1978). The majority of studies, however, suggest that both generalization and instance matching are used in classifying new instances.

A study by Hayes-Roth and Hayes-Roth (1977) exemplifies this final type of study. The categories used were two fictional clubs, Club 1 and Club 2. The experimenters did not tell subjects what attributes of people predicted their membership in a club. Rather they just showed them many, many examples (102 to be precise) of people who belonged to these two clubs. (This may be like what happens to young children when they learn vocabulary. Usually, no one tells them "A cat is a furry, small animal that says meow." Rather they see many examples of cats and hear their parents label the examples.)

The examples of club members were displayed on computer terminals and subjects were directed to study each example. A typical sequence for a subject might be first to read:

Susan Smith, 40 years, junior high,

married, bowls, Club 1

and then to read on the next display:

Jack Brown, 50 years, senior high, single, fishes, Club 2

and then to read on the next display:

Jane Doe, 50 years, college, single,

paints, Club 2

According to J. R. Anderson's description of generalization (Anderson, Kline, and Beasley, 1980), if the instances *Jack Brown* and *Jane Doe* are active in working memory simultaneously, the subject might form a general production of the form:

IF PERSON is 50 years old

And PERSON is single

THEN Classify PERSON as member

of Club 2.

That is, the subject would find conditions in common across two situations that led to the same action. In this example the conditions in common are age and marital status.

The majority of people in Club 1 that were presented to subjects were thirty years old. The majority were also junior-high educated. Finally, the majority of members were married. However—and crucial to the experiment—there was no Club 1 member who was thirty years *and* junior-high educated *and* married. Table 5.5 shows the patterns of age, education, and marital status that were presented for the members of each club. You can see from that table that the majority of members of Club 2 were fifty years old, the majority were college educated, and the majority were single. However, once again, no one member was fifty years old *and* college educated *and* single.

According to generalization theory, the exposure to the examples of club members should lead subjects to form the two productions shown in Table 5.6. For the action of P_1 to take place, the conditions of thirty years, junior high, and married should all be present. For the action of P_2 to take place, the conditions of fifty years, college, and single

Table 5.5. The membership of Club 1 and Club 2 presented to subjects. Notice that the frequency of certain age, education, marital status patterns varies. For example, ten members of Club 1 were thirty, junior high, single, whereas only one member was thirty, senior high, and married. Also, notice that the majority of members of Club 1 were thirty, the majority were junior high educated, and the majority were married. However, no one member of Club 1 was thirty and junior high educated and married. (From Hayes-Roth and Hayes-Roth, 1977 as described in J. R. Anderson, 1980.)

CLUB 1	CLUB 2
A. 10 instances of 30 years, junior high, single	M. 10 instances of 50 years, college, married
B. 10 instances of 30 years, college, married	N. 10 instances of 50 years, junior high, single
C. 10 instances of 50 years, junior high, married	O. 10 instances of 30 years, college, single
D. 1 instance of 30 years, junior high, divorced	P. 1 instance of 50 years, college, divorced
E. 1 instance of 30 years, senior high, married	Q. 1 instance of 50 years, senior high, single
F. 1 instance of 40 years, junior high, married	R. 1 instance of 40 years, college, single
G. 1 instance of 30 years, senior high, divorced	S. 1 instance of 50 years, senior high, divorced
H. 1 instance of 40 years, junior high, divorced	T. 1 instance of 40 years, college, divorced
I. 1 instance of 40 years, senior high, married	U. 1 instance of 40 years, senior high, single
J. 5 instances of 30 years, senior high, single	V. 5 instances of 30 years, senior high, single
K. 5 instances of 40 years, college, married	W. 5 instances of 40 years, college, married
L. 5 instances of 50 years, junior high, divorced	X. 5 instances of 50 years, junior high, divorced

should all be present. These two generalizations would be formed because they represent the most typical situation for a member of a given club. Other generalizations representing combinations of two of the three crucial attributes or only one crucial attribute would also be formed.

To find out whether some general representation had been formed, Hayes-Roth and Hayes-Roth tested subjects on both old and new instances. On the test only information about age, education, and marital sta-

Table 5.6. Two productions formed through generalization while learning about members of two clubs.

IF PERSON is 30 years old
and PERSON has junior high education
and PERSON is married
THEN PERSON is in Club 1.

IF PERSON is 50 years old
and PERSON has college education
and PERSON is single
THEN PERSON is in Club 2.

tus was presented. (That is, members' names and hobbies were not presented.) The subjects were asked to state the club membership of each test instance.

There were two crucial new instances on the test. These were:

30 years, junior high, married

50 years, college, single

Neither instance had been seen before, but they matched perfectly the general description for membership in Club 1 and Club 2, respectively. Thus, if subjects are using their memories for previously seen instances to judge the category membership of test instances, they should not do very well in categorizing these crucial instances. However, if they are relying on a generalized representation to judge category membership, then they should do quite well on the crucial instances because of the match between these crucial instances and the generalized representation. The results were that subjects were better at classifying the crucial instances correctly than they were at classifying previously seen instances. This suggests, then, that people do form general procedures to classify new examples of categories.

However, the subjects also used instance memory to make some judgments. In addition to being asked to classify the test instances, subjects were also asked to indicate whether or not each test instance was previously studied and how confident they were in their judgment. As you can see in Table 5.5, some age, education, marital status patterns had been seen ten times (each time in conjunction with a different name and hobby) whereas others had been seen only once. The subjects were more confident of having seen a test instance before if it had been studied ten times than if it had been studied only once. If all that the subjects had stored in memory during the study period was a general representation for membership in each club, then one would not expect them to show sensitivity to the frequency with which they had encountered specific instances. Therefore, these data suggest that subjects store instance representations *and* general representations.

From a functional point of view, it makes sense for humans to store both instance and general information. The advantage of the general category information is cognitive speed and economy: the more things we can classify correctly, the more appropriate actions we can take. The advantage of instance information is that when general category information fails, we have other information available in memory that may suggest alternatives. Thus, it is adaptive to keep both instance and category information in memory.

Instructional Support for Generalization

When students learn new concepts in any subject they are acquiring pattern-recognition procedures and are likely to use generaliza-

tion. Teachers and instructional materials can enhance this process by selecting appropriate examples of a concept for presentation. Also, students become better independent learners if they know how to seek or generate the right kinds of examples. If two examples are presented one right after the other and if these two examples differ widely on irrelevant attribute values, then the appropriate generalization is most likely to develop.

Successive Presentation of Examples. A teacher, textbook, or computer program might present an example of a concept, then some anecdotal information that is not too germane, and then another example of the concept. When examples of concepts are separated in time, they are less likely to be active in working memory at once, and therefore generalization is not as likely. It might be better for the teacher to present two examples of the concept in rapid sequence or else to leave the first example on the blackboard for the student's referral.

Presentation of Examples That Vary Widely on Irrelevant Attributes Values. In generalization one looks for common elements among productions that have the same action. If two examples for which a student develops two specific productions have conditions in common other than the crucial ones for category membership, generalization will include these similarities and therefore will form too limited a generalization. For example, an elementary school child who encounters several pictures of construction workers, all male, may include maleness in a representation of construction workers. To prevent the formation of too-restricted generalizations, it is important to provide examples that vary widely on irrelevant attributes (Houtz, Moore, and Davis, 1972; Klausmeier and Feldman, 1975; Tennyson, 1973). Thus, if this child had encountered an example of a male construction worker followed by an example of a female construction worker, he or she would not have included maleness in a representation of construction workers.

Tennyson, Woolley, and Merrill (1972) demonstrated the importance of presenting examples that vary widely on irrelevant attribute values for the concept of trochaic meter. Trochaic meter in poetry has each regular beat (called a "foot") consisting of a stressed syllable followed by an unstressed syllable. For example, the word áp•ple consists of a stressed syllable followed by an unstressed syllable. Other types of meter are an unstressed syllable followed by a stressed syllable (as in a•bóve), a stressed syllable followed by two unstressed syllables (as in "cóme to the"), or two unstressed syllables followed by a stressed syllable (as in "to the séa"). Thus, the crucial attributes for classifying a line of poetry as trochaic meter are (1) two syllables in each foot and (2) the sequence of stressed syllables preceding unstressed.

If a teacher presented examples of trochaic meter that were all written by one poet, all from the Romantic period, or all two lines long, the student might form a too-restricted representation such as that shown at the top of Table 5.7. The bottom of Table 5.7 shows the correct general representation for trochaic meter. Students who learned the general representation shown at the top of the table would fail to classify correctly modern poems with trochaic meter. In other words, they would undergeneralize.

Tennyson et al. (1972) had college students read through instructional materials on trochaic meter. Different groups were presented with different examples of trochaic meter poetry, but all groups received a definition of trochaic meter at the beginning of instruction. Then some students received examples that did not vary widely on values

Table 5.7. Two productions that classify examples of trochaic meter. The production on top will apply only to examples of trochaic meter from the Romantic period. The production on the bottom will apply to all examples of trochaic meter.

IF POEM is from Romantic period
  and each FOOT has two SYLLABLES
  and stressed SYLLABLE precedes
    unstressed SYLLABLE
THEN Classify POEM's meter as trochaic.

IF Each FOOT has two SYLLABLES
  and stressed SYLLABLE precedes
    unstressed SYLLABLE
THEN Classify POEM's meter as trochaic.

given to irrelevant attributes. Two of the examples they saw are shown in Table 5.8. Both are from the Victorian period in British poetry and both are two lines long. Other students received examples that did vary widely on irrelevant attributes, as is shown in Table 5.9. The first example in that table is by an American poet and is two lines long; the second is by a British poet and is only one line long.

Table 5.8. Examples of trochaic meter that do not vary widely on irrelevant attribute values. Even though the period of poetry and number of lines are irrelevant to the definition of trochaic meter, these two examples have the same values on these irrelevant attributes. They are both from the Victorian period and they both have two lines. (Adapted from Tennyson, Woolley, and Merrill, 1972.)

There they are, my fifty men and women,
Naming me the fifty poems finished!

R. Browning

Wailing, Wailing, Wailing, the wind over
land and sea —

Tennyson

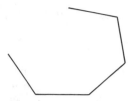

Table 5.9. Examples of trochaic meter that vary widely on irrelevant attribute values. The first example is by an American poet and is two lines long. The second is by a British poet and is one line long. (Adapted from Tennyson, Woolley, and Merrill, 1972.)

Out of childhood into manhood
Now had grown my Hiawatha

> Longfellow

Pansies, lilies, kingcups, daisies.

> Wordsworth

After studying several examples, all the students took a test in which they were asked to classify new examples of poetry as having trochaic meter or not. The students who had received a wide variety of examples during instruction were much less likely to undergeneralize on the test than were the students who had received examples that did not vary widely on irrelevant attributes. Thus, it appears that exposure to examples that vary on irrelevant attribute values is important for the facilitation of generalization.

Discrimination

Whereas generalization *increases* the range of situations to which a procedure applies, discrimination *restricts* this range. According to J. R. Anderson's theory, discrimination results in adding to the condition side of a production (J. R. Anderson, Kline, and Beasley, 1980). To return to the example given in Table 5.4, suppose that the student has created a production like P_3 that classifies all two-dimensional figures with equal sides as polygons. Then suppose that this student encounters the following figure. Since this figure is two dimensional and all of its sides are equal, the student would classify it as a polygon. The teacher might then tell the stu-

dent that he or she is wrong, because the figure is not closed. The student would then revise production P_3, to make the following production:

P_4 IF FIGURE is two dimensional

and FIGURE is closed

and all sides are equal,

THEN Classify FIGURE as polygon.

P_4 has three conditions whereas P_3 in Table 5.4 had only two. The new condition restricts the range of situations in which polygons are recognized to those involving closed figures.

Discrimination is stimulated when a known procedure does not work. (In the preceding example, the known procedure for classifying polygons met with negative feedback.) This failure motivates the learner to understand what is different about the situation in which the procedure did not work and the many previous situations in which it did work. Here the student received help from the teacher. In other situations a student might do additional reading or might make some trial-and-error application of the procedure. The goal is to identify what distinguishes situations where the procedure is successful from those where it is not. Once the difference is identified, it will be added to the production as a necessary condition for application of that production.

Now try your hand at generating some more discriminating productions:

5.3. IF FIGURE is two dimensional

and FIGURE has three sides

and SIDES are straight

THEN Classify FIGURE as a triangle.

This production recognizes patterns of stimuli as triangles. Suppose that students who have this production are confronted with the figure shown. Will they classify this figure as a triangle?

yp

5.4. Suppose that, through further experience, these students realize that they are correct in calling:

triangles, but incorrect in calling:

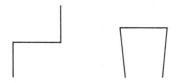

triangles. What condition would be added to the condition side of their production to make it correct? *closed*

5.5.   IF LETTER has tall, vertical

LINE

and tall, vertical LINE is on

left

THEN Classify LETTER as "bee."

Students who have this production see the printed letter b. Would they classify this letter as "bee"? *Yes*

5.6. The students see the letter w. Would they classify it as "bee"? *no*

5.7. The students see the letter h. Would they classify it as "bee"? *yes*

5.8. Write a production that has more conditions than the one in 5.5 and that correctly discriminates the letter b from all other printed letters in the English alphabet. *the bottom part of vertical line closes a semi-circle to its right*

Instructional Support for Discrimination

In generalization the selection and sequencing of *examples* are important for increasing the probability that a learner will form the correct pattern-recognition production. In discrimination it is the selection and sequencing of *nonexamples* that are important. A nonexample is an instance that is not an example of the concept being learned. Thus, a square is a nonexample of the concept of triangle.

Simultaneous Presentation of an Example and a Nonexample of a Concept. For discrimination to occur, situations in which a classification is and is not correct need to be active simultaneously in working memory so that the crucial differences between the two types can be identified. This simultaneity can be achieved in a variety of ways. The teacher or instructional materials can present an example immediately followed by a nonexample. The teacher can list a set of examples and a set of nonexamples on an overhead. Students can be asked to give examples of a concept. If a student gives a nonexample, the teacher can stop soliciting examples and explain why the student's supposed example is really a nonexample. There are many other ways of ensuring that students are comparing examples and nonexamples.

Selection of "Matched" Nonexamples. A "matched" nonexample varies in only one way from the example it is paired with: it lacks one of the crucial attribute values for being a member of a class (Houtz, Moore, and Davis, 1972; Markle, 1975). It is matched to its paired example in all other ways. That is, it has all the other crucial attribute values of the concept and also the same irrelevant attribute values as are possessed by the particular example with which it is paired.

"Minimal contrasts" used in phonics instruction are pairs of examples and matched nonexamples. In Figure 5.1 *fate* is paired with *fat* and *rode* is paired with *rod*. The pattern to be learned is that a vowel, consonant, and silent e at the end of a word mean that the vowel has a long sound. The matched nonexamples (*fat* and *rod*) both have the vowel and consonant, which are two of the crucial aspects of the pattern, but they lack the silent e. Also, they have the same vowel and consonant as the examples with which they are paired. What the vowel and consonant are in the pattern is irrelevant. However, matched nonexamples keep the same irrelevant attribute values as the example with which they are paired.

By holding constant everything between an example and a matched nonexample except one crucial attribute one focuses on this crucial aspect. In discrimination one looks for crucial differences between successful and unsuccessful applications of a production, and creates a new production that adds this difference as a condition. If the only difference to be found is a crucial one, the production created will be correct.

Suppose that instead of *fate* and *fat*, one presented *fate* and *fan*. The student might think that a crucial condition for a long vowel sound is the absence of the letter n at the end of a word. He or she might form the production:

> IF VOWEL in last syllable of word
>
> and it is not followed by an n
>
> THEN Classify VOWEL as long.

By presenting *fate* and *fat*, however, one prevents the student from deriving an incorrect

Figure 5.1. The use of minimal contrasts in phonics instruction is a case of using examples and matched nonexamples. The example and its matched nonexample differ in only one crucial way—whether the word ends in silent e or not.

production. The production would probably be the correct one:

> IF VOWEL in last syllable of word
>
> and VOWEL followed by con-
>
> sonant, and silent e
>
> THEN Classify VOWEL as long.

The nonexample *fan* is not as good as the nonexample *fat* because it varies in more than one crucial way from its paired example.

Tennyson et al. (1972), in their study of how to teach the concept of trochaic meter, gave one group of students nonexamples that were matched with their paired examples, as shown in Table 5.10. At the top of the table is an example that is a list of four things and is one line long. It is matched with a nonexample that is also a list of four things and one line long. The nonexample, like the example, has a stressed syllable at the beginning of each foot, but unlike the example, it has three syllables per foot. The second example in the table is a two-line fragment by a British poet. Its matched nonexample is also a two-line fragment by a British poet. This nonexample has two syllables per foot, but the unstressed syllable precedes the stressed. Thus, irrelevant attribute values, such as period of po-

Table 5.10. Two pairs of examples and matched nonexamples. In the first pair the main difference between the two is the number of syllables per foot—the nonexample has three, the example has two. Both have the stressed syllable preceding the unstressed syllable, both are one line long, and both are a list of four words. In the second pair, the example and nonexample share many irrelevant attribute values such as being two lines long, being by a British poet, and ending in an exclamation point. They also have one crucial attribute value in common—having two syllables per foot. However, the nonexample lacks the correct sequence of stressed and unstressed syllables. (Adapted from Tennyson, Woolley, and Merrill, 1972.)

PAIR 1

Example: Pán·sies,/ lí·lies,/ kíng·cups,/ dái·sies.

Wordsworth

Matched nonexample: Mó·ther·ly,/ Fá·ther·ly,/ Siś·ter·ly,/ Bró·ther·ly!

Unknown

PAIR 2

Example: Máid of/ Ath·ens,/ 'ere we/ párt
Gíve, oh/ gíve me/ báck my/ heárt!

Byron

Matched nonexample Sure só/·la·cér/ of hú/·man cáres,
And swéet/·er hópe/ when hópe/ de·spaírs!

Bronte

etry, nationality of author, and length are kept constant across an example and a matched nonexample. All that varies is the value of one of the crucial attributes. The effect of seeing examples and matched nonexamples is to focus attention on crucial attributes.

Table 5.11 shows the type of nonexample presented to another group of students. These nonexamples sometimes had different irrelevant attribute values than the example with which they were paired—such as different periods of poetry. Also, they sometimes lacked both of the crucial attribute values rather than just one. As in the example of minimal contrasts, the use of unmatched nonexamples can produce misconceptions about the definition of a concept.

In the classification test that Tennyson et al. (1972) gave following training, the students given unmatched nonexamples showed far more misconceptions than did those given matched nonexamples. The group given matched examples performed quite well. These data, then, support the notion that the provision of examples and matched nonexamples facilitates discrimination.

Table 5.11. An example of trochaic meter (top) and an unmatched nonexample (bottom). The two differ on the number of syllables per foot, whether the stressed syllable precedes the unstressed syllables in a foot, and the period in which the poem was written.

Thére they/ aŕe, my/ fíf·ty/ mén and/ wó·men,
Nám·ing/ mé the/ fíf·ty/ pó·ems/ fín·ished!

R. Browning

If the heárt/ of a mán/ is de·préssed/ with caŕes,
The míst/ is dis·pélled/ when a wó/·man ap·péars.

Gay

The Role of Schooling in Teaching Pattern-Recognition Procedures

In the previous sections, evidence was given for the principle that correct generalization is facilitated by exposure to examples that vary widely on irrelevant attribute values. This prevents an irrelevant attribute value from being encoded as part of the condition of the pattern-recognition production. Evidence was also presented to support the principle that correct discrimination is facilitated by exposure to examples paired with matched nonexamples. A matched nonexample varies in only one crucial way from the example and hence encourages the addition of this crucial aspect to the condition of a new production.

Because of the powerful effect of the nature and timing of examples and nonexamples, formal schooling can substantially increase the number of pattern-recognition productions that people acquire. People do acquire new pattern-recognition procedures through informal interaction with the environment. They do so because newly encountered examples stimulate the retrieval of information about previously encountered examples and hence create the minimal conditions for generalization and discrimination. However, there is nothing in the "natural" environment to ensure that the new examples and the remembered examples vary widely on irrelevant attribute values or that new nonexamples and remembered examples will be matched. In fact, examples are not likely to vary widely because, for many concepts, examples in the real world have correlated irrelevant attribute values (such as male for construction workers). It is also highly unusual for examples and nonexamples in the real world to have only one crucial difference between them. Thus, one place that a teacher can make a large difference in learning is in the careful selection of examples and nonexamples.

5.9. Assume that you want a student to develop the following pattern-recognition production:

IF ANIMAL has hair

and ANIMAL has mammary glands

and ANIMAL has placenta

THEN Classify ANIMAL as a placental mammal.

(For your information, mammals are all animals with both hair and mammary glands. There are two classes of mammals: one (including the majority of mammals) has placentas, the other does not. The nonplacental class includes the orders *marsupial* and *monotremes*. Marsupials and monotremes, like all other mammals, have hair and mammary glands. However, monotremes lay eggs, and marsupials give birth to very immature young and have no placentas. Instead, they have external pouches in which they carry the very young animals.)

One thing that would help the student to form the above production would be to present examples that encourage generalization and nonexamples that encourage discrimination. Choose from the following list of examples and nonexamples of placental mammals:

a. Two examples that vary widely on irrelevant attribute values.
b. An example and a matched nonexample.
   1. An opossum. Small. Long tail. No placenta. Hair. Mammary glands. Eats garbage. Walks on four feet.
   2. A human. Large. Walks on two feet. Hair. Mammary glands. Placenta.
   3. A koala bear. Medium size. Walks on four feet. Hair. Mammary glands. No placenta.
   4. A rat. Small. Long tail. Placenta. Hair. Mammary glands. Eats garbage. Walks on four feet.
   5. A whale. Very large. Lives in the water. Hair. Mammary glands. Eats plankton. Placenta.

ACQUIRING ACTION-SEQUENCE PROCEDURES

Pattern-recognition procedures often set the stage for action sequences that follow. We do not classify things simply for the intellectual fun of classification. We do so because it helps us make predictions or carry out actions. Thus, pattern-recognition and action sequences are intimately connected in performance. However, during learning the two can be separated.

The learning of action sequences is a slow process, characterized by many errors. If you have ever studied either computer programming or a foreign language you may recall how slowly and awkwardly you worked at first. Most objectives in typical programming and language courses are action sequence ones. You can tell this from the types of assignment given. The assignment to "write a program to find the square root of any number" requires that many symbolic actions be carried out. So does the assignment to "change these ten French sentences from the present to the future tense."

According to J. R. Anderson's theory (1982), action sequences are learned in the following manner. First the learner represents a sequence of actions in declarative (propositional) form. Then a procedural representation of the action sequence develops with experience in trying to produce the action sequence. A familiar example of this process is learning to drive a stick-shift car. At first one guides oneself verbally by stating (or thinking) each step and then carrying out that step. Then, after many attempts to drive with a stick shift, the learner drives smoothly and without any conscious cuing from declarative knowledge.

The process of changing from performance of a sequence of actions guided by declarative knowledge to performance guided by procedural knowledge is called, by J. R. Anderson, *knowledge compilation*. The term suggests an analogy to computers. Computer programs can run in one of two forms—compiled or interpreted. In an interpreted form, each individual line of the program is translated into machine code at the time that the program is run; in a compiled form, a program is loaded into the computer in a pre-translated form so that it runs quite rapidly. Knowledge compilation thus is the process of building a representation for action sequences that leads to smooth and rapid performance.

Knowledge compilation is said to be comprised of two subprocesses: proceduralization and composition. *Proceduralization* is the dropping out of cues from declarative knowledge, while *composition* is the collapsing of several procedures into one procedure.

Proceduralization

Many of the action sequences that we learn begin as declarative knowledge. We read rules in textbooks or the teacher writes a sequence of steps on the board that we endeavor to follow. Also, we observe the action sequences of others and represent their actions declaratively. Later we retrieve this declarative knowledge in an attempt to imitate significant others. Thus, the initial step in learning action sequences is creating a propositional representation for the procedure. The second step is creating one production to represent each step in the action sequence. Both steps occur during proceduralization.

Consider, for example, the rule for adding fractions, shown at the top of Table 5.12. While reading the steps in this rule, one creates propositional representations for them, some of which are shown at the bottom of Table 5.12. Then one translates these propositions into productions. Table 5.13 shows productions for the first three steps in the procedure. Thus proceduralization involves (1) generating a propositional description of a sequence of actions, and (2) translating this propositional description into a set of productions.

Proceduralization would be a straightforward process were it not for two obstacles: limitations on working memory capacity and lack of prerequisite knowledge.

Limitations on Working Memory. The most efficient representation for adding fractions would be one large production that had for its conditions (1) the goal of adding fractions, and (2) the existence of fractions to add, and had for its actions the nine steps listed at the top of Table 5.12. This representation is efficient because it carries out nine transformations without propositional representation of anything but the intermediate results. Having a separate production for each step is not as efficient, because after each step is carried out a complete propositional representation of the situation must be reinstated before the next production can apply. (Recall that for a production to apply, each of its conditions must be represented in the active portion of the propositional network.) As an example, for P_3 in Table 5.13 to take place the propositions that my goal is to add fractions, that there are two fractions to add, and that I have RESULT 1 must all be active. If one large production was controlling performance all that would be needed to move from step 2 to step 3 would be RESULT 1. In other words, a series of small productions is less efficient than one large production because more working

Table 5.12. The steps involved in adding fractions and propositional representations for the first two steps.

1. Find the least common denominator.
2. Divide the denominator of the first fraction into the least common denominator.
3. Multiply the result of step 2 by the numerator of the first fraction.
4. Write the result of step 3 above a line and the least common denominator below that line.
5. Repeat steps 2–4 for the second fraction.
6. Add the numerators of the two fractions written down in step 4.
7. Write the result of step 6 as a numerator.
8. Write the least common denominator as the denominator.
9. If the numerator and denominator have a common factor, divide them by this factor and write the result.

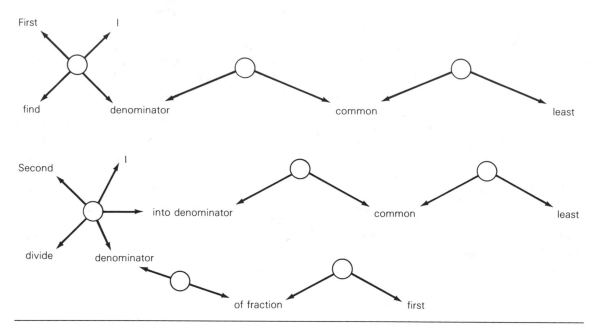

memory capacity is taken up with unnecessary representation of information.

If productions with a large action clause are more efficient then why don't people immediately create such productions from declarative knowledge? The reason is limited-capacity working memory. Productions are forged in working memory. When they are forged from propositions a good deal of working memory's capacity is taken up by the propositions. Also, some capacity is taken up by the operations used to translate propositions into productions. There is simply not enough room to create large productions at first. So, initially, small productions are created, one for almost each step in a procedure. Later, during composition, larger productions are created from small ones.

Lack of Prerequisite Knowledge. Almost all procedures refer in their conditions and actions to other procedures (either pattern-recognition or action-sequence procedures) that are presumed to be available to the learner.

Table 5.13. Production representations for the first three steps in adding fractions shown in Table 5.12.

P_1 IF   My GOAL is to add FRACTIONS and there are two FRACTIONS to add
THEN   Set SUBGOAL to find LEAST COMMON DENOMINATOR.

P_2 IF   My GOAL is to add FRACTIONS and there are two FRACTIONS to add and LEAST COMMON DENOMINATOR is known
THEN   Divide DENOMINATOR of FRACTION 1 into LEAST COMMON DENOMINATOR to get RESULT 1.

P_3 IF   My GOAL is to add FRACTIONS and there are two FRACTIONS to add and I have RESULT 1
THEN   Multiply NUMERATOR of FRACTION 1 by RESULT 1.

Table 5.14. A production for computing the least common denominator.

IF   GOAL is to find LEAST COMMON DENOMINATOR and there is more than one FRACTION
THEN   Multiply all DENOMINATORS to get PRODUCT
Identify COMMON FACTORS among DENOMINATORS and PRODUCT
Divide PRODUCT by COMMON FACTORS.

This is somewhat analogous to computer programs that refer to subroutines or to other programs that are supposed to be available in the computer's library. If such procedures are not available, then the new procedure cannot operate.

One example of reference to other procedures is provided by the first production shown in Table 5.13. In that production the action is to set a subgoal of finding the least common denominator. This action, in order to operate, must call up the relevant procedure. For example, the production shown in Table 5.14 finds least common denominators. Its actions are (1) multiply all the denominators, (2) identify common factors among the denominators and their product, and (3) divide the product by the common factors.

If this production was not already known to the person who created the first production shown in Table 5.13, then he or she would not be able to proceed to the other productions in the sequence because their conditions would not be met. For example, production P_2 has one condition that the least common denominator be known. Since one has no way of knowing the least common denominator, P_2 cannot take place. Thus, lack of prerequisite procedural knowledge creates an obstacle to learning new procedures.

Evidence for Proceduralization

As knowledge moves from a declarative to a procedural representation, the performance it underlies speeds up dramatically. Retrieval of propositions is a slow process, relying on spread of activation, but retrieval of productions is rapid since the action of one production often creates the conditions for another production to apply.

Perhaps the most persuasive evidence for proceduralization comes from thinking-aloud protocols of students as they acquire a new action sequence. One example of this is provided by J. R. Anderson (1982). He observed a student reading the side-angle-side (SAS) postulate shown in Figure 5.2 and then attempting to do a problem (shown in Figure 5.3) requiring the use of this postulate. Here is what the subject said as he attempted to solve the problem:

> If you looked at the side-angle-side postulate (long pause) well *RK* and *RJ* could al-

POSTULATE 14 If two sides and the included angle of one
(SAS POSTULATE) triangle are congruent to the corresponding
parts of another triangle, the triangles are congruent.

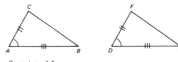

According to Postulate 14:

If $\overline{AB} \cong \overline{DE}$, $\overline{AC} \cong \overline{DF}$, and $\angle A \cong \angle D$,
then $\triangle ABC \cong \triangle DEF$.

Figure 5.2. The description given for the side-angle-side postulate in the textbook being studied by a high school student. The textbook is *Geometry* by R. C. Jurgensen, A. J. Donnelly, J. E. Maier, and G. R. Rising. Boston: Houghton Mifflin, 1975, p. 122. Copyright 1975 by Houghton Mifflin Co. Reprinted by permission. (From J. R. Anderson, 1982.)

most be (long pause) what the missing (long pause) the missing side. I think somehow the side-angle-side postulate works its way into here (long pause). Let's see what it says: "two sides and the included angle." What would I have to have to have two sides. *JS* and *KS* are one of them. Then you could go back to *RS* = *RS*. So that would bring up the side-angle-side postulate (long pause). But where would Angle 1 and Angle 2 are right angles fit in (long pause) wait I see how they work (long pause)

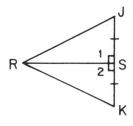

Given: $\angle 1$ and $\angle 2$ are right angles
     JS = KS

Prove: $\triangle RSJ \cong \triangle RSK$

Figure 5.3. The first problem a student encountered after reading about the side-angle-side postulate. (From J. R. Anderson, 1982, p. 382.)

JS is congruent to *KS* (long pause) and with Angle 1 and Angle 2 are right angles that's a little problem (long pause). OK, what does it say—check it one more time: "If two sides and the included angle of one triangle are congruent to the corresponding parts." So I have got to find the two sides and the included angle. With the included angle you get Angle 1 and Angle 2. I suppose (long pause) they are both right angles, which means they are congruent to each other. My first side is *JS* is to *JK*. And the next one is *RS* to *RS*. So these are the two sides. Yes, I think it is the side-angle-side postulate. (pp. 381–82)

One can see in this protocol several things that are characteristic of the proceduralization process. First, there are some false starts. For example, toward the middle of the protocol, it looks as though the student is about to match the SAS postulate. He recognizes the two congruent sides and only has to find that the included angles are congruent. However, what he says at this point is "Angle 1 and Angle 2 are right angles that's a little problem." Why they are a problem is not clear. This type of false start may be due to the heavy load on working memory.

Another aspect of proceduralization is that the learner is constantly having to remind him- or herself of the declarative statement of the rule. At two places in the preceding protocol the student goes back to reread the statement of the SAS postulate in his text.

Finally, the translation aspect of proceduralization is obvious in this protocol, especially in the second half, where the student explicitly matches each part of the postulate with something in the problem being solved. The explicit nature of this matching process suggests that the procedure is still in declarative form, because once it is in procedural form it will be performed without verbalization. The student will simply look at a problem and think of SAS automatically. The student whose protocol was just quoted went on to do four more practice problems, two of which involved the use of the SAS postulate and two of which did not. After that he started to work on another problem that involved the use of the SAS postulate. His entire protocol for this problem was:

> Right off the top of my head I am going to take a guess at what I am supposed to do: Angle DCK is congruent to Angle ABK. There is only one of two and the side-angle-side postulate is what they are getting to. (J. R. Anderson, 1982, p. 382).

Notice that the student no longer makes false starts, reminds himself of the postulate, or appears to go through a translation process. Rather, he appears to immediately apply the postulate. His behavior seems to emanate from procedural knowledge.

Encouraging Proceduralization

Instructional events that encourage proceduralization help overcome the obstacles to proceduralization: limited-capacity working memory and lack of prerequisite knowledge.

Memory Support. Apparently there has been little research on how to support memory during proceduralization, so what is said in this section is speculative. However, it seems logical to expect that easy-to-use sequences would be helpful for proceduralization. It also seems logical that requiring students to memorize, in declarative form, the steps in an action sequence, would *not* be useful. The declarative representation serves as a way station on the road to a procedural representation and so there seems to be little point to fixing this information in long-term memory. Time might be better spent in many practice trials, with lists of steps or other prompts available for reference as long as is necessary. For most procedures the aversiveness of having to look back at the list to rein-

state the declarative representation should provide ample motivation for proceduralizing the knowledge. Thus, it seems that there should be little danger that prompts will be relied on forever.

Not all procedures can be neatly described in words. This is true, for example, for the subtle thought processes involved in drawing inferences, checking the logic of some information, or coming up with an original solution to a problem. When steps cannot be verbalized completely, a teacher can model the questions he asks himself when engaged in thinking. In other words, a model thinking-aloud protocol can help one create a rough propositional representation of a procedure that is difficult to make completely explicit. Figure 5.4 shows a thinking-aloud protocol for proceduralizing a logic-checking procedure.

Ensuring Knowledge of Prerequisites. Although there has been little or no research on instructional support for working memory during proceduralization, there is a good deal of work that demonstrates how one can be given the needed prerequisite knowledge. One thing to do, of course, is to ensure that the prior knowledge has been learned. This is part of the rationale for individualized mastery instruction. Individualized mastery instruction allows each student to proceed at his or her own rate and tests for student mastery of each objective. If an objective is not mastered following instruction, alternative instruction is provided until the objective is mastered. This type of instruction ensures that each student has learned the necessary prior knowledge for any given new skill.

In general, individualized mastery instruction has been found to produce greater achievement gains than traditional instruction (Bloom, 1976; Torshen, 1977). In traditional group instruction if an individual fails to master a given objective, instruction

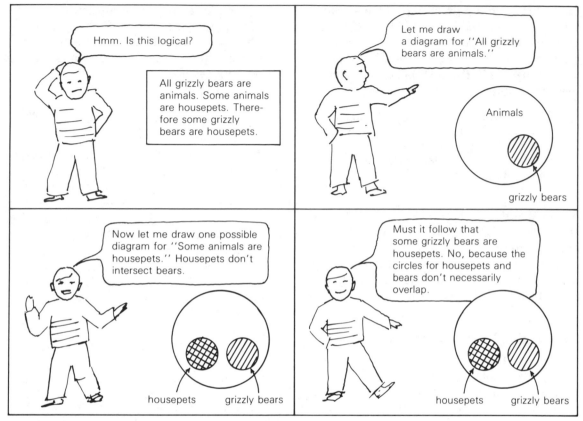

Figure 5.4. A cartoon showing an action sequence used for deciding whether or not a particular conclusion necessarily follows from two premises. Such cartoons (or teacher modeling) are useful prompts for students while they learn action sequences.

proceeds to the next topic anyway. Thus some individuals may not have the required prerequisite knowledge for learning new skills. One study compared these two forms of instruction in an introductory college physics course (Moore, Hauck, and Gagné, 1973). Many of the objectives of this course were action sequence ones. Students were randomly assigned to a section that received individualized mastery instruction or traditional lectures. Both groups took the same final exam, which was judged to not be biased in favor of either group. The individualized mastery group received an average of 120 points on the exam; the traditional group averaged 99 points. Probably a major reason for the superior performance of the individualized mastery group was that proceduralization of new action sequences was facilitated by knowledge of prerequisites.

We often learn procedures without having adequate prior knowledge. In such situations we learn the prerequisites concomitantly with the new procedures. This slows down the learning process. Resnick, Siegel, and Kresh (1971) demonstrated this idea in an experiment in which kindergarten children were trained to classify objects according to attributes. The experimenters focused on the two tasks shown in Figures 5.5 and 5.6.

The task shown in Figure 5.5 was called *placing*. The children were presented with a 3×3 matrix of empty cells. Each row in the matrix was associated with a different color, and each column was associated with a different shape. The color was indicated to the left of each row and the shape was indicated at the top of each column. These indicator cells were called "attribute" cells. The children were given nine objects (e.g., blue car) to place correctly in the cells of the matrix.

The task shown in Figure 5.6 was called *inferring*. Children had to infer the attributes associated with each row and column of the matrix before placing the object in its correct cell. The children were given a partially filled matrix that had no attribute cells. They were also given nine objects. Then they were told to select from the nine objects the object that

correctly filled each of the empty cells in the matrix.

Resnick et al. (1971) thought that the inferring task was more complex than the placing task. Moreover, they thought that the inferring task required many of the same procedures as did the placing task, but that it also required more procedures. In other words, the skills used in the placing task were prerequisite to the skills used in the inferring task. One way to represent the relationship between the two tasks is to describe the production sets that would underlie performance on each task and then compare them. Tables 5.15 and 5.16 show these production sets for the placing and inferring tasks, respectively.

Production 1 in each set is similar in that each functions to set the main goal and to identify the starting conditions. In P_1 for placing there are only two conditions, whereas in P_1 for inferring there are three. The first con-

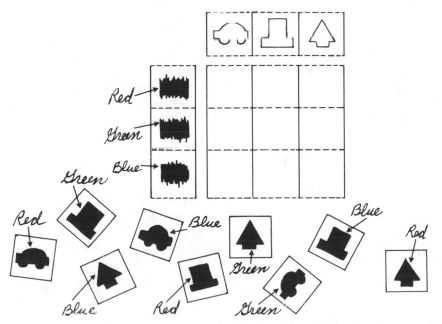

Figure 5.5. The placing task presented to kindergarten children. (From a verbal description in Resnick, Siegel, and Kresh, 1971.)

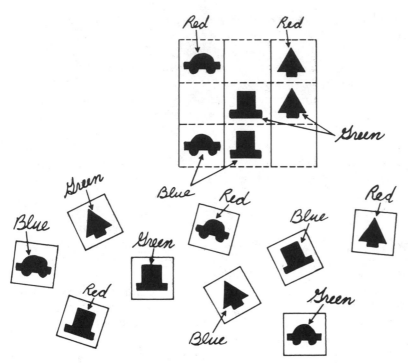

Figure 5.6. The inferring task. Children were directed to select the correct objects to fill each empty cell in the matrix. (From a verbal description in Resnick, Siegel, and Kresh, 1971.)

dition is similar for placing and inferring and the second conditions are complements of one another: for placing, the attributes are known, for inferring, they are not known. The actions of the first production in placing and inferring are similar, though not identical. For placing, the action is to set the subgoal of identifying the color of the *object*, whereas for inferring, the action is to set the subgoal of identifying the color associated with the *cell*. If P_1 in placing had been learned before P_1 in inferring many of the procedures implied by P_1 in inferring would already be proceduralized. For example, the procedure for identifying attributes would be known as would the procedure for setting up a subgoal to identify color.

A similar analysis of productions 2 and 3 for each task shows a similar relationship be-

tween the two tasks. For placing, P_2 and P_3 observe the color and shape of an object, respectively, and assign variable names to the color and shape observed (i.e., COLOR 1 and SHAPE 1). For inferring, P_2 and P_3 perform these same operations for two objects. In addition, they perform the action of moving the finger along a row (P_3) or a column (P_4) in order to identify the two objects to be observed. If placing's P_2 and P_3 had been learned before inferring's P_2 and P_3, then many of the operations in these latter productions would already have been proceduralized.

In general, then, many of the inferring procedures include placing procedures. In that sense, the placing procedures are prerequisite to the inferring procedures. Resnick et al. (1971) hypothesized that children who

Table 5.15. A hypothetical set of productions underlying performance on the placing task.

P_1
 IF GOAL is to place OBJECT 1 in correct CELL
   and ATTRIBUTES of ROWs and COLUMNs are known
 THEN Set SUBGOAL to identify COLOR of OBJECT 1.

P_2
 IF SUBGOAL is to identify COLOR of OBJECT 1
 THEN Observe OBJECT 1
   Let COLOR of OBJECT 1 be COLOR 1
   Set SUBGOAL to identify SHAPE of OBJECT 1.

P_3
 IF SUBGOAL is to identify SHAPE of OBJECT 1
 THEN Observe OBJECT 1
   Let SHAPE of OBJECT 1 be SHAPE 1
   Set SUBGOAL to identify ROW for COLOR 1.

P_4
 IF SUBGOAL is to identify ROW for COLOR 1
 THEN Scan three ATTRIBUTEs for ROWs
   Find match of ATTRIBUTE and COLOR 1
   Let matching ROW be ROW X
   Set SUBGOAL to identify COLUMN 1 for SHAPE 1.

P_5
 IF SUBGOAL is to identify COLUMN for SHAPE 1
 THEN Scan three ATTRIBUTEs for COLUMNs
   Find match of ATTRIBUTE and SHAPE 1
   Let matching COLUMN be COLUMN Y
   Set SUBGOAL to find INTERSECTION CELL.

P_6
 IF SUBGOAL is to find INTERSECTION CELL
 THEN Move finger from START of ROW X to right
   Move finger from TOP of COLUMN Y down
   Call CELL where fingers meet CELL 1
   Set SUBGOAL to place OBJECT 1.

P_7
 IF SUBGOAL is to place OBJECT 1
 THEN Place OBJECT 1 in CELL 1.

learned the placing task before they learned the inferring task would learn the inferring task faster than children who learned the inferring task without first learning the placing task. The results confirmed this hypothesis, with children who learned placing before inferring taking an average of 6.86 trials to learn the inferring task and children who learned the inferring task without first learning the placing task taking an average of 8.85 trials to learn the inferring task.

One might argue that the children who learned the placing task first did better on inferring not because they had learned prerequisite procedures but because they were used to matrix problems. If this were the case, then the number of trials to learn both tasks, regardless of the order in which they were learned, should be equal because either task could serve as a warmup for the other. However, the children who learned placing first and inferring second learned the two tasks in fewer trials (11.21) than the children who learned inferring before placing (14.23 trials).

Table 5.16. A hypothetical set of productions underlying performance on the inferring task.

P_1	IF GOAL is to identify OBJECT that fits in CELL 1 and ATTRIBUTES of ROWs and COLUMNs are not known and there are at least two OBJECTs in each ROW and each COLUMN THEN Set SUBGOAL to identify COLOR of CELL 1.
P_2	IF SUBGOAL is to identify COLOR of CELL 1 THEN Move finger along ROW to which CELL 1 belongs until two OBJECTs have been found Observe the two OBJECTs Let COLOR of two OBJECTs be COLOR 1 Set SUBGOAL to identify SHAPE of CELL 1.
P_3	IF SUBGOAL is to identify SHAPE of CELL 1 THEN Move finger along COLUMN to which CELL 1 belongs until two OBJECTs have been found Observe the two OBJECTs Let SHAPE of two OBJECTs be SHAPE 1 Set SUBGOAL to find OBJECT.
P_4	IF SUBGOAL is to find OBJECT THEN Scan array of nine OBJECTs Find OBJECT with COLOR 1 and SHAPE 1 Let OBJECT be OBJECT 1 Set SUBGOAL to place OBJECT 1.
P_5	IF SUBGOAL is to place OBJECT 1 THEN Place OBJECT 1 in CELL 1.

In other words, learning a complex procedure without first learning some of its components, slows down the learning process.

Composition

The other subprocess involved in learning action sequences is called *composition* (J. R. Anderson, 1982). During composition several productions are combined (composed) into one. As was mentioned previously, the productions that result from proceduralization are small because working memory does not have room for the direct creation of large productions from declarative knowledge. However, once a set of small productions exists, larger productions can be created from them. This is accomplished during composition.

For composition to take place, a sequence of two productions must be active in working

memory at the same time. The system then "notices" that the action of the first production creates the condition for the second production. The result is a new production that has the condition of the first production and the actions of both productions. The condition of the second production is dropped out as unnecessary information.

Tables 5.17 and 5.18 show an example of composition. Table 5.17 contains four productions that underlie the skill of sounding out unfamiliar printed words. P_1 breaks the word into syllables, P_2 pronounces each syllable, P_3 searches memory for a match between the sounds produced in P_2 and a known word, and P_4 pronounces the known word. Table 5.18 shows two new productions, one composed of P_1 and P_2 from Table 5.17, and one composed of P_3 and P_4. The one composed of P_1 and P_2 keeps the condition of P_1 (encoun-

Table 5.17. Four small productions that take place in a sequence in sounding out a word that is unfamiliar in print but is available in a person's aural vocabulary.

P_1 IF   Encounter WORD that I don't recognize
THEN   Break WORD into SYLLABLEs.

P_2 IF   WORD is broken into SYLLABLES
THEN   Pronounce each SYLLABLE.

P_3 IF   Each SYLLABLE in WORD has been pronounced
THEN   Match SOUNDS of SYLLABLEs to a word I have heard.

P_4 IF   SOUNDS of SYLLABLEs are matched to a word I have heard before
THEN   Say the word that I have heard before.

ter a word that I don't recognize), and has as its actions the actions of P_1 and P_2 in that order (break words into syllables, then pronounce syllables). The condition of P_2 (word is broken into syllables) has dropped out.

The two productions shown in Table 5.18 will accomplish the sounding out of a new word more rapidly than will the four in Table 5.17. This is because there is an activation time for each production and also because

Table 5.18. Two composed productions created from the four small productions shown in Table 5.17. The first production was created from P_1 and P_2 in Table 5.17. The second was created from P_3 and P_4.

IF   Encounter WORD that I don't recognize
THEN   Break WORD into SYLLABLEs
     and pronounce each SYLLABLE.

IF   Each SYLLABLE in WORD has been pronounced
THEN   Match SOUNDS of SYLLABLEs to a word I have heard
     Say the word I have heard.

working memory is less burdened when fewer conditions have to be represented.

Composition could easily continue to operate on the two productions shown in Table 5.18. The result would be one large production (shown in Table 5.19) to represent the entire skill.

Problems with Composition

While composition is useful in some situations, it can also be a detriment as it can produce what has been called the "set effect" or the "Einstellung effect." The set effect (Luchins, 1942) is the situation in which someone applies a less-than-optimal procedure to a new problem because that procedure has become composed. Lewis (1978) demonstrated the set effect in college students solving letter-replacement problems. A sample problem is shown in Table 5.20. Here students are given the goal of producing a letter string that contains the letter G. They are also given some rules for letter replacement: (1) if an I occurs, then change it to a D, (2) if both D and M occur, then replace them with L and O, and (3) if two O's occur, then replace them with G and C. Given the starting string Q M X L M, a student can first use rule 1 to produce Q M X D M, then use rule 2 to produce Q M X L O, then use rule 1 to produce Q M X D O, then use rule 2 to produce

Table 5.19. One production created from the two productions shown in Table 5.18. During composition, intermediate conditions in a sequence of actions are dropped and the entire action sequence is encoded into one production.

IF   Encounter WORD that I don't recognize
THEN   Break WORD into SYLLABLEs
     and pronounce each SYLLABLE
     and match SOUNDs of SYLLABLEs to a word I have heard
     and say the word I have heard.

Table 5.20. A letter replacement problem and two solutions — one with three rules and one with a fourth rule. The goal is to produce a letter string containing the letter G. (Adapted from Lewis, 1978).

REPLACEMENT RULES

1. If L, replace with D.
2. If both D and M occur, replace with L and O.
3. If two Os occur, replace with G and C.

        Start: Q M X L M
        Step 1: Q M X D M
        Step 2: Q M X L O
        Step 3: Q M X D O
        Step 4: Q L X O O
        Step 5: X L X G C

ADDITIONAL REPLACEMENT RULE

4. If both M and O occur, replace with G and V.

        Start: Q M X L M
        Step 1: Q M X D M
        Step 2: Q M X L O
        Step 3: Q V X L G

Table 5.21. The individual productions that would result from proceduralization of the replacement rules shown in Table 5.20. After much practice on problems containing L, M, and M, the composed production would take over control from the individual productions.

INDIVIDUAL PRODUCTIONS

    If LETTERSTRING contains L
    THEN Replace L with D.

    IF LETTERSTRING contains D
    and LETTERSTING contains M
    THEN Replace D and M with L and O.

    IF LETTERSTRING contains two Os
    THEN Replace Os with G and C.

COMPOSED PRODUCTION

    IF LETTERSTRING contains L, M, and M
    THEN Replace M and M with G and C.

Q L X O O, and finally use rule 3 to produce a string with the letter G in it: Q L X G C.

At first students may proceduralize each of the three rules into a separate production and apply each in a stepwise fashion as described previously. Three productions that encode these rules are shown at the top of Table 5.21. However, with extended practice on a set of problems that all contain L, M, and M at the start (e.g., L M X Q M, T M L Q M, and M Q L X M), students may form a composed production such as the one shown at the bottom of Table 5.21.

If a new replacement rule that reduces the number of steps needed to solve the problem is introduced after extended practice, it may not be heeded. For example, the new rule—(4) if both O and M are in the string, replace them with G and V—can shorten the number of steps in problems that contain L, M, and

M at the start, such as Q M X L M. First, one applies rule 1 to get Q M X D M, then one applies rule 2 to get Q M X L O, and then one applies rule 4 to get a string with the letter G in it: Q V X L G. This solution took three steps, whereas the solution without the new rule took five. If students are applying rules 1–3 in a stepwise fashion they can easily change when rule 4 is introduced because the necessary conditions for rule 4—the presence of O and M—will occur after step 2. However, if students have created a composed production such as the one shown at the bottom of Table 5.21, then the conditions needed for rule 4 will never occur.

Lewis introduced rule 4 to subjects after no practice with rules 1–3, or after twenty practice problems of the type L, M, M, or after fifty practice problems of the type L, M, M. He then gave some new L, M, M problems and observed whether or not students used the new rule (rule 4). He found an increase in resistance to using the new rule as a function of amount of practice without the new rule. Of those with no practice, only 5 percent failed to use the new rule. Of those with twenty practice trials, 63 percent failed to use the new rule, and for those with fifty practice trials, 78 percent failed to use the new rule. These are the results that one would expect if the procedure for solving L, M, M problems had become composed with practice.

The Lewis study shows that composition can make behavior more rigid. If individuals habitually solve a given type of problem in one way, the solution used becomes composed. Once it is composed learning alternative solutions is difficult because the conditions that trigger the productions in the alternative solutions never enter working memory. This suggests that we should be thoughtful in deciding what procedures should be learned to the point of composition. Two criteria for procedures that should be composed are (1) that they are unlikely to be changed, and (2) that they are used so often that speed in their use is beneficial. The procedures that underlie decoding skill in reading meet both of these criteria· the rules of letter-sound correspondences are unlikely to change substantially and these rules are used constantly in reading. No doubt there are many other skills which meet these criteria and hence it is important to know how to provide instructional support for composition

Instructional Support for Composition

Although not all skills need to be learned to the level of composition, some do. In particular, certain basic reading, arithmetic, and writing skills should become composed so that working memory can be used for higher-level thinking processes. In arithmetic, Tait, Hartley, and Anderson (1973) found that slowness in recalling basic number facts was related to poor computation of complex arithmetic problems. In reading, Perfetti and Lesgold (1979) have found that slow word decoding is related to poor comprehension. In both cases it appears that working memory is being cluttered with awkward attempts to perform basic procedures and that this leaves less room in working memory for solving the arithmetic problem or comprehending the passage.

For skills that should become composed practice and feedback are effective. Each practice attempt represents a chance to have two potentially related productions active in working memory simultaneously and hence represents a chance for composition.

Suppes and his colleagues (Suppes, Jerman, and Brian, 1968; Suppes and Morningstar, 1972) conducted a large-scale study of the effects of practice and feedback on arithmetic achievement. The procedures that children practiced included those involved in addition, subtraction, fractions, long division, multiplication, and percentages and ratios. They practiced on a computer terminal for about ten minutes a day for an entire school year. The difficulty of items was adjusted according to how well the student was doing. Immediate feedback was provided.

The students who received practice did significantly better than students who did not receive practice on a standardized achievement test given at the end of the school year. The improved performance on computational subtests may be due to the fact that the students who practiced had a greater number of composed (faster) procedures and hence could get through the timed subtests faster. Moreover, achievement gains on problem-solving subtests may be due to the fact that students with composed computational skills had more room in working memory to think about the problems and to monitor their execution of solutions.

Learning to Recognize Situations for Which a Given Action Sequence is Appropriate

Sometimes students learn a set of action sequences well but do not know when to use them. For example, children may be able to perform addition, subtraction, multiplication, and division rapidly and accurately when told to, but may not know which of these operations to use for a given "story" problem.

Action sequences are not fully effective until they become associated with pattern-recognition procedures. For example, one pattern for which addition is appropriate has the conditions (1) that there are two quantities, and (2) that one wants to know the quantity that would result from the merging of these two. One pattern for which subtraction is appropriate has the conditions (1) that there are two quantities, and (2) that one wants to know the quantity that would result from taking the amount represented by one quantity away from the other quantity.

Learning to recognize the patterns that are associated with a given action sequence involves the same generalization and discrimination processes as any pattern-recognition learning. Teaching should therefore proceed by giving examples that vary on irrelevant attribute values (e.g., the quantities in word problems could refer to candy, marbles, or inches) and by mixing examples with matched nonexamples (e.g., an addition problem involving candy followed by a subtraction problem involving candy).

Some arithmetic books teach addition, give practice in addition, teach subtraction, give practice in subtraction, teach multiplication, give practice in multiplication, teach division, give practice in division, and then stop. They fail to take the crucial final step of giving mixed sets of problems to help students create pattern-recognition procedures and associate them with appropriate action-sequence procedures.

Tennyson and Tennyson (1975) examined tenth graders' ability to use two grammatical rules following exposure to instances that varied widely or not so widely on irrelevant attribute values. Students given broad exposure performed 30 percent better than those given a narrow range of instances. The researchers also compared performance following exposure to matched versus unmatched nonexamples of rule use and found 30 percent better performance among students who had been presented with the matched nonexamples. This study demonstrates that action sequences must become linked to relevant pattern-recognition knowledge if they are to be useful.

COMMON STRATEGIES IN TEACHING PROCEDURAL KNOWLEDGE

Practice and Feedback

So far in this chapter, I have emphasized the unique aspects of generalization, discrimination, proceduralization, and composition. These unique aspects imply different teaching strategies for their support. However, there is also a common strategy that supports the learning of any procedural knowledge: practice followed by feedback. If the procedure is pattern recognition, then opportunities to classify new examples of the pattern should be given. The feedback should not only show whether one performed correctly, but also, if the answer was incorrect, it should identify precisely what parts of the answer were incorrect and what parts correct. If the procedure is an action sequence, problems should require the application of the procedure and feedback should identify precisely how the application was incorrect or precisely how fast a correct procedure was applied.

The types of problem presented and the nature of feedback vary depending on the learning process being tapped. For example, for proceduralization feedback about accuracy is more appropriate than feedback about speed. For composition feedback about speed is appropriate. Also, for proceduralization attention should be given to the sequencing of practice problems so that problems using prerequisite skills precede problems using more complex skills. For composition several similar problems should be given together. For generalization practice on examples that vary widely on irrelevant attributes should be given, whereas for discrimination practice on examples and matched nonexamples is called for. Thus, the nature of practice and feedback vary, even though *all* procedures require practice and feedback for their acquisition.

In contrast, practice and feedback are not required for learning declarative knowledge. In fact, when we use practice and feedback (in the form of rote rehearsal) for learning declarative knowledge, we remember this knowledge less well than when we "practice" this knowledge only once but try to comprehend it, elaborate on it, and/or organize it.

Analogies

Recently there has been some formal analysis of the role that analogies may play in the learning of new procedures. Rumelhart and Norman (1981) use the example of learning kinship classifications by analogy. Using their way of representing procedural knowledge, mother is defined as:

define mother (:x)

   return female parent :x

If someone had already learned this classification rule for mother, then the rule for classification of fathers could be produced by analogy rather than from scratch. All that this person would need to be told is *"father* is like *mother* with *male* for *female."* Given this information, the person could copy his or her rule for mother, replacing *female* with *male* and get:

define father (:x)

   return male parent :x

Learning new procedures by analogy to known procedures should be faster than learning them from scratch, because the simple process of copying bits of cognitive structure is used rather than the more complex processes of generalization, discrimination, proceduralization, or composition. Although formal analysis suggests that learning procedures by analogy should be helpful, there has been little research on this topic.

SUMMARY

Procedural knowledge, or knowing how, underlies skilled, routine intellectual performance. It is a type of knowledge that does not need to be searched for in long-term memory. Rather, patterns of conditions (representing both internal and external states) automatically activate it, and, once it is activated, its actions occur automatically.

Pattern-recognition procedures and action-sequence procedures work together in performance, but they can be distinguished by the types of learning processes that generate them. Generalization and discrimination are processes that, respectively, broaden and restrict the application of pattern-recognition procedures. Proceduralization and composition are processes that affect the acquisition of action sequences. Proceduralization leads to dropping cues from declarative knowledge. Composition puts several pieces of procedural knowledge together.

All of the learning processes associated with procedural knowledge depend on practice and feedback. Thus, it should not be surprising that it takes years to develop expertise in any area of intellectual performance, be it reading, chess, writing, or physics. We all need plenty of opportunities for practice of procedures, because it is only through practice that the procedure will develop.

ADDITIONAL READINGS

Theory and Research Related to Procedural Knowledge

Anderson, J. R. (1981). *Cognitive skills and their acquisition.* Hillsdale, N.J.: Lawrence Erlbaum Associates.
———.(1982). Acquisition of cognitive skill. *Psychological Review,* 89, 369–406.
Gagné, R. M. (1962). Acquisition of knowledge. *Psychological Review,* 69, 355–65.
LaBerge, D. and Samuels, S. J. (1974). Toward a theory of automatic information processing in reading. *Cognitive Psychology,* 6, 293–323.

Instructional Support for the Acquisition of Procedural Knowledge

Gagné, R. M., and L. J. Briggs, (1974). *Principles of instructional design.* New York: Holt, Rinehart and Winston.
Markle, S. M., and P. W. Tiemann (1969). *Really understanding concepts.* Champaign, Ill.: Stipes.
Merrill, M. D., and R. D. Tennyson (1977). *Teaching concepts: An instructional design guide.* Englewood Cliffs, N.J.: Educational Technology Publications.

ANSWERS TO EXERCISES

5.1.   IF There is a two-dimensional FIGURE
And the FIGURE is closed

And all points on the line of the FIGURE are equidistant from an imaginary center
THEN Classify the FIGURE as a circle.

(The generalization process kept the three common conditions and deleted the unique conditions having to do with the color of the figure.)

5.2.   IF MUSIC has harpsichords
And MUSIC has trio form
THEN Classify MUSIC as baroque.

(The generalization process kept common conditions and the common action and deleted the unique condition that the music be composed by one particular person. I do not claim that this is a "correct" classification procedure. Nonbaroque music can have a trio form and harpsichords. Nonetheless, it is plausible that someone who has never studied music formally might create this procedure through hearing pieces of music that were labeled as "baroque.")

5.3. Yes. This figure is two dimensional and has three sides, all of which are straight. Therefore, all the conditions of the production are met and its action will take place.

5.4. and FIGURE is closed. In addition to being two dimensional, with three straight sides, the figure must be closed to be correctly classified as a triangle.

5.5. Yes. A b has a tall, vertical line on the left. All the conditions of the production are met so its action will take place.

5.6. No. A w has no tall, vertical line. The conditions of the production are not met, so its action will not take place.

5.7. Yes. An h has a tall, vertical line on the left. All the conditions of the production are met, so its action will take place (even though the result is incorrect).

5.8.   IF LETTER has tall, vertical LINE
and tall, vertical LINE is on left
and short, curved LINE attaches
to tall, vertical line at bottom
THEN Classify LETTER as "bee."

(The condition you added may not use the same words as the third condition here, but it should describe the curved part of the letter b in a way that distinguishes it from h, k, and p.)

5.9. a. Whale and rat are the best two examples. They diverge on almost all irrelevant attribute values such as size, where they live, how they locomote, and what they eat.

b. Rat and opossum. Both are small, have long tails, and eat garbage. Both have hair and mammary glands. However, the opossum lacks a placenta.

Chapter

6

Problem Solving and Transfer

SUMMARY

1. A problem consists of a goal state, a starting state, and the set of all possible solution paths leading from the starting state to the goal state.

2. No matter what the type of problem, three cognitive processes that occur during problem solving are *problem representation, knowledge transfer,* and *evaluation.* The way people represent problems is crucial because it determines what knowledge will be activated.

3. *General* problem-solving strategies apply to a wide variety of problems, independent of their content, whereas *domain-specific* strategies apply only within a given domain of problems.

4. Some general problem-solving strategies, such as working forward and means-ends analysis, are helpful in *limiting* the search for solutions to those

which have the highest probability of success. Other strategies, such as reasoning by analogy and brainstorming, are helpful in *expanding* the search for solutions.

5. Expert problem solvers in a given domain have both more domain-specific knowledge and better organized knowledge than do inexpert solvers. This better organization helps them search efficiently through their knowledge while attempting to solve problems.

6. Transfer may be mediated by pattern-recognition productions that partially match a problem representation or by declarative knowledge activated by the problem representation.

7. Training programs that teach general problem-solving strategies are not always effective in producing transfer. One program that did work appeared to provide the appropriate conditions for generalization: a variety of example problems.

8. Training programs that support elaboration and organization appear to be successful in obtaining broad transfer of problem-solving skills.

This chapter is about how people achieve goals for which they do not have an automatic solution (problem solving), and about what facilitates the application of knowledge learned in one situation to a somewhat different situation (transfer). These two concepts are related in that transfer is one of the component processes of problem solving.

The ultimate goal of schooling is for students to transfer what they have learned in school to problems they encounter outside of school. Unfortunately, it is difficult to measure how much people use knowledge obtained from school in solving everyday problems, because knowledge acquired in and out of school is not segregated into neat packets in the mind. Subjectively, many people estimate that what they use of knowledge learned in school is small. Of course, it is obvious that people use the basic literacy skills learned in elementary school. But benefits of schooling are less clear when one thinks about middle and high school. Flanagan (1978) interviewed a representative sample of

1000 people about the effects that high school had on their adult lives. The conclusion of this study was that people perceived very little benefit from their high school years.

Although people's subjective estimates of their use of knowledge acquired in school may not be accurate, it still seems safe to say that some school knowledge that has potential transfer value is never transferred. It is therefore important to ask, How can we increase the probability of transferring knowledge to everyday life?

The question has no well-proven psychological answer. Psychologists have found problem solving and transfer to be difficult areas to study. It is hard to measure qualitative differences in the mental processes people go through to reach a solution. The Gestalt school of psychology was an early attempt at understanding problem solving, but it did not make much progress because it lacked methodological and theoretical tools for analyzing problem-solving processes. The tools now available to cognitive psychologists, discussed in Chapter 2, appear to be aiding the study of problem solving. For example, thinking-aloud protocols are used frequently as a way of finding out about the mental processes of a person solving a problem. So now there is a renewed interest in the study of problem-solving processes.

Because of the insufficient state of psychological knowledge, I will give no definitive answers to the question of how to teach for problem solving and transfer. Instead, I will describe an information-processing framework for viewing problem solving, and indicate possible—though far from proven—implications.

AN INFORMATION-PROCESSING VIEW OF PROBLEMS

A problem is said to exist whenever one has a goal and has not yet identified a means for reaching that goal. The problem may be wanting to answer a question, to prove a theorem, to be accepted, or to get a job. In each of these situations, there is a goal and, at least for a moment, no identified way to reach the goal.

The same problem may be more or less difficult depending on the individual. For example, for you or me to add 25 and 36 is almost trivial, but for a first grader it is almost impossible. Our well-practiced pattern-recognition productions immediately recognize the familiar pattern of numbers to be added, and these patterns are the conditions for the action sequences of addition to occur. Thus, for literate adults, simple addition problems are problems for only an instant.

The standard information-processing framework for viewing problems includes a goal state, a starting state, and all possible solution paths for reaching the goal. These three elements are called the "problem space" (Newell and Simon, 1972). Figure 6.1 shows

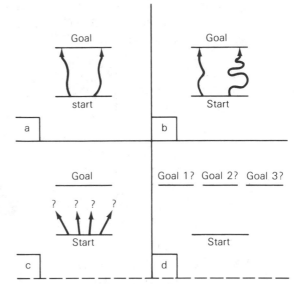

Figure 6.1. A problem consists of a starting state, a goal, and a set of solution paths for reaching the goal. These panels show several types of problem space.

several possible problem spaces. In panel a, there is a goal and two solutions of equal efficiency for reaching the goal. An example of this might be performing long division with one of two standard long-division procedures. In panel b there is a goal for which one solution path is clearly much more efficient than another. An example of this would be a child's goal of understanding a story. An efficient way to reach this goal is to read the story (if the child can read). A less efficient way would be to try to find someone to read to her. In panel c there is a person at one point and a goal at another point and no known path between the starting point and the goal. This is a common situation for people trying to solve novel problems. They can think of actions to try but there is little assurance that what is tried will lead them closer to their goal. Finally, in panel d there is a problem in which there are either several possible goals or unclear goals. This situation exists in "ill-defined" problems (W. Reitman, 1964), where the initial step of problem solving is to decide on one's goal. Once the goal is decided on, such problems then revert to being like the problems in panels a, b, and c. (Ill-defined problems will be discussed in greater detail in Chapter 10.)

PROBLEM-SOLVING PROCESSES

No matter what the characteristics of the problem space for a given problem, the same processes occur during problem-solving. Initially, the solver *forms a representation* of the problem. It may consist of propositions or images in working memory and may also include some external representations on paper, chalkboard, etc. For example, when given a story problem in algebra, people may create propositions in WM that assign values to certain variables, and they may also write down these equations on paper. This problem representation then activates related knowledge. For example, a symbolic representation of a story problem may activate various mathematical processes such as combining like terms and substituting equivalent elements. The activated knowledge is applied to the new situation. Activation and application of knowledge together are called *transfer*. Finally, there is an *evaluation* of the success of the solution.

These processes are interactive. For example, after forming an initial problem representation and activating knowledge that is relevant to that representation, one may find that the knowledge does not apply. One will then form a new representation and activate different knowledge. These interactions continue until a problem is solved or the solver gives up. As an example of these interactions, consider a teacher who wants a student to improve his C grade in history. The teacher

may initially think such things as "He is bright, so he should be able to do better," and "Therefore, he must be lazy." These thoughts form the initial representation of the problem. The knowledge activated by this representation might be ways of motivating "bright, lazy" students—perhaps a challenging assignment. The teacher might apply this idea by having the student do a research project on the causes of World War II. If this fails to motivate the student, the teacher might change her initial problem representation, thinking "Maybe he's not as bright as I thought. He seemed to copy his research paper out of an encyclopedia. Maybe he has poor reading comprehension." The new representation would activate knowledge of how to improve comprehension skills, which would be applied and the results evaluated. This dynamic interaction would continue until the teacher found an adequate solution.

As can be seen, the problem representation is most crucial to the success of problem-solving, because the representation determines what knowledge will be activated in long-term memory. Recent research comparing expert and novice problem solvers shows dramatic differences in how they represent problems initially. The expert's representation goes quickly to fundamental principles, whereas the novice represents the problem in terms of superficial, but perceptually salient, attributes. For example, for the assignment of writing a story, one seventh grader may activate knowledge about how long stories should be and thus may represent the problem as producing a written document of two pages. Another may activate story scenes that she has previously imagined and thus may represent the problem as capturing on paper her imagined scenes. The first student is behaving like a novice in representing the problem in terms of a perceptually salient aspect of the solution—length. The other student has a more meaningful problem representation and is therefore acting more like an expert. Throughout the rest of this book, we will be seeing examples of differences between experts' and novices' problem representations.

GENERAL VERSUS DOMAIN-SPECIFIC PROBLEM-SOLVING STRATEGIES

A strategy is a goal-directed sequence of mental operations. In solving problems, people behave as if they have selected a particular strategy. They do not have to be aware of the strategies they are using because, like other kinds of procedural knowledge, well-learned strategies may be activated automatically.

General strategies can be applied to a variety of problems independent of content, whereas *domain-specific* ones are appropriate only within a particular content area. For example, the strategy of trying to remember an analogous situation can be applied to the problems of planning study time, improving the yield of a crop, or smoothing over a difficult social situation. Therefore solving problems by analogy is said to be a general strategy. On the other hand, skimming the headings of a textbook chapter before reading the chapter works only for textbook reading problems. It would not be useful, say, for solving a difficult social situation or improving the yield of a crop.

In the next section some general problem-solving strategies are described. Following this is an example of problem-solving using a domain-specific strategy. A major point to be inferred from these two sections is that novel problems are more likely to produce a general problem-solving strategy and familiar ones are more likely to suggest a domain-specific strategy.

SOME GENERAL PROBLEM-SOLVING STRATEGIES

General problem-solving strategies are activities that can improve the search for a solution across a wide variety of problems. Sometimes the search becomes too random; there seem to be too many possible solutions and no way to judge which possibility is most likely to lead to success. In such situations a strategy for *limiting* the search is needed. At other times search seems to be quite impoverished. The solutions that have been thought of do not seem to work. Here a strategy for *expanding* the search is needed.

Limiting Search

Consider a "cryptarithmetic" problem such as the one shown in Table 6.1 (Newell and Simon, 1972). In cryptarithmetic the goal is to find out what number is represented by each letter. In this problem you are told that D = 5 and your goal is to find what numbers are signified by the other letters. Try this problem and think aloud while you do so. The answer may be found at the end of the chapter.

There are a third of a million possible an-

Table 6.1. A cryptarithmetic problem. The goal is to find what number to assign to each letter such that when added together and translated back to letters, they would produce the name ROBERT. (From Newell and Simon, 1972.)

$$
\begin{array}{c}
D\ O\ N\ A\ L\ D \\
+\ G\ E\ R\ A\ L\ D \\
\hline
R\ O\ B\ E\ R\ T
\end{array}
$$

Given: D = 5

swers to this problem (Simon, 1978), because there are 9! ($9 \times 8 \times 7 \times 6 \times 5 \times 4 \times 3 \times 2 \times 1$) possible assignments of nine numbers to nine letters. This is quite a large set of solutions to consider. A large computer might be able to go through it systematically within a reasonable time period, but a human cannot. Although most real-world problems do not have this many possible solutions, they often have more solutions than can be fit into human working memory. Therefore humans need strategies to limit their search to solutions that are most likely to be correct.

One way to limit the search for a solution is to "work backward" from the desired goal. This is what mathematics students are doing when they ask themselves, "What is the unknown?" because the unknown is the desired goal. A powerful form of working backwards is called *means-ends analysis*. Another way to limit search, which is not as powerful as means-ends analysis, is called *working forward* and involves performing whatever actions occur to one in response to a given problem.

Means-Ends Analysis. Means-ends analysis involves these steps:

1. Find the difference between the goal and the current situation.

2. Find an operation that is relevant to that difference.

3. Perform the operation to reduce the difference.

4. Repeat steps 1–3 until the problem has been solved.

Consider the following problem. A student shows a great deal of anxiety about speaking in front of his peers. His teacher would like him to be less anxious in this situation. The difference between the goal and

the current situation is one of anxiety. The operations that are relevant to reducing anxiety are based on classical conditioning (e.g., systematic desensitization or modeling). The teacher selects systematic desensitization as a procedure. First, she asks the student very easy questions that require short answers, and she asks these when the class has broken up into small groups. When the student states the answer correctly, she accepts it but does not emphasize the correctness of the answer (it could cause future anxiety if the student learned that being correct had great importance). Gradually the teacher increases the number of students in front of whom she asks questions of the target student; she also increases the length of the required answer and the difficulty of the question. In short, the teacher pairs a relaxed, learning-oriented (as opposed to evaluation-oriented) attitude with the student's speaking aloud in front of peers. Through classical conditioning the student comes to associate speaking aloud in front of peers with positive, relaxed emotions.

This teacher used means-ends analysis. She first thought of the goal (getting the student to relax while speaking in front of peers) and then of a relevant operation to reduce the difference between the student's situation (tenseness) and the goal. Classical conditioning techniques are relevant to problems involving anxiety. Finally the teacher applied these techniques and solved the problem.

Many problems that are solved by means-ends analysis involve several cycles, each of which focuses on a different difference. For example, consider this problem:

John started running at 4:05 and finished at 4:45. He ran 3.5 miles in that time. What is his running speed?

If one uses means-ends analysis to solve this problem, one starts out by saying, "What is the difference between the goal (to know speed) and the current situation?'' The difference is one to which the operation speed = distance/time is relevant. One starts to apply this operation by letting distance = 3.5. But then one realizes that there is no value stated in the problem for time. This leads one to the subgoal of finding a value for time. Again, one asks, ''What is the difference between my goal (to know time) and the current situation?'' The difference is one to which the operation of subtraction is relevant. Specifically, if one subtracts the time that John started to run from the time when he stopped running one gets the desired value for time. After performing this operation, one can return to the first goal of solving for speed in the formula speed = distance/time: speed = 3.5/.67 hour = 5.22 m.p.h.

Working Forward. Working forward is much simpler than means-ends analysis. One examines the current situation and performs operations to change it. The operations one selects are not constrained by the goal as they are in means-ends analysis; therefore they may sometimes lead one in fruitless directions.

In the problem of the anxious student, a teacher who uses a working-forward strategy might say to the student, after he has shown nervousness in speaking, ''Don't get so uptight.'' This statement seems much more direct than the elaborate means-ends analysis. Unfortunately, it is also much less likely to work. It is based on a superficial analysis of the problem: the teacher recognizes the student's anxiety but fails to use knowledge of what reduces anxiety.

In the ''speed'' problem, working forward may work because only a few operations are suggested by the problem statement even when the solver does not keep the goal in mind. The first sentence in the problem almost begs the solver to subtract start time from stop time, which would be the first step performed in working forward. Then the resulting value could be brought to bear as the solver reads the second sentence, which would cause him or her to think of the formula speed = distance/time.

Thus, working forward works when the operations suggested by the current situation are the ones that lead to the goal. If the current situation suggests misleading operations, working forward will not lead to the goal. Then means-ends analysis is more powerful, because it selects only goal-relevant operations.

Means-ends analysis requires more knowledge than does working forward. The crucial step in means-ends analysis is selecting an operation that reduces a functional difference between the current situation and the goal. If one does not possess knowledge of such operations or cannot activate one's knowledge, one cannot use the means-ends strategy. For example, if the teacher in the earlier example had not known the relationship between classical conditioning and anxiety reduction, she could not have applied these principles to the problem. An important aspect of means-ends analysis is that its success depends on the quality of one's declarative knowledge. If one's declarative knowledge of functional operations in a given domain is deficient, one will have difficulty performing means-ends analysis.

Expanding the Search

Means-ends analysis and working forward are strategies for limiting the search for solutions. However, sometimes a problem can be solved best by *expanding* the search. This is particularly true when known solutions to a problem are inadequate, as is often the case for global and national problems, complex personal problems, scientific and artistic problems, and some teaching problems. Two strategies that may be used in expanding the search for solutions are *reasoning by analogy* and *brainstorming*.

Reasoning by Analogy. Reasoning by analogy is often used when people have a problem in a domain for which they have little knowledge. It involves representing the problem, using the representation to access knowledge in a familiar domain relevant to the current situation, and then evaluating the utility of the accessed knowledge. Many examples of reasoning by analogy can be seen when one observes computer-naive adults learning to use a microcomputer for word processing (cf. Rumelhart and Norman, 1981). Such learners solve editing problems as they would on a typewriter and thus they fail to take advantage of the computer's memory. Here analogical reasoning does not lead to effective problem solving.

In other situations, however, an analogy leads to effective solutions to novel problems. For example, when Kekulé was trying to discover the molecular structure of benzene, he dreamt of a snake eating its tail (Glass, Holyoak, and Santa, 1979). This image provided a visual analogy for the ring of carbon atoms in the benzene ring, and it led Kekulé to propose that the basic structure of benzene was a ring of carbon atoms. There are many such anecdotes about the use of analogical reasoning in creative problem solving (e.g., Koestler, 1964).

Although analogical reasoning is generally thought to be an important problem-solving strategy, people do not seem particularly good at using it. In various studies researchers have ensured that subjects could perform one problem correctly. They then gave them a second problem that was superficially different, but whose solution process was the same as for the first problem. The results have shown that subjects do not tend to see the analogy between the two problems unless it is pointed out to them (J. Hayes and Simon, 1976; Reed, Ernst, and Banerji, 1974).

Analogical reasoning can also be difficult. The conditions that favor effective analogical reasoning are not known, but the anecdotes suggest that an important one is the solver's knowledge of both the domain in which the problem exists and the analogous domain. Kekulé knew chemistry and he had visual experience of snakes eating their tails. On the other hand, the computer-naive adults had little knowledge of the domain of computers. Therefore, they may have formed an inadequate representation of their editing problems. The notion that level of knowledge determines the effectiveness of analogical reasoning needs to be studied experimentally.

Brainstorming. Another strategy for increasing the number and quality of solutions to a problem is called *brainstorming* (Osborn, 1963). The steps in brainstorming are:

1. Define the problem.
2. Generate, without criticism, as many solutions as possible, however bizarre they may seem at first.
3. Decide on criteria for judging the solutions generated.
4. Use these criteria to select the best solution.

Brainstorming includes elements of both working forward and means-ends analysis and thus has the advantages of both. Step 2 essentially involves working forward: one simply responds to the problem statement with operations that could change the situation. Steps 3 and 4 usually involve some means-ends analysis: the criteria one develops certainly include meeting the goal.

If the teacher with the shy student had used brainstorming to solve the problem, she would first have generated a list of possible solutions. For example, she might list these:

1. Tell him to relax.

2. Ask the school psychologist to do something.

3. Make him practice speaking out loud every day.

4. Give him tranquilizers.

5. Use systematic desensitization.

6. Have self-confident students model a relaxed attitude.

7. Don't ask him to speak out loud.

After generating a list, she would then think about criteria for a good solution. These might include (1) that it was likely to reach the goal of having the student relax, (2) that it was feasible, and (3) that it was legal. Solutions 1, 3, and 7 do not have as high a probability of success as do 2, 4, 5, and 6. Solution 2 may not be feasible if the school psychologist is already overworked, and solution 4 may not be legal. This leaves solutions 5 and 6 as the ones that best meet all the criteria.

In this example one of the solutions selected by brainstorming was also the solution selected by means-ends analysis. However, in many situations brainstorming may lead to a better solution than that reached through means-ends analysis. Although studies have not directly compared brainstorming and means-ends analysis strategies, they have compared brainstorming to strategies spontaneously adopted by individuals. These studies sometimes show that brainstorming results in higher-quality solutions than whatever techniques individuals use spontaneously (cf. Parnes and Meadow, 1959). For

brainstorming as for analogical reasoning, the quality of solutions seems affected by the amount of relevant declarative knowledge. Parnes (1961), for example, found a correlation between the number of ideas one produced and the originality of one's ideas.

Summary. General problem-solving procedures are used when the solution to a problem is not obvious. They may expand or limit the search for solutions. Some procedures for limiting the search are means-ends analysis and working forward. Means-ends analysis is powerful because it selects only goal-relevant operations. However, the success of means-ends analysis depends on the quality of the problem solver's knowledge of functional relationships. Two procedures for expanding search are the use of analogies and brainstorming. The success of both of these techniques also appears to depend on the extent of knowledge that a solver can access.

There are many other procedures for limiting and expanding search and for other aspects of problem solving. These are described in many books and articles, some of which are listed at the end of this chapter. The main point of this discussion is that there are general strategies that work independent of the content of a problem and that many of these strategies affect the search for solutions.

EXPERTISE IN SOLVING PROBLEMS

The preceding section might suggest that expertise in problem solving could be developed by training people to use general strategies such as means-ends analysis, analogical reasoning, and/or brainstorming. However, studies comparing expert and novice problem solvers lead to a quite different conclusion. They suggest that expertise in problem solving can be developed best by helping people acquire *domain-specific* knowledge. In the section on instruction, we will look at studies of the effectiveness of training people to use general problem-solving strategies. First, however, let us see how expert and novice problem solvers differ.

General Problem-Solving Strategies

Initially, psychologists thought that experts in a given field would use more powerful general problem-solving strategies than would novices and that this would account for their greater success at problem-solving. However, they have found that novices, not experts, use what is considered to be the more powerful strategy (Chi, Glaser, and Rees, 1982). For example, chess masters quickly select their next move in response to the pattern of players on the board. This behavior looks like a working-forward strategy: the master reacts to the situation at hand and does not appear to take the time to consider whether the selected action will meet the goal of winning the game. Novice chess players take much longer to select a move and appear consciously to consider whether different moves will bring them closer to the goal.

It seems surprising that the expert would use the simpler working-forward strategy and the novice the more powerful means-ends analysis. However, the expert's working-forward strategy is based on a great deal of experience in which he or she has learned which moves work at what times. In some sense, the expert's behavior is not strategic at all. Rather, he or she is automatically recognizing known patterns and applying the action sequences associated with those patterns.

Thus it does not seem that expert and novice problem solvers differ much in the general strategies they use. If a chess master were confronted with an unusual configuration on the chessboard, he or she would probably use the means-ends strategy that the novice uses more frequently. Elstein, Shul-man, and Sprafka (1978) have found that expert and novice problem solvers do not differ in their general strategies.

Domain-Specific Knowledge

If experts and novices do not differ dramatically in general problem-solving strategies, how do they differ? They seem to differ a great deal in both the quantity and quality of domain-specific knowledge that they possess. Experts seem to have more and better-organized long-term memory structures for their areas of expertise (Akin, 1980; Chase and Simon, 1973a, 1973b; Egan and Schwartz, 1979). The better organization of knowledge makes search through the problem space efficient.

Consider the hypothetical knowledge structure shown in Figure 6.2. This structure might be possessed by a doctor with twenty years of clinical experience in diagnosing congenital heart disease. For the moment, do not concern yourself with the meanings of the terms in the structure. (Each term refers to either a symptom of a disease or the name of a disease.) For now just pay attention to the structure of links between the labels and contrast this structure with that shown in Figure 6.3. It is the analogous structure for a novice in the diagnosis of congenital heart disease (e.g., a fourth-year medical student who has read a textbook chapter on congenital heart disease and has had a little bit of clinical experience with such diseases). One difference is that the expert has more domain-specific knowledge than does the novice.

Another difference that is at least as important as the quantity of knowledge is the organization of knowledge. Notice that the hierarchical organization of the expert's knowledge is missing from the novice's. For example, the expert's structure has six levels, whereas the novice's has only two. The two levels in the novice's structure look very

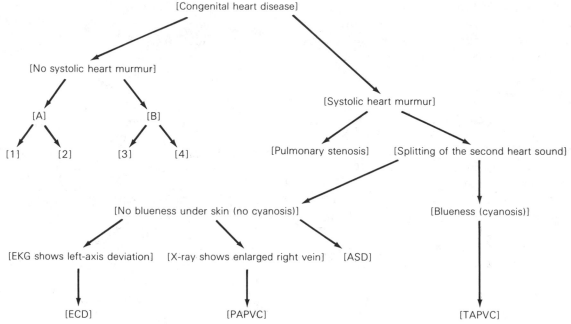

Figure 6.2. A hypothetical memory structure for an expert diagnostician of congenital heart disease.

much like textbook entries: they consist of symptoms at one level and the names of diseases associated with a given symptom at another level. The symptoms in the novice's structure are found at various levels in the expert's structure. For example, the x-ray

symptom appears at the level second from the bottom and the systolic heart murmur appears at the level second from the top.

In the expert's memory structure, relationship is indicated by closeness in the hierarchy. For example, [EKG shows left axis

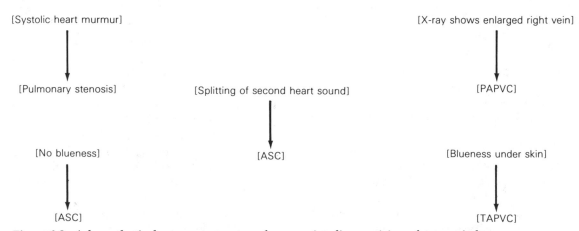

Figure 6.3. A hypothetical memory structure for a novice diagnostician of congenital heart disease.

deviation = ECD] is more distant from [Blueness = TAPVC] than from [X-ray shows enlarged right vein = PAPVC]. Specifically, to go from [EKG shows left-axis deviation] to [X-ray shows enlarged right vein], two links must be traversed, whereas to go from [EKG shows left-axis deviation] to [Blueness under skin], three links must be traversed. If this knowledge is embedded in a propositional network, then spread of activation is more likely between the pair with only two links separating them than between the pair with three links separating them. In the novice's memory structure, there are no links between isolated bits of knowledge, and hence activation will not spread from one area of knowledge about congenital heart disease to another.

There is converging evidence from many experiments that novices' and experts' memories differ in the quality of organization of domain-specific knowledge. However, the difference in knowledge structures does not explain why experts are better problem solvers. It just suggests that we should look for an explanation based on this difference. The next question, therefore, is, How might these knowledge differences affect the problem-solving process?

The Role of Domain-Specific Knowledge in Problem Solving

How does the knowledge structure of experts allow them to solve problems better than novices? Before I discuss some answers to this question, let us consider an example of expert versus novice problem solving. The example comes from medical diagnosis of congenital heart disease so it is first important to review some facts about the circulatory system.

Congenital Heart Disease. The normal circulatory system is shown schematically in Figure 6.4. As described by Feltovich (1981),

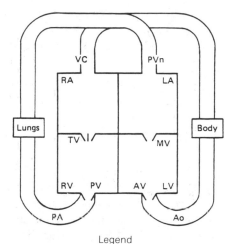

Legend

Ao = Aorta	PV = Pulmonary valve
AV = Aortic valve	PVn = Pulmonary veins
LA = Left atrium	RA = Right atrium
LV = Left ventricle	RV = Right ventricle
MV = Mitral valve	TV = Tricuspid valve
PA = Pulmonary artery	VC = Vena Cavae

Figure 6.4. The normal circulatory system. (From Clancy and Shortliffe, 1984.)

the following events take place in the normal system:

> Starting on the right side of the heart, the right ventricle (RV) of the heart pumps blood across the pulmonary valve (PV), through the pulmonary artery (PA), and into the lungs where the blood receives oxygen. Blood then returns to the heart via the pulmonary veins (PVn) into the left atrium (LA). From the left atrium, oxygenated blood proceeds across the mitral valve (MV) into the left ventricle (LV), where it is pumped across the aortic valve (AV), through the aorta (Ao), and to the body. In the body, oxygen is extracted from the blood which then flows back to the right atrium (RA) of the heart via the vena cavae (VC). Deoxygenated blood from the right atrium flows across the tricuspid valve (TV) into the right ventricle and the cycle repeats. The "upper" chambers of the heart, the atria, are normally separated by the atrial septum, while the "lower" chambers, the ventricles, are normally separated by the ventricular septum.

Congenital heart diseases are anatomic or physiologic abnormalities within the heart and cardiovascular system (e.g., holes in heart septa, tight valves, or electrical conduction problems). These basic abnormalities alter the flow, pressure, or resistance patterns of the system and produce the patient manifestations (signs, symptoms, laboratory test results) that the physician must utilize in diagnosis [pp. 53, 55].

There are several types of heart abnormality with which infants can be born. One type, which we will be especially concerned with, is called total anomalous pulmonary venous connections (TAPVC). In this disease all four pulmonary veins connect to the right atrium (see the top of Figure 6.5) rather than the left atrium, which is the normal site of connection. The child appears bluish (cyanotic) under the skin, because oxygenated blood and deoxygenated (blue) blood are mixed together before being pumped to the body.

Other diseases that are similar to TAPVC are also shown in Figure 6.5. One is partial anomalous pulmonary venous connection (PAPVC), in which only part of the pulmonary vein goes incorrectly to the right atrium while the other part goes correctly to the left atrium (the bottom of Figure 6.5). Children with PAPVC do not appear bluish, because blood pumped to their bodies is oxygenated. The other diseases, shown in the middle of Figure 6.5, are called atrial septal defect (ASD) and endocardial cushion defect (ECD). In both diseases an abnormal hole occurs in the heart wall that separates the left and right atria. The hole allows blood in the left atrium to be improperly shunted to the right atrium. The difference in the two diseases is in the placement of the hole: in ASD it is in the up-

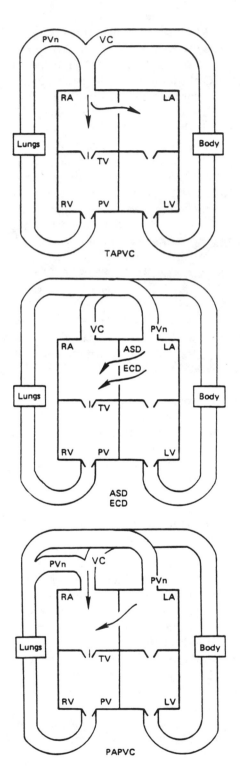

Figure 6.5. Four congenital heart disease syndromes. (From Clancy and Shortliffe, 1984.)

per portion of the wall, whereas in EDC it is in the lower portion. Like PAPVC, these diseases do not produce cyanosis, because blood going to the body is oxygenated. Thus, of these four diseases (TAPVC, PAPVC, ASD, and ECD) the only one to produce cyanosis is TAPVC.

The four diseases present the same abnormal heart sound (ausculum) when a doctor listens to the heart through a stethoscope. First, there are two murmurs—one associated with increased blood flow across the tricuspid valve (TV), the other with increased flow across the pulmonary valve (PV). There is also a fixed splitting of the second heart sound. All of these sounds indicate a volume overload on the right side of the heart, which is produced by all four diseases.

To distinguish among the four possible diseases associated with the same ausculum, then, a doctor needs additional evidence. Cyanosis distinguishes TAPVC from the other three diseases. Among the remaining three ECD is indicated if the electrocardiogram (EKG) shows an abnormal left-axis deviation. PAPVC is indicated if an x-ray shows an unusual shadow on the right side, suggesting an enlarged right vein. Otherwise ASD is indicated.

An Example of Domain-Specific Problem Solving. Now that you have assimilated some new information about congenital heart disease, let us return to how knowledge structures influence problem-solving. To study this question Feltovich (1981) gave expert and novice diagnosticians the same case. It was an actual report of a child with TAPVC. The subjects were given a file containing four categories of information: history, observations from a physical examination, x-ray description, and EKG description. Each category contained one or more items of information. The most crucial items are shown in Table 6.2. These included observations of

Table 6.2. Some of the items in the case file read by expert and novice diagnosticians. (From Clancy and Shortliffe, 1984.)

HISTORY

7. The mother, who has two younger children, has noted that in the last two years when the child is cold her lips turn blue. In the last year the mother has noted dusky nail beds but cannot relate this to any specific conditions.

PHYSICAL EXAM

11. She shows minimal circumoral cyanosis. Fingernails appear minimally cyanotic with slight watch-crystal formation of fingernails.
17. Auscultation of the heart shows a first heart sound with a very loud component. The second heart sound is widely split all the time and appears fixed. The pulmonary component is a little prominent.
18. A grade 2–3 over 6 systolic ejection type murmur is present along the upper left sternal border, the murmur being as loud or perhaps even louder over the left upper back.
19. A grade 2 over 6 mid to late diastolic murmur is present along the left sternal border.

X-RAY

21. The chest x-ray shows moderate cardiomegaly and markedly increased pulmonary vasculature. There is an insufficient amount of barium in the esophagus on the lateral view to adequately evaluate the size of the left atrium. There is an unusual shadow seen in the right side representing, very likely, an anomalously coursing pulmonary vein.

EKG

22. The EKG shows right axis deviation of +120 degrees, a wandering atrial pacemaker, right atrial enlargement, and right ventricular hypertrophy. There is an rsR's' pattern in lead V1.

---

an abnormal heart sound (17, 18, and 19), which could be associated with any of the four diseases just described, information suggesting cyanosis (7 and 11), which is associated only with TAPVC; x-ray information (21) suggesting an enlarged right vein; and EKG information (22) ruling out ECD, because there is no abnormal *left*-axis deviation.

The two experts were specialists in congenital heart problems who had at least twenty years of clinical experience. The four novices were fourth-year medical students who had covered congenital heart disease in a course and had observed twenty-five to fifty patients with congenital heart disease. The subjects were asked to think aloud as they read through the case information. Thus the researcher had a record of what hypotheses the subjects were entertaining at what points during the problem-solving process. After reading the case file, the subjects were asked for a diagnosis. Both experts gave the correct diagnosis, whereas none of the novices did.

One expert mentioned ASD, PAPVC, and TAPVC as possibilities after reading items 17–19. The other mentioned ASD and ECD as possibilities after reading those items. Then after reading item 21, which contained strong evidence against ASD, this latter expert mentioned PAPVC and TAPVC. Thus, both experts seemed to entertain more than one hypothesis at once, and the hypotheses they entertained were consistent with the data they had read up to that point.

The novices tended to entertain only one hypothesis at a time, changing hypotheses when a new bit of information suggested another disease. For example, some novices mentioned ASD after reading items 17–19 but failed to mention any of the other possibilities that fit with the same heart sound data (ECD, PAPVC, and TAPVC). After reading 21 the novices changed their hypothesis to PAPVC because of the association between the reported x-ray pattern and PAPVC. As Feltovich (1981) says,

> This indicates a strong data-driven dependence in the diagnosis by these subjects: that

is, the subjects are pushed from hypothesis to hypothesis depending upon the most recent strong disease cue in the data, and when new hypotheses are generated, these are not strongly enough associated with other [similar diseases] to activate these other diseases. (p. 86)

Other novices mentioned a disease called pulmonary stenosis after reading item 18. In pulmonary stenosis a systolic heart murmur, such as that described in item 18, occurs. However, this disease is not associated with a splitting of the second sound (item 19) or with other symptoms shown in the case. To deal with these other symptoms, these novices went on to postulate a multiple-disease syndrome. For both sets of novices, problem-solving behavior is characterized by reacting to the latest bit of information without keeping prior information in mind.

Feltovich (1981) proposes that novices take this piecemeal approach to problem solving because their knowledge structures about the symptoms of congenital heart disease are not as well organized as are those of the experts. As was shown in Figures 6.2 and 6.3, the expert's structure seems to be more interconnected and more hierarchical than the novice's. In the expert's structure every bit of information shown about congenital heart disease is connected, however remotely, with every other bit. Furthermore, diseases with similar symptoms are closer together in the knowledge structure than are diseases with different symptoms. For example, ECD and PAPVC, which both present the same heart sound and the same lack of blueness, are quite close in the knowledge structure, whereas pulmonary stenosis and PAPVC are much further apart. The novice's knowledge structure shows several pairs of associations between symptoms and diseases, but no relationships between one disease and another, and no hierarchical organization.

How would such knowledge structures affect the problem-solving process for the case of TAPVC that was studied? Hierarchical organization seems to allow solvers to keep all of the appropriate hypotheses in mind while considering additional data. Both experts considered more than one hypothesis after reading items 17–19, whereas the novices narrowed to only one hypothesis at this point. Furthermore, the hierarchy allowed the experts to find alternative hypotheses that were still consistent with the data when information disconfirming to their current hypotheses was presented. This was seen when one expert found disconfirming evidence about ASD in the x-ray data and immediately mentioned PAPVC and TAPVC as still being consistent with the data.

By contrast, the novice's structure does not allow for efficient management of memory. When a novice reads about a symptom, he or she retrieves the disease associated with that symptom in memory. When another symptom is read about that cues another disease, that disease is assumed to be the correct one, even though it may not be consistent with prior information.

It appears, then, that expert diagnosticians are more successful because their knowledge is qualitatively different from that of novices. Specifically, the experts' knowledge seems to be more hierarchically organized. In Chapters 9, 10, and 12 other examples of the role of knowledge structure in domain-specific problem-solving will be described. In all of these cases the experts' knowledge structure appears to be better organized than the novices'.

One must keep in mind, however, that experts and novices also have different amounts of domain-specific knowledge. In many cases sheer quantity of knowledge probably accounts for observed differences in problem solving. However, Mayer (1975, 1980) has conducted studies in which the effect of organization of knowledge has been demonstrated even when quantity of knowledge is controlled.

TRANSFER

As was previously stated, transfer is one of the key parts of problem solving (along with problem representation and evaluation). Transfer is the activation and application of knowledge in new situations. It is at the heart of successful problem solving.

Two early theories of transfer focused on the two sides of transfer processes. The "identical elements" theory (Thorndike and Woodworth, 1901) stated that probability of transfer was a function of the number of identical elements in the new situation and in the ones where the knowledge to be transferred had previously been used. Identical elements were perceptual (not cognitive). Thus, the identical elements theory predicts very little transfer at a conceptual level and is therefore a rather pessimistic theory.

A more optimistic theory was the "formal discipline" theory, which claimed that very general mental processes learned in one situation would transfer to other situations. This theory was used in the early 1900s to justify teaching Latin and Greek. Even though Latin and Greek are dead languages, it was argued, students will develop their mental facilities while studying these languages, making them more capable in general. (A recent version of this theory is used to justify the teaching of LOGO to elementary school children because it will help them with general problem-solving skills.)

These early theories focused on what type of knowledge can transfer (e.g., concrete versus abstract). In current views of transfer one assumes that both concrete and abstract knowledge can be transferred under certain conditions and focus more on the conditions that facilitate transfer.

The previous section on medical problem solving suggests that one crucial condition for transfer is the quality of knowledge organization. Both the medical students and the experienced clinicians had the facts needed to make the correct diagnosis, but the students failed to activate all of the right facts at the right time. There are now studies from several domains that point to this same conclusion: organization of knowledge mediates transfer. This view of transfer is different from the earlier views in assigning more importance to what the person brings to the situation than to the situation itself (Royer, 1980).

Another question of current interest is how best to characterize the transfer process. For example, is it mediated through pattern-recognition productions that partially match the problem representation? Or is it mediated through knowledge stored in the propositional network in long-term memory that is activated by the problem representation? Or do both forms of knowledge mediate transfer, depending on the situation? Answers to these questions await further research.

INSTRUCTION

We have, so far, two conflicting suggestions about what to teach to increase people's problem-solving capability. One suggestion is to teach general strategies. The assumption that general strategies help people solve problems underlies many modern science curricula in which strategies such as generating hypotheses and designing tests of hypotheses are taught. Another suggestion, derived from the description of expert/novice differences in problem solving, is that if people could be taught well-organized domain-specific knowledge, then they would become better problem-solvers.

Which of these views is correct? Or do they both have some merit? The hypothesis that teaching general strategies improves problem-solving has a longer research history than does the other hypothesis. However, the results of this research are not yet clear. There are many anecdotal reports of the success of teaching general strategies (e.g., Tuma

and Reif, 1980), and Torrance's (1972) review of experimental evidence concludes that the teaching of general strategies is successful. However, Mansfield, Busse, and Krepelka's (1978) review of experimental evidence comes to the opposite conclusion.

The argument centers on the criterion validity of measures of success. Many studies of training in brainstorming, for example, use as a criterion a standardized test of creative thinking that has not been shown to predict creative production in the "real world." Thus, even though the trained groups do better than controls on the standardized test, it is not clear that this means that they will be better problem solvers. However, Torrance (1981) has shown that elementary school children's scores on the Torrance Test of Creative Thinking (one of the standardized tests used in training studies) predicts their creative production as adults. Since there is no consensus yet on the validity of the criterion test, this leaves the success of teaching general problem-solving strategies unproven as well.

Despite its briefer history, research on the effect on problem solving of teaching organized knowledge seems to yield more consistently positive results. However, little research has been conducted on this question so it would be premature to conclude that the teaching of organized knowledge leads to improved problem solving under all conditions.

With the tentative nature of instructional implications in mind, I will describe one training program for general strategies and one for domain-specific knowledge organization. At this point, both approaches still seem to merit consideration.

Training in General Problem-Solving Strategies

One of the most carefully developed and evaluated programs for teaching general problem-solving strategies is *The Productive Thinking Program* developed by Covington,

Crutchfield, and Davies (1966) and supplemented by Olton and Crutchfield (1969). The program is a set of sixteen self-instructional booklets designed to teach fifth and sixth-graders such skills as (1) generating original ideas, (2) working in a systematic manner, (3) trying to look at a problem in a different light when one gets "stuck," (4) attending to important facts or events, (5) asking questions that further problem solving, and (6) avoiding jumping to conclusions. Each booklet contains a story, presented in cartoon fashion, about two children who live with their bachelor uncle. The children become involved in a series of mysteries, which they try to solve with some hints from their uncle. At various points in each booklet, the student is invited to respond, just as the children in the cartoon are responding.

Figure 6.6 shows some pages from a booklet designed to teach students how to avoid jumping to conclusions. Specifically, the children's uncle suggests that to avoid jumping to conclusions one can pick out each

important thing and try to figure out why it was important. This can be done by first listing each important item and then thinking about why each one might be important. At this point readers are directed to write their own list of important things for the mystery that is being solved. Later they are directed to write down why each item on their list might be important. This procedure is brought up in other booklets so that students practice it more than once.

If we were to put the skill of considering all potentially important items into production system language, it might look something like Table 6.3. The first production in this system applies when an individual has a "mystery" to solve and when he or she wants to avoid jumping to conclusions. The action it takes is to set a subgoal of identifying potentially important items. The second production applies when the subgoal is to identify potentially important items and the item being considered is an object or a person. If these conditions occur, the action taken is to

Table 6.3. A production system for avoiding jumping to conclusions by paying attention to all important information.

P_1	IF	MYSTERY exists
		And GOAL is to avoid jumping to conclusions
	THEN	Set SUBGOAL of identifying potentially important ITEMS.
P_2	IF	SUBGOAL is to identify potentially important ITEMS
		And ITEM is an OBJECT or PERSON
	THEN	Classify ITEM as potentially important
		And write ITEM down on LIST.
P_3	IF	SUBGOAL is to identify potentially important ITEMS
		And there are no more ITEMS to consider
	THEN	Set SUBGOAL to think of significance of each ITEM on LIST.
P_4	IF	SUBGOAL is to think of significance of each ITEM on LIST
	THEN	Read ITEM on LIST
		And infer how ITEM could cause MYSTERY
		And write down inference.
P_5	IF	SUBGOAL is to think of significance of each ITEM on LIST
		And there are no more ITEMS on LIST
	THEN	Stop.

Uncle John notices Jim's silence:

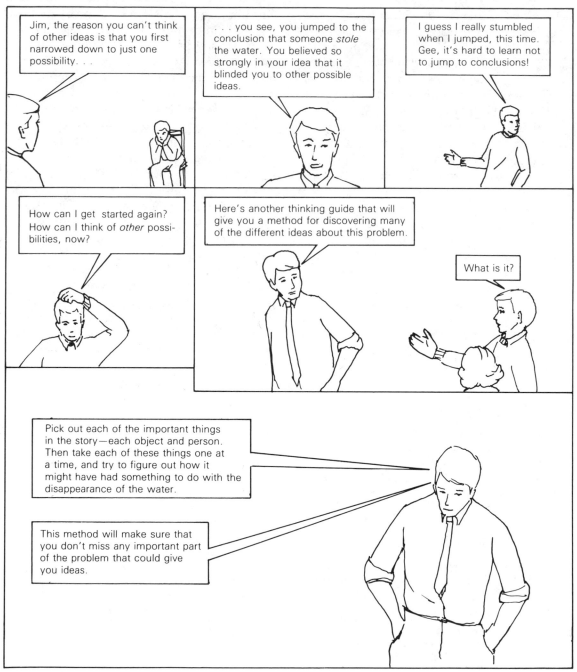

Now, what will happen as Jim and Lila take Uncle John's advice? Turn the page to find out.

You try making a list too. Go back to pages 8 and 9 and read the story
again. Then pick out each of the main things in the story and write it down:

_____   _____

_____   _____

_____   _____

Figure 6.6. Some pages from the *The Productive Thinking Program* designed to teach
problem-solving skills to children. These pages are designed to teach children how to
avoid jumping to conclusions. (From Covington, Crutchfield, and Davies, 1966.)

write that item on a list. The third production applies when the subgoal is to identify potentially important items but there are no more items to consider. Under these conditions, a new subgoal—thinking of the importance of each item—is set. The fourth production applies when the subgoal is to think of the significance of an item on the list. The actions it takes are (1) to read the item, (2) to infer how the item could have caused the mysterious situation, and (3) to write down the inference. Finally, the fifth production applies when the subgoal is to think of the significance of an item on the list, but there are no items left. It causes the system to stop.

Most of the elements of these procedures are stated either explicitly or implicitly in the materials shown in Figure 6.6 or the rest of the booklet from which those materials were taken. For example, in the first panel in Figure 6.6, the uncle states the condition to be avoided that forms part of the conditions of P_1 in Table 6.3: "You jumped to the conclusion, . . ." and the boy states this condition in another way: "How can I think of *other* possibilities, now?" The other condition of P_1—that there is a mystery to be solved—is implicit in the booklet. The action of P_1 is stated in the second panel, when the uncle says, "Pick out each of the important things in the story."

The conditions of P_2 are the subgoal of picking out the important things and the requirement that the things be objects or persons. These conditions are described by the uncle in the second panel ("Pick out each of the important things in the story—each object and person.") One of the actions of P_2 (classifying each object and person as potentially important) is also implied by the uncle's statement. The second action—writing the item down on a list—is explicitly stated by the boy in the third panel ("Let's make a list of them!") and is demonstrated in the fourth

panel with the picture of the boy and girl making the list. Finally, the student is directed to carry out the action of this production him- or herself. Additional pages of the booklet describe the conditions and actions in productions P_4 and P_5.

The main learning process supported by these materials is proceduralization. The goal is that the students translate a sequence of mental and/or physical actions from declarative to procedural form. To support that goal, most of the conditions and actions relevant to each step are explicitly stated. Also, the children in the cartoon model proceduralization. Finally, the student is required to perform the procedure, which forces her or him to translate the verbal description of the process into an action sequence. The process of composition in this example might involve a collapsing of some of these productions into one large production such as the following:

> IF GOAL is to solve MYSTERY
>
> and I want to avoid jumping to
>
> conclusions
>
> THEN I identify objects and persons
>
> in MYSTERY until there are
>
> no more to consider
>
> And I infer how each object or
>
> person could cause MYS-
>
> TERY until there are no more
>
> to consider.

In this production there are four actions: (1) Identifying objects and persons in the mystery comes from the condition side of the original P_2. (2) Stopping identification, comes from the condition side of P_3. (3) Inferring the causal connection comes from the action side of P_4. (4) Stopping the process includes the action side of P_5. The actions of writing things down have been stopped during composition, presumably because one can now keep track of items in memory without writing them down, because one has fewer productions to monitor.

The Productive Thinking Program provided support for the composition process by providing opportunities for practice and feedback on each of the skills that it taught. For example, after the students learned what to do to prevent jumping to conclusions, they practiced this in other mysteries.

How did the *Productive Thinking Program* support the learning of pattern-recognition procedures? One pattern that it was important for students to learn was *when* to use the action sequences that were being learned. Since all the learning situations involved children solving mysteries, one might expect that the students would use the new skills they were learning only when confronted with mysteries of the type found in mystery books. Production 1 in Table 6.3 suggests this restricted application of avoiding jumping to conclusions, since one of its conditions is that a mystery exists.

The authors of the program realized that their instructional materials might not promote generalization of the skills being taught, and so they wrote some supplementary materials that involved not mysteries but real-world problems such as conserving resources, managing waste, and combatting poverty. After the students learned a particular skill using the cartoon mystery booklets, they then practiced it on one or more real-world problems. For example, for the skill of thinking about a problem in a different way, students were given a description of the problem of waste management. At the end of the description the directions said, ''The experts have been asking themselves, 'How can we *destroy* the waste material?' But a new way to look at the problem would be to ask the question _____.'' Students might answer,

''What can be done to *transform* the waste materials into something useful?'' The students' answers were discussed during class and the point was made that looking at the problem in a new way led to thinking of new solutions.

It was hoped that the supplementary materials would show the students that any problem could be attacked using the skills being learned (that the pattern-recognition procedure learned would be quite general). Giving a wide variety of problems for practice should have facilitated the generalization process.

Several large-scale, carefully controlled studies of the effectiveness of *The Productive Thinking Program* suggest that students who receive the training program generate more ideas for solving problems, have higher-quality ideas, are better at asking relevant questions, and are more successful in solving problems (Covington and Crutchfield, 1965; Crutchfield, 1966; Olton and Crutchfield, 1969; Wardrop et al., 1969). Furthermore, Olton and Crutchfield (1969) demonstrated that the skills learned transfer to quite different types of problems and that they are retained six months after training.

Thus, it appears that general problem-solving strategies can be taught in the same way as other procedures. If adequate support is given to the processes of generalization, discrimination, proceduralization, and composition, then these strategies can be acquired.

Many programs designed to teach general problem-solving strategies fail to obtain impressive transfer, and this has been frustrating since the assumption behind teaching these strategies is that they transfer quite broadly. This is an important area for research. Since some programs, such as the one described here, have obtained good transfer results, there is reason to hope that others can also. Our knowledge of the transfer process is just becoming sophisticated enough to use in identifying what aspects of training increase the probability of transfer.

Training That Affects Domain-Specific Knowledge Organization

Another way to enhance problem-solving ability is to teach domain-specific knowledge so that it is stored in long-term memory accessibly. The more accessible knowledge is, the more likely one is to apply it to new problems. We saw in Chapter 4 that both elaboration and organization make declarative knowledge more accessible. Here we will see that this accessibility leads to broader transfer of knowledge to new situations.

Mayer (1975) studied the effects on problem solving of two kinds of knowledge acquisition. He taught college students some elements of the FORTRAN programming language and then tested their ability to both interpret and generate computer programs. The two types of presentation of FORTRAN were called *model* and *rule*. Both presentations were in the form of booklets that the students read. The model program was designed to encourage students to integrate new knowledge with prior knowledge, whereas the rule program was designed *not* to encourage knowledge integration.

The model booklet started with a diagram (model) of the functional units of a computer and described these units by using analogies to familiar objects. Specifically, the input unit of a computer was likened to a ticket window, the output unit was likened to a message pad, the list of program statements was likened to a shopping list, and the erasable memory was likened to a scoreboard. The seven FORTRAN statements to be learned were introduced after the presentation of the model. They were presented one at a time, with a definition, an example, and an explanation of the statement in terms of

the model. For instance, the statement $P6$ GO TO $P4$ was explained by saying that the pointer would move from the sixth to the fourth statement on the "list." Or, $A3 = 0$ was explained by saying that the computer would erase whatever was on its "memory scoreboard" for $A3$ and write a zero instead.

The rule booklet simply presented each of the seven statements, one at a time. As in the model booklet, each statement was defined and exemplified, but no model was presented and no interpretations of statements in terms of a familiar model were given. Thus, the difference between the two booklets was in whether or not it provided a meaningful framework for interpreting statements.

The model and rule booklets were randomly distributed to students, who read through the booklets at their own rate. When they finished reading, they took a test consisting of two types of problem: (1) a problem in which students were asked to *generate* a program language to perform some function, and (2) one in which students were shown some new program statements and asked to *interpret* them. The interpretation problems were considered to be a measure of "far" transfer because they were not as similar to what the students had been exposed to in the booklets as were the generation problems.

Each type of problem was presented at three levels of complexity. The simplest was a one-line statement, which the student was asked to generate or interpret. Of medium complexity were nonlooping programs, and of greatest complexity were looping programs. The looping programs were also considered to demand the farthest transfer because they were least similar to the booklet materials.

Table 6.4 shows the proportion of problems solved correctly by students in the model and rule groups. For generation problems, the two groups performed similarly on questions requiring the generation of one

Table 6.4. Proportion of problems solved correctly by subjects who read the model and rule booklets. (Adapted from Mayer, 1975.)

	GENERATION			INTERPRETATION		
	STATEMENT	NONLOOPING PROGRAM	LOOPING PROGRAM	STATEMENT	NONLOOPING PROGRAM	LOOPING PROGRAM
Model	.63	.37	.30	.62	.62	.09
Rule	.67	.52	.12	.42	.32	.12

statement. For generating nonlooping programs, the rule group outperformed the model group, whereas for generating looping programs, the model group outperformed the rule group: Mayer (1975) explains that the rule group had a "rote learning set" in which they learned how to use FORTRAN statements in ways that were similar to the examples given during training and the model group had a "meaningful learning set" in which they related new knowledge to prior knowledge. Thus, the rule group excelled at problems that did not require much transfer, but the model group excelled on transfer problems.

The results for the interpretation problems are consistent with this explanation. The model group outperformed the rule group on interpretation of statements and on interpretation of nonlooping programs, but both groups did poorly on the looping programs. The model group presumably did better because they could use the familiar model they had learned to help them interpret new programs.

In the terminology used in this book, Mayer (1975) is arguing that the model group did better because they elaborated more on new information. Although this explanation is plausible, Mayer did not have a direct measure of elaboration processes. In a later study, however, he did (Mayer and Bromage, 1980). In this study all students were given the model, but half received it *after* reading about the program statements and half received it

before. Those who read about the model after the other material would not have it available while they were encoding the new information, so they would be unable to use it to generate elaborations while acquiring new declarative knowledge.

After the students read through their booklets, instead of solving problems as in the previous study, they were asked to recall the definition and explain each of the statements about which they had learned. Their answers were examined to see if the ideas presented were different for the model-before and model-after groups. Idea units were classified as giving *technical* information (such as "/ means divide"), *format* information (such as "an address name goes in parentheses"), or *concepts* (such as "an address name is a space in the computer's memory"). In addition, intrusions in the answers were categorized into *text appropriate* (additions that made sense), *text inappropriate* (ones that did not make sense), and *model* intrusions (additions based on the model).

Table 6.5 shows the differences that were found. The subjects who studied the model before learning the programming statements gave more conceptual information, more appropriate intrusions, and more model intrusions, whereas the subjects who did not study the model first gave more technical and format information and more inappropriate intrusions.

These data provide more direct evidence that students who study a model before

Table 6.5. Types of ideas in protocols of subjects given a meaningful model either before or after learning some programming statements. (Adapted from Mayer and Bromage, 1980.)

	IDEA UNITS			INTRUSIONS		
MODEL	TECHNICAL	FORMAT	CONCEPT	APPROPRIATE	INAPPROPRIATE	MODEL
Before	5.0	1.9	6.6	1.2	1.5	3.0
After	5.9	2.8	4.9	.7	2.4	.5

studying programming statements organize their knowledge differently from other students. Specifically, their knowledge seems to be organized around the functional concepts suggested by the model. Thus the Mayer and Bromage (1980) results lend further support to the notion that breadth of transfer is facilitated by elaboration and organization.

SUMMARY AND PREVIEW

The information in this chapter sets the stage for much of the rest of this book, because each of the chapters that follow shows how people solve problems in a specific domain (reading, math, science). For example, trying to understand what a writer is communicating is a problem, as is trying to design an experiment. In either case a person has a goal and is searching for a means to reach that goal. Thus it is useful to keep in mind, as one reads further, the processes of problem representation, knowledge transfer, and evaluation. Although the terminology may sometimes differ, these processes will be found frequently in the pages to come.

One of the main points of this chapter has been that the quality of the problem representation affects the quality of problem solution. This point will be echoed in several other chapters. We will see, for example, that good and poor writers represent the writing problem differently. Also, good problem solvers in math represent problems differently than their less able peers.

We also saw that problem solving is af-

fected by how the solver's domain-specific knowledge is organized. This point also will be echoed later in the book. For example, Ph.D. physicists have been shown to have a different knowledge structure than do first-year physics students (Chi, Feltovich, and Glaser, 1981).

These ideas about the role of problem representation and knowledge organization in problem solving are new ones and therefore much research still needs to be done. We do not know, for example, the mechanisms by which problem representation and knowledge organization operate during problem solving. The coming years should give us a better understanding of problem solving and how it can be improved during the school years.

ADDITIONAL READINGS

Gagné, R. M. (1980). Learnable aspects of human thinking. In A. E. Lawson (ed.), *The psychology of teaching for thinking and creativity*. 1980 Yearbook of the Association for the Education of Teachers in Science Education.

Greeno, J. G. (1978a). Natures of problem-solving abilities. In W. K. Estes (ed.), *Handbook of learning and cognitive processes*, Vol. 5 (pp. 239–70). Hillsdale, N.J.: Lawrence Erlbaum Associates.

Hayes, J. R. (1981). *The complete problem solver*. Philadelphia: Franklin Institute Press.

Hill, C. C. (1979). *Problem solving: Learning and teaching (an annotated bibliography)*. New York: Nichols.

Johnson-Laird, P. N., and P. C. Wason, eds.

(1977). *Thinking: Readings in cognitive science.* Cambridge, England: Cambridge University Press.

Mayer, R. E. (1983). *Thinking, problem solving, and cognition.* San Francisco: Freeman.

Newell, A., and H. A. Simon (1972). *Human problem solving.* Englewood Cliffs, N.J.: Prentice-Hall.

Polson, P., and R. Jeffries (1978). *Problem solving as search and understanding.* In R. J. Sternberg (ed.), *Advances in the psychology of human intelligence* (pp. 367–411). Hillsdale, N.J.: Lawrence Erlbaum Associates.

Scandura, J. M. (1977). *Problem-solving: A structural process approach with instructional implications.* New York: Academic Press.

Tuma, D. T., and F. Reif eds. (1980). *Problem solving and education.* Hillsdale, N.J.: Lawrence Erlbaum Associates.

ANSWER TO CRYPTARITHMETIC PROBLEM

1. T, E, R, A, L, G, N, B, and O are, respectively, 0, 9, 7, 4, 8, 1, 6, 3, and 2.

You can verify this result by substituting the numbers for the letters in DONALD and GERALD, then adding, and then translating the results back into letters. You should get ROBERT when you perform the translation.

Basic Skills and Subject Matter Areas

Chapter 7

Reading

SUMMARY

1. Reading processes can be divided into *decoding, literal comprehension, inferential comprehension,* and *comprehension monitoring.*

2. Decoding involves using the printed word to activate word meanings in memory, either through a direct association of the printed word and its meaning or through the intermediate step of representing letter-sound correspondences.

3. Literal comprehension involves putting activated word meanings together to form propositions.

4. Inferential comprehension involves going beyond the idea explicitly stated to summarize and/or elaborate on these ideas.

5. Comprehension monitoring involves setting a reading goal, checking to see if it is being reached, and implementing remedial strategies when it is not being reached.

6. Less skilled and younger readers differ from more skilled and older readers in decoding, literal-comprehension, inferential-comprehension, and comprehension-monitoring skills.

Reading is a tremendously valuable basic skill. The ability to read opens up the world of jungle animals to an urban six-year-old and the world of sophisticated technology to a ten-year-old villager in Ghana. It allows adults to change careers through independent study. It provides people of all ages with an inexpensive way of finding out about the variety of ideas and landscapes in our world.

In information-based societies such as our own, reading is not only valuable, it is necessary for adequate functioning. Diehl and Mikulecky (1980) have found that the percentage of time spent reading in various job categories is higher than one might expect: across a wide sampling of job categories, including both white- and blue-collar jobs, the average time spent reading per day is two hours. The fact that reading skill is needed for many jobs may explain in part why there is a positive association between criminality and illiteracy (Silberberg and Silberberg, 1971). If people who cannot read have a more difficult time getting jobs, they may be forced to commit criminal acts in order to get money.

Despite the importance of reading, over 33 percent of the world's adult population (750 million people) is illiterate (Huss, 1970). In America 13 percent of high school graduates are functionally illiterate and another 17 percent are barely competent (National Commission on Excellence in Education, 1983). Thus we are failing to teach adequate literacy skills to about 30 percent of all high school graduates.

Why should this be so? One possibility is that teachers are directing students to spend time on trivial aspects of reading and thus are not getting students to put the majority of their efforts into important aspects. But how can one know which aspects of reading are most important? One way is to study what is known about differences between skilled and less skilled readers. If skilled readers, for example, are better at guessing words, then this is probably an important process to teach less skilled readers. If, on the other hand, readers at different levels of skill are equally good at getting word meanings from contexts, then it would be a waste of time to teach this process. In this chapter we will review current knowledge about the differences between skilled and less skilled readers. But first we will look at a model of reading that organizes the information about how skilled and less skilled readers differ.

COMPONENT PROCESSES OF SKILLED READING

Skilled reading is a highly complex capability involving many processes. It is, therefore, no wonder that many persons have difficulty learning to read. Problems can occur in any one of the processes or in a combination of them. Fortunately, however, teachers who understand enough about these processes can help solve reading problems.

Reading processes can be divided into four groups: decoding, literal comprehension, inferential comprehension, and comprehension monitoring. At any time during reading, processes included in all of these subgroups are likely to be going on in parallel (Frederiksen, 1982; Thibedeau, Just, and Carpenter, 1982).

Decoding

Decoding means cracking a code, and this is exactly the function of decoding processes—they crack the code of print to make print meaningful. According to Ehri (1982) there are two main decoding processes. One is *matching* the printed word to a known pattern for the word, which activates the word's meaning in long-term memory. Matching is used in recognizing words in one's sight vocabulary. The other decoding process is *recoding*, which is involved in "sounding out" a word. During recoding the printed word is translated into sound patterns and then the sound patterns activate the word's meaning in long-term memory.

Matching. All readers acquire a *sight vocabulary*—a set of words that they recognize quickly in print. Words that are in a person's sight vocabulary do not need to be sounded out or guessed. The knowledge structure underlying sight vocabulary can be conceived of as a set of highly specific pattern-recognition productions. For example, to recognize the word "cat" in print, a reader may use the production shown in Table 7.1. In this production there are two conditions: the letter c and the pair of letters *at*. (Since a and t frequently occur together in English, they are

Table 7.1. A production that might underlie the ability to recognize the word "cat" in print.

IF	First LETTER is c
	And second and third letters are a, t
THEN	Activate concept of cat in LTM
	And activate sound pattern for cat.

probably recognized as a unit). The actions in the production are activation of the meaning and sound for *cat* stored in LTM.

Matching, then, can be conceived of as the process of matching the condition clauses of word-specific productions. When these condition clauses are matched, both the meaning and the sound of the word are activated automatically. The reason for conceiving of matching in production terms is that productions are automatic and hence they capture this important aspect of matching.

Recoding. In matching the external print directly activates meaning. In recoding the print is first translated into a string of sounds and the string of sounds are then used to activate meaning. The steps in recoding are:

1. Partition the unfamiliar words into syllables.

2. Generate a sound pattern for each syllable.

3. String the sounds together.

4. Use the sounds generated in step 3 to activate meaning in LTM.

For example, a student who did not recognize the word *tiger* through matching, would, (1) divide the word into two syllables (ti-ger), (2) generate the sound corresponding to *ti* (tī) and the sound corresponding to *ger* (gĕr), (3) string these two sounds together (tīgĕr), and (4) use this sound pattern to activate the meaning of *tiger* stored in long-term memory.

One can conceptualize the knowledge underlying recoding skill as being a set of productions that encode the knowledge of letter-sound correspondence of the language being read. A subset of these productions would have to do with syllabification. For example, a production that would correctly segment words such as *letter*, *runner*, and *jagged* would be:

> IF WORD has six LETTERS
>
> And LETTERS 3 and 4 are CONSONANTS
>
> And LETTERS 3 and 4 are the same
>
> THEN Divide WORD between LETTERS 3 and 4.

Another subset of productions would have to do with what sounds were represented by what letters. For example:

> IF SYLLABLE is last in WORD
>
> And SYLLABLE begins with VOWEL
>
> And SYLLABLE ends with E
>
> And CONSONANT is between VOWEL and E
>
> THEN Pronounce long form of VOWEL
>
> And pronounce regular form of CONSONANT
>
> And do not Pronounce E.

This production encodes the "silent e" rule. A final set of productions would have to do with the blending of sounds. For example, when a *dle* syllable ends a two-syllable word (cradle, ladle, etc.), the d is scarcely pronounced. A production representing this knowledge might have the form:

> IF WORD has two SYLLABLES
>
> And second SYLLABLE is DLE
>
> THEN Pronounce first SYLLABLE
>
> And attentuate D in pronouncing second SYLLABLE.

Of course, people's productions do not contain words like "attentuate" or "pronounce." They contain whatever abstract symbol a person uses to produce attentuation or pronunciation. The words used here were chosen to communicate the effect, not the form, of the productions that might underlie recoding skill. Also, remember that productions represent knowledge of how to act automatically under given conditions. The conditions are recognized and the actions take place without reflection.

Literal Comprehension

The patterns of print or sound that are identified during decoding are part of the input that stimulates literal comprehension processes (the other part comes from higher-level processes such as one's expectations about the passage). The function of literal comprehension is to derive literal meaning from print. It is composed of two processes: *lexical access* and *parsing*.

Lexical Access. During lexical access, the meanings of words are identified. The term comes from the notion that humans have mental dictionaries (lexicons) that are accessed during language comprehension. The propositional network of declarative knowledge discussed in Chapters 2 and 3 may well include this dictionary. Lexical access is the end result of decoding. That is, when patterns of print or sound are recognized, the meanings associated with these patterns are activated in long-term memory.

Exactly what is activated in LTM depends very much on one's store of declarative knowledge. For example, Figure 7.1 shows two sixth graders' mental dictionaries for *oxygen*. One student's dictionary has a single entry ("ve need it to breathe"), whereas the other's has several entries ("a constituent of air," "a gas," "burns with a blue flame,"

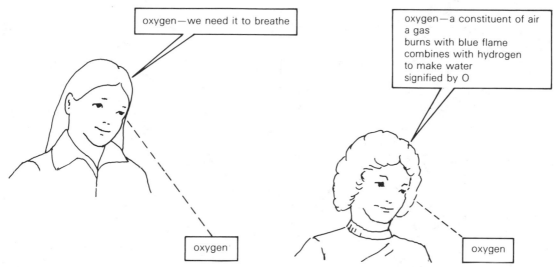

Figure 7.1. A comparison of the mental lexicons of two students who are equally skilled at decoding.

"combines with hydrogen to make water," and "signified by O"). As we shall see presently, a difference in what is activated during the lexical access process can greatly affect inferential comprehension.

Parsing. The function of the parsing process is to put various word meanings together in their appropriate relationships. The result is a proposition—that is, a unit of declarative knowledge (discussed in Chapter 3). Figure 7.2 shows the propositions that are created by parsing for the sentences:

> John called Sally.
>
> Sally called John.

The parsing mechanism uses cues from word order, word endings, and other sources to decide whether *John* or *Sally* is the subject of the sentence. If *John* occurs first (in an active sentence), it is considered to be the subject; if *Sally* occurs first, that is the subject. Without parsing, the relationships in these two sentences could not be distinguished.

Parsing processes can operate on word labels as easily as on word meanings. Therefore, we can create propositions for such sentences as Lewis Carroll's famous *Jabberwocky* sentences:

> 'Twas brillig, and the slithy toves
> Did gyre and gimbel in the wabe:

Even though we have no idea what "toves" are, we recognize them as the actors in the sentence because they precede the verb (which we detect from "did"). Thus we can create a proposition such as that shown in Figure 7.3. The only difference between this proposition and those shown in Figure 7.2 is that the end nodes are word labels rather than word meanings. (This is signified by the quotation marks around the word labels in Figure 7.3.)

Thus parsing provides some understanding of sentences, but the understanding is incomplete. Lexical access provides another type of understanding, but it is also incomplete. The two processes working together provide literal comprehension.

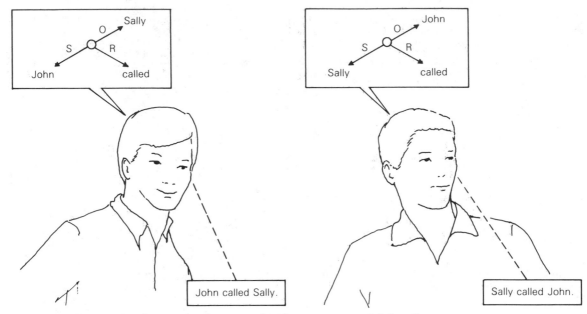

Figure 7.2. Propositional structure for two printed sentences containing the same words.

Inferential Comprehension

Literal comprehension is sufficient for tasks such as reading a bus schedule or reading a description of a process in order to perform it. However, going beyond the information literally stated in text—inferential comprehension—gives the reader a deeper and broader understanding of the ideas about which he or she is reading and is therefore

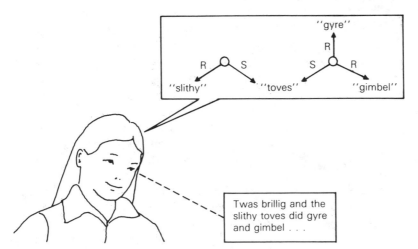

Figure 7.3. Propositional structure for a sentence in which the word meanings are unknown.

an important aspect of reading. The processes involved in inferential comprehension include *integration, summarization,* and *elaboration.*

Integration. Integration processes result in a more coherent mental representation of the ideas in the text than would otherwise occur. Suppose, for example, that a third grader reads the sentences:

The bear walked toward John.

He ran.

On the surface, the ideas in these two sentences are not necessarily related. *He* might refer to someone other than John. And the running might occur for the fun of it, for participation in a race, or to catch a thief. A skilled reader, however, assumes that the sentences in a text are related to one another. When their relationship is not explicitly stated, it is inferred. In our example the skilled reader uses accepted rules of pro-

nomial reference to infer that *he* in sentence 2 refers to *John* in sentence 1. Further, the reader uses prior knowledge about what one does when one sees a bear to draw the inference that John ran because the bear was walking toward him. In fact, the final mental representation of the two sentences might be this inference. Notice that this combined idea is more coherent than the two separate ideas explicitly communicated by the text. The skilled reader tries to integrate text ideas because it makes the text more meaningful and in so doing lessens the load on memory.

Summarization. The function of summarization is to produce in the reader's memory a "macrostructure" (Kintsch and van Dijk, 1978) for the main ideas of a passage. A macrostructure is like a mental outline and can be thought of as a set of propositions that represent the main ideas.

Figure 7.4 shows a paragraph about the climate in Mala (from Rickards, 1976) and a macrostructure for that paragraph: "Mala has

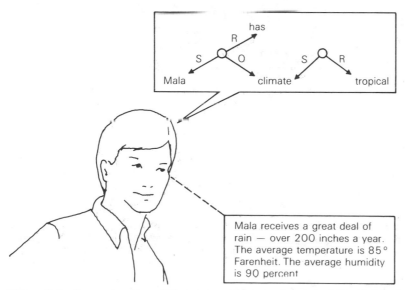

Figure 7.4. A paragraph and the macrostructure developed by the reader for that paragraph.

a tropical climate." Notice that this idea is not explicitly stated in the paragraph. The idea represented by the macrostructure is often not explicitly stated. As in integration, the mental product in summarization is often inferential rather than literal.

Summarization processes rely on both word and meaning cues. Phrases such as "in summary," "in conclusion," and "in general," cue the reader that a summary statement is coming. The reader is then likely to create a macrostructure based on this statement. On the other hand, there may be no word or phrase cues, as in Figure 7.4. In such situations, the reader is attentive to internally produced meaning cues. For example, the meanings for "Rainfall is over 200 inches per year," "85 degrees," and "humid" are all associated with the idea of a tropical climate. The skilled reader uses the activated LTM nodes to help generate a macrostructure for the paragraph.

Other cues for macrostructure come from the reader's knowledge of the structure of different types of text. For example, the prototypical structure for stories, discussed in Chapter 4, is a series of episodes, each consisting of an exposition about an actor and his or her goal, actions taken to meet that goal, a complication or obstacle, and a resolution of the complication (Kintsch, 1977).

Expository texts also have typical structures. B. J. F. Meyer (1975) has identified the five structures for expository text that are shown in Table 7.2. The examples in that table have been condensed into two or three sentences for space-saving reasons. More typically, an entire essay or textbook chapter or section can be classified into one of these five structures for expository text. These structures are used by skilled readers when they form summaries.

Elaboration. Whereas integration and summarization organize new information by building a coherent meaning representation, elaboration adds to this meaning representation by bringing prior knowledge to bear on it. In other words, the main processes involved in inferential comprehension are the same as those involved in learning declarative knowledge (organization and elabora-

Table 7.2. Expository text structures and examples of each.

STRUCTURE	DEFINITION	EXAMPLE
Antecedent/ Consequent	Shows a causal relationship between topics.	"If you had two eggs this morning you're already over the daily cholesterol limit; eating the eggs resulted in boosting you over the cholesterol limit."
Comparison	Points out similarities and differences between two or more topics.	"You should be as careful choosing a puppy food as you are in choosing a baby food. Puppies, like babies, have special needs due to their fast growth."
Collection	Shows how ideas are related.	"A cowboy has two jobs. He herds cattle and he brands them."
Description	Gives examples, details, or settings for topic.	"When liquid is heated to its boiling point some of it changes into a gas. An example of this is boiling water."
Response	Presents a problem and solution or question and answer.	"The nation is increasingly confronted with the need for renewable energy sources. One such source is solar energy."

tion, discussed in Chapter 4). This makes sense since the most common goal of reading is to acquire new declarative knowledge.

Some types of elaboration are shown in Table 7.3. The first elaboration gives an example of a general class. The second continues a story. The third adds details. And the last is an analogy. In each of these examples, the reader's thoughts are called elaborations because they use prior knowledge to add to the ideas gleaned from the text.

As we saw in Chapter 4, elaborative processes are particularly useful when the reader's goal is to remember or reconstruct information at a later date. By tying new information to something familiar one can more easily retrieve the new information later on. Elaboration also appears to increase the probability of transfer of knowledge (cf. Mayer, 1980).

Comprehension Monitoring

Comprehension monitoring ensures that the reader is meeting his or her goals effectively and efficiently. The processes involved in comprehension monitoring—*goal setting, strategy selection, goal checking*, and *remediation*—are analogous to the executive processes that occur in any situation involving setting cognitive goals and attempting to meet them efficiently. This broader set of skills has been called "metacognition" (Flavell, 1979) and refers to one's awareness of one's own cognitive processes.

Goal Setting and Strategy Selection. In skilled readers, comprehension monitoring begins at the start of a reading event and continues throughout. At the start of reading the reader sets a goal and selects a reading strategy to use in meeting the goal (this is probably done fairly automatically in skilled readers). The goal might be finding a particular piece of information, in which case the appropriate strategy might be skimming for a key word associated with the desired information. Or, the goal might be getting an overview of a chapter, in which case one might skim the chapter headings.

Goal Checking and Remediation. The purpose of goal checking is to test that the reader's goals are being met. For example, if a goal is to find out when the American Civil War started, a check of the goal would be whether or not the reader could answer the question "When did the American Civil War start?" If, on the other hand, the reader's goal was to pass an essay test on the American Civil War, a test for this goal would be his or her ability to answer potential essay questions.

As reading proceeds, the goal-checking process may disrupt the normal flow, and re-

Table 7.3. Some types of elaborations and an example of each.

TYPE	WHAT THE TEXT STATED	WHAT THE READER ADDED (ELABORATION)
Example	"A credenza is a low side cabinet in an office."	"My uncle has a credenza in his office."
Continuation	"And so Tom returned to his home after his trip around the world."	"Tom later became an ambassador due to all his experience in travelling."
Detail	"Jane hit the nail and hung the picture on the wall."	"Jane used a hammer and hit the nail hard."
Analogy	"A credenza is a low side cabinet in an office."	"It's like a bureau because it holds things, but it's in an office, not a house."

mediation will be activated to deal with whatever caused the break in comprehension. This disruption can be observed when a word with two meanings is encountered and the wrong meaning is adopted at first. For example, when people read the sentence "There were tears in her brown dress," they first interpret *tears* to be water from the eyes (Carpenter and Just, 1981). But when they encounter *dress* a signal from the goal checker is put out indicating lack of understanding. Then the readers disrupt the normal flow of reading and backtrack with their eyes to *tear*, this time accessing the other meaning of tear (a rip). The sentence now passes the goal checker and reading proceeds.

THE DYNAMICS
OF SKILLED READING

It would be useful if teachers knew exactly which component process was taking place during reading at any given time. If a teacher knew, for example, exactly when a student was decoding the word "somnolent," he or she could ask the student questions that would stimulate recoding processes, such as "What is the first letter?" When so well timed, such questions would be quite useful. However, what if the student had already decoded the words in the sentence and was now integrating the meaning of the sentence with the meanings of previous sentences? In that case, asking "What does the first letter sound like?" would be interfering rather than helpful.

Although it is difficult to know exactly what processes are occurring and when, Just and Carpenter (1980) have a model of reading dynamics in the skilled reader that provides some good approximations. These researchers had college students read passages from *Scientific American* and measured their average gaze time on each word in the passage. Table 7.4 shows the average number of milliseconds spent looking at each word for two sentences in their study.

Several interesting observations can be made about these data. First, there is a large difference between the fixation time on unfamiliar words, such as *flywheel* (1566 msec) and familiar words, such as *the* (0 msec). This is because it takes longer to recode *flywheel* than to match *the*. A second observation is that the gaze time on words at the ends of sentence constituents, such as *engine* at the end of the noun phrase "Every internal combustion engine" (684 msec), is longer than the gaze times at words in the middle of such phrases, such as *combustion* (517 msec). This suggests that parsing tends to occur at the ends of major sentence constituents. A final observation is that, in general, the fixation time is longer for words at the ends of sen-

Table 7.4. Average duration of eye fixations (in milliseconds) while reading a text for understanding. (From Just & Carpenter, 1980.)

1566	267	400	83	267	617	767	450	450	400	616	517
Flywheels	are	one	of	the	oldest mechanical	devices	known	to	man.	Every internal	combustion

684	250	317	617	1116	367	467	483	450	383	284
engine	contains	a	small	flywheel	that converts	the	jerky	motion of the	pistons into	the	smooth

383	317	283	533	50	366	566
flow	of	energy	that	powers	the	drive shaft.

tences than for equally or less familiar words in the middles of sentences. For example, *man* is a very familiar word, more familiar than *oldest*. Yet *man*, occurring at the end of sentence 1, is looked at for an average of 450 milliseconds, whereas *oldest*, occurring in the middle of sentence 1, is looked at for only 267 milliseconds. This suggests that time is taken at the ends of sentences for summarization, integration, and elaboration.

Thus, these observations suggest that skilled readers decode and lexically access words as they are fixating them. They parse phrases as their eyes reach the ends of sentence constituents. Finally, as their eyes reach the ends of sentences, they take time to integrate the ideas represented by the sentence with ideas already represented in their mind.

The time spent on various component processes varies depending on the reader's goals. Carpenter and Just (1981), for example, found that readers who expected a test in which they had to write down what they remembered spent more time integrating ideas in the sentences than did readers who expected a multiple-choice test. Or, for example, readers who are skimming for the main idea may spend little time processing any sentences other than the first and last sentences in each paragraph.

It is important to realize that what is represented in working memory during reading is constantly changing depending on what component processes are taking place. This idea is illustrated in Figure 7.5. The circle around the A in the center of that figure represents attention. The arrows going out from the circle imply that intermediate products may be active in working memory at any given time. In this example, readers read the sentence "The cat is black" and represent either the visual image of the words in working memory (matching) or the sound patterns associated with the letters (recoding). Next, the visual or sound representation activates

the word meanings (lexical access). For example, "cat" stimulates the recall of images and/or propositions about cats. After all the word meanings for this sentence have been activated, a proposition is constructed to represent the relationships among the word meanings (parsing). At this point literal comprehension of the sentence "The cat is black" is complete.

When propositions from two or more ideas have been constructed, they are integrated. For example, the idea that the cat is named Mike (obtained from a previous sentence) is connected to the idea that the cat is black because both ideas refer to the same specific cat. Elaboration of the idea that the cat is black may also take place. For example, the reader may use prior knowledge that cats like to chase birds to generate the elaboration that this cat named Mike likes to chase birds. Summarization is also possible although it is not shown in Figure 7.5. The propositions developed from parsing, integration, elaboration, and summarization processes are deposited in long-term memory.

Of course, depending on both the goals and the skills of different readers, some of the states represented in Figure 7.5 may be skipped. Also, some processes may occur simultaneously or in a different sequence from the one presented. The main point is that several transitory states and processes occur as reading proceeds.

DIFFERENCES BETWEEN SKILLED AND LESS SKILLED READERS

It would be nice if it could be shown that reading problems were confined to one or two of the component processes described in the previous sections. Then research and instruction could emphasize these problem areas. Unfortunately, skilled readers appear to be substantially better than less skilled readers in almost all reading processes. This

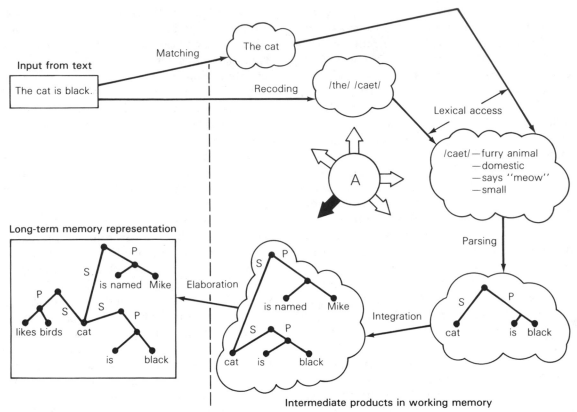

Figure 7.5. Many of the component processes of reading and the intermediate products they generate in working memory. The A in the circle represents attention, which is a limited resource. The dark arrow from attention signifies that attention is currently focused on the ideas that the cat is black and named Mike. (Once a given process is fully automatic, its intermediate products are no longer heeded in working memory.) The arrows represent one logical sequence for the flow of information, but, in reality, there is a flow of information in the other direction as well.

section describes some of the evidence that supports this general statement.

Decoding

Skilled and less skilled readers have been shown to differ in both matching and recoding processes. They do not differ so much in terms of errors as in terms of the speed with which they typically perform these processes. Speed is important because if it takes

a long time to decode a word, one may have forgotten previous words and, therefore, will have more difficulty in generating a meaningful representation.

Matching. Ehri and Wilce (1983) studied the speed with which skilled and less skilled elementary school children could read familiar printed words such as "hat," "boy," and "car." They compared this speed with the time it took to read familiar one-digit numbers such as 3, 4, or 8. The results are shown in Figure 7.6. Less skilled readers in the first and second grades were substantially slower at reading words than digits. By fourth grade, however, their word and digit reading times were equal. For skilled readers, there was no difference in word and digit reading time at any grade level. These data imply that, especially in the early years at school, the matching process in poor readers is not as fast as it is in good readers.

Recoding. By far the most research on differences between skilled and less skilled readers has focused on recoding processes. By now there is ample evidence that skilled readers can perform recoding faster than less skilled readers.

In a typical study of recoding, subjects read aloud words or pronounceable nonsense words (such as *noke* and *pight*). The time between presentation of the stimulus and voice onset (called vocalization latency) is recorded. Presumably, the faster a subject can "sound out" a word, the faster the response time will be, especially for a nonsense word (pseudoword) that is completely unfamiliar. Frederiksen (1981) found that high school students with very high reading ability were twice as fast at starting to say pseudowords as were students of very low reading ability. Figure 7.7 shows the vocalization latencies for high school students at four levels of reading ability. The lowest ability group took 1.2 seconds on the average to start to say a pseudoword, whereas the highest ability group took an average of .6 second. Other studies

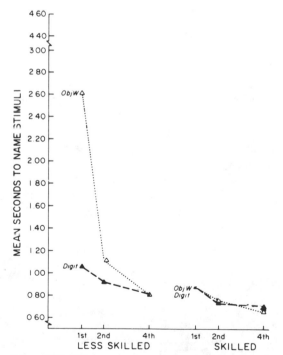

Figure 7.6. Mean number of seconds to identify digits and familiar object words as a function of grade and reading skill. (Adapted from Ehri and Wilce, 1983.)

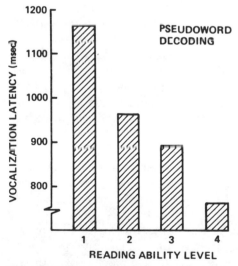

Figure 7.7. Mean speed of voice onset in the pronunciation of pseudowords as a function of reading ability level (1 = lowest ability level, 4 = highest level). (From Frederiksen, 1981, p. 369.)

have obtained similar results with younger readers (Curtis, 1980; Perfetti and Hogaboam, 1975; Perfetti, Finger, and Hogaboam, 1978).

The ability to pronounce unfamiliar words or pseudowords can be broken down into a pattern-recognition component and an action-sequence component. Studies of these components also reveal differences between skilled and less skilled readers.

Frederiksen (1981) measured speed of pattern recognition by asking subjects to name the letters seen in briefly exposed letter bigrams. Bigrams are letter pairs that occur together normally in language (e.g., *sh* and *ck* are bigrams; *fp* and *xb* are not). A subject was seated before a computer terminal screen watching a continuous flow of bigrams, each displayed for 100 milliseconds and then masked. The subject called out the name of each letter in turn.

Performance on this task can be conceptualized as involving either four or five processes, depending on whether or not an individual has mastered a given pattern-recognition procedure. If such a procedure has been mastered, the processes would be (1) perceive the letter bigram as a unit (pattern recognition), (2) retrieve letter names from LTM, (3) say letter name 1, and (4) say letter name 2. If the pattern-recognition procedure has not been mastered, then the processes would be (1) perceive letter 1, (2) perceive letter 2, (3) retrieve letter names from LTM, (4) call out letter name 1, and (5) call out letter name 2. Less skilled readers may be less likely than skilled readers to have developed pattern-recognition procedures for bigrams. If this is so, they would call letters more slowly, because they would use more mental operations.

Figure 7.8 shows the results obtained by Frederiksen (1981). His subjects were high school students arranged into four levels of reading skill as measured by scores on the

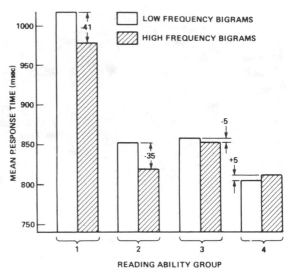

Figure 7.8. Mean latency to call letters in bigrams that vary in their frequency of occurrence in English words. Group 1 is the lowest reading ability level and Group 4 is the highest. (From Frederiksen, 1981, p. 365.)

Nelson-Denny reading test. The dark bars represent latencies of response to bigrams that occur very frequently in natural language and the light bars represent latencies to bigrams that occur less frequently. The lowest ability group was slower to call letters. Also, the two lowest ability groups showed differences in their response times to more versus less familiar bigrams, whereas the two higher ability groups did not show such differences. Frederiksen interprets these results to show that skilled readers are more efficient at pattern-recognition than are less skilled readers.

The action sequence part of recoding has been studied by Calfee, Lindamood, and Lindamood (1973). They gave students in grades K–12 a test requiring them to represent sequences of sounds (Subtest I) and blends of sounds (called Subtests II and III). Figure 7.9 shows their results. Readers were divided into those who were in the upper and lower

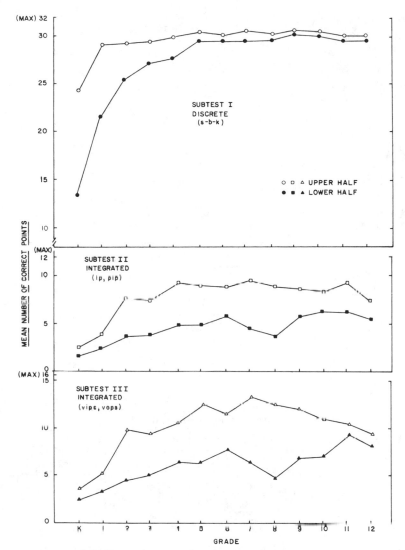

Figure 7.9. Mean number correct on tests of recoding skill as a function of grade and reading skill level (open symbols = above-average skill, closed symbols = below-average skill). Subtest I requires students to represent sequences of sounds, whereas Subtests II and III required them to represent blends of sound sequences. (From Calfee, Lindamood, and Lindamood, 1973.)

halves of the range of scores for their grade on the Reading and Spelling subtests of the Wide Range Achievement Test. In grades K–4, the less skilled readers were significantly worse than the skilled readers at representing sequences of sounds and, in all grades, the less skilled were worse at representing blends than were the skilled readers.

Are the differences in recoding skill between good and poor readers fixed, or can they be reduced with practice? Venezky and Johnson (1973) have some data that can be used to address this question. These researchers were interested in the development of young children's abilities to pronounce pseudowords that contained either long or short a (e.g., "gāne" versus "găn") or hard or soft c sound (e.g., "bact" versus "bace"). They grouped first, second, and third graders into three reading ability groups, according to their scores on the Gates-MacGinitie comprehension test. All students were shown pseudowords on flash cards, and the correctness of their responses was noted.

Figure 7.10 shows the results for each ability group at each grade level for long and short a sounds. You can see that the initially large differences (roughly 45 percent) be-

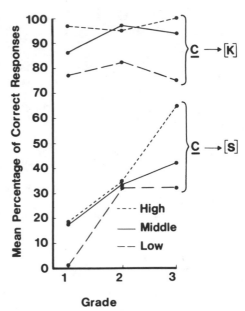

Figure 7.11. Mean correct pronunciation of hard and soft c as a function of grade and ability. (From Venezky and Johnson, 1973, p. 113.)

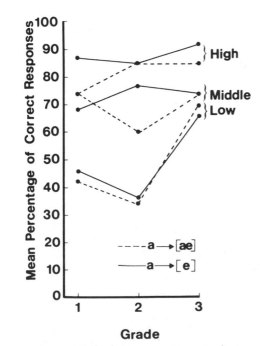

Figure 7.10. Correctness of pronunciation of pseudowords containing long or short a sounds as a function of grade and reading ability. (From Venezky and Johnson, 1973, p. 112.)

tween the high- and low-ability groups in the first and second grades substantially reduced (to roughly 25 percent) by the third grade. These data demonstrate that the differences between ability groups in the letter-sound correspondences for long and short a sounds narrows over time.

What about differences in pronunciation of hard and soft c sounds? Figure 7.11 shows the percentage correct for high- and low-ability children for these sounds. In contrast to the pattern of data for the a sound, these data do not show a consistent reduction of differences between skill levels over time. For the hard c sound, the low-ability students lag behind the high-ability students by about 20 percent in each grade. For the soft c sound, they lag behind high-ability students in the first and third grades, though not in the second. These data, then, suggest that the differences between high- and low-skill students do not decrease over time.

The discrepancy in patterns for the a and c sound can be explained by differences in (1) the amount of direct instruction given to these children on these sounds, and (2) the frequency with which words occurred in the children's readers that contained the sounds. The researchers report that in the schools attended by their subjects:

> both long and short a correspondences are introduced early in Grade 1 and reinforced frequently. The distinction between the two patterns is pointed out by a variety of mechanisms, including contrastive pairs like *can:cane, at:ate,* and *cap:cape.* (p. 115)

In contrast, they report that for the letter c, the hard sound in the initial position is introduced early in the first grade, but the soft sound is often never covered. In addition, few words with soft c sounds occur in the beginning reading material of these children. These facts suggest one reason for the decrease in difference between high- and low-ability students on pronunciation of the letter a: the direct instruction in the letter-sound correspondences benefited the low-ability students more. The lack of such instruction for the soft c sound left the low-ability students at their initial disadvantage.

The ways in which instruction can improve the performance of students of low reading ability will be discussed more in a later section of this chapter. Here we see that there are clear differences between skilled and less skilled readers on recoding ability.

The Relationships Between Decoding Skills and Comprehension. Some theorists argue that decoding skills are unimportant for skilled reading performance. They say that skilled reading is "conceptually driven"—we use the context and prior knowledge to predict words. If we do this, then it really does not matter if we think "car" when the book actually says "automobile," because we are getting the correct meaning. Therefore, decoding is unimportant.

Although this argument has logical consistency, it is challenged by studies that show a strong relationship between decoding and reading comprehension. Curtis (1980), for example, found an average correlation between word matching (matching) scores and reading comprehension scores of .51. She found an average correlation of .55 across elementary grades between word vocalization speed (recoding) and comprehension. Across grades 1–3, Venezky and Johnson (1973) found an average correlation of .70 between letter-sound (recoding) ability and reading comprehension.

Correlations, of course, do not imply causality. However, when there is a good causal explanation for a correlation, the correlation at least is not contradictory to that explanation. There are at least two causal explanations of the relationship between decoding speed and comprehension. The first explanation assumes that some decoding is necessary before higher comprehension processes can occur. If this is true, the faster decoding occurs, the sooner comprehension processes can become active and the more one can comprehend in a unit of time. Slow decoders, therefore, are slower to start up their comprehension processes and therefore comprehend less in a unit of time. The second explanation is based on the fact that active knowledge, if not attended to, becomes inactive rather quickly. If much of working memory's capacity is being used for decoding, less will be available for keeping knowledge active. This implies that a slow decoder will have less information available to integrate, and his or her comprehension may suffer as a result.

Besides the correlational data that suggests a relationship between decoding and comprehension skill, most evidence suggests that children who are taught recoding skills perform better on reading comprehension tests than do children who are not taught recoding (Pflaum, Walberg, Karegianes, and Rasher, 1980). Those who argue that good decoding skills are unnecessary for good comprehension must explain these data.

Literal Comprehension

Lexical Access. One question that is currently being examined by cognitive psychologists is whether or not individuals differ in their speed of activation of long-term memory—that is, speed of lexical access. Such a speed difference might be a "hardware" difference, for which instruction could do little, or it might be one that could be reduced with practice.

Hunt, Davidson, and Lansman (1981) studied the relationship in college students between activation speed and Nelson-Denny reading test scores. Activation speed was measured by several tasks, all of which required retrieval from long-term memory. In one task, for example, subjects saw two words on a cathode ray screen: (1) a superordinate category label (e.g., *furniture*) and (2) an item that 50 percent of the time was a member of the category specified (e.g., *chair*) and 50 percent of the time was not a member of the category specified (e.g., *peach*). The subjects were to respond by pressing different response keys depending on whether or not the item was a member of the category specified. To decide about category membership, the subjects had to retrieve information from long-term memory.

The results were that speed in deciding about category membership correlated about −.30 with the comprehension subtest score for the Nelson-Denny reading test. Results similar to this have been found in other studies (e.g., Goldberg, Schwartz, and Stewart, 1977; Hunt, Lunneborg, and Lewis, 1975), but Hogaboam and Pellegrino (1978) failed to find significant correlations between activation speed and comprehension, so there is still some controversy.

Using Context to Speed Lexical Access. Lexical access can be speeded when the context provides clues that constrain activation to certain parts of long-term memory. For example, try to predict the word that goes in the blank in the following sentences:

1. I reminded her gently that this was something she really wanted to
   _____.

2. Grandmother called the children over to the sofa because she had quite a story to_____.

You probably thought of many possibilities for the first sentence (do, buy, take, see, read, try), but only one or two for the second (tell, relate). This is because *wanted to* is appropriate to many contexts and reading *wanted to* therefore does not constrain activation. By contrast, *story* is almost always found in the context of *tell*, and therefore *story* will constrain activation to the neighborhood of *tell* in LTM, allowing for quicker processing than if activation was not constrained.

Skilled readers appear to be better than less skilled readers at taking advantage of context to predict words and therefore speed up literal comprehension. Frederiksen (1981) showed this with high school students. He had the students read sentences with blanks at the ends of them, such as the ones just shown. When they had read them, they pressed a button and saw the word that fit in the blank. They were to pronounce it as fast as they could. If they were expecting the word, they should pronounce it faster than if they were not expecting it.

Sentence 1 was said to provide a "weak context" whereas sentence 2 provides a "strong context." Frederiksen (1981) wondered if good readers benefited more from having the strong context than poor readers. If so, then they should show a greater acceleration in reaction time between weak and strong context sentences. Figure 7.12 shows what they found. The high-ability readers showed greater acceleration in reaction time because of having a strong context and this was especially true for less frequently occurring words. Frederiksen believes that skilled readers automatically activate several word meaning possibilities at once and are ready to pronounce any one of them, whereas poor readers deliberately search for one word at a time and if it is the wrong word (as would be likely for low-frequency words) they must discard it and search for another one, thus slowing down pronunciation.

Whatever the cause of the difference, it is clear that skilled readers are better able to take advantage of context in speeding up literal comprehension than are less skilled readers.

Inferential Comprehension

Integration. Skilled readers' ability to take advantage of context may be due to their greater ability to integrate propositions both within and between sentences. The Frederiksen (1981) study demonstrated within-sentence effects of context. A study conducted by Perfetti and Roth (1981) illustrates between-sentence context effects. In this study the subjects were eight to ten years old. Less skilled readers scored below the fortieth percentile on the Metropolitan Achievement Test comprehension subtest and skilled read-

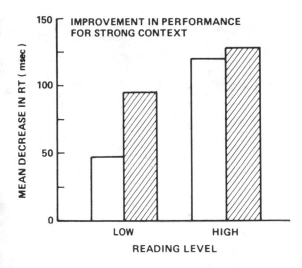

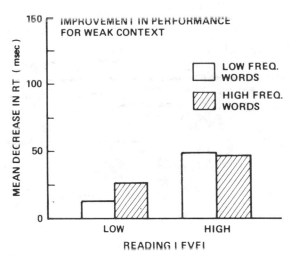

Figure 7.12. Average decrease in reaction time due to context. The high-ability readers show a greater benefit from a strong context than the low-ability readers. (From Frederiksen, 1981, p. 372.)

ers scored above the sixtieth percentile. All subjects had average or above-average intelligence.

The subjects' task was to listen to pairs of related sentences and predict the last word in the second sentence. By having the subjects

is wt this still recoding — a part of decoding

listen rather than read, the researchers were able to separate comprehension processes from decoding processes. The first sentence provided either a high constraint, a moderate constraint, or a low constraint for predicting the missing word in the second sentence. For example, two moderate-constraint pairs were:

Lenny wanted to write a letter to his friend. He opened the drawer and looked for a_____.

When I got home from work, I wanted to eat a fruit. I went to the refrigerator and got a_____.

Not surprisingly, as can be seen in Table 7.5, the skilled and less skilled readers were equivalent in their performance in high- and low-constraint situations. However, in the moderate-constraint situation, the skilled readers were about 8 percent more accurate than the less skilled readers. In examining the errors, the researchers noticed that the less skilled readers were more likely to produce words that did not fit with the constraints of the first sentence (e.g., pizza is not a fruit). It was as if the less skilled readers forgot the first sentence as they were making their predictions.

As we discussed previously, one impor-

tant part of integration is solving problems of pronoun reference. How do skilled and less skilled readers compare on this aspect of integration? Frederiksen (1981) has found several interesting differences in high school readers of varying reading levels.

In one study subjects read text aloud and researchers determined their mean reading time per syllable. Some sentences repeated the noun phrase from a previous sentence, whereas others substituted a pronoun reference, and others only indirectly referred to the topic of the previous sentence. If the process of determining the referent of the second sentence is more difficult for a pronoun or an indirect reference than for a repeated noun phrase, this should slow down reading. Frederiksen (1981) found that this process slowed down reading, especially for the lowest ability group (below the fortieth percentile on the Nelson-Denny reading test). The results are displayed as average differences in reading time for repeated noun phrases versus pronouns (left side of Figure 7.13) and for repeated noun phrases versus indirect reference (right side). The lowest ability group (group 1) shows the greatest average difference, and hence the most slowing, for both pronouns and indirect references.

In a second study Frederiksen (1981) found that low-skill readers were slowed down much more than high-skill readers by sentences in which the pronoun was not "foregrounded" by an implicit reference in a previous sentence. Thus, in general, less skilled readers appear to be slower at integration processes than are skilled readers.

These studies of integration give the impression that less skilled readers have smaller WM capacity than do skilled readers. That is, their "hardware" may be deficient in this regard. However, this idea has not received unequivocal support. Some studies show a relationship between WM capacity

Table 7.5. Percentage of correct predictions of the final word in a sentence as a function of constraint provided by a previous sentence. Notice that skilled readers perform better than less skilled readers in the moderate-constraint condition. (Adapted from Perfetti and Roth, 1981, p. 281.)

	SKILLED READERS	LESS SKILLED READERS
High constraint	92.9	94.4
Moderate constraint	23.7	15.2
Low constraint	0.2	0.1

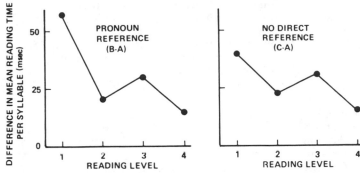

Figure 7.13. The left-hand graph shows the difference in reading time between reading a pronoun referent for a noun phrase and reading the noun phrase repeated. The right-hand graph shows the difference between reading an indirect reference to the noun phrase and reading the noun phrase repeated. The larger the difference, the more the pronomial or indirect reference is slowing down the reader. Poor readers (level 1) are slowed down more than good readers. (From Frederiksen, 1981, p. 377.)

and reading skill (e.g., Badian, 1977), whereas others do not (e.g., Guyer and Friedman, 1975). The apparent WM deficit may really occur because less skilled readers perform some of the simpler comprehension operations less automatically and therefore devote more room in working memory to them, leaving less capacity for other processes (Daneman and Carpenter, 1980). This view is a very hopeful one from an educational standpoint. Whereas memory capacity is more or less fixed, automaticity of skills is quite variable depending on the amount of practice.

Summarization. Several studies have demonstrated that more competent readers are better at using the structure of a passage to develop a summary of the passage ideas (Bartlett, 1978; B. J. F. Meyer, Brandt, and Bluth, 1980; Taylor, 1980). The typical study in this area presents readers with well-structured text and has them freely recall what they can after reading.

Meyer, Brandt, and Bluth (1980) used this technique with ninth graders. They had the students read two expository passages, one

with a comparison structure (see page 172) and one with a problem-solution structure. One of the passages used is shown in Table 7.6. After reading, the students wrote down all they could remember from the passages.

Table 7.7 shows the average number of students who used the same organizational structure as the author's in their recall as a function of reading skill (good, average, and poor readers as measured by the Stanford Achievement Test). About three-fourths of the good readers, about one-half of the average readers, and less than one-fourth of the poor readers used the text structure in recall. Students who did not use the text structure tended to list ideas from the passage in a variety of orders. Meyer et al. (1980) also found that the use of the text structure was a substantial predictor of the overall amount recalled. This is probably because the text structure organized encoding and retrieval processes.

Although the poor readers in the Meyer et al. study seem not to recognize text structure, this may not be the case. They may recognize it but fail to use it for organizing recall. A study by Brown and Smiley (1977), how-

Table 7.6. Passage read and recalled by students. The italicized words show the most important ideas, not italicized in student's version. (Adapted from Meyer, Brandt, and Bluth, 1980.)

SUPERTANKERS

A problem of vital concern is the prevention of oil spills from supertankers. A typical supertanker carries a half-million tons of oil and is the size of five football fields. A wrecked supertanker spills oil in the ocean; this oil kills animals, birds, and microscopic plant life. For example, when a tanker crashed off the coast of England, more than 200,000 dead seabirds washed ashore. Oil spills also kill microscopic plant life which provide food for sea life and produce 70 percent of the world's oxygen supply. Most wrecks *result from the lack* of power and steering equipment to handle emergency situations, such as storms. Supertankers have only one boiler to provide power and one propeller to drive the ship.

The solution to the problem is not to immediately halt the use of tankers on the ocean since about 80 percent of the world's oil supply is carried by supertankers. *Instead, the solution lies in the training of officers of supertankers, better building of tankers, and installing ground control stations to guide tankers near shore.* First, *officers of supertankers must get* top *training* in how to run and maneuver their ships. Second, tankers should be *built* with several propellers for extra control and backup boilers for emergency power. Third, *ground control stations should be installed* at places where supertankers come close to shore. These stations would act like airplane control towers, guiding tankers along busy shipping lanes and through dangerous channels.

ever, suggests that there is a developmental sequence in the ability to distinguish important and less important parts of a text's structure. Thus, some of Meyer et al.'s subjects were probably developmentally behind others.

A. Brown and Smiley (1977) had students in the third, fifth, and seventh grades and college students read unfamiliar folk tales and rate each idea unit in the tales for importance to the overall theme. They found that college

Table 7.7. Average number of students using the structure of the text in their recall protocols. Average scores on the Stanford Achievement Test (Comprehension Subtest) were 84th, 58th, and 32nd percentile, respectively, for the good, average, and poor comprehenders. (Adapted from Meyer, Brandt, and Bluth, 1980.)

	STRUCTURE OF RECALL	
	SAME AS TEXT	DIFFERENT FROM TEXT
Good comprehenders	23.5	8.5
Average comprehenders	16.5	18.5
Poor comprehenders	6.5	28.5

students clearly differentiated among four levels of importance that had been previously established for the ideas. Fifth graders could distinguish the most important ideas but could not distinguish among ideas at the other three levels. Third graders could not distinguish any levels of importance. Table 7.8 shows these results. Brown and Smiley also found that recall of passages increased with age, suggesting that recall increases because students are learning how to organize passage information in storage and retrieval.

In summary, skilled versus less skilled readers differ in their use of text structure in recall and mature versus less mature readers differ in their ability to distinguish the hierarchy of ideas contained in a text. Knowledge and use of text structure are important in the summarization process. If less skilled students could be trained to recognize text structures and to generate summaries of text using such structures, their summarization would likely improve. B. J. Bartlett (1978) has demonstrated a successful training program in this area.

Elaboration. Elaboration is the reading process during which the reader makes the material meaningful to him- or herself by re-

Table 7.8. Mean importance ratings for different levels of importance of ideas as a function of the age level of the reader. (Adapted from A. Brown and Smiley, 1977.)

GROUP	IMPORTANCE LEVEL			
	1 (LEAST)	2	3	4 (MOST)
Third grade	2.41	2.52	2.51	2.56
Fifth grade	2.42	2.35	2.46	2.76
Seventh grade	2.02	2.36	2.58	3.05
College	1.61	2.09	2.78	3.52

lating the new ideas being read about to known information. C. Weinstein (1978) has studied the use of elaboration by students who are more and less successful, as measured by grade point average, and by students at various grade levels. She gave students the questionnaire about elaboration shown in Table 7.9. Notice that this questionnaire not only asks if a student has used a particular type of elaboration but also requires a specific example. If a student can provide a specific example, his or her response is probably valid.

Weinstein (1978) summarizes the results of her studies: "More successful learners, and those with more years of schooling, use meaningful elaboration strategies in preference to more rote, or superficial strategies." Although these results do not speak directly to reading skill differences, since reading skill is highly correlated with success in school, it is likely that skilled readers are better at elaborative processing than are less skilled readers.

Comprehension Monitoring

Complex skills that are optimally developed appear to have built-in tests for progress. Since the goal of most reading is comprehen-

Table 7.9. Questions asked to students about their elaboration processes. (Adapted from C. Weinstein, 1978.)

Please try to think of an example of how you would use this method. If you can't, it's OK. Check the method anyway.

_____ A. Think about the purpose or need for the material. Example:
_____ B. Relate it to your experience or characteristics. Example:
_____ C. Relate it to your beliefs or attitudes. Example:
_____ D. Think about your emotional reactions to the content. Example:
_____ E. Relate it to people in general. Example:
_____ F. Think about the ideas that you have as you read it. Example:
_____ G. Think about other people's reactions to the content. Example:
_____ H. Relate it to what you already know. Example:
_____ I. "Free associate" to the topic or ideas. Example:
_____ J. Think about implications of what is stated. Example:
_____ K. Look for common sense or logical relationships. Example:
_____ L. Relate the content to the theme. Example:
_____ M. Relate key words or concepts to ideas. Example:
_____ N. Discussion with other people. Example:

sion, it is important for readers to assess whether comprehension is occurring. Moreover, when a test indicates noncomprehension, the reader must then use some strategy to remediate the problem, such as rereading, looking up words in a dictionary, or asking someone for help (T. H. Anderson, 1979). Most of the research on monitoring and remediation has compared readers at different levels of maturity rather than those at the same level of maturity but different skill levels. However, older readers on the average have greater reading skill than younger readers, so we can use age comparisons to get ideas about reading skill differences. In so doing we must recognize the possibility differences with age may be due to maturation or general experience rather than skill.

Goal Checking. More and less mature readers differ in awareness of their failure to comprehend (Markman, 1979). Harris, Kruithof, Terwogt, and Visser (1981) showed this by having third- and sixth-grade children read stories, some of which contained an anomalous sentence. Table 7.10 shows a sample of one of the stories used, and two titles for the story. The title *John at the Dentist* made the fourth sentence ("he sees his hair getting shorter") anomalous and was therefore called the *conflicting title*. The title *John at the Hairdresser's* made the fourth sentence easy to in-

Table 7.10. A sample story with a conflicting and an appropriate title. The conflicting title renders sentence 4 anomalous. (From Harris, Kruithof, Terwogt, and Visser, 1981.)

Appropriate Title: John at the Hairdresser's

Inappropriate Title: John at the Dentist

1. John is waiting
2. There are two people before him.
3. After a while it is his turn.
4. He sees his hair getting shorter.
5. After a while he may get up.
6. He can go home.

terpret and was therefore called the *appropriate title.* The titles of stories were counterbalanced across the two age groups so that story content would not be a confounding variable.

Each child read three stories and his or her reading time for each sentence was recorded. After all three stories were read, the experimenter asked each child, "Did you notice in one of the stories a line that did not fit in with the rest of the story?" If the answer was yes, the child was asked to recall the line. If he or she could not recall the line, the experimenter showed the stories to the child again and asked the child to point to the line. Finally, for those children who said they had not noticed a problem, the experimenter showed them the stories again and asked them to point to a line that did not fit in very well.

The results showed that both age groups were faster at reading a line when the title was appropriate than when it was conflicting. For the appropriate title, the average reading time was 3.3 seconds, whereas for the conflicting title, the average reading time was 4.2 seconds. The two age groups differed, however, in how many children noticed the problem sentence. Even when they were allowed to look back over the stories, 30 percent of the third graders still could not identify the problem sentence. Only 11 percent of the sixth graders were unable to identify the problem sentence. Also, 44 percent of the sixth graders said that they noticed a problem sentence and could recall this sentence without any prompts. Only 11 percent of the third graders could do this.

The different results for reading time and ability to identify problem sentences suggests that the younger children are producing signals that comprehension is faltering. They lack the ability to monitor these signals. That is, the third graders slowed down while reading a sentence that was incongruent with the story title, and this cued them that their comprehension was failing. However, since third graders frequently could not identify problem sentences, this suggests that they do not monitor the cues available to them. In other words, they are not as skilled at goal checking as are sixth graders.

Remediation. The recognition of problems precedes their solution. If this is correct, we should find that low-skill readers neither recognize comprehension problems nor have remedial strategies to solve them, whereas medium-skill readers recognize problems but do not yet know how to deal with them, and finally high-skill readers both recognize and know how to remediate comprehension problems.

Garner and Reis (1981) found just such a pattern when they examined age and reading ability differences in the use of the "look-

Table 7.11. Passage and questions used to study the look-back strategy. Each passage and the questions that followed it were printed on a separate page. The questions marked with asterisks are those for which relevant information occurred on a preceding page. (From Garner and Reis, 1981.)

Bill lived in Maryland, but this summer he was staying at Camp Wildwood in New York. His cabin was Number 11. He shared the cabin with five other boys: Tom from Maine, Sam from Vermont, David from New York, and Richard and Joseph from Pennsylvania. Only Richard and Joseph had known each other before the summer began. Bill enjoyed spending long days outdoors. He especially enjoyed fishing for trout and catfish in Big Bear Lake and for bass in Blue Pond. Bill was the best fisherman in cabin Number 11.

1. Where was Camp Wildwood?_____
2. How many boys were in cabin Number 11?_____
3. What was Bill's favorite camp activity?_____

After one week at Camp Wildwood, nearly everyone had received mail from home. Letters with Vermont, New York, Maryland, and Pennsylvania postmarks arrived almost daily. None of the guys got really homesick. They were too busy. Tom had discovered swimming. Richard had learned how to paddle a canoe. Bill fished from morning until night. One day Bill caught 12 fish in Blue Pond, and the Number 11 group had fresh fish for dinner instead of hamburgers. All six of the boys became close friends.

*4. Which of the boys did not receive mail?_____(Sect. 1)
5. How many fish did Bill catch for dinner?_____
*6. What kind of fish were they?_____(Sect. 1)

It finally came time for the boys to leave camp and return home. They were all sad. As parents arrived at camp to pick them up, each boy promised to write the others. Joseph's mother was not happy when she had to delay her return to Pennsylvania. Her extra rider had decided to take one last canoe trip for the summer. However, by the end of the day, sports equipment was packed away, all the boys were on the road, and cabin Number 11 was closed for the season. Bill had reminded the others that they would all try to get the same cabin next summer at Wildwood.

*7. Which boy made Joseph's mother wait?_____(Sect. 1 or 2)
8. What had been packed away?_____
9. What was Bill's reminder?_____
*10. Where did Bill fish other than at Blue Pond?_____(Sect. 1)

back'' strategy. The look-back strategy involves looking back in a text when one realizes one needs information from preceding pages. It is certainly useful, but apparently not all readers possess it.

The children in this study were good and poor comprehenders in grades 4–10. They read passages such as the one shown in Table 7.11 and answered the questions shown. Some of the questions could be answered by referring to the paragraph just read, whereas others required the reader to look back to (or possibly remember) information from preceding paragraphs. For example, question 10 could be answered by looking back to the first paragraph, which was on a separate page.

Garner and Reis (1981) counted the number of spontaneous expressions of problems (evidence of goal checking) and also the number of look-backs to solve the problems. Expressions of problems included such verbalizations (after reading a question) as ''hmm'' or ''let's see'' or ''I don't know'' and also such nonverbal expressions as shrugging or head shaking. Poor comprehenders expressed problems on only 7 percent of the questions requiring look-backs, whereas good comprehenders expressed problems on 60 percent of these questions. The good comprehenders looked back on an average of 30 percent of the look-back questions, whereas the poor comprehenders looked back only 9 percent of the time. Finally, the six oldest good comprehenders used a look-back strategy almost 80 percent of the time. Thus, it seems that poor comprehenders neither recognize their problems nor use a look-back strategy very often, whereas younger good comprehenders recognize their problems over half the time and use a look-back strategy about a third of the time. Older good comprehenders consistently recognize comprehension problems and employ strategies to solve them. In a developmental sense, then, problem recognition does precede the learning of problem-solving strategies.

DECLARATIVE KNOWLEDGE DIFFERENCES

The preceding sections have described many types of procedural knowledge that differentiate people with higher and lower reading skill. Differences in declarative knowledge can also be a source of reading-skill differences. Declarative knowledge is activated during lexical access and during summarization and elaboration. As one has more stored information relevant to a word, one's lexical access should be more sensitive to shades of meaning (Curtis, Collins, Gitomer, and Glaser, 1983). Also, one's summarization and elaboration of new information about the topic should be better.

Spilich, Vesonder, Chiesi, and Voss (1979) studied this latter possibility by using a text on baseball, a topic about which people have widely differing amounts of declarative knowledge. The text used is shown in Table 7.12. The subjects in this study were divided into groups of high and low declarative knowledge on the basis of a forty-five-item test of baseball knowledge, which included questions about terminology, rules, and procedures of baseball. The high-knowledge group had an average score of 42 on this test whereas the low-knowledge group averaged only 19 correct. The groups were equivalent on the Davis Reading Test, so they did not differ on reading skill.

Subjects listened to the baseball text and wrote down as much as they could remember from the passage. The results showed great quantitative differences in recall, with the high-knowledge subjects recalling an average of forty-eight propositions and the low-knowledge subjects recalling an average of only thirty-one. There were also interesting qualitative differences in recall. High-knowledge subjects recalled more information about actions that produced significant changes in the game and they were more likely to recall events in the correct order. Also, they re-

Table 7.12. The baseball text used to study knowledge effects on comprehension. (From Spilich, Vesonder, Chiesi, and Voss, 1979.)

The Ridgeville Robins are playing the Center City Cougars. The Robins are leading 5–3 with the Cougars at bat in the last half of the fifth inning. The sky is getting darker, and the rain that has started is becoming heavier. The Cougars' first batter, Harvey Jones, is taking his time coming to plate. The umpire steps back from behind the plate and tells him to step into the batter's box.

Jones, the hitter, is left-handed, and has a batting average of .310. Claresen, the pitcher, has allowed only four hits, has walked one, and has struck out six. This performance is about average for Claresen since this left-hander has an earned-run average of 6.00 and typically strikes out quite a few batters.

Claresen now adjusts his cap, touches his knee, begins his windup, and delivers a high fastball that the umpire calls "Ball One." The Robins' catcher, Don Postman, returns the ball, and Claresen takes the sign. The next pitch is swung on and hit to centerfield. Maloney comes in and catches it for the first out.

The next batter is the powerful hitter, Fred Johnson, who leads the league in home runs with 23. Claresen no doubt is glad to face him with no one on base. Claresen is now getting his sign from the catcher, begins his windup, and throws a curveball breaking into a right-hand batter at the knees. The umpire calls it a strike. Claresen is now getting ready again, winds up and throws, and Johnson hits it off to right and into the stands, a foul ball. The count is now 0 and 2. Claresen rubs up the new ball, takes his sign, and throws a fastball which just misses the bill of Johnson's cap. Johnson took one step toward the mound, but then came back. Johnson stepped out of the batter's box, and put some resin on his hands; the bat is no doubt slippery from the rain. Claresen is ready again, winds up and throws a slider which breaks inside, making the count 2–2. Once more Johnson steps out of the batter's box and gets some resin on his hands. He steps back in and the Claresen starts his motion and throws. Johnson swings and has a line drive down the left-field line. Ferraro runs over to get the ball as Johnson rounds first and goes toward second. Ferraro's throw is late and Johnson is safe on second with a double.

Beck, the left-handed relief pitcher, is warming up in the bull pen. The next hitter for the Cougars is the right-hand hitting Carl Churniak, a .260 hitter who is known to hit well in the clutch. Claresen takes his sign, delivers, and Churniak takes the pitch for a ball. Claresen again is ready and pitches, and Churniak swings and hits a slow bouncing ball toward the shortstop. Haley comes in, fields it, and throws to first, but too late. Churniak is on first with a single, Johnson stayed on second.

The next batter is Whitcomb, the Cougars' left-fielder. He is a left-hander hitting .255. Claresen wipes his forehead with his sleeve and takes his sign. Claresen looks toward first, where Manfred is holding the runner. He stretches, looks at second, and throws a high fastball for a strike. The catcher returns the ball and Claresen once more gets ready. Claresen throws a low curveball. It bounces into the dirt and past the catcher. Johnson moves to third and Churniak to second before the catcher can retrieve the ball. The ball is returned to Claresen. He gets the sign and winds up, and throws a slider that Whitcomb hits between Manfred and Roberts for a hit. Dulaney comes in and picks up the ball. Johnson has scored, and Churniak is heading for the plate. Here comes the throw, and Churniak is heading for the plate. Here comes the throw, and Churniak is out. Churniak argues, but to no avail. The batter reached second on the throw to the plate.

The next batter is Rob Williams, the Cougars' catcher. He is hitting .230. Claresen is rubbing up the ball and now is ready to pitch. The rain is coming down in sheets. Claresen delivers and Williams takes a curve over the inside corner for a strike. Working rapidly Claresen again delivers and Williams takes a ball, low and outside. Claresen again gets the sign, stretches, and throws a fastball, which Williams swings and misses. The catcher returns the ball and Claresen is ready. The pitch is a curveball which Williams swings at and misses for his third strike.

The umpires now are meeting and they signal that the game is being called.

ported larger chunks of information. For example, whereas a low-knowledge subject might state that someone "got a double," a high-knowledge subject would say, "The batter lined a double down the left-field line." The high-knowledge subject's chunk contains more information that is significant to the unfolding of the game. These qualitative differences show the important role of declarative knowledge in summarization and integration of text.

The researchers also noted a greater tendency for high-knowledge subjects to elaborate on text information. For example, the text stated that the pitcher struck out many batters and was left-handed. One high-knowledge subject called the pitcher a "big, fastballing lefthander" even though "big" and "fastballing" were not in the text. However, it is a fact that pitchers who get a lot of strikeouts tend to be large and throw fastballs, so the elaboration is quite appropriate.

Here, then, is a situation in which students who have the same reading skill level show large differences in comprehension. What if these low-knowledge subjects had taken a college admissions test for reading comprehension on a series of baseball texts? They might not have been admitted to college! Fortunately, standardized tests of reading comprehension sample a wide variety of topics, so knowledge differences among test takers are likely to "average out" across the entire test. Nonetheless, some students may score poorly on reading tests not because of procedural knowledge deficits, but rather because of extensive declarative knowledge deficits. This would seem to be a possible cause of reading difficulties for students from either unstimulating environments or rich, but culturally different environments in which much declarative knowledge was acquired but it did not overlap much with topics of reading comprehension passages found on standardized tests.

INSTRUCTION

The research on differences between skilled and less skilled readers suggests a variety of reasons for less skilled readers' low performance. Many low-skill individuals (even in the twelfth grade) lack adequate recoding skills. Also, some low-skill individuals are poor at integrating, summarizing, and elaborating on information. Some do not monitor their comprehension and do not have strategies to deal with comprehension problems. Finally, some may lack a rich base of declarative knowledge to use in comprehension. One implication for instruction, then, is that reading curricula should emphasize several goals and should provide diagnostic tests so that each student's strengths and weaknesses can be determined.

In addition to emphasizing several goals, instruction should be designed to increase the probability of reaching a given goal. For learning declarative knowledge, this means presenting information in organized and meaningful ways, so that students engage in organization and elaboration. For learning new pattern-recognition procedures, this means providing a wide variety of examples to promote generalization, and matched nonexamples to promote discrimination. For learning new action sequences, this means providing practice and feedback so that proceduralization and composition can occur.

At the beginning of this chapter it was stated that knowledge of how skilled and less skilled readers differ may help in efforts to improve reading instruction. In this section this notion will be exemplified. Two training studies will be reported—one that focuses on decoding skills and one that focuses on inferential comprehension and comprehension-monitoring skills. Both studies are attempts to train students in skills that have been demonstrated to be lacking in poorer readers.

Teaching Decoding Skills

Automaticity of decoding, which seems to be so important for skilled reading (LaBerge and Samuels, 1974), is developed through practice and feedback. Recently some experimental attempts to produce automaticity in less skilled readers have met with some success (Samuels, 1979). Some of these attempts have used microcomputers to present text to readers and give feedback on the readers' increase in speed and accuracy (Carver and Hoffman, 1981; Frederiksen et al., 1983). Microcomputers seem well suited to stimulating the extensive practice needed to automate a skill.

J. R. Frederiksen and his colleagues (Frederiksen et al., 1983) designed some effective computer games that exemplify how extended practice and feedback can be made interesting. One of the games they developed was designed to improve the speed with which readers recognized common multiletter units (e.g., *un, ism, tion, pro*) within words. This skill is logically prerequisite to recoding, since a single sound unit is associated with each of the multiletter units used by Frederiksen et al. This game gave students practice in recognizing sixty of the most frequent multiletter units in the English language. The units were embedded in real words, equally often at different locations within words. For example, for the unit *gen*, some of the words presented to the students were *gen*erous, re*gen*cy, and indul*gen*ce.

During each "run" of the game, the students focused on only one multiletter unit. They saw many words, some of which contained the unit and some of which did not, and they indicated by pressing a response key, whether or not each word contained the target unit. The goal of the game was to increase the speed of responding (the speed of recognizing units) without adversely affecting accuracy. The game itself had a car race theme. Since subjects were high school males (with decoding deficiencies), this theme was appropriate.

Figure 7-14 shows the types of display that the student might see during one run of the game. At the start (panel 1) the student

is shown the target unit (*gen*), the initial speed, and the goal speed. An initial speed of "60 per minute" means that the run would start with a presentation rate of sixty words per minute. A run commences with a display such as the one shown in panel 2. The student sees the target unit at the top of the display and a word (e.g., "gelatinized") in the box just below the middle of the display. The *error lights* show the number of errors that the subject has made so far for a particular run. Up to five errors are permissible. If more than five errors are made, then the display in panel 4 is shown (a crash which terminates the run). The limitation on number of errors prevents students from responding randomly to increase their speed.

If less than five errors have occurred, the run continues for a maximum of 100 words, half of which contain the target unit and half do not. Each time a correct response is made within the current presentation speed, the speed is increased. The increase is shown by the spedometer at the bottom of panel 2. Thus, throughout the run, the student receives continuous feedback about how near he is to his goal speed and how near he is to crashing. A student who reaches his goal speed within a run sees the display shown in panel 3. If not, he sees a "Yea, you finished" display.

Later, after runs with other multiletter units, the student repeats runs for any units on which he did not reach the goal. Each repeat run adjusts the initial speed upward somewhat depending on the student's final speed during the first run. Thus, the number of runs depends on the individual. Each performs on as many runs as necessary to get him to the goal speed.

What were the effects of this training? Students were given pre- and posttests on recognition speed for both the sixty trained units and twenty other common multiletter units. The results for recognition speed are

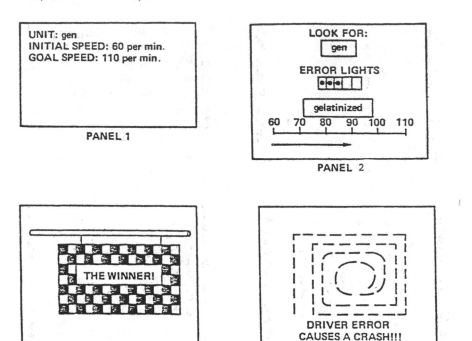

```
UNIT: gen
INITIAL SPEED: 60 per min.
GOAL SPEED: 110 per min.



            PANEL 1
```

```
            LOOK FOR:
              gen

          ERROR LIGHTS

            gelatinized
        60  70  80  90  100  110


            PANEL  2
```

```
            THE WINNER!



            PANEL  3
```

```
            DRIVER ERROR
          CAUSES A CRASH!!!
            PANEL  4
```

Figure 7.14. Displays seen by students in a microcomputer game designed to teach recognition of common multiletter units. (From Frederiksen et al., 1983.)

shown in Figure 7.15. For both two- and three-letter units, the reaction time decreased by about 75–100 milliseconds between the pre- and posttests. Not only did the students' reaction time decrease, but at the end of training, their times were comparable to those of high school students in the top 10 percent on reading achievement test performance.

It is interesting that the reaction time decreased for untrained units as well as for trained units. This finding suggests that a general attentional skill is being learned. It has been shown that poor readers attend mainly to the initial letters in a word (Harris and Sipay, 1975). To perform well in this game, however, attention must be distributed across all letters. The students thus learn to allocate attention more effectively.

Besides taking pre- and posttests on detecting multiletter units, students also took pre- and posttests on pseudoword decoding. (You will recall that pseudoword decoding involves pronouncing phonetically regular nonwords). Figures 7.16 and 7.17, respectively, show the students' average reaction times and accuracy on the pseudoword decoding task. As you can see, whereas reaction time decreased from the pre- to the posttest, accuracy increased. These results give empirical support to the logical assumption that multiletter unit detection is prerequisite to recoding skill.

The students in this study probably learned both pattern-recognition and action-sequence procedures during their thousands of trials at multiletter-unit detection. The pattern-recognition procedures that may have been formed are specific to each of the sixty trained units. Conditions were provided that promoted generalization and discrimination.

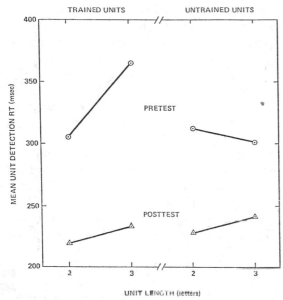

Figure 7.15. Reaction time for identification of multiletter units before and after training. (From Frederiksen et al., 1983.)

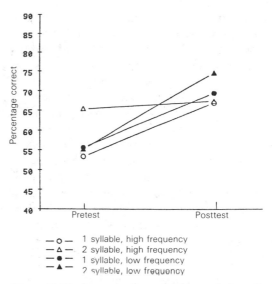

Figure 7.17. Accuracy for pseudoword decoding before and after training. (From Frederiksen et al., 1983.)

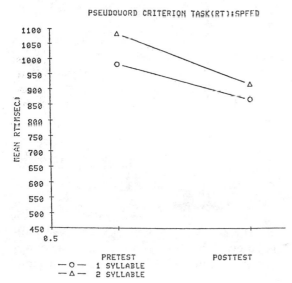

Figure 7.16. Reaction time for pseudoword decoding before and after training. (From Frederiksen et al., 1983.)

That is, the examples of the units varied widely in that the units were embedded in fifty different words and their position within words varied. This variety should have promoted generalization. Also, many of the distractor words were close to being matched nonexamples. For instance, "germane" has two of the three crucial letters of *gen*, forcing attention to the n by its absence. Also, "grenadiers" has all three crucial letters, but they do not occur together, forcing attention to the need for the letters in the unit to occur together. Although these words were not completely matched with words in which the target unit appeared, they were similar enough to promote discrimination.

The action-sequence procedure that may have been learned was one of quick visual scanning of an entire word. This procedure apparently replaced the less effective procedure of focusing on initial letters only. Proceduralization is not relevant as a learning process for this action sequence because translation from declarative to procedural form does not seem to be involved. However, composition is highly relevant, and important conditions for composition are practice and feedback, with feedback including information about both speed and accuracy. In Frederiksen et al.'s (1983) game feedback on speed and accuracy was displayed continuously over the thousands of practice trials.

In summary, this study demonstrates the success that can be achieved by using known principles of learning to teach skills that learners are known to lack. It also demonstrates a creative use of microcomputers in reading instruction.

Teaching Inferential Comprehension and Comprehension-Monitoring Skills

Recall that skilled readers are better at detecting the main ideas in passages and at monitoring their own comprehension than are less skilled readers. Palincsar and Brown (1984) conducted a series of studies on teaching less skilled readers to detect main ideas, and to monitor their own comprehension through making predictions, asking questions, and looking out for unclear portions of text. They worked with middle school students who had good decoding skills but performed poorly on comprehension tests.

In these studies teacher and students took turns being the "teacher." The teacher's role was to ask questions both before and after the group read a segment of expository text. If the segment was at the beginning of a passage, the teacher would ask the group to make predictions from the title or to say what the title made them think of. After the group had read a segment, the teacher would ask a question about the main point of the segment. If there were unclear phrases, the teacher asked the group for clarification.

At the start of each session, the real teacher was responsible for the first reading segment and hence could model good questions before the students took their turns as teacher. Also, the real teacher gave feedback to the students about their responses. Depending on the quality of the response, the real teacher might say, "You asked that question well; it was very clear what information you wanted"; "Excellent prediction, let's see if you're right"; or "That was interesting information. It was information that I would call detail in the passage. Can you find more important information?" Palincsar and Brown, 1984, (p. 131). After feedback the teacher might again model a response and say something like, "A question I might ask would be . . ." or "I would summarize by saying . . ."

Another feature of instruction was showing the students the reason for learning to summarize, predict, ask questions, and clarify, and the importance of always doing these things when reading. The students were given weekly feedback on their improvement on comprehension test questions, which they answered every day after the practice session was over. This feedback lent credibility to the teachers' claims that the skills would help them improve comprehension.

Figure 7.18 shows the results for four classes of middle school children taught by four different teachers. The first portion of each graph (baseline) is the performance of the students prior to training. Performance was the percentage correct on comprehension questions over passages that were read silently. As you can see, all groups were averaging 50 percent or less correct before training. During the training (called "reciprocal teaching"), they gradually improved to about 80 percent or more correct. This high level of performance was maintained on the days immediately following training and also appeared on comprehension tests given eight weeks later.

The teaching method emphasized modeling followed by a great deal of practice and

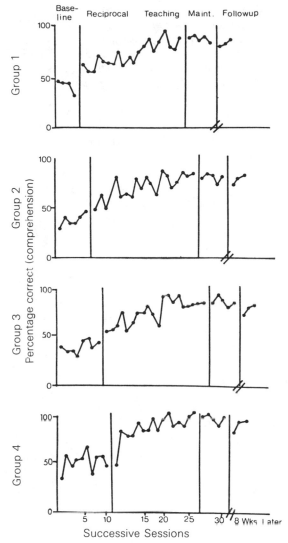

Figure 7.18. Scores on comprehension tests before, during, and after training in four classes. Maint. = maintenance after training stopped. (From Palincsar and Brown, 1984.)

informative feedback. As we discussed in Chapter 5, modeling, practice, and feedback are important conditions for learning action-sequence procedures. Another technique that was used in this study was calling attention to the reasons for learning the skill and dem-

onstrating the improvements that resulted from learning. Making students aware of why they are learning something, how it will lead to success, and when it will be useful appear to be key elements in obtaining transfer (A. Brown, 1978).

As with the Frederiksen et al. (1983) study, the Palincsar and Brown (1984) study demonstrates that significant improvements can be made by (1) identifying students who lack skills that have been shown to be possessed by more competent individuals, and (2) facilitating the learning and transfer of these skills by providing appropriate learning conditions. These are demonstration studies, not designed to test hypotheses about specific instructional variables (e.g., amount of practice). Instead they used a combination of instructional variables that had been shown in other studies to be effective. Thus, these studies demonstrate what creative teachers and instructional designers can do by combining variables in teaching important skills to individuals who lack them.

SUMMARY

Reading is an important skill for adequate functioning in society and for the greatest appreciation of life, yet many people lack this skill. The information-processing model of reading suggests that problems can occur in one or more component reading skills and there is evidence that good and poor readers differ on almost all these skills. Several lines of evidence suggest that automaticity of decoding is needed in order to carry out higher comprehension processes and that poor readers' decoding skills are not as automatic as are good readers'. Practice and feedback should increase automaticity and therefore help less skilled readers. In addition, providing support for generalization, discrimination, proceduralization, and composition of inferential comprehension skills and comprehension monitoring skills should help less skilled readers become more skillful.

ADDITIONAL READINGS

Baker, L., and A. L. Brown (1984). Metacognitive skills and reading. In D. Pearson (ed.), *Handbook of Reading Research*, pp. 353–94. Newark, Del.: International Reading Association.

Just, M. A., and P. A. Carpenter, eds. (1977). *Cognitive processes in comprehension*. Hillsdale, N.J.: Lawrence Erlbaum Associates.

Lesgold, A. M., and C. A. Perfetti, eds. (1981). *Interactive processes in reading*. Hillsdale, N.J.: Lawrence Erlbaum Associates.

Resnick, L. B., and P. A. Weaver, eds. (1979). *Theory and practice of early reading*, (Vols. 1–3). Hillsdale, N.J.: Lawrence Erlbaum Associates.

Spiro, R. J., B. C. Bruce, and W. F. Brewer, eds. (1980). *Theoretical issues in reading comprehension*. Hillsdale, N.J.: Lawrence Erlbaum Associates.

Chapter 8

Writing

SUMMARY

1. Writing can be divided into planning, translating, and reviewing. Planning can be further divided into setting goals, generating ideas, and organizing ideas.

2. In planning, skilled writers are more likely than less skilled writers to focus on the goal of communicating meaning. Less skilled writers focus on avoiding mechanical errors or on retrieving knowledge of a given topic.

3. Mature writers generate more ideas than immature writers, apparently because they have internal cues for idea generation. Immature writers are used to external (conversational) cues to continue idea production.

4. Mature writers have greater mastery over the organizational devices used to establish cohesion and coherence than have less mature writers.

5. During translation less skilled writers are thinking about spelling, grammar, and punctuation, whereas skilled writers are thinking about cohesion and communication. The less skilled writers do not appear to have spelling, grammar, and punctuation skills at an automatic level.

6. Skilled writers are more likely to recognize problems when they review their written products and are also more likely to know how to remediate these problems. They are also more likely to make meaning-related revisions than are less skilled writers.

7. Persons of equal writing skill will vary on the quality of their written products if they possess different amounts of declarative knowledge of the topic about which they are writing.

Writing is the rendering of ideas in the printed symbols of a given language. In some ways it is the opposite of reading, which is the comprehension of ideas expressed in the printed symbols of a given language. Writing serves many purposes. On the job it is an important means of communicating and recording what has been communicated. In one's personal life it is a means of expression and a technique for thinking through problems. In intellectual and political arenas writing is a powerful means of persuading others to change their ideas or to take some action. Like all other basic skills, it is liberating for the one who possesses it, and its lack restricts options.

There has been a great deal of concern over the past decade that the quality of writing of high school graduates is deteriorating. The National Assessment of Educational Progress, for example, showed a significant decline in the quality of writing for thirteen- and seventeen-year-olds between 1969 and 1974 (R. Brown, 1981). Here is a composition written by a college freshman (Perl, 1979):

> All men can't be consider equal in America base on financial situation. Because their are men born in rich families that will never have to worry about financial difficulties. And then theyre are another type of Americans that is born to a poor family. and alway may have some kind of fina—difficulty. Especially nowadays in New York city With the bugdit Crisis and all. If he is able To get a job. But are now he lose the job just as easy as he got it. So when he loses his job he'll have to try to get some fina—assistance. Then he'll probley have even more fin—diffuicuty. So right here you can't see that In America, all men are not create equal in the fin—sense.

There are obvious "mechanical" errors in this composition—errors of spelling, punctuation, and agreement. But more grievous than the mechanical errors is the fact that the essay is incoherent.

What can be done to improve students' writing? Applebee (1982) attributes the decline in writing quality to both the nature and the small quantity of writing instruction in grades 1–12. One way to increase the quantity of writing required of students is to encourage teachers in almost all subject areas and all grade levels to have students write.

In this chapter we will discuss the components of writing skill. A knowledge of these components will help teachers focus instruction on important aspects of writing that have been neglected.

A MODEL OF WRITING

In school writing usually begins when a teacher gives some students a writing assignment. Assignments vary in length, amount of originality expected, type of discourse (e.g., description or persuasion), and topic. Variations depend on the age of the student, the subject matter being studied, and the goals of instruction (see Applebee, 1982, for a description of writing tasks). Across all this variation, however, some components and dynamics of writing remain constant.

Components

Flower and Hayes (1981*a*) have proposed a model for writing, which is shown in Figure 8.1. Although this model has not been validated in its entirety, it serves as a useful outline of the components of writing skill. These include *planning, translating,* and *reviewing.* Planning refers to *setting goals* and *generating* and *organizing ideas.* Translating refers to transforming the ideas in one's head into strings of words on a piece of paper or a cathode ray screen. Reviewing refers to *evaluating* what one has written and possibly *revising* it.

According to Flower and Hayes (1981*a*), these component skills are guided by the rhetorical problem (that is, the writer's interpretation of the assignment), by the text that has been generated so far, and by the writer's declarative knowledge of the topic, the audience, and the writing process. For example, if the text produced so far does not match the writer's goals, he or she will probably revise

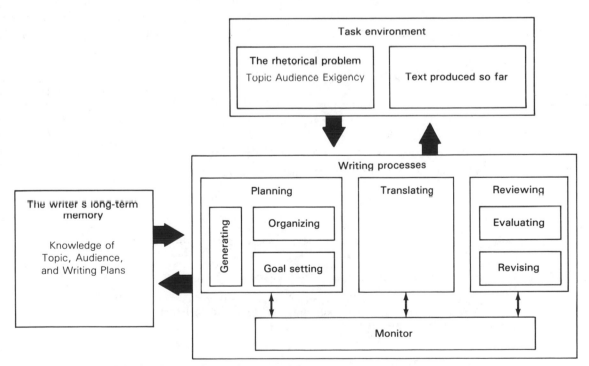

Figure 8.1. A model of writing. (From Flower and Hayes, 1981*a*.)

extensively. However, if there is a good match, revision will not be as extensive.

Dynamics

Anyone who has attempted writing knows that it does not proceed in a linear sequence from planning to translating to reviewing. Typically it starts with a brief period of pre-planning, followed by a writing phase in which all the component skills—planning, translating, and reviewing—are used. Plans made before writing may be revised or elaborated in light of what has been written. Detailed plans for achieving cohesion may be formulated during writing rather than before it. Reviewing may occur even before writing starts, as when someone thinks of an idea, then evaluates it and modifies it. Reviewing typically continues throughout writing, as when a writer stops to reread and evaluate what has been written to that point.

To get a feel for the dynamics of writing, it is useful to examine thinking-aloud protocols, collected as writers are composing. Table 8.1 shows one such protocol in which the writer, a teacher, has been asked to pretend that she is also a freelance writer. Her task is to write an article for *Seventeen* magazine describing her jobs to an audience of teenage girls. The numbers above words in the protocol indicate where the writer paused and the duration of the pause in seconds. Flower and Hayes (1981b) had judges divide this protocol into episodes defined by shifts in attention.

In episode 1 the writer reads the assignment (the words underlined twice) and reacts to it. In episode 2 she tries to solve the problem of writing about a job she is not familiar with (freelance writing). She decides to invent a formula for the job. Episode 3a involves a great deal of translation (the underlined words are those which were written down) in which the plans made in episode 2 are transformed into word strings.

Table 8.1. A thinking-aloud protocol as a writer plans and writes. Each episode has a different focus. (From Flower and Hayes, 1981b.)

Episodes in an Expert Writer's Protocol

Episode 1 — My Job²for a young²—Oh I'm to describe <u>my job for a young thirteen to fourteen year-old teenage female audience</u>—Magazine —Seventeen. -a- My immediate reaction is that it's utterly impossible. I did read Seventeen, though—I guess I wouldn't say I read it -a- I looked at it, especially the ads, so the idea would be to describe what I do to someone like myself when I read— well not like myself, but adjusted for—well twenty years later. -a- Now what I think of doing really is that—until the coffee comes I feel I can't begin, so I will shut the door and feel that I have a little bit more privacy,//

Episode 2 — -um- Also the mention of a free-lance writer is something I've —I've no experience in doing and my sense is that it's a—a formula which I'm not sure I know, so I suppose what I have to

do is -a- invent [2] what the formula might be, and—and then try
[3.8] [4.2]
to -a- try to include—events or occurrences or attitude or ex-
[3.6]
periences in my own job that would -a- that could be—that

Episode 3a could be conveyed in formula so let's see -// [2] I suppose one
would want to start—by writing something—that would -a-
attract the attention of the reader—of that reader and -a- [2] I
suppose the most interesting thing about my job would be that
it is highly unlikely that it would seem at all interesting to
someone of that age [2] —So I might start by saying something like
—Can you imagine yourself spending a day—Many days like
this—waking up at 4:30 a.m., making a pot of coffee . . .
looking around . . . my—looking around your house, letting in
your cats . . . -a- walking out—out with coffee and a book and
watching the dawn materialize . . . I actually do this . . . although
4:30's a bit early, perhaps I should say 5:30 so it won't seem—
although I do get up at 4:30 -a- watching the dawn materialize
and starting to work—to work by reading—reading the manuscript—of a Victorian writer . . . with a manuscript of a . . . a
Victorian writer . . . a person with a manuscript of a student
—Much like yourself—Much like—Much like -a- a student or
a book by Aristotle they've heard of Aristotle or—who could
I have it be by—Plato probably When it gets to be—When
you've . . . -a- finished your coffee and whatever you had to
do (Oh thanks)—whatever—now I've just gotten coffee—finished
your coffee (mumbling) . . . when you've finished your coffee
[3] [2]
and -a- foreseen—and -a- ummmmmm—when you've finished your
coffee, you dress and drive—about three miles to the university
where you spend another—where you spend—you spend hours
—you spend about—oh what—four or five—supposed to be four
hours—about three hours a day—about three hours teaching—
many more hours talking to students—talking to—talking to
[6.8]
Episode 3b other teachers . . . Um -/ should I (mumble)—the thing is
about saying teachers—the—the teenage girl is going to think
teachers like who she has, and professor I always feel is sort of
pretentious and a word usually—usually I say teacher, but I
[2] [7.6]
know that means I . . . It's unfortunate now in society we
Episode 3c don't—but that that isn't prestige occupation./ Talking to other
people like yourselves—that's whoever it may be—other people
at your job—other—other people like yourself—uh a lot like
yourself but—talking to other people like yourself—going to
meetings . . . committee meetings . . . and doing all this for nine
months so that the other three . . . and doing all this for three
months—okay—nine months . . . If you can imagine that . . .

Episode 3*b* involves more planning in light of an audience of teenage girls. The problem being addressed is how these readers will interpret *teacher* versus *professor*. Finally, episode 3*c* involves further translation activity.

In this example the tempo of writing seems to be to plan some, then write some, then plan some more, then write some more. Long pausing is often associated with the beginning of a planning episode. This protocol was produced by a fairly sophisticated adult writer. Less skilled and younger writers tend not to engage in as much planning activity. However, all writers alternate among the components of writing throughout the course of producing a written document.

INDIVIDUAL DIFFERENCES IN WRITING PROCESSES

Research shows that individuals differ in their abilities to plan, translate, and review a written product. Within planning they differ in the types of goals they set, in how they generate ideas, and in how well they organize ideas.

Goal Setting

One of the most important differences between more and less skilled writers is in the type of goals they set for themselves in writing. So far, researchers have distinguished three types of goals. The goal that is characteristic of skilled writers of any age is to communicate meaning. Another goal, which is characteristic of immature writers, occurs in what Bereiter (1980) calls "associative writing." This goal is simply to dump on paper the contents of one's memory relevant to a given topic. A third goal, which is typical of poor writers at middle, high school, and college levels, is to avoid making errors (cf. Atwell, 1981; Birnbaum, 1982; Perl, 1979).

How are writers' goals inferred? Re-searchers base their inferences on several sources of data. They use "data triangulation," which means that after collecting several types of data, they check inferences based on each type against one another. If the inferences are consistent across data types, then the researchers are fairly confident that their conclusions are correct. Usually the data are collected by giving more and less skilled writers (or older and younger writers) a writing task, letting them compose either aloud or silently and either with or without a videotape recorder, and then asking them afterward to say what was going through their minds while composing. If the subjects' verbal reports match their overt behavior (for example, pauses), these reports are considered valid.

Error Avoidance. Using this technique, Birnbaum (1982) compared skilled and less skilled writers in the fourth and seventh grades and concluded that although "less proficient writers' behaviors seemed rooted in the expectation that they conform to an externally imposed task with little meaning," more proficient writers' "processes seemed rooted in their intention to re-present meaning to self and others" (p. 253).

Also using this technique, Atwell (1981) compared ten college students who were good writers, according to standardized tests, with ten who were in a remedial writing class. She categorized the statements they made in their retrospective reports according to the level of discourse that was being heeded: structural (whole text), syntactic, word, or affect. As Table 8.2 shows, the good writers made 50 percent of their comments about the whole text (for example, whether or not they had gotten their meaning quite right), whereas only 30 percent of the remedial writers' comments were at this level. By contrast, 51 percent of the remedial writers' comments were about word choice or surface consider-

Table 8.2. Retrospective comments classified according to the level of discourse being heeded. (Adapted from Atwell, 1981.)

	GOOD WRITER	REMEDIAL WRITER
Discourse/structural	50%	30%
Word/surface	27%	51%
Syntax	14%	9%
External/affect	9%	10%

ations such as those of spelling and punctuation; only 27 percent of the good writers' comments were at this level.

Atwell (1981) also found that the good writers were more likely to interrupt writing at sentence boundaries, whereas remedial writers were more likely to interrupt writing *within* words. Table 8.3 shows these results. Atwell interpreted both sets of results as showing that the better writers were concerned with meaning or structure, whereas the less skilled writers were concerned with penmanship and the surface appearance. In other words, the good writers had the goal of conveying meaning, whereas the remedial writers had the goal of avoiding mechanical errors.

Differences in goals between more and less skilled writers has also been inferred for high school students. Stallard (1974) had

Table 8.3. Percentage of interruptions of writing that occurred at a sentence boundary, within a word, or at other places in a sentence. (Adapted from Atwell, 1981.)

	GOOD WRITER	REMEDIAL WRITER
Interrupt writing at sentence boundary	29%	21%
Interrupt writing within a word	13%	17%
Interrupt writing at other places	58%	62%

thirty twelfth graders write on a current news topic, stating their opinion. He compared the retrospective reports of fifteen skilled writers with those of fifteen randomly selected writers. The skilled writers scored at or above the ninetieth percentile on the STEP Essay Writing Test. Stallard found that 93 percent of the skilled writers versus only 53 percent of the randomly selected writers reported having thought about the purpose of their essay before starting to write. This is what one would expect if the skilled writers have the goal of conveying meaning and some of the randomly selected writers have the goal of avoiding errors. Although one needs to think ahead to convey meaning, one does not need to think ahead about avoiding mechanical errors.

Associative Writing. Whereas older poor writers do not write fluently because of their obsession with mechanics, young writers write fluently but fail to produce what adults judge to be good compositions. Young students appear to think that the goal of writing is to recall all one can about a given topic. This goal is evident in the following composition produced by a ten-year-old when asked to write on the topic "Should school children be allowed to choose their own subjects?"

> I think children should be able to choose what subjects they have in school.
> I don't think we should have to do language, and art is a bore a lot. I don't think we should do novel study every week. I really think 4s and 3s should split up for gym. I think we should do a lot of math. I don't think we should do diary. I think we should do French. (Burtis, Bereiter, Scardamalia, and Tetroe, 1983).

From an adult point of view, this young writer does not comply with the assignment. To an adult, the assignment implies that one should state an opinion and then argue in support of that opinion. In persuasive writing, skilled adult writers adopt the goal of communicating an argument to persuade the reader. This young writer states his opinion but does not support it. Rather, he lists what subjects he would like to take in school. This type of writing appears to be governed by the goal of retrieving information.

The associative writing goal of immature writers appears to be closer to the goal of communicating meaning than is avoidance of error (the goal of unskilled older writers). This is because associative writing and communicating meaning both focus on *meaning*. Associative writing, however, lacks an emphasis on *communication*. One can imagine that a teaching strategy that encourages young writers to add audience awareness to their meaning-oriented goals might rather easily move them toward the goal of communicating meaning. On the other hand, the writer with the error-avoidance goal cares neither for meaning nor for communication; hence teaching such a person to adopt meaning communication as a goal may require more extended and complex efforts than are needed for immature writers.

Idea Generation

People vary in the amount of ideas they can generate. Young children produce fewer ideas in writing than do older children. For example, when Scardamalia, Bereiter, and Goelman (1982) gave fourth- and sixth-grade children a writing assignment, the sixth graders produced an average of ninety words, whereas the fourth graders produced only fifty-seven words on the average. Average writers in high school produce shorter essays than do highly skilled writers (Stallard, 1974). In college, persons with low verbal SAT scores produce essays with fewer ideas, than do persons with average verbal SAT scores (Glynn, Britton, Muth, and Dogan, 1982).

Why do some people produce longer es-

says than others? There are probably many reasons, including differences in declarative knowledge (Voss, Vesonder, and Spilich, 1980), and differences in management of demands on working memory (Glynn, Britton, Muth, and Dogan, 1982). Another reason, that seems to account for the findings of Scardamalia et al. (1982) with young children, is that some people do not know how to cue themselves to continue writing. In particular, younger children, being more familiar with conversation than with composition, rely more on social cues to continue to produce ideas. In conversation the listener nods or gives some other cue that gives the speaker "permission" to continue. When young writers are asked to write rather than speak their ideas, they stop after very little production, not because they have run out of ideas, but because they have no cues to keep them going. More mature writers have internal cues. For example, they may continue to produce ideas as long as their ideas are cohesive. When cohesion deteriorates, this cues them to stop.

If this argument is correct, then cuing young children to write more should cause them to write more and should also lead to greater cohesiveness of what is written. That is, if children rely on external cues to continue idea generation, and if such external cues are lacking, they may stop generating ideas before the end of a cohesive chain of ideas. On the other hand, if children rely on their own internal cues, then they should continue producing ideas on their own, whether or not they are cued, until they reach the end of a cohesive chain.

Scardamalia et al. (1982) tested these speculations by cuing fourth and sixth graders to continue writing by saying, after a child appeared to be finished writing, "You're doing fine," or "Can you write some more?" Both fourth and sixth graders increased the quantity of writing following cuing. However, in terms of coherence and clarity of the product, only the fourth graders' compositions improved from the additional writing. These results support the idea that the fourth graders had ceased writing before they had completed a cohesive chain of ideas. Thus, when they were cued to continue, they completed the chain, causing the ratings of their compositions to improve.

In very young writers, then, a constraint on idea generation appears to be lack of internal cues to generate more. It would be interesting to see if teachers' modeling of a self-questioning strategy would help young children acquire such internal cues. For example, a teacher could write part of a short composition on the board, then step back and ask him- or herself out loud, "Have I finished? Do I have more to say?" and then add some more. Children viewing this process might well internalize it if they also saw that it led to an improved product.

Organization

The organization of a written product is important in communicating meaning. Readers expect organization at both local and global levels of discourse. Organization reduces the burden on working memory for the reader (recall the Kintsch and van Dijk model of reading comprehension described in Chapter 2) by grouping related ideas. It facilitates both comprehension and retrieval of information (cf. Britton, Meyer, Hodge, and Glynn, 1980). In writing, organization is communicated through cohesive ties between sentences and through a coherent structure across paragraphs.

Cohesion. An organizational skill that develops early is using cohesive ties. Cohesive ties are linguistic devices that tie one idea in a text to neighboring ideas. (For a more technical discussion of cohesion, see Halliday and Hasan, 1976.) There are several classes of cohesion, including referential, conjunctive,

and lexical. Table 8.4 shows some examples of each of these types. *Referential* cohesion uses pronouns, demonstratives, and definite articles to refer to a previously mentioned item. *Conjunctive* cohesion uses conjunctions such as *and, or* to indicate relationships between ideas. *Lexical* cohesion uses word meanings, rather than syntax, to establish ties between ideas.

Cohesive ties vary in their dependence on the reader's declarative knowledge. Ties that are signaled by syntax (referential and conjunctive ties) do not depend much on declarative knowledge. Even if a sentence had

Table 8.4. Examples of referential, conjunctive, and lexical cohesion. Referential and conjunctive cohesion use syntax to indicate ties between sentences. Lexical cohesion uses semantics (word meanings) to indicate ties.

REFERENTIAL COHESION

John went to the store. *He* bought a newspaper. (Pronominal reference)

It is important to exercise every day. *This* establishes a routine. (Demonstrative reference)

There were two boys at the game, one quite tall, the other of average height. *The* tall boy took the lead. (Definite article)

CONJUNCTIVE COHESION

Jane read about sailing *and* imagined what it would be like. (additive)

Jane read about sailing *but* she couldn't imagine what it would be like. (adversative)

Jane read about sailing *because* she was about to go on her first sailing expedition. (causal)

LEXICAL COHESION

Tony *ran* down the road. He *ran* so fast he missed the turnoff. (repetition)

Tony *sped* down the road. He *ran* so fast he missed the turnoff. (synonyms)

There are several *swimming strokes*. In the *crawl stoke*, the flutter kick is used. (superordinate)

Sandra was *starting at a new school*. She went to the *principal's office* to get her *class schedule*. Then she went to her *homeroom* where the *teacher introduced her to the class*. (collocation)

nonsense words in it, referential and conjunctive ties would signal the relationships between the nonsense words. For example, "The jix fimed, but the sowel exclated," signals that *jix* and *sowel* have been previously referred to (otherwise "*a* jix" and "*a* sowel" would have been used). Also, *but* signals a contrast between what the jix did and what the sowel did.

Lexical ties always depend on the reader's declarative knowledge of word meanings and facts. For example, a synonym of a previously used word is used to indicate that the same topic is still being discussed. In collocation a reader without an organized knowledge structure (schema) may be at a disadvantage. Consider the example of collocation shown in Table 8.4. A person (say someone from a nonliterate culture) who does not have a "first-day-at-new-school" schema would fail to understand the relationship between going to the principal's office and getting a class schedule or between going to a homeroom and being introduced. The sequence of events would seem arbitrary for such an individual. However, for most people in literate cultures, the description is cohesive, because the lexical items occur in a predictable order.

Young writers have difficulty writing cohesively. One mistake they make, apparently as a carryover from oral language, is to assume that the reader knows what is being referred to even if the referent has never been specified. Here, for example, are three sentences written by a kindergartener, along with their translations (King and Rentel, 1981):

Kindergartener's Sentences	Translations
I like Hm	I like him.
Day maj	He did magic.
He jagdo	He juggled.

The referent for "him" and "he" in these sentences is never given. The child seems to assume that the reader will know that she is referring to a juggler she has just seen. King and Rentel found that for kindergarteners and first graders, 34 percent of all attempts at cohesive ties made did not specify the referent. By second grade, however, nonspecified referents were down to 5 percent.

Nonetheless, problems using cohesive ties in a clear way continue throughout the school years. For example, Collins and Williamson (1981) found that weak essays in grades 4, 8, and 12 failed to specify referents twice as often as did strong essays. Looking at all types of cohesion (not just referential cohesion), McCutchen and Perfetti (1982) found that the percentages of unsuccessful cohesive ties were 51, 38, 13, and 18, respectively, in grades 2, 4, 6, and 8.

In college the liberal use of successful cohesive ties results in a higher-quality product. Witte and Faigley (1981) had ninety freshmen write on "Changes in behavior." They then compared the cohesiveness of the five top-rated essays and the five lowest-rated essays. In the best essays 32 percent of the words contributed to explicit cohesive ties, whereas only 20 percent of the words in the worst essays contributed to cohesion. The best essays contained more of almost every type of cohesive tie and a greater variety of subtypes as well. One exception to this finding was that the worst essays contained more cohesive ties that were established by word repetition than did the best essays. Perhaps this is because word repetition, although establishing cohesion, makes for uninteresting reading.

The top-rated essays used collocation three times as often as the lowest-rated essays. This finding suggests that the writers of the best essays may have had more knowledge about the topic than did the writers of the poor essays. For example, students who had taken a high school course in psychology might have some psychology schemas about changes in behavior that could allow for collocation as a cohesive device, whereas students who lacked such schemas would not have this source of help. Although we do not know exactly how organizational processes interact with schemas, it makes sense that processes dependent on schemas as input would fail to operate when such input is lacking. Whatever the cause of the differences, however, it is clear that writers of poor essays use fewer cohesive ties than do writers of good essays.

Coherence. The use of cohesive ties establishes organization at the sentence level. At the level of an entire text, coherent structures create organization. By coherence is meant the degree to which an entire piece of writing fits together in an organized way.

One example of variation in coherence is shown in the essays in Figures 8.2 and 8.3. These were written in response to the assignment to write an essay that begins with the sentence: "There are many things about ___ that make it fun and exciting," and that ends with the sentence: "So while _____ can be fun, there are those dangers that we must watch out for so that the fun is not spoiled." The topic filling in the blank was selected by the student.

The essay diagrammed in Figure 8.2 is more coherent than the one in Figure 8.3 because the overall structure of the text is

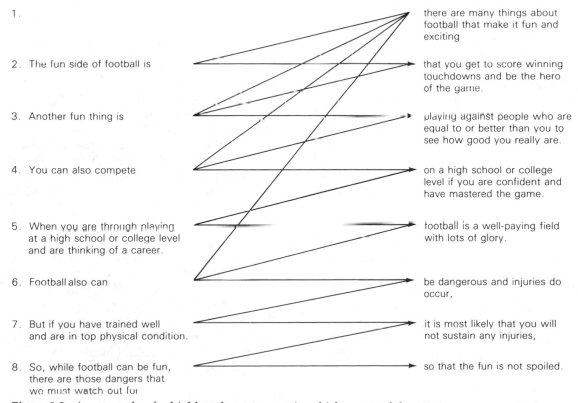

1.

2. The fun side of football is

3. Another fun thing is

4. You can also compete

5. When you are through playing at a high school or college level and are thinking of a career.

6. Football also can

7. But if you have trained well and are in top physical condition.

8. So, while football can be fun, there are those dangers that we must watch out for

there are many things about football that make it fun and exciting

that you get to score winning touchdowns and be the hero of the game.

playing against people who are equal to or better than you to see how good you really are.

on a high school or college level if you are confident and have mastered the game.

football is a well-paying field with lots of glory.

be dangerous and injuries do occur,

it is most likely that you will not sustain any injuries,

so that the fun is not spoiled.

Figure 8.2. An example of a highly coherent essay in which many of the sentences relate back to both the previous and the topic sentences. (From McCutchen and Perfetti, 1982.)

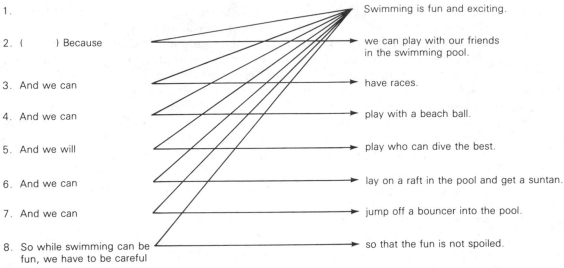

1.

2. ( ) Because

3. And we can

4. And we can

5. And we will

6. And we can

7. And we can

8. So while swimming can be
fun, we have to be careful

Swimming is fun and exciting.

we can play with our friends
in the swimming pool.

have races.

play with a beach ball.

play who can dive the best.

lay on a raft in the pool and get a suntan.

jump off a bouncer into the pool.

so that the fun is not spoiled.

Figure 8.3. An essay that is less coherent than the essay shown in Figure 8.2 because each sentence refers back to the topic sentence only (and not to the previous sentence). (From McCutchen and Perfetti, 1982.)

tighter. The tightness is due to the fact that most of the sentences have ties to both the previous sentence and the topic sentence, as is indicated by the arrows going from ideas in the left column to ideas in the right column. Most of the sentences in the less coherent essay have ties only to the topic sentence.

Just as there are developmental differences in the establishment of cohesion, so are there developmental differences in the establishment of coherence. McCutchen and Perfetti (1982) found that only 44 percent of fourth graders' essays had the tighter structure shown in Figure 8.2, whereas 67 percent and 60 percent of sixth and eighth graders' essays, respectively, were tighter in form.

Mastery over coherent form varies with the subject matter and function of writing. Applebee, Durst, and Newell (1984) studied coherence of writing among high school students in "summary" and "analysis" passages written in science and social science classes. A summary passage was one that

provided a generic description of a recurrent pattern of events. An analysis passage provided a "generalization or classification related to a situation, problem, or theme, with logical or hierarchical relationships among generalizations implicit or explicit."

The coherence scores for student essays were compared with scores given to typical science and social science textbooks. As can be seen in Table 8.5 there is no substantial difference between textbooks' and students' summaries in either the social sciences or sciences; nor is there much of a difference for analyses in the social sciences. However, the textbook analysis passages in science were much more coherent than the student analysis passages.

Figure 8.4 shows coherence graphs for an analysis passage from a typical science textbook and from a typical science student. The textbook passage has symmetry in describing two alternative types of trees, but the student's passage shows extreme lack of symmetry. The student's passage starts out by

Table 8.5. Average coherence scores for textbook and student passages of two forms (summary and analysis) in the social sciences and sciences. (From Applebee, Durst, and Newell, 1984.)

	TEXTBOOKS		STUDENTS	
	SUMMARY	ANALYSIS	SUMMARY	ANALYSIS
Social science	72.9	72.9	60.0	61.0
Science	67.2	69.3	69.4	37.9

stating that two alternative types of engines will be discussed, but only one is described in any detail.

Thus, at times, students have difficulty writing in a coherent, organized fashion. This may be due to their lack of procedural knowledge about how to create an organization or to their lack of declarative knowledge from which an organization can be created. Later in this chapter we will see how declarative knowledge influences coherence. For the moment let us consider some specific procedural knowledge that might be useful in generating coherent text.

McCutchen and Perfetti (1982) argue that to generate coherent text one must satisfy several constraints at once and it is the satisfaction of all constraints that leads to the structure of the text fitting together. For example, their subjects were asked to satisfy the following constraints in the compositions they were writing:

1. The topic must be something that is fun.

2. The topic must also be something that is dangerous.

3. Enough must be known about the fun and dangerous components of the topic to support the claims that it is fun and dangerous.

Once the subjects had identified such a topic in their memory, they could produce a coherent text by writing down the contents of memory in a specified order. Thus, the important procedural knowledge is recognition of all constraints. Fourth graders were not able to write as coherent a text as sixth and eighth graders because their procedures were not as complete.

The difference in procedural knowledge just described can be expressed in production system terms. Production systems for a typical fourth grader and a typical eighth grader are shown in Table 8.6. The differences begin with how they represent the assignment. The fourth grader represents the goal as one of arguing that a given topic has a given property (P_1). To do this, he or she must search for a topic that has the property and also has enough components with the property for supporting arguments to be presented (P_2). Once an area of knowledge is identified that satisfies these constraints, the relevant propositions are tagged (P_2) and the tags are used to guide the process of translating ideas into written form (P_3).

Eighth graders' procedural knowledge is more elaborate. It has two parts (to argue that a topic has one property and to argue that it also has a contrasting property). To meet the two-part goal, eighth graders must search their memory for a topic that satisfies four, rather than the fourth grader's two, constraints: the topic must have property A, some components that have property A, property B, and some components that have property B (P_5). The relevant propositions are tagged (P_5) and form the basis of writing (P_3).

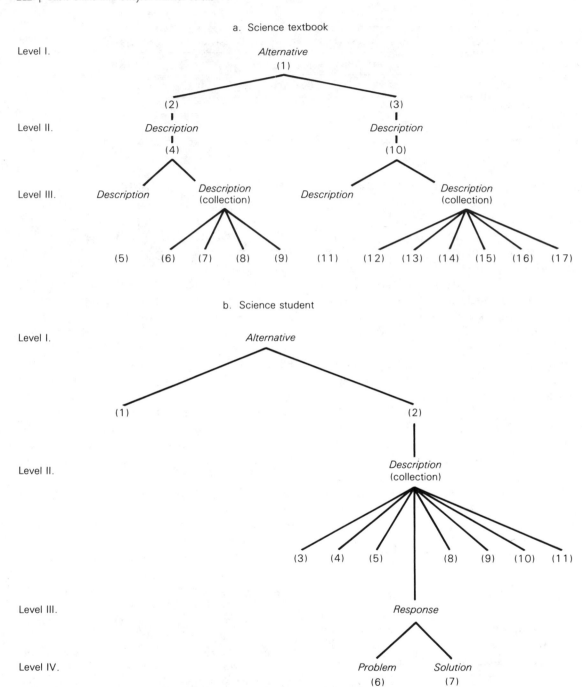

Figure 8.4. The structure of two analysis passages, both starting with an alternative argument. The top passage, from a science text, has a much more balanced structure than does the bottom passage, written by a student. (Adapted from Applebee, Durst, and Newell, 1984.)

Table 8.6. Production systems for fourth- and eighth-grade text generation.

FOURTH GRADE

P_1 IF GOAL is to argue that TOPIC has PROPERTY A
THEN Set SUBGOAL to search memory for TOPIC that has PROPERTY A and COMPONENTS.

P_2 IF SUBGOAL is to search memory for TOPIC that has PROPERTY A and COMPONENTS.
THEN Identify NODE that has PROPERTY A and two or more COMPONENTS
And tag the proposition that NODE has PROPERTY A as SENTENCE 1
And tag the proposition that COMPONENT 1 has PROPERTY A as SENTENCE 2
And tag the proposition that COMPONENT 2 has PROPERTY A as SENTENCE 3
And set SUBGOAL to write ARGUMENT.

P_3 IF SUBGOAL is to write ARGUMENT
And propositions tagged as sentences exist
THEN Write SENTENCES 1–N.

EIGHTH GRADE

P_4 IF GOAL is to argue that TOPIC has PROPERTY A but also has PROPERTY B
THEN Set SUBGOAL to search memory for TOPIC that has PROPERTY A and COMPONENTS with PROPERTY A and has PROPERTY B and COMPONENTS with PROPERTY B.

P_5 IF SUBGOAL is to search memory for TOPIC that has PROPERTY A and COMPONENTS with PROPERTY A and has PROPERTY B and COMPONENTS with PROPERTY B
THEN Identify NODE that has PROPERTY A and two or more COMPONENTS
Identify NODE that has PROPERTY B and two or more COMPONENTS
Tag the proposition that NODE has PROPERTY A as SENTENCE 1
Tag the proposition that COMPONENT 1 has PROPERTY A as SENTENCE 2
Tag the proposition that COMPONENT 2 has PROPERTY A as SENTENCE 3
Tag the proposition that NODE has PROPERTY B as SENTENCE 4
Tag the proposition that COMPONENT 3 has PROPERTY B as SENTENCE 5
Tag the proposition that COMPONENT 4 has PROPERTY B as SENTENCE 6
And set SUBGOAL to write ARGUMENT.

P_3 IF SUBGOAL is to write ARGUMENT
And propositions tagged as sentences exist
THEN Write SENTENCES 1–N.

McCutchen and Perfetti (1982) tested their model of procedural knowledge differences by comparing the output of a computer simulation with the performance of elementary school children. They put into the computer the declarative knowledge representation shown in Figure 8.5. Then they ran a simulation using the model of fourth graders' procedural knowledge, which ignores some constraints, and another simulation using the model of eighth graders' procedural knowledge. (You may wish to think through the simulation by predicting how the production systems shown in Table 8.6 would operate on the knowledge structure shown in Figure 8.5). The fourth-grade model produced a text with the listlike structure exemplified in Figure 8.3, whereas the eighth-grade model produced a text with the zigzag structure exemplified in Figure 8.2.

An interesting aspect of this model is that the same declarative knowledge representation resulted in qualitatively different essays because of procedural knowledge differ-

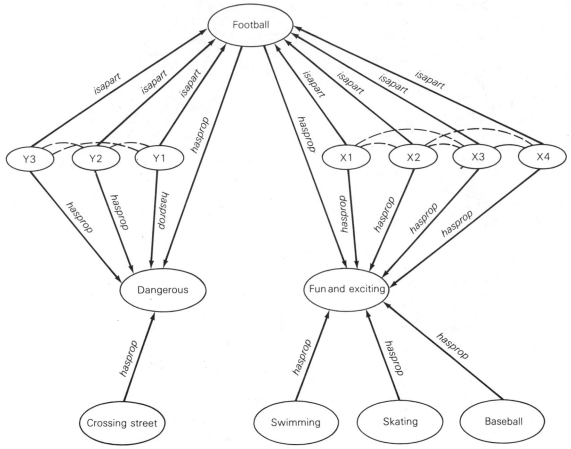

Figure 8.5. Declarative knowledge available to the computer in a simulation of writing skill. (From McCutchen and Perfetti, 1982.)

ences. This suggests that at least sometimes the individual differences we observe in the coherence of writing are due to variations in procedural knowledge. Specifically, the variations are in the differentiation of the writing goal, which in turn affects the number of constraints imposed on the memory search.

In summary, good and/or mature writers are more successful at organizing their ideas both in sentences and whole texts. We do not know yet what mental representations and processes underlie differences in organization. One possibility is that a more differen-

tiated goal representation and more constrained memory search affect organization, but much more research needs to be done before this possibility or others are validated.

Translation

Translation involves the actual generation of text. It starts from a mental representation and ends with words on paper or in a computer file. The mental representation may be a goal and an organized plan for meeting that goal, or it may be a single idea. Whatever it is, it is assumed to be represented in either propositional or image form in working memory. Since such forms do not carry the details of spelling, punctuation, and grammar demanded by the conventions of written language, translation involves many operations that fill in these details.

Translation can stretch working memory's capacity to its limits. The writer is typically trying to keep many things active in memory at once: the goals and plans for the text, ideas for content, and memory for what has just been written (so that cohesive ties can be established). Just as automatic decoding skills help substantially in reading, so too automatic skills help a great deal in writing. In reading, automatic decoding allows more attention to be devoted to comprehension. In writing, the abilities to spell and punctuate automatically allow for more attention to be devoted to cohesion and coherence. Younger and/or less skilled writers have to pay attention to activities that, for older and/or more skilled writers, are automatic.

Attention to Motor Skills. The most basic set of skills to be composed in writing are the motor skills of holding a pencil and forming letters with it on paper. Children in early elementary school grades mouth each word as it is written, suggesting that their motor skills require a great deal of attention. After about third grade, however, this behavior disappears, suggesting that by third grade most children have automatic control over the motor aspects of writing.

Attention to Mechanics. Several studies suggest that unskilled writers pay more attention to spelling, grammar, and punctuation while they are translating than do skilled writers (Atwell, 1981; Birnbaum, 1982; Pianko, 1979). Pianko, for example, found that remedial college writers spent more time

writing each word than average college writers and, when asked what they were thinking about during writing, the majority reported thinking about spelling, punctuation, or word choice. The average writers wrote faster, suggesting that they were not consciously spelling out most words as they wrote them. Also, the majority of average writers reported paying attention to style and purpose during pauses in writing. In a previous section, data like these were interpreted as indicating that unskilled writers have a different goal (avoiding errors) than do skilled writers (communicating meaning). These data may also mean that unskilled writers must attend to mechanics because these skills are not yet composed. Further research is needed before the reason for verbal report differences can be identified.

External Support for Writing Cohesively. Cohesiveness of ideas may be established or refined during translation. For less skilled writers, the ability to maintain cohesion during writing is quite fragile. This was demonstrated by Atwell (1981). Atwell had more and less skilled college writers write a personal essay. For the first half of the writing session the students could see what they had written; however, for the second half they used inkless pens. What they wrote was recorded by means of carbon paper, but they were blind to it.

Writing blind caused the compositions of the less skilled writers to lose cohesion, but it had little effect on the cohesiveness of skilled writers. This result is illustrated in Figure 8.6, which shows the propositional structure of a typical essay from the skilled (top of figure) and less skilled groups. Each circle denotes a proposition, and the lines between circles indicate relationships between propositions. The more lines interconnecting circles, the greater the cohesiveness of the essay. The left half of the figure shows the part of

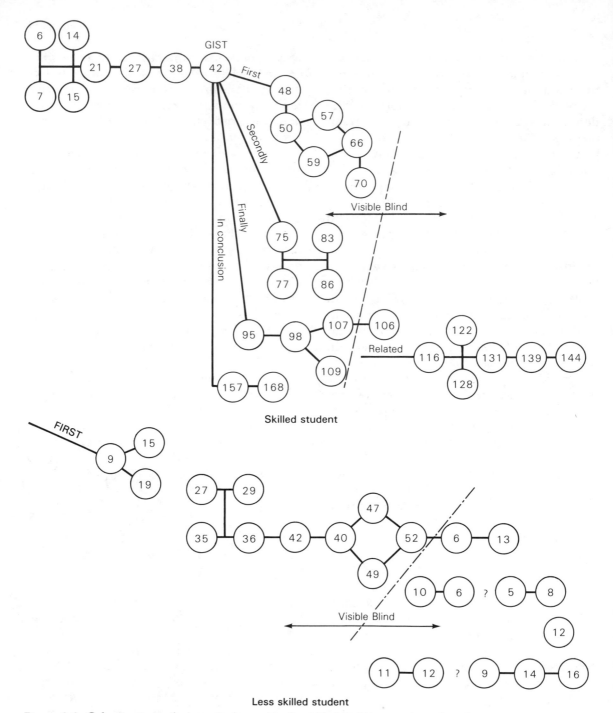

Figure 8.6. Cohesiveness of essays before and after blind writing was introduced. Circles indicate propositions and lines indicate relations between propositions. After blind writing was introduced, the cohesion of the less skilled writer's essay (bottom of figure) deteriorated. (From Atwell, 1981.)

the composition written before writing became blind. Both compositions show cohesiveness there. However, after the blind writing was introduced (right half), cohesion in the less skilled writer's composition breaks down dramatically.

These data demonstrate that less skilled writers need to read what they have just written if they are to maintain cohesion. Skilled writers do not depend as much on this external support. The reason for this difference is unknown. Perhaps skilled writers generate cohesive text because they have cohesive plans. Or, because they spell and punctuate automatically, they have more room in working memory to keep active what they have just written. They can thus use this active residue to decide what cohesive ties must be generated. Less skilled writers, because they must take up space in working memory to make decisions about mechanics, lose their representation of what they have just said. Normally they can look back to see what they have written, but in blind writing they no longer have this external cue.

In summary, although the details of the events of translation are not well known, it is clearly a time when a writer's possession of automatic skills can come in handy. In particular, composition of motor skills, spelling, punctuation, and grammar seem to free writers to attend to larger issues such as cohesion, coherence, and purpose.

Writer's Block. Other obstacles to translation are getting started and keeping going. At one time or another almost everyone experiences difficulty getting started with a writing task or completing the task. Sometimes the ''block'' is due to a need for more knowledge of the topic, in which case more information gathering should alleviate the problem.

Another source of writer's block is the rules of thumb that writers acquire to guide their writing. Rose (1980) compared five college students who often experienced writer's block with five who wrote more easily. The students were equivalent in general ability and writing skill. Rose asked the students to report retrospectively what they were thinking while writing. The students who experienced writer's block were using rigid rules (given to them by teachers) to guide their behavior. One, for example, was guided by the rule that a good essay always grabs the reader's attention immediately. With this rule in mind, she had trouble going beyond the first sentence! Another student was using the rule ''You must always make three or more points in an essay, or it won't be a strong essay.'' When that student had one point to make and elaborate, he felt defeated. Using rules like these can understandably lead to writer's block, since many essays will not fit such exacting standards.

The students who wrote easily used rules that facilitated, rather than blocked, the writing process, such as ''When stuck, write.'' Also, the rules they used were not stated in such absolute terms—for example, ''*Try* to keep your audience in mind'' is less absolute than ''*You must* keep your audience in mind.'' These findings suggest that teachers should think carefully about the rules they explicitly give to students.

Reviewing

Reviewing consists of evaluating what has been written to determine how well it meets one's goals and then remediating unsatisfactory parts of the product.

Young Children's Reviewing Processes. During the elementary school years, children first become proficient at recognizing that their writing has problems (evaluating) and then later at remediating (revising) such problems. Table 8.7, for example, shows data from a study in which children wrote a composition

Table 8.7. Percentages of children correctly evaluating and revising their compositions as a function of grade level. (Adapted from Scardamalia and Bereiter, 1983.)

	APPROPRIATE EVALUATION	INAPPROPRIATE EVALUATION
Grade 4	85%	15%
Grade 6	93%	7%
Grade 8	100%	0%

	APPROPRIATE REVISION	INAPPROPRIATE REVISION
Grade 4	23%	77%
Grade 6	47%	53%
Grade 8	64%	36%

and were asked to evaluate and remediate each sentence as they went along (Scardamalia and Bereiter, 1983). The evaluations and the success of the revision strategies were then judged by expert adult writers. Table 8.7 shows that even fourth graders are fairly good at recognizing when something is wrong (85 percent success rate). However, only older elementary school children are predictably successful at revising the problem they have recognized. Over 70 percent of the time fourth graders do not successfully remediate problems they recognize. Table 8.8 shows a

Table 8.8. Percentage of children correctly evaluating and revising ambiguous references in text. (Adapted from E. J. Bartlett, 1982.)

	ABOVE-AVERAGE WRITERS	BELOW-AVERAGE WRITERS
Correct evaluation		
Grade 5	62%	37%
Grade 6	72%	57%
Grade 7	75%	59%
Correct revision		
Grade 5	17%	6%
Grade 6	32%	17%
Grade 7	36%	21%

similar pattern of results for evaluating and revising ambiguous references in text (E. J. Bartlett, 1982).

This developmental sequence in reviewing is reminiscent of the developmental sequence in comprehension monitoring described in Chapter 7. Recall that for comprehension monitoring, the youngest children did not even recognize that they had not understood something. Slightly older children realized they were not understanding but did not know what to do about it. Still older children could both recognize and remediate comprehension problems. This correspondence in development of reading and writing skills is expected, since much of the procedural knowledge involved in language processing should apply equally well whether one is receiving or generating language.

High School and Adult Reviewing Processes. Like young writers, some unskilled older writers fail to recognize problems in what they have written. Perl (1979) had five unskilled college writers think aloud while composing. By comparing what was said with what was written, Perl could identify incidences of reading something that had not actually been written—for example, reading one word when another word had been written or reading a correct word ending when the ending had been left off in the written product. The discrepancies strikingly correlated with the number of unresolved problems in the compositions, suggesting that the problems remained unresolved not because of lack of strategies to resolve them but because of the writer's failure to recognize their existence.

The types of problem that skilled and less skilled writers focus on when they review differ in the same way that their goals differ. Stallard (1974) compared the writing behavior of fifteen high school seniors who scored in the ninetieth percentile on a standardized writing test with that of fifteen randomly selected seniors. Of the revisions made by the top group 82 percent were revisions in meaning rather than mechanics, whereas only 41 percent of the revisions made by the randomly selected group were for meaning. Bridwell (1980) found a similar result.

One type of revision that is strikingly absent from the writing of less skilled writers is that which alters the structure of an entire essay. Faigley and Witte (1981) found that the frequency of such changes was only about one per 1000 words among remedial college writers, whereas among skilled college writers and professional writers the frequency of such changes was about twenty per 1000 words.

Thus, less skilled writers are deficient in rereading carefully enough to identify problems and, the problems they do find are mechanical. Skilled writers make more meaning-related revisions.

Quantity of Revision. One might expect skilled writers to revise more than unskilled writers. This persistence in revision would then account for the higher quality of the product. On the other hand, one might expect that less skilled writers revise more because they make more errors that need to be remediated. In fact, neither of these expectations is consistently supported by experimental data

Stallard (1974) had his high school subjects write a persuasive essay, defending their position on a current news topic. His top writers made an average of 12.24 revisions, whereas his randomly selected writers made an average of 4.26 revisions. These data suggest that good writers revise more. However, Bridwell (1980) found no relationship between number of revisions and quality of descriptive essays written by high school students. Perhaps descriptive essays on familiar topics are easier to write, and under

such conditions good writers do not revise more than poor writers. However, when the topic is less familiar or the task more demanding, they may revise more.

Thus, it seems that sometimes skilled writers revise more than less skilled writers and sometimes there is no difference in the amount of revision. However, less skilled writers do not seem to revise more than skilled writers. For students who think that revision is a sign of lack of skill, it might be useful to inform them that there is no evidence to support this idea.

DO ARCHITECTURAL DIFFERENCES AFFECT WRITING PROCESSES?

As we discussed in Chapter 2, the human information-processing system has a basic architecture within which learning takes place. Architecture is analogous to hardware in computer systems. It includes a long-term memory store, receptors, effectors, and, most crucial, a limited-capacity, short-duration working memory.

There is a great deal of evidence from digit span tasks that from birth to about age fifteen, working memory capacity seems to increase. Three-year-olds, for example, typically can only remember one digit long enough to repeat it back to you, whereas seven-year-olds can remember three or four digits, and people above age fifteen can remember about seven digits. It is not yet clear whether this developmental sequence reflects maturation of the nervous system, in which case it would be an age-related difference in architecture, or increased strategic knowledge of how to manage one's own memory, by grouping or rehearsing, for example. Quite possibly, both maturation and learning contribute to increases in working memory's capacity.

Assuming for the moment that architecture differences exist, what effect might these have on writing? Because writing, like reading, seems sometimes to stretch the limits of working memory, one might predict that the size of working memory would be correlated with writing success. This prediction was tested by Tetroe (1984). Tetroe measured her subjects' working-memory capacity using a memory-for-digits test. She then had her subjects write narratives for which the final sentence was given. The final sentences varied as to the number of constraints they imposed (for example, the sentence "That's how Melissa came to be at the laundromat with a million dollars in her laundry bag" has two constraints). Her data, shown in Figure 8.7, show that subjects were most successful at meeting all constraints when the number of constraints matched their WM capacity.

It is important to be careful in interpreting this finding. One interpretation is that individuals have a fixed WM capacity that determines, or at least limits, their writing ability. Such an interpretation can be used to justify giving up trying to teach an individual how to write.

Neither the interpretation nor the decision it is used to justify are necessarily warranted. There are other interpretations of Tetroe's findings (cf. Case, 1978; Chi, 1978). For example, the ability to group numbers in a memory-for-digits task may develop in tandem with the ability to group constraints in a writing task. Grouping leads to better memory for digits and better memory for constraints. Even if Tetroe's findings do show architecture differences in the human information-processing system, this does not justify giving up in trying to teach an individual. Rather, it challenges the teacher to work within limitations that have been identified. If WM capacity appears to be a problem, one might use external memory supports such as outlines or notes.

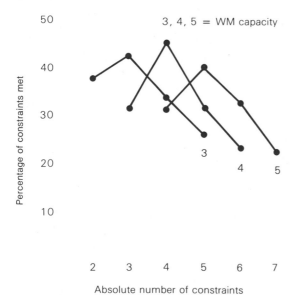

Figure 8.7. The relationship between WM capacity and number of constraints met in a writing task. The most constraints were met when this number matched the individual's WM capacity. (Adapted from Tetroe, 1984).

DO DECLARATIVE KNOWLEDGE DIFFERENCES INFLUENCE WRITING?

Recall the study by Spilich, Vesonder, Chiesi, and Voss (1979) described in Chapter 7, in which it was found that readers of the same skill level differed in their comprehension of a passage about baseball, depending on how much general knowledge about baseball they possessed. Those with much knowledge recalled more from the new passage than did low-knowledge individuals. It seems reasonable to suppose that a similar phenomenon might occur in the domain of writing. That is, people of the same skill level, but with differing amounts of declarative knowledge about the topic of an essay, should produce essays of differing quality.

Voss, Vesonder, and Spilich (1980) examined this hypothesis using college students of equal verbal ability but with different levels of knowledge about baseball. They asked these students to write a fictional account of half an inning of baseball. One result was that the task representation of high- and low-knowledge individuals differed somewhat. All the high-knowledge people successfully complied with the task, but only seven of the ten low-knowledge people did. Of the three who were not successful, one wrote about cricket, one wrote about less than half an inning, and one wrote about more than half an inning. Thus their lack of knowledge led to a misrepresentation of the task.

The compositions of the successful students were analyzed into propositions and then each proposition was categorized as being about (1) the setting, (2) significant states of the ball game, (3) game actions, (4) auxiliary actions, (5) relevant nongame actions, and (6) irrelevant nongame actions. Game actions were major events in the game that produced changes in the state of the game. For example, "The batter hit a ground ball" is a game action because it changes the status of the game. Auxiliary actions elaborated the game actions. For example, "The batter hit a ground ball that went between the third baseman and the bag and rolled down the left-field line," contains two auxiliary actions about where the ball went. Relevant nongame actions were relevant to the game but did not change the game state (e.g., "the catcher signaled the pitcher"). Irrelevant nongame actions were such things as descriptions of what the fans were doing.

The results of this analysis are shown in Table 8.9. High- and low-knowledge students did not differ in the proportion of setting, significant states, and game action statements written. However, the high-knowledge compositions contained a higher proportion of auxiliary actions (.39 for high knowledge versus .22 for low knowledge) and the low-knowledge compositions contained a higher proportion of irrelevant non-

Table 8.9. Proportion of types of statements written by high- and low-knowledge individuals. (Adapted from Voss, Vesonder, and Spilich, 1980.)

	PROPORTION OF PROPOSITIONS IN CATEGORY	
	HIGH KNOWLEDGE	LOW KNOWLEDGE
Setting	.30	.25
Significant states	.09	.16
Game actions	.10	.09
Auxiliary actions	.39	.22
Relevant nongame	.04	.03
Irrelevant nongame	.08	.24

game actions (.24 for low knowledge versus .08 for high knowledge). Since auxiliary actions provide elaborative detail (whereas irrelevant actions shift the topic), high-knowledge students' compositions were probably more cohesive and coherent than were those of the low-knowledge students.

It seems, then, that declarative knowledge not only affects the quality of the meaning representation developed in a comprehension task; it also affects the quality of production in a writing task. Inadequate declarative knowledge clearly constrains the effectiveness of procedural knowledge.

INSTRUCTION

So far in this chapter, we have seen that people may differ in many ways in writing skill; such as control of mechanics, goals for writing, and focus during revision. They may also differ in possession, access, and organization of relevant knowledge. Writing is not unique in its complexity. We have seen equal complexity in reading, and we will see it again in mathematics. However, since writing is not always included in the core curriculum, variation in writing skill within a group of grade-

and ability-level peers may be greater than variation in reading or math skill. Therefore, a major problem in writing instruction is how to handle variation.

Conferencing

"Conferencing" refers to a type of writing instruction that includes, as an important component, conferences between the teacher and each student (Duke, 1975). The focus of these conferences is the quality of the student's written product, the processes used by the student, and the relationship between process and product. The teacher questions the student on these topics and gives verbal reinforcement for ideas, expressed by the student, that the teacher wishes to encourage. For example, the following is a verbatim transcript of part of a conference between a teacher and a freshman composition student (Freedman and Swanson-Owens, 1983). The student (S) is reading aloud to the teacher (T) a composition that he has written about bus transportation at the university. The teacher has invited him to stop at any point during reading to comment on both strengths and weaknesses of the composition:

S: [Student finishes reading his paragraph.] That was the second paragraph. It might be a little short in development.

T: Can you think of anything offhand that you would want to develop more. Or, as you read it, when you say, oh, I've left the reader hanging?

S: I think it just touches very lightly on each of the things like too many buses and going one route, and it doesn't say anything about express buses and having and not having enough express buses, and, uh, yeah [unclear]

T: Do you see any other places for development?

S: [long pause] Why the people are discour-

aged when taking the bus cause of the time.

T: How would you develop that?

S: Uh, examples. How long people have to wait and, uh, and how far they have to go to their bus stop, whatever, allowing for transfers and stops.

T: Great, good.

S: And I had those in my one of my drafts, I think, but, uh, I thought I would get overdevelopment. It wouldn't develop the topic sentence if I used all that. (p. 23)

As you can see in the last statement made by the teacher, she strongly praises the student's generation of ideas for how to improve on his written product. The praise informs the student both that the thinking processes he is going through (self-evaluation and remediation) and the details he comes up with to develop his ideas are good. Because feedback is provided when the processes occurred, the student learns the processes. Typically, feedback on compositions occurs long after the thinking process and is thus less likely to be informative.

Besides allowing for immediate feedback on composing processes, conferencing allows the teacher to raise questions or give "mini-lectures" to help the student consider alternative writing strategies. For example, in one conference studied by Freedman (1981), the following exchange took place:

S: See I saw a lot of things when I was doing the rewrite. But I just couldn't put it down into words.

T: Um, that's interesting. Did you make any, uhm kind of outline on the side trying to get your ideas plugged into an organization? (p. 83)

If this student has never tried using an outline or other organizational strategy during revision, the teacher's suggestion may stimulate her to try it. Since instruction in conferences depends on the learner's needs, it is likely to be heeded.

Conferencing is often combined with classroom instruction on rhetoric and composition, reading of a rhetoric text, writing essays, and receiving peer evaluation of essays in addition to teacher and self-evaluation. If teachers do not have time for out-of-class conferences, they may conduct them during class time while the other students are engaged in in-class writing or peer-group conferences. Conferencing has been used successfully in elementary schools (Graves, 1982), as well as high schools and colleges, for writing in social science, science, and math classes (cf. Healy, 1981; Marshall, 1984) not just in English classes.

How does this technique help solve the problem of individualization? It does so by helping both the student and teacher focus on problems that are unique to that student. When the student recognizes a problem, he or she can then seek solutions from the available instructional resources—text, lectures, feedback from peers, and feedback from the teacher. The conference thus sensitizes the student to personal objectives and encourages him or her to work toward those objectives throughout the course.

One example of this instructional process can be seen in what happened to "Cee," a freshman studied by Freedman and her student (Freedman, 1981; Freedman, 1982; Freedman and Swanson-Owens, 1983). Several changes in Cee's writing and writing behavior occurred during the semester in which she took freshman composition from a teacher who was skilled in conferencing. First, the quality of her writing improved. Two of Cee's compositions, one from the beginning of the semester and one from the end, are shown in the appendix at the end of this chapter. Although the essay written late in the semester has some problems, including a change of focus between paragraphs 3

and 4, it is far more substantial than the essay written at the beginning of the semester.

Cee's self-evaluation also changed. Early in the semester only one-third of the comments she made during conferences were on the organization and development of her essays. The rest were on mechanics and sentence structure. Late in the semester, however, all of her comments were on organization and development. A final change that was observed was in the extensiveness of Cee's revisions. She spent more time revising at the end of the semester and made many more changes.

Exactly what happened to produce these changes is not clear, but there are hints in the data provided by Freedman on what the teacher did during her conferences with Cee. First, the teacher responded to Cee's concerns about mechanics either neutrally or negatively. A neutral response was one in which she answered Cee's direct question, but did not evaluate Cee's writing in any way. A negative response was one in which the teacher shifted the discussion away from the topic of grammar or spelling that had been raised by Cee. Positive responses occurred when Cee focused on discourse level concerns, as the following example illustrates:

T: Any other things that offhand you think make the paper good or bad?
S: Let's see. Yeah, I know there was sup posed to be um, one of those things— comma, not a comma . . .
T: Apostrophe?
S: Apostrophe there. And I had a hard time trying to keep track. Uh, I can't think of a correct word for it, but like sometimes I read, go back and say "businesswoman," and then I go on and say "they" when it should have been like "her," so I had to write everything back to plural—to the plural form . . . And let's see . . . And you mentioned something yesterday about

how the last paragraph should come together. What I was saying like in the first paragraph of my thesis that it should end with the . . . well, come to a conclusion of what I said earlier. And, I felt that this last paragraph here wasn't what I said up here. And I wasn't too sure about this ''male species believe that women, especially ones with children devote more of their time worrying over the family's welfare, welfare, than over the company's.'' And that sort of left it hanging in a way. I should have continued it and expanded it more as to why I said that.

T: Okay good . . . Are there any other places where when you went back a little while ago and read, reread the essay, that you felt you should have developed it you mentioned that you were worried about development? Any other places aside from that place?

S: Let's see . . . in the third paragraph I should have said why, what kind of a assignment that women can handle that men are already handling. That should have been expanded more. And and then needed the I wasn't sure about, uh, the apostrophe on this husband's career. (Freedman and Swanson-Owens, 1983, p. 26)

Even though Cee returned to her concern for apostrophes, she also focused on the discourse level in her self-evaluations. Because her attention was on the discourse level, she was probably open to instruction that helped her with discourse goals. One instructional sequence directed at discourse concerns, which took place during a conference with Cee, is recorded here:

S: But it, its's easier to talk it out than write it down on a piece of paper
[A few lines are deleted here]

T: And start out that way, then you can cross off those extra words. Remember how

Trimble suggests that you do that. Just talk. Pretend like you're explaining to a friend.

S: No, it's much more different talking to a friend because you can put in your own ideas. You don't have to watch out too much about the little grammar errors or spelling errors or anything like that. Just say right out or you could maybe exaggerate a little bit more, and everything's just flowing right out. But when you're talking on, to a piece of paper, you're talking, but then you might forget something or you might all of a sudden change it. Because I have a habit of changing everything in mid air. Like I might have an essay al-almost done to type up and then maybe one or two days before it's due, I change the whole essay or go to a new topic because I don't like the form of my essay.

T: Okay. Uhm the only thing I can say about that is that if if it would help you get ideas on to the paper to think you were talking, let those grammar errors come out and then when you do your editing you can go back and correct it at a different stage. So the point I just wanted to make for you was that I, that it's possible, maybe, now maybe you're, you're saying that just the speech and putting anything down on paper is really different.

S: Oh yeah.

T: Which it is to a degree, but sometimes if people feel like they're just writing to a friend or they're explaining something to their audience is somebody that's a friend and they're writing out their ideas they can get more out on paper and it flows more smoothly.

S: Like I was writing to a friend recently. And I was telling him about the BART [Bay Area Rapid Transit]. I said I'm crazy about BART. And I was just telling all these little things and how they're having fights in Daly City and it really came out. So maybe I should pretend that I'm writing to somebody about the M & M's ad.

T: Yeah do. Um, pretend like you and I are, are old buddies and I happen to be in the business now of, producing M & M's and you're the president of another corporation of an advertising corporation and you're just explaining to me about this ad, and then your editing stage, later, once you get all your ideas out.

S: Yeah.

T: Then go back and look at the grammar, but don't worry about that when you're getting your ideas on the paper.

S: I think that's what I do. I worry too much about the grammar and how it comes out the first time around, and maybe that's the main cause that I worry about that too much, that I don't really worry about how the paper would turn out in the sense of is this the right ideas, will the reader find that she can relate to this ad, can she visualize the picture? (Freedman, 1981, pp. 85–87)

Cee had problems producing ideas as was seen in the brevity of her first essay. In this conference the teacher attempts to discover why Cee has this problem (she tries to make the first draft perfect). The teacher suggests pretending that one is talking to a friend as a way of getting ideas down on paper.

There is evidence that this instruction "took," since Cee's compositions are much longer at the end than at the beginning of the quarter. Also, she makes greater changes during revision at the end of the quarter, perhaps because she is no longer trying to make her first draft perfect.

In summary, Cee had unique writing problems that she identified with the help of her teacher. She then found ways to solve these problems and improve her writing as a result. Conferencing allows for individuali-

zation within a classroom. Moreover, since students are practicing self-monitoring during conferences, they learn a way to continue improving their writing when the teacher is absent.

Teaching Revision Strategies

As we saw in the section on reviewing, less skilled and younger writers make fewer revisions in their compositions than do more skilled and older writers. In particular, they make fewer meaning-oriented revisions. Because younger writers appear to not revise for meaning, Cohen and Scardamalia (1983) designed a training program to teach young children some revision strategies.

The children were twenty-one sixth graders who received nine days of instruction (for forty-five minutes per day) in revision. Instruction on days 1, 2, 3, 5, and 6 started with having the students write a brief essay on an assigned topic. Then the teacher introduced one or two diagnostic statements to the class as a whole. The entire set of diagnostic statements is shown in Table 8.10. For example, on day 1 one of the diagnostic statements discussed was "Part of the essay does not belong here." After introducing each statement,

Table 8.10. Diagnostic statements introduced to sixth graders and training day on which each statement was introduced. (Adapted from Cohen and Scardamalia, 1983.)

DAY	DIAGNOSTIC STATEMENT TAUGHT
1	1. Too few ideas.
	2. Part of essay does not belong here.
2	3. Introduction does not explain what the essay is about.
	4. Idea said in a clumsy way.
3	5. Conclusion does not explain ideas.
5	6. Incomplete idea.
	7. Ignored a strong point on other side.
6	8. Weak reason.
	9. Needs an example to explain idea.

the teacher presented an essay designed to illustrate the problem identified by that statement. The class as a whole judged the essay in light of the statement and suggested revisions. For example, for "Part of the essay does not belong here," students identified a part of the essay that was out of place and then suggested where that part might better fit within the essay. Finally, students were directed to apply the diagnostic statements of that day to the essays they had written at the beginning of class and to revise their essays accordingly.

On day 4 there was a general discussion, and on days 7, 8, and 9 the class as a group practiced revising essays that had been written by some of the students. These practice sessions were directed by students.

The training program was evaluated by having students write and revise an essay before training and then do a second revision of the same essay after training. The essays and revisions I and II were rated globally for quality on a five-point scale by a person who did not know whether a revision had been produced before or after training. When these ratings were compared statistically, the researchers found that the original essay and revision I (written before training) did not differ in quality. However, revision II (written after training) was better than either the original essay or revision I.

The two revisions were compared for the types of revisions made: mechanical, word, phrase, or idea. Table 8.11 shows that students increased most in their revision of ideas and least in their revision of mechanics. Since the diagnostic statements that formed the

core of the training were focused on ideas, it is not surprising that this is where the greatest increase in revisions was found.

Finally, the idea revisions were further divided into those which changed the introduction, clarified an idea, expanded an idea, added more ideas, deleted ideas, or changed the conclusion. Table 8.12 shows the frequency with which each of these subgroups was observed. By far the most frequent revision was the addition of more ideas, a revision that is cued by the diagnostic statement "too few ideas."

What is most interesting about these results is that all of these changes are what one would expect if the students used the diagnostic statements to cue their revisions. For example, changes in the introduction would be cued by "Introduction does not explain what the essay is about," and clarification would be cued by "Idea said in a clumsy way."

Taken as a whole, these data suggest that the students learned to recognize problems at the meaning level in their essays and learned ways to remediate these problems. This learning led to higher-quality essays. The instruction that facilitated this learning clearly included opportunities for practice and feedback, an important condition for learning procedural knowledge. Probably the instruction also included both examples and nonexamples of writing problems, and a wide variety of examples. The examples and nonexamples probably occurred during the group revision sessions, when students proposed that a given part of an essay had a particular problem such as "too few ideas." The teacher

Table 8.11. Number of changes in revisions I and II. (Adapted from Cohen and Scardamalia, 1983.)

	MECHANICAL	WORD	PHRASE	IDEA	TOTAL
Revision I	4	13	3	5	25
Revision II	8	29	15	47	99

Table 8.12. Frequency of types of idea change. (Adapted from Cohen and Scardamalia, 1983.)

	INTRODUCE	CLARIFY	EXPAND	ADD	DELETE	CONCLUDE
Revision I	0	1	1	1	0	1
Revision II	3	3	2	28	1	3

presumably gave feedback on the students' proposals. Positive feedback signified an example. Negative feedback signified a nonexample. Since the details of this part of training were not described, however, these ideas about examples and nonexamples are just speculation. It would be interesting to study more systematically the role of examples and matched nonexamples in teaching students to evaluate their own essays.

CONCLUSION

In this chapter we have seen what is known about cognitive differences between successful and unsuccessful writers. Successful writers have the goal of communicating meaning, enough declarative knowledge to communicate, and greater knowledge of text structure. They also seem to have more mechanical and sentence-level cohesion skills under automatic control. Finally, they appear to revise for meaning and are thus willing to make drastic changes when such are needed.

What we do not know is how writers' goals determine their strategies. Is each goal automatically associated with a given strategy, or are there a variety of strategies from which the writer selects on the basis of audience, time constraints, and other factors? We also do not know much about the relationship between text-structure pattern-recognition knowledge and the use of text structure in generating text. Are these two types of knowledge stored separately? Or is one form constructed from the other when needed? These are just a few of the questions

that remain to be answered through research on writing processes.

ADDITIONAL READINGS

Britton, J., T. Burgess, N. Martin, A. McLoed, and H. Rosen (1975). *The development of writing abilities (11–18)*. London: Macmillan.

Faigley, L., and A. Skinner (1982). *Writers' processes and writers' knowledge: A review of research* (Tech. Rep. No. 6). Austin: University of Texas, Writing Program Assessment Project.

Frase, L. T., ed. (1982). Special issue: The psychology of writing. *Educational Psychologist* 17.

Frederiksen, C. H., and J. F. Dominic, eds. (1981). *Writing: Process, development, and communication*. Hillsdale, N.J.: Lawrence Erlbaum Associates.

Gregg, L., and E. Steinberg, eds. (1980). *Cognitive processes in writing: An interdisciplinary approach*. Hillsdale, N.J.: Lawrence Erlbaum Associates.

Humes, A. (1983). Research on the composing process. *Review of Educational Research* 53, 201–16.

Kroll, B., and C. G. Wells, eds (1983) *Explorations in children's development in writing*. Chichester, England: John Wiley and Sons.

Nystrand, M., ed. (1982). *What writers know: The language, process, and structure of written discourse*. New York: Academic Press.

Scardamalia, M., and C. Bereiter, (1985). Written composition. In M. C. Wittrock (ed.), *Handbook of research on teaching*, vol. 3.

APPENDIX

Cee's early writing:

A person who believes that time spent in a company or in a trade school will enhance his knowledge in greater than in an university. He will be able to obtain first hand the essentials of his chosen field and learn the ups and downs, the moans and the groans of working in his area. A person is able to learn much quicker what the subject material is about in a work environment. (Freedman and Swanson-Owens, p. 58)

Cee's later writing:

SNOOPY

The Peanuts character Snoopy is the best representative for America. Snoopy shows how the American people attitude's are a bit childish. Snoopy's character in the strip tells the public that they are lazy and spoiled.

People in the United States are known to love the easy way of living which is being lazy. People do not particularly like to work but must do so in order to pay for living expenses such as food, clothes, entertainment, and housing payments. If an organization were to do a survey on whether a person likes to work, the company would find that about 66% of the public would prefer to relax and enjoy life as it comes and devote more time to traveling, gardening, visiting freinds and relatives, and attending sports events. Snoopy has the same attitudes of the American public because he shows the reader that life should be fun and exciting, not boring like working in a company or going to school. Thus, this is why we never see Snoopy mowing the lawn, fixing his own dinner, or doing homework.

Another reason why Snoopy represents America is that he shows the American people that they are spoiled rotten by throwing tantrums and by not appreciating what they have or what is given to them.

For example, Snoopy throws tantrums when Charlie Brown does not put some type of food decoration such as parsley or croutons in his dinner, and when Charlie Brown does not serve Snoopy his dinner on the patio, otherwise, if Snoopy did not have these "services," he would not eat his dinner until everything is to his satisfaction. Thus, Snoop's attitude reflects the attitude of the people who do not appreciate what they had in the past and what they have now, especially with the current gas crisis. The people did not believe there was a gas crisis until they went to a gas station and found them either closed or with a limited supply. This gas crisis has hit the people right where it hurts the most—in their beloved gas tank.

Hopefully with the current gas crisis, people will use other forms of public transportation such as BART, Muni, AC Transit, Samtrans, and the railroad system and will continue to use these systems when the gas crisis is over. Even if there was no crisis, people are still spoiled by having BART, Muni, and the other public transportations, because other counties and states are not as fortunate as to have these "rides" as the San Francisco-Bay Area. The people who live in San Francisco and the outlying areas take all these services such as public transportations, gas, televisions, for granted until they no longer there to service the people's needs.

In order for a person to get something what he desires, he must appreciate that he is fortunate to have several types of services available to him and that he is lucky to live in the United States as compared to the people in Vietnam who have little or nothing available to them such as public transportation, good food, a house over their head, and gas. As the famous saying goes, "Appreciate what you are lucky to have before it goes out of style or out of order." (Freedman and Swanson-Owens, pp. 62–63)

Chapter

9

Mathematics

SUMMARY

1. Mathematics competence comprises two broad areas—computational skill and conceptual understanding.

2. Students may have trouble with computation because they are using an incorrect procedure. If this is the case, verbal instructions or corrective feedback can often lead students to use correct procedures.

3. Another reason that students have trouble with computation is failure to master prerequisite skills. To correct this problem teachers should assess students' knowledge of prerequisites and teach prerequisite skills that students do not already possess.

4. Inefficient computation may be due either to using a less-than-optimal procedure, in which case a more optimal procedure might be pointed out; or to

not having a composed procedure, in which case practice and feedback should lead to composition.

5. Differences in mathematical understanding are caused in part by differences in the way people organize knowledge. This organization influences what people attend to in problems, what they recall about problems, and therefore how they solve problems.

6. Skill in estimation allows people to monitor their answers to problems and thus is an important aspect of mathematics competence.

Most people agree that reading and writing are essential skills. Fewer agree that competence in mathematics is essential for getting along in our culture. Some people argue that the ubiquitous presence of calculators means that computational skill is unnecessary for daily consumer transactions. Further, they argue, the need for mathematics beyond the level of blind computation is not pervasive: only a few persons in highly technical engineering and scientific jobs really need it.

The facts, however, refute this argument. Saunders (1980) interviewed persons in 100 job categories representing the entire economic range in our society. He found that knowledge of basic arithmetic was necessary for 62 percent of these jobs and that knowledge of statistics was essential for 65 percent. Czepiel and Esty (1980) found that 93 percent of articles on the front page of *The New York Times* cannot be fully comprehended without fundamental mathematical competence. Further, Graziano, Musser, Rosen, and Shaffer (1982) found that children's mathematical competence was related to their use of fairplay standards: those who could not divide could not distribute rewards equitably among winners of a game. In general, our knowledge of quantity and space (that is, our knowledge of mathematics) has a pervasive effect on how well we function in society and the number of opportunities open to us.

Ironically, as technology (and its silent partner, mathematics) becomes increasingly important in daily life, students appear to have less, rather than more, mathematical literacy. The average quantitative SAT score significantly decreased from 1963 to 1980 (National Commission on Excellence in Education, 1983). Also, the National Assessment of Educational Progress showed significant declines in the mathematical competence of eleven- and sixteen-year olds over the same period. The causes of these declines are unknown. They may reflect poorer or less teaching, changing demographics of student populations, or less informal education by parents. Whatever the causes, the only solution over which teachers have control is the improvement of instruction in mathematics and, more likely than not, if instruction is substantially improved, student competence in mathematics will increase.

It is well documented that elementary school children spend much less time engaged in arithmetic tasks than they do engaged in reading tasks (Fisher et al., 1978). Elementary school teachers may be less comfortable with mathematics than with reading and therefore may avoid teaching it. It might be better for teachers to confront the sources of their discomfort. Are they uncomfortable because they do not understand certain topics in mathematics themselves? If so, they should seek further training or at least explanations from colleagues who do understand these topics. Or are they uncomfortable because they have difficulty communicating mathematics concepts to students? If so, they should seek the reasons for students' difficulty. As one who has taught elementary school, I do not mean to single out elementary school teachers as villians. Many secondary school teachers of mathematics may also feel uncomfortable with math because they were trained in other disciplines. Also, sometimes those who are trained in mathematics feel most frustrated in their attempts to teach it.

In this chapter I will describe some information-processing analyses of mathematical competence. For readers who lack confidence in their own mathematical competence, these examples may give you fresh insights into your own cognitive processes. Readers who are discouraged in attempts to teach mathematics may gain new ideas here about students' cognitive processes. Readers who are not primarily involved in teaching mathematics should be stimulated to think more about the commonalities between mathematics competence and competence in other domains.

TYPES OF MATHEMATICAL COMPETENCE

Most mathematics educators agree on the distinction between the computational aspect of mathematics ("algorithms," "computation," "rules") and the conceptual aspect ("heuristics," "problem-solving," "understanding"). Table 9.1 shows some problems in each category. The problems in the left column require the student to carry out one or more operations to transform the given information. The needed operation is either explicitly stated or strongly implied in the problem statement. For example, the first problem says "add" and the third says "find

the area." Number 2 does not say, "Add like terms" but little else could be done; and number 4 does not say "Use the equation distance = rate × time to find rate," but this direction is strongly implied. To get the correct answer to these problems the student must perform action-sequence procedures correctly.

The problems in the right-hand column use the same operations as the corresponding problems on the left. However, they do not tell the student what operation to select. For example, in the first problem the student is not told that addition is the way to find out how many marbles John has. Similarly, in the third problem students are not told to find the area of the triangle *ABD* and multiply this by 2. These problems are considered to be more difficult than the problems in the left-hand column of Table 9.1 because they require more insight or understanding.

Roughly speaking, then, mathematical competence is composed of two subsets, which will be called computation and understanding. Educators argue over the relative value of these subsets. Some say that as computers become almost universally available, computational ability will become less important and understanding will become more important because people will have to understand what they want computers to do. Others argue that even with computers computational skill is a prerequisite to understanding.

A psychological answer to this issue is not available. However, psychological knowledge is available about the cognitive underpinnings of both the computational and conceptual aspects of mathematics performance. These will be discussed in separate sections of this chapter. Just because computation and understanding are segregated for discussion here does not imply that they should be segregated during instruction. They are probably best taught together.

Table 9.1. Some examples of mathematics problems. The problems on the left emphasize computation. Those on the right require both understanding and computation.

1. Add the following:

$$28$$
$$+ \ 32$$

1. If John has 28 marbles and he wins 32 more, how many marbles does he have?

2. $3x + 2x =$ _____

2. Penny has three times as many stamps as Sue, and Jane has two times as many stamps as Sue. Together Penny and Sue have 150 stamps. How many stamps does Sue have?

3. Find the area of a triangle with a base of 3 inches and a height of 1 inch.

3. *Given:* Triangle *ABD* is equal to triangle *ACD*. Height of triangle *ACD* is equal to 1 inch. Base of triangle *ACD* is equal to 3 inches.
   Find: The area of triangle *ABC*.

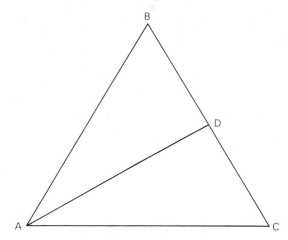

4. Distance = 40 miles
   Time = 2 hours
   Rate = ?

4. A cyclist went 40 miles in 2 hours. At what rate was she traveling?

COMPUTATION

No matter whether computation or understanding is emphasized in a given mathematics program, at least some computational procedures are taught. Both speed and accuracy are prized components of computational skill. We do not especially admire an individual who gets accurate results at an incredibly slow rate, or one who computes rapidly but incorrectly. We do, however, admire fast and accurate calculation. Psychologists have examined the cognitive causes of both accuracy and speed of computation, and we will consider some of their findings in this section.

Successful Computation

Before teachers attend to students' speed in computation, they usually attend to students' accuracy. Many areas of computing are known to give students difficulty, including carrying, borrowing, computing percentages, adding fractions, manipulating exponents, and solving algebraic equations. The types of errors students make in computing often give clues to the cognitive reasons for their lack of accuracy. Errors are rarely random, but rather show patterns that observant teachers will notice.

Two classes of error can be usefully distinguished. One consists of errors in the target skill (the skill being taught) and the other consists of errors in subskills that are consid-

ered to be prerequisite to the target skill. Table 9.2 shows these two classes for a test in fractions. The target skill, addition of fractions, is measured by items 1 and 2. Items 3 and 4 test for prerequisite knowledge of what the terms "denominator" and "numerator" signify, whereas items 5 and 6 test for skill in determining common denominators, which is one component of adding fractions.

At the bottom of Table 9.2 are the answers to these problems given by two students, Carl and Mack. Both gave incorrect answers to problems 1 and 2, but Carl was correct on all other problems whereas Mack also missed items 5 and 6. Carl's errors are only on the target task. He seems to be adding the two numerators and then adding the two denominators to get an answer (Vinner,

Table 9.2. Two students' responses to a test in the area of fractions. Carl's errors are only on the addition items. Mack's errors are on addition items and items asking him to find a common denominator. The error patterns suggest distinct reasons for each student's failure to add fractions correctly.

Name_____

1. $\frac{1}{3} + \frac{3}{1} = ?$ 2. $\frac{4}{5} + \frac{1}{5} = ?$

3. Circle the denominator in $\frac{4}{5}$.

4. Circle the numerator in $\frac{3}{7}$.

5. Find the common denominator for $\frac{3}{7}$ and $\frac{1}{3}$.

6. Find the common denominator for $\frac{1}{4}$ and $\frac{2}{3}$.

Carl	Mack
1. 4/6	1. 4/5
2. 5/8	2. 5/6
3. 4 /⑤	3. 4 /⑤
4. ③/ 7	4. ③/ 7
5. 21	5. 9
6. 12	6. 3

Hershkowitz, and Bruckheimer, 1981, found that this is a typical misconception that students have about adding fractions). In other words, Carl has an incorrect procedure for adding fractions. Mack's errors on the first two problems do not show a pattern, but rather appear to be guesses. However, his errors on the items that test prerequisite knowledge do show a pattern. He does not know how to find common denominators. Clearly, Mack needs to learn this skill before he can learn the more complex skill of adding fractions.

Thus the two classes of errors are associated with different causes: errors only on items measuring target performance are probably due to an *incorrect procedure* for the target task; errors on items that measure prerequisite skills as well as on items that measure the target performance suggest that lack of success on the target items is due to *lack of prerequisite skill.*

Incorrect Procedures. In subtraction with borrowing students seem to be good at coming up with incorrect procedures. For example, the errors on the problems shown in Table 9.3 suggest an incorrect procedure. Stop reading here and see if you can figure out what (incorrect) rule the student is using.

If you hypothesized that the student was

Table 9.3. A hypothetical student's answers to some subtraction problems. The mistakes made are due to the student's use of an incorrect rule.

234	387	462
− 153	− 124	− 234
121	263	232
615	723	493
− 351	− 258	− 289
344	535	216

subtracting the smallest from the largest number in each column, *independent* of whether the number was on top or on the bottom, you are probably right. In the first problem, for example, the student correctly subtracts 3 (bottom) from 4 (top) to get 1. Then he or she *incorrectly* subtracts 3 (top) from 5 (bottom) to get 2. Finally 1 (bottom) is correctly subtracted from 2 (top) to get 1.

J. S. Brown and R. Burton (1978) found that in a sample of 1325 students in the fourth, fifth, and sixth grades, 54 students (or about 4 percent) consistently used this incorrect procedure. Another 4 percent used an incorrect rule when borrowing from zero. When confronted with a problem such as 205 − 32, these students would change the 0 to 9, but then would fail to reduce the number in the next column to the left:

$$
\begin{array}{r}
9 \\
2\cancel{0}5 \\
-\ 32 \\
\hline
263
\end{array}
$$

Table 9.4 shows 14 of the incorrect rules discovered by Brown and Burton in their study of children's errors on subtraction problems.

Brown and Burton (1978) refer to students' incorrect rules as "bugs," a term that comes from computer programming. In developing a program, after the initial program is written, it often needs to be "debugged" before it will run. Debugging involves systematically finding the incorrect part of the program code. Brown and Burton believe that if students could learn to think of their procedural knowledge as being analogous to a set of computer programs, and to think of their errors as being due to some incorrect or incomplete program statement, they could become much more independent in learning new procedures. As they put it, students begin to "see their own faulty behavior not as being a sign of their stupidity, but as a source

Table 9.4. Incorrect procedures used by students in solving subtraction problems. (From Brown and Burton, 1978.)

The 14 most frequently occurring bugs in a group of 1325 students

57 students used: BORROW/FROM/ZERO (103 − 45 = 158)
    When borrowing from a column whose top digit is 0, the student writes 9, but does not continue borrowing from the column to the left of the 0.

54 students used: SMALLER/FROM/LARGER (253 − 118 = 145)
    The student subtracts the smaller digit in a column from the larger digit regardless of which one is on top.

50 students used: BORROW/FROM/ZERO and LEFT/TEN/OK (803 − 508 = 395)
    The student changes 0 to 9 without further borrowing unless the 0 is part of a 10 in the left part of the number.

34 students used: DIFF/0 − N = N and MOVE/OVER/ZERO/BORROW
    Whenever the top digit in a column is 0, the student writes the bottom digit in the answer, i.e., $0 - N = N$. When the student needs to borrow from a column whose top digit is 0, he skips that column and borrows from the next one.

14 students used: DIFF/0 − N = N and STOPS/BORROW/AT/ZERO
    Whenever the top digit in a column is 0, the student writes the bottom digit in the answer; i.e., $0 - N = N$. The student borrows from zero incorrectly. He does not subtract 1 from the 0 although he adds 10 correctly to the top digit of the current column.

13 students used: SMALLER/FROM/LARGER and 0 − N = 0 (203 − 98 = 205)
    The student subtracts the smaller digit in each column from the larger digit regardless of which one is on top. The exception is that when the top digit is 0, a 0 is written as the answer for that column; i.e., $0 - N = 0$.

12 students used: DIFF/0 − N = 0 and MOVE/OVER/ZERO/BORROW
    Whenever the top digit in a column is 0, the student writes 0 in the answer; i.e., $0 - N = 0$. When the student needs to borrow from a column whose top digit is 0, he skips that column and borrows from the next one.

11 students used: BORROW/FROM/ZERO and DIFF/N − 0 = 0
    When borrowing from a column whose top digit is 0, the student writes 9, but does not continue borrowing from the column to the left of the 0. Whenever the bottom digit in a column is 0, the student writes 0 in the answer; i.e., $N - 0 = 0$.

10 students used: DIFF/0 − N = 0 and N − 0 = 0 (302 − 192 − 290)
    The student writes 0 in the answer when either the top or the bottom digit is 0.

10 students used: BORROW/FROM/ZERO and DIFF/0 − N = N
    When borrowing from a column whose top digit is 0, the student writes 9, but does not continue borrowing from the column to the left of the 0. Whenever the top digit in a column is 0, the student writes the bottom digit in the answer; i.e., $0 - N = N$.

10 students used: MOVE/OVER/ZERO/BORROW (304 − 75 = 139)
    When the student needs to borrow from a column whose top digit is 0, he skips that column and borrows from the next one.

10 students used: DIFF/N − 0 − 0 (103 208 − 105)
    Whenever the bottom digit in a column is 0, the student writes 0 in the answer; i.e., $N - 0 = 0$.

10 students used: DIFF/0 − N = N (140 − 21 = 121)
    Whenever the top digit in a column is 0, the student writes the bottom digit in the answer; i.e., $0 - N = N$.

9 students used: DIFF/0 − N = N and LEFT/TEN/OK (908 − 395 = 693)
    When there is a 0 on top, the student writes the bottom digit in the answer. The exception is when the 0 is part of 10 in the left columns of the top number.

of data from which they can understand their own errors'' (p. 172).

In order to discover the bugs in children's subtraction procedures, Brown and Burton (1978) first developed a model of competence in subtraction. Their model is a set of interrelated procedures, shown in Figure 9.1. Procedures higher in the figure are composed

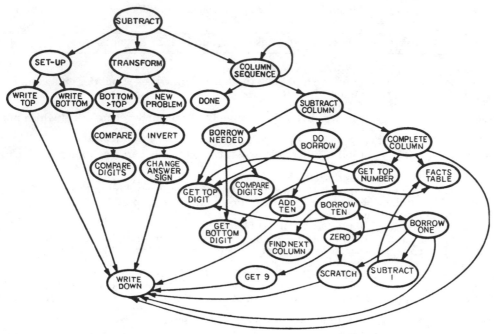

Figure 9.1. A procedural network for subtraction. (From Brown and Burton, 1978.)

of procedures lower in the figure. For example, on the left, the SET-UP procedure, which sets up the problems, is composed of two smaller procedures: WRITE TOP (write the top number) and WRITE BOTTOM (write the bottom number). Also, some of the smaller procedures are used by more than one larger procedure. For example, the procedure of focusing on the top digit in a specified column (GET TOP DIGIT) is used by the procedure for deciding if borrowing is needed (BORROW NEEDED) and also by the actual performance of borrowing (DO BORROW). In other words, the skill of focusing on the top digit is a lower-level skill that is integrated into more than one higher-level (more complex) skill.

This set of procedures was translated into a computer program that was capable of performing subtraction problems with 100 percent accuracy. Then various changes were made in the program in order to mimic the

errors made by children. If the altered program made the same pattern of errors as a child made, then it was a good bet that the child had in mind the same incorrect rule as had been written into the program.

This method of diagnosing the reason for errors by matching them with errors that would be produced by an hypothesized underlying misconception may seem to be too detailed and therefore too time-consuming for teachers. However, if classroom microcomputers do the detailed work in the future, then analyses such as these can become a regular part of teaching. A teacher could use diagnostic information produced by a computer analysis of student errors to select the specific remedial instruction needed for a particular student. Much of the waste in education is caused because one cannot match instruction to student capabilities. Cognitive analyses such as the one performed by Brown and Burton (1978) on subtraction, provide a map for more specific diagnosis of students' misconceptions and therefore pave the way for more efficient instruction.

Lack of Prerequisite Skills. Incorrect procedures or "bugs" are one source of poor performance on computation problems. Another is lack of prerequisite skills. When students perform poorly on test items that measure a target skill because they lack prerequisite skills they will also perform poorly on test items that measure some or all of the prerequisites.

R. M. Gagné and N. E. Paradise (1961) demonstrated this cause of poor performance in solving linear equations of the type shown in Table 9.5. Stop reading here and try solving these problems in order to refresh your memory for the processes involved. Try to observe your own mental processes as you solve the equations. What rules do you think you are using? (Some people collect all the elements containing the same variable on one side of the equation and move all other elements to the other side of the equation. Another operation is to simplify by reducing fractions to least common denominators).

Gagné and Paradise (1961) performed a *rational task analysis* on the task of solving linear equations in order to decide what skills were prerequisites for successful performance. Rational task analysis starts with this

question: "What would an individual have to know how to do in order to achieve successful performance of this class of task, assuming he were given only instructions?" There were three answers to this question for solving linear equations: (1) simplify an equation by adding and subtracting terms to both sides, (2) simplify an equation by multiplying, dividing, adding, and subtracting numbers to both sides, and (3) simplify an equation by multiplying and dividing both sides by terms. If one can do these three acts, one should be able to solve linear equations. Therefore, these three capabilities are prerequisite to solving linear equations. The prerequisite relationships are indicated in Figure 9.2. In a box at the top of the figure is the task of solving linear equations. Underneath this box are the three tasks just mentioned, each with a line connecting it to the top box.

The task analysis proceeds by focusing on the three prerequisite skills identified in the first step. Each skill is now treated as if it were the final task, and the question that was asked above is asked again. The answers are another set of skills (shown across from II in Figure 9.2) for which one can again ask the question, "What would an individual have to know how to do in order to achieve successful performance of this class of task, assuming he were given only instructions?" The questionning process is iterated until one

Table 9.5. Some of the problems solved by students in R. M. Gagné and N. E. Paradise's study of solving linear equations. (Adapted from Gagné and Paradise, 1961.)

1. Solve for b:

   $2b - 3 - 8b - 4 + 3b = 13 - 6 - 3b - 2 - 6b$

2. Solve for x:

   $\frac{4x}{2} = 6x - 8$

3. Solve for x:

   $7x + 4x = 3a + 3a + 2a - x$

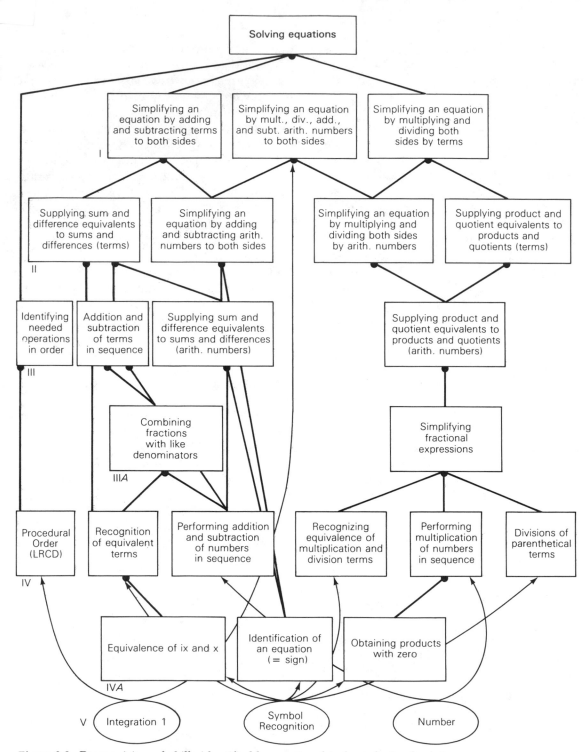

Figure 9.2. Prerequisite subskills identified by a rational task analysis of solving equations. (From R. M. Gagne and N. E. Paradise, 1961.)

reaches a level at which one expects most or all students to already have skill. In Figure 9.2 this is level V, which contains number concepts, symbol recognition, and the ability to integrate information. Since Gagné and Paradise were working with seventh graders, it was reasonable to assume that most of their subjects could identify number concepts, recognize symbols, and integrate information.

This analysis suggests that people who do poorly at solving linear equations may lack one or more of the prerequisite capabilities. For example, if a person cannot add and subtract terms in a sequence (line III in Figure 9.2), such as $6a + 2a - a$, then he or she will not be able to add and subtract terms in an equation.

The idea that lack of prerequisite skill was a major source of failure in learning was rather radical in 1961, when most people assumed that failure in learning was due to low intelligence. Indeed, the idea is still controversial today. As a challenge to the notion that global intelligence accounted for learning, Gagné and Paradise (1961) proposed that speed of learning new skills and achievement of new skills would relate better to a student's possession of relevant prerequisite skills than to intelligence.

To test their hypothesis these researchers gave about 100 seventh graders a verbal knowledge (intelligence) test and then a programmed instruction unit on solving linear equations. After completing the unit, the students were tested on achievement with equations similar to those they had been asked to solve while completing instruction. Finally, the students answered test items that measured their achievement of each of the prerequisite skills identified by the task analysis.

Some of the findings of this study are shown in Table 9.6. The predictions were supported: students' prerequisite skills were highly related to their time to complete the unit of instruction ($r = .78$) and their overall

Table 9.6. Correlations between vocabulary and prerequisite skill tests and learning speed and achievement on a unit designed to teach students how to solve linear equations. (Constructed from R. M. Gagné and N. E. Paradise, 1961.)

	TIME TO COMPLETE UNIT	ACHIEVE-MENT TEST SCORE
Vocabulary test	.18	.22
Prerequisite Skills test	.78	.82

achievement ($r = .82$), whereas their vocabulary knowledge, which is supposed to be a good stand-in measure of intelligence, was only slightly related to learning speed ($r = .18$) and achievement ($r = .22$).

These results show that in learning to solve linear equations prerequisite skill is more helpful than is general intelligence. However, the results do not show whether the prerequisites are *necessary* to achievement of the higher-level skills. The task analysis shown in Figure 9.2 implies that the skills lower in the hierarchy must be mastered before higher-level skills can be learned.

There was a way to examine the necessity of prerequisites in the Gagné and Paradise data. The researchers knew for each student exactly which of the subskills he or she could perform. There were four logical combinations of success and failure on subskills that were at adjacent levels in the hierarchy: (1) higher-level item correct and prerequisite item correct $(+ +)$, (2) higher-level item wrong and prerequisite item wrong $(- -)$, (3) higher-level item correct but prerequisite item wrong $(+ -)$, and (4) higher-level item wrong and related prerequisite item correct $(- +)$. Of these four possibilities, 1, 2, and 4 are consistent with the notion that prerequisite skill is necessary for learning a higher-level related skill. However, the third possibility is not consistent with this notion. That is, if a prerequisite skill is necessary for achievement of a higher-level skill, it should not be possible to fail a test of the prerequisite while passing a test of the higher-level skill.

Gagné and Paradise (1961) looked at the frequencies with which each of these four patterns occurred in their data. What they found is shown in Table 9.7. The pattern that is inconsistent with the necessity assumption is shown in the third column. In general, there are far fewer entries in this column than in any other column and therefore the notion that the prerequisite skills identified by the task analysis are necessary for higher-level learning is supported.

The data in Table 9.7 also suggest that for some pairs of skills the prerequisite is not as necessary as for others. One example of this is the relationship between skill IIIA2 and IV4, IV5, and IV6, where 10 out of 118 students were able to perform the higher-level skill without demonstrating prerequisite knowl-

edge. Perhaps the rational task analysis was incorrect for this relationship. This demonstrates the importance of empirical validation of rational task analyses.

It is interesting to represent as a production system some of the skills involved in solving equations, because this representation makes clear the prerequisite relationships among skills. Table 9.8 shows four production systems, called *collect terms, transpose terms, collect numerals,* and *transpose numerals. Collect terms* consists of two productions: $P1.1$ adds like terms and $P1.2$ subtracts like terms. The second system, transpose terms, also has two productions: $P2.1$ operates when the largest term for the target variable is on the left side of the equation and $P2.2$ operates when the largest term for the target variable is on the right side of the equation. Production systems 3 and 4 are analogous to systems 1 and 2 except that they operate on numerals rather than on terms.

Table 9.7. Pass-fail patterns of achievement between adjacent lower- and higher-level skills. (Adapted from Gagné and Paradise, 1961.)

| SKILL | | FREQUENCY OF PASS-FAIL PATTERN—HIGHER, LOWER | | | |
HIGHER	LOWER	+ + (1)	− − (2)	+ − (3)	− + (4)
IV2 from IVA1		110	0	0	8
IV5 from IVA3		113	0	0	5
IIIA1 from IV2, IV3		85	0	7	26
IIIA2 from IV4, IV5, IV6		94	5	10	9
III1 from IV1		45	9	1	63
III2 from IV3, IIIA1		68	30	6	14
III3 from IVA2, IV3		75	25	7	11
III4 from IIIA2		62	40	4	12
II1 from IV2, III2, III3		34	70	3	11
II2 from IVA2, III3		41	60	2	15
II3 from III4		37	72	3	6
II4 from III4		9	85	0	24
I1 from II1, II2		25	78	2	13
I2 from II2, II3		28	80	3	7
I3 from II3, II4		6	104	0	8
	Total	832	658	48	232

Table 9.8. Productions for solving simple linear equations.

COLLECT TERMS

*P*1.1   IF More than one like term is on same side
      And like terms are related by addition
   THEN Add like terms.

*P*1.2   IF More than one like term is on same side of equation
      And like terms are related by subtraction
   THEN Subtract like terms.

TRANSPOSE TERMS

*P*2.1   IF Only one like term exists on each side of equation
      And left side term is more than right side term
   THEN Subtract like term on right side from itself
      And subtract same from like term on left side.

*P*2.2   IF Only one like term exists on each side of equation
      And right side term is more than left side term
   THEN Subtract like term on left side from itself
      And subtract same from like term on right side.

COLLECT NUMERALS

*P*3.1   IF More than one numeral exists on one side of equation
      And numerals are related by addition
   THEN Add numerals.

*P*3.2   IF More than one numeral exists on one side of equation
      And numerals are related by subtraction
   THEN Subtract numerals.

TRANSPOSE NUMERALS

*P*4.1   IF There is only one term in equation
      And term and numeral exist on same side of equation
      And relationship of numeral to term is subtract
   THEN Add numeral to both sides of equation.

*P*4.2   IF There is only one term in equation
      And term and numeral exist on same side of equation
      And relationship of numeral to term is add
   THEN Subtract numeral from both sides of equation.

To examine an example of the prerequisite relationships implied in production system notation, look at productions 4.1 and 4.2. Notice that the first condition in both of these productions is that the target variable be represented in only one term. For the variable to be so represented, the student must have already collected like terms and put like terms on one side of the equation. In other words, the skills embodied in COLLECT TERMS and TRANSPOSE TERMS must already be mastered. As another example, look at the condition side of *P*1.1. Each of the words in these conditions implies a concept that the student must already recognize. If the concept of ''like term'' (by whatever label) is not known, then the production will not apply. The concept of ''like term'' can itself be represented by a pattern-recognition production of the form:

IF Letters exist in equation

And more than one element

contains the same letter

THEN Classify elements containing

same letter as like terms.

The production system notation is one way to represent competence underlying performance. The procedural set of Brown and Burton (1978) and the task analysis of Gagné and Paradise (1961) are alternative methods. Each makes the relationships among skills explicit, but the production system notation is best at showing the dynamics of these relationships during performance. Also, unlike the other two methods, the production system notation makes explicit the conditions that must exist for a particular skill to operate. These conditions imply a set of prerequisite concepts that the learner must already possess.

Summary. People often get incorrect results when computing or manipulating symbols; the question is, Why? Since pencil and paper are typically available, the problem is unlikely to be the overloading of working memory. One cause seems to be the possession of incorrect procedures. Incorrect procedures can often be identified by close examination of the types of errors one makes on test items that assess the target skill.

Besides having incorrect procedures, students may lack prerequisite procedures. Lack of prerequisites can be identified by examining student performance on test items designed to test knowledge of various prerequisites.

Efficient Computation

The goals of speed and accuracy in computing are worthy ones. People who find that computing takes a lot of time are less likely to use computing in their daily lives, and so will benefit less from having a skill than will people who are speedier. For example, people who routinely compute the unit cost of comparable products when they shop probably do so in part because their computation skills are efficient.

Just as there are several causes of unsuccessful computation, so there are several causes of inefficient computation. In the early stages of learning a new skill, computation may be inefficient because the skill is stored in declarative rather than procedural form—that is, the knowledge underlying the skill has not yet been proceduralized (proceduralization was discussed in Chapter 5). However, even after a skill has been proceduralized there are still sources of inefficiency. One is that the procedure itself may not be the most efficient one for reaching some goal, because it has more steps than it needs. Another is that several small skills have not yet been combined into a larger unit that deletes some of the redundancies in the set of smaller skills. That is, the skill may not yet be composed.

The Number of Steps in a Procedure. An interesting example of efficient versus inefficient procedures has been demonstrated in young children's procedures for solving simple addition problems. Before they know their addition facts, young children are often required to find the sum of two small, single-digit numbers, for example, 4 + 3 = _____. Older children and adults solve such problems by retrieving the appropriate number fact (4 + 3 = 7) from long-term memory. But preschool and first-grade children do not yet know their number facts. These children are nonetheless quite successful at performing simple addition problems. Groen and Parkman (1972) found an average 97 percent success rate among first graders for sums whose answer was 9 or less. What procedures do young children use that yields such great success?

As Groen and Parkman (1972) have suggested, children might use one of several procedures, all of which involve counting by ones and keeping track of what has been counted. These procedures could be performed mentally or both mentally and with the help of fingers or other physical representations of items that have been counted. The five variants of the counting procedure studied by Groen and Parkman were:

1. Count one by one until the first addend is reached. Continue counting one by one until the second addend is reached. (This will be referred to as the COUNT BOTH procedure.)

2. Start at the first addend and count one by one for the number of times indicated by the second addend. (This will be referred to as the COUNT FROM FIRST procedure.)

3. Start at the second addend and count one by one for the number of times indicated by the first addend. (This will be referred to as the COUNT FROM SECOND procedure.)

4. Start at the minimum of the two addends and count one by one for the number of times indicated by the maximum of the two addends. (This will be referred to as the COUNT FROM MINIMUM procedure.)

5. Start at the maximum of the two addends and count one by one for the number of times indicated by the minimum of the two addends. (This will

be referred to as the COUNT FROM MAXIMUM procedure.)

The most efficient of these five procedures is COUNT FROM MAXIMUM, because it requires the least amount of counting. COUNT BOTH is by far the least efficient because in it, unlike the other four procedures, both numbers are counted. COUNT FROM FIRST and COUNT FROM SECOND would be most efficient when the first and second number, respectively, in the sum was the maximum. The COUNT FROM MINIMUM procedure, using the minimum for a starting point, is inefficient because the greater of the two numbers must be counted. The question posed by Groen and Parkman (1972) was whether or not youngsters used what was objectively the most efficient procedure.

To study this question they collected latency data on thirty-seven first graders solving problems of the form $m + n = $ _____, where the answer was less than or equal to nine. They then examined the match between the actual form of the data and the form that would be expected for each of the five procedures proposed. For example, if the children were using COUNT BOTH, their speed of response should be a function of the sum of m and n, because the smaller this sum, the fewer times they would have to count one more and the larger this sum, the more times they would have to count one more. On the other hand, if children were using COUNT FROM MAXIMUM, latency should be a function of the size of the minimum addend. This is because all the child is counting in this case is the minimum addend—the larger this number is, the longer the child will take to count it.

The only match that Groen and Parkman (1972) found was for COUNT FROM MAXIMUM. None of the other procedures was matched by the data from any of the children, whereas the latencies of twenty-five of the children (or 68 percent) matched the form expected for COUNT FROM MAXIMUM. Figure 9.3 shows the observed response times as a function of the size of the minimum addend and also the predicted response times for COUNT FROM MAXIMUM (called "Model 5" by Groen and Parkman). The match of the predicted and observed results is clear in this figure.

It is interesting to think about the few problems that did not fit predictions very well. Looking at Figure 9.3, you can see that the problems 2 + 2, 3 + 3, and 4 + 4 were all solved faster on the average than one would predict if the children were counting on from the maximum addend. Groen and Parkman (1972) speculate that for these problems—ones in which a number is added to itself—the children had already learned the associated number fact and therefore, to answer these problems, they simply retrieved the fact from long-term memory. This seems plausible, since the children who participated in the study were at the end of the first grade.

Whereas Groen and Parkman (1972) used latency data to infer what addition algorithms were used by young children, Houlihan and Ginsburg (1981) used retrospective reports. They gave first and second graders problems similar to those used by Groen and Parkman. After a child gave an answer the researcher said, "Tell me how you got your answer to this problem." The answers were categorized into two groups: one group was like the COUNT BOTH procedure and the other group included all procedures that involve starting with one addend and counting on from there (COUNT ON). Since Houlihan and Ginsburg always presented the maximum addend first, they could not distinguish between the COUNT FROM FIRST and the COUNT FROM MAXIMUM procedures identified by Groen and Parkman.

Houlihan and Ginsburg's (1981) results, summarized in Table 9.9, showed that the first graders used COUNT BOTH 31 percent of the time and COUNT ON 34 percent of the time. On only 4 percent did they use retrieval

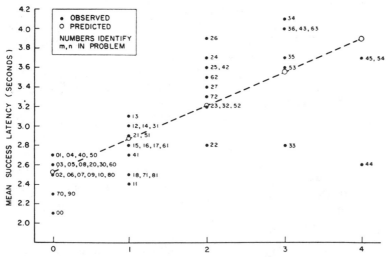

Figure 9.3. Latencies of response as a function of the minimum addend. The dark circles indicate observed latencies. The open circles indicate predicted latencies. Both observed and predicted latencies increase with the size of the minimum addend, showing a good match of the data with predictions from the COUNT FROM MAXIMUM procedure. (From Groen and Parkman, 1972.)

from long-term memory. However, the second graders used retrieval for 29 percent of the problems. Also, they used COUNT BOTH on only 3 percent of the problems. They used COUNT ON for 49 percent of the problems. From these data it appears that second graders have found more efficient procedures overall than have first graders. They either retrieve information from long-term memory, which is the most efficient procedure, or, if they must resort to a counting procedure, they are efficient in that they count on from one addend rather than counting both addends.

Unlike Houlihan and Ginsburg (1981), Groen and Parkman (1972) did not find any first graders who appeared consistently to use COUNT BOTH. The difference may have occurred because Groen and Parkman studied upper-middle class children with above-average IQ scores, whereas Houlihan and Ginsburg studied children from low- and middle-income families. Despite the differences, both studies reveal that many of first graders use an efficient procedure for finding sums.

Composed versus Fragmented Procedures.

As we just discussed, one reason for people's improvement in speed of computation is their learning of new procedures that require fewer steps than previously used procedures. An

Table 9.9. Percentage of time that students used different procedures for solving single digit addition problems. (Adapted from Houlihan and Ginsberg, 1981.)

	RETRIEVAL FROM LTM	COUNT BOTH	COUNT ON	OTHER
First grade (N = 26)	4%	31%	34%	31%
Second grade (N = 31)	29%	3%	49%	19%

other reason is that several procedures applied in a sequence come to be combined into one procedure that removes any redundancies. An example of this is given in Figure 9.4, which shows two hypothetical written answers to the problem: $6x - 12 - 12 + 6x = 11x - 12$. The top answer clearly shows a sequential procedure in which the student first collects all like terms on either side of an equation and then transposes the x terms to one side of the equation and the numerals to the other side. The bottom answer suggests a procedure in which collection and transposition are performed together. In the top answer it is as if the student must write down the intermediate results in order to remind himself or herself of what to do next, whereas in the bottom answer, the student does not seem to need such a reminder.

What cognitive change might underlie this performance change? Table 9.10 shows at the top two productions (COLLECT and TRANSPOSE) that might underlie the sequential performance shown at the top of Figure 9.4. At the bottom of Table 9.10 is a production that combines the actions of COLLECT and

$6x - 12 - 12 + 6x = 11x - 12$

$$12x - 24 = 11x - 12$$
$$x = 12$$

$6x - 12 - 12 + 6x = 11x - 12$

$$x = 12$$

Figure 9.4. Two students' written answers to the same linear algebra problem. The first student writes down intermediate results, and the second does not. The second student may have a composed procedure for solving such problems and therefore does not need to write down intermediate results.

Table 9.10. Productions for solving linear equations. COLLECT and TRANSPOSE are two productions that must occur in sequence (COLLECT first, then TRANSPOSE). COLLECTRANSPOSE is a composed production that captures the sequence of COLLECT and TRANSPOSE by putting the actions of collection before the actions of transposition in its action sequence.

COLLECT

IF Goal is to solve for x
   And more than one term with x exists on one side of equation
   And more than one numeral exists on one side of equation
THEN Combine terms with x on each side of equation
   And combine numerals on each side of equation.

TRANSPOSE

IF Goal is to solve for x
   And only one term with x exists on each side of equation
   And only one numeral exists on each side of equation
THEN Subtract the term with x on the right side of equation from itself and from the term with x on the left side of equation
   And subtract the numeral on the left side of equation from both sides of the equation.

COLLECTRANSPOSE

IF Goal is to solve for x
THEN Combine terms with x on each side of equation
   And combine numerals on each side of equation
   And subtract the term with x on the right side of equation from itself and from the term with x on the left side of equation
   And subtract the numeral on the left side of equation from both sides of the equation.

TRANSPOSE (and is therefore called COLLECTRANSPOSE). This production might underlie the integrated performance shown at the bottom of Figure 9.4. Notice that TRANSPOSE will operate only after COLLECT because two of the conditions of TRANSPOSE are that only one term contain x and that one numeral be on each side of the equation. These are exactly the conditions created by the actions of COLLECT: it combines all terms containing x and all numerals on each side of the equation. When students write down the intermediate step $12x - 24 = 11x - 12$, it is easy for them to recognize the conditions of TRANSPOSE so that TRANSPOSE can operate.

By contrast to the intermediate set of conditions needed to reach the answer with COLLECT and TRANSPOSE, COLLECTRANSPOSE requires only one initiating condition to obtain an answer—the goal of solving for x. The first two actions performed by COLLECTRANSPOSE, which are exactly the same as those performed by COLLECT, in fact produce the conditions needed for TRANSPOSE. The third and fourth actions performed by COLLECTRANSPOSE are the same as those performed by TRANSPOSE. Thus, COLLECTRANSPOSE keeps all of the actions of COLLECT and TRANSPOSE but reduces the number of conditions. The lost conditions are still generated, but one no longer needs to attend to them consciously.

This process of making larger productions from smaller ones is part of what underlies the development of efficiency. It is very similar to the acceleration in motor skills that occurs when a need for cuing intermediate steps lessens. If you recall when you learned to drive, you will probably remember a stage in which you thought to yourself, "First, make sure the car is in neutral; second, put the key in the ignition; third, turn the key; fourth, put the clutch down; fifth, put the car in gear," etc. Later, the whole sequence was performed as a unit without the need for one step to cue the next.

One hallmark of expertise is speed. If having more composed procedures is one element of faster performance, then experts should show evidence of having more of such procedures than novices have. Lewis (1981) looked for such evidence for the task of solving linear equations. His experts were five mathematicians who worked at an IBM research lab, and his novices were ten university students who performed rather poorly on a pretest of skill in solving linear equations. He gave both groups fourteen new problems to solve and then counted the number of written steps in the correct solutions. The novices wrote down an average of 3.7 steps per correct solution, whereas the experts wrote down an average of 2.7 steps. Of course, the difference in the number of steps written down might reflect differences in WM capacity: mathematicians may have a larger capacity than university students and therefore, even if both groups are using the same procedures, the mathematicians may have less need to write down intermediate results. However, the results could also mean that the experts have developed composed procedures in which certain intermediate results never need to be represented in working memory. Since, as we discussed in Chapter 7, there is little evidence to support large differences in absolute WM capacity, the differences found by Lewis probably reflect differences in procedural knowledge.

Summary. In everyday computation tasks it is important to be not only effective but also efficient. Why are some people more efficient at computation than others? Besides the initial inefficiency in performing skills that comes from translating declarative into procedural knowledge, other sources of inefficiency are using a procedure of more steps than are needed and using procedures that require noticing more than a minimum number of conditions.

UNDERSTANDING

Computation can be performed fast and accurately, but inappropriately—as when someone adds correctly all the numbers in a "story problem," although the numbers should have been multiplied. In talking about knowledge of when to use one procedure or another to solve a mathematics problem, we are moving into an area that teachers often call "understanding." A person who really understands algebra or geometry or place value can use the rules and concepts in these domains flexibly and with a sensitivity to their appropriateness. This understanding may be encoded as a set of propositions, as a set of pattern-recognition productions, or as some mixture of these. Because the exact representations that influence understanding are not known, I will use a theoretically neutral term—*knowledge organization*—to refer to these representations. I encourage you to think more explicitly about the details of knowledge organization even though I avoid being explicit here. Clearly, future research must move toward greater explicitness in this area.

Knowledge Organization

As we saw in Chapter 6, domain-specific knowledge organization influences problem solving within a given domain because it guides the search for a solution. It helps us find our way through cognitive territory much as maps help us find our way through physical territory. When one is lost in the mountains, one can usually find one's way out faster with the help of a good map of these mountains than without one. When one is "lost" in a mathematics problem, one can usually solve it faster with a good knowledge organization than without one.

Differences in the Knowledge Organization of Experts and Novices

The knowledge organizations of experts and novices in mathematics (as in other domains) differ. Typically, experts' knowledge organization is more consistent with the accepted structure of a subject matter than is novices'. How do we know this? How can we observe something mental such as knowledge organization? The answer is that we cannot really observe knowledge organization; mental representations must always be inferred. A standard technique for inferring organization is to find out how strongly certain concept labels are associated for a given person, for example by having him or her free associate to the concept label. Try this on yourself by writing down now the first five words that come to your mind when you read "add." Then write down the first five words that come to your mind when you read "subtract." Finally, write down the first five words that come to your mind when you read *exponent.*

Figure 9.5 shows my responses to those three words. Notice that "add" and "subtract" both caused me to think of the other, but neither caused me to think of "exponent." Also, I did not think of "add" or "subtract" in response to "exponent." With responses such as these from several individuals, psychologists use various statistical techniques to determine how close these words (and, by inference, the concepts to which they refer) are in mental space.

Essentially, the statistical techniques involve counting the frequency with which concept labels of interest are grouped or share some third linking concept label. In Figure 9.5 the lists headed by "add" and "subtract"

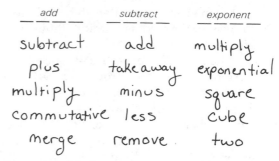

add	subtract	exponent
subtract	add	multiply
plus	take away	exponential
multiply	minus	square
commutative	less	cube
merge	remove	two

Figure 9.5. My free associations for add, subtract, and multiply. Concepts whose labels share associations (e.g., add and exponent share multiply) are thought to be closer in memory than concepts whose labels do not share any associations (e.g., subtract and exponent have no common associations).

share two words ("add," "subtract"), those headed by "add" and "exponent" share one word ("multiply"), and those headed by "subtract" and "exponent" share no words. Thus, the concepts of *add* and *subtract* are said to be closer together in my mental space than the concepts of *add* and *exponent,* which in turn are closer together than the concepts of *subtract* and *exponent.* A map of these relationships is shown in Figure 9.6. Notice that *add* and *subtract* are directly linked to each other because they cued each other's recall.

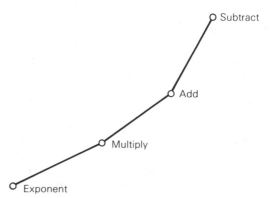

Figure 9.6. The arrangement of four mathematical concepts in mental space.

Add and *exponent,* on the other hand, are linked only indirectly through the concept of *multiply* because they did not cue each other's recall, but both cued the recall of *multiply.* In this manner, the organization of knowledge is inferred from subjects' associations or groupings of concept labels.

Geeslin and Shavelson (1975*a*) used a word-association test to examine knowledge organization of eighth graders for the domain of probability. The concept labels used were "probability," "event," "independent," "zero," "interaction," "trial," "experiment," "mutually exclusive," and "outcome." Each student generated associations to these labels three times: immediately before a unit of mathematics instruction (pretest), immediately after the unit (posttest), and two weeks later (retention test). A randomly selected half of the students studied a programmed unit on probability that covered the concepts (experimental group), whereas the other half studied a programmed unit on prime numbers (control group). Geeslin and Shavelson predicted that, after instruction, the students who studied the probability unit would arrange probability concepts in their minds in a manner similar to the arrangement reflected in the programmed unit, whereas the other students would not.

The results confirmed their prediction. Figure 9.7 shows the average distance between the organization of the concepts found in the instructional material and the organization inferred from the students' responses on the free-association test. On the pretest, both groups show a similar distance (.04) between their knowledge organization and the content organization. However, on both the posttest and the retention test, the experimental group's organizations are significantly closer to the content organization than the control group's are.

The researchers also gave the students a thirty-five item achievement test on probability concepts and problems. Table 9.11 shows the performance of the two groups on this test. On the pretest both groups performed equally poorly, but the experimental group performed much better than the con-

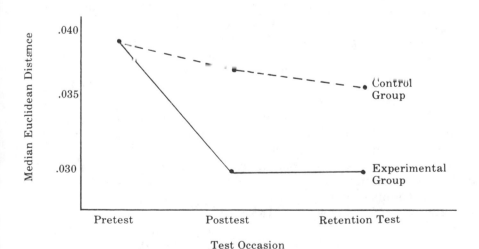

Figure 9.7. Median distances between students' knowledge organization and the organization of the content of instruction. (From Geeslin and Shavelson, 1975*a*.)

Table 9.11. Means and standard deviations of scores on achievement tests for students with different knowledge organization. (From Geeslin and Shavelson, 1975a.)

TREATMENT GROUP	PRETEST	POSTTEST	RETENTION TEST
Experimental	$\overline{X} = 3.65$ $\sigma = 2.45$ $n = 43$	$\overline{X} = 15.54$ $\sigma = 5.74$ $n = 41$	$\overline{X} = 16.21$ $\sigma = 6.32$ $n = 43$
Control	$\overline{X} = 3.00$ $\sigma = 1.90$ $n = 42$	$\overline{X} = 3.73$ $\sigma = 2.46$ $n = 40$	$\overline{X} = 4.16$ $\sigma = 3.06$ $n = 43$

trol group on the posttest and retention test. Thus the "experts" in probability (those who performed well on the achievement test) had an organization of knowledge different from the "novices" (those who did not perform well on the achievement test). Geeslin and Shavelson (1975b) replicated this study using high school students and obtained similar results.

Knowledge organization has also been studied for "word problems." Silver (1981) studied how seventh graders grouped sixteen word problems that independently varied on content and on the process used to solve the problem. For example, the following two problems have similar content (farming) but are solved using different procedures:

9.1. A farmer is counting the hens and rabbits in his barnyard. He counts a total of 50 heads and 140 feet. How many hens and how many rabbits does the farmer have?

9.2. A farmer is counting the hens and rabbits in his barnyard. He counts 6 coops with 4 hens each, 2 coops with 3 hens each, 5 cages with 6 rabbits each, and 3 cages with 4 rabbits each. How many hens and how many rabbits does the farmer have?

Take a minute to try to solve these two problems. Did you use the same procedures? The solutions are given at the end of the chapter.

Another problem used by Silver (1981) was:

9.3. Bill has a collection of 20 coins that consists entirely of dimes and quarters. If the collection is worth $4.10, how many of each kind of coin are in the collection?

Clearly, this problem has different content from problems 9.1 and 9.2. However, it is solved using the same procedure as was used to solve problem 9.1.

Silver (1981) asked students to sort sixteen such problems into groups that were "mathematically related." He then asked them to solve twelve of the problems they had sorted. On the basis of their problem-solving performance, he divided the students into good, average, and poor problem solvers. He was most interested in whether or not students sorted problems differently (by content or process) at different levels of expertise in word problems.

Table 9.12 shows the results. If students are categorizing completely on the basis of one dimension or the other, their problem-sorting score for that dimension would be 24. However, the good problem solvers were

Table 9.12. Categorization of word problems by good, average, and poor problem solvers. (Adapted from Silver, 1981.)

	DIMENSION USED IN SORTING	
	PROCESS	CONTENT
Good problem solver	17.8	0.6
Average problem solver	12.0	3.4
Poor problem solver	6.3	8.9

more likely to use process to categorize problems, whereas the poor problem-solvers were more likely to use content. These results suggest that the good problem solvers' knowledge is organized around problem solution processes and the poor problem solvers' knowledge is not.

THE ROLE OF KNOWLEDGE ORGANIZATION IN COGNITIVE PROCESSING

The fact that skilled and less skilled persons differ in knowledge organization for a given mathematics domain might be quite unimportant for performance, just as one's hair color is irrelevant to one's quantitative skill. However, there is growing evidence that knowledge organization (also called cognitive structure) has a pervasive influence on cognitive processing. It influences what is attended to, what is recalled, and therefore, ultimately, how problems are solved. In Chapter 6 we saw one example of how organization influences problem solving (medical diagnosis) and in Chapter 10 we will see another. Here we will focus on the role of knowledge organization in attention and recall.

The Role of Organization in Attention. Robinson and Hayes (1978) studied the role of knowledge organization in attention. They

reasoned that if students have organized knowledge about algebra word problems, they should be able to use it to decide what parts of the problem statement are relevant or irrelevant (that is, to decide what to attend to).

One type of word problem commonly found in high school algebra is the "river current" type in which the speed of a boat depends on the rower's strength, the speed of the current, and the direction of the boat with respect to the current. Robinson and Hayes (1978) used an analog of this type of problem involving headwinds and tailwinds rather than current. Their problem is shown in Table 9.13.

These researchers had college students who were good algebra students read this problem, segment by segment, and judge which segments of the problem statement were relevant and which were irrelevant to the solution. In fact, only three elements of

Table 9.13. The word problem used by Robinson and Hayes (1978). The question that went along with this problem was "What was the plane's speed in each direction?"

A crop-dusting plane carries 2,000 pounds of Rotenone dusting compound, 250 pounds of high test fuel, a pilot highly skilled in low-altitude flying, and a duster-machinery operator, the pilot's younger brother. The plane must dust a rectangular tobacco field 0.5 miles wide by 0.6 miles long. The dusting compound must be spread with a density of 200 pounds per 0.001 square mile. Further, the compound must be spread between 6 A.M. and 9 A.M., when there is sufficient light and before the morning dew has evaporated, to assure the adherence of the compound to the plants. The plane can dust a 44 foot wide strip at one time. The plane flies the length of the field with a 6 m.p.h. tailwind and back against the same headwind. With the wind, the plane uses fuel at the rate of 80 pounds per hour. The ratio of flying time against the wind to time with the wind is 9:8. The duster operator must try to spread the compound uniformly on the ground despite varying speed.

the statement were essential to finding the solution: (1) "with a 6 m.p.h. tailwind," (2) "back against the same headwind," and (3) "ratio of flying time against the wind to time with the wind is 9:8." If the students are using some cognitive structure they have for solving this type of problem, one would expect them to judge these three elements to be relevant more often than they judged other elements of the problem to be relevant.

The researchers also thought that whether the problem question was seen first (before the statement) or last would influence students' judgments of relevance. The problem question provides a big clue to the type of problem and therefore to what knowledge to activate. Finally, they thought that students' judgments might change from a first to a second reading of the statement, especially if the problem question had been read last.

Table 9.14 shows the results. Overall, the data supported their predictions: the relevant segments (1) were judged to be relevant by a higher proportion of the students than were any of the irrelevant segments. Also, the students who had read the problem question first were more likely to judge relevant segments as being relevant on the first reading (.93) than were students who read the problem question last (.84). Improvement in correctly classifying relevant segments on the second reading (pass 2) was restricted to the students who read the problem question last (they went from .84 correct on pass 1 to .89 correct on pass 2).

The data in this table also show interesting differences between different types of irrelevant segment. Some of the irrelevant segments dealt with space, some with weight, and some with nonmathematical matters such as the type of dusting compound used. Students were good at recognizing the nonmathematical segments (4) that were irrelevant, but were often fooled by the space and weight segments. Robinson and Hayes (1978) speculate that some students are fooled by space and weight segments because their organization of knowledge does not provide for these distinctions.

The Role of Organization in Recall. If people pay attention to information that matches their knowledge organization and ignore other information, they should be more likely to recall the needed information. Mayer (1982) examined students' recall of algebra story problems in light of this hypothesis. Some of the problems he used are shown in Table 9.15. His word problems could be solved differently as could Silver's (1981). For example, the first problem in Table 9.15 is solved by using the formula Distance = rate × time, and the second by setting up some algebraic equations and then solving for each unknown. In all, Mayer studied sixteen problem types. He knew from a previous study (Mayer, 1981) the relative frequencies with which each type occurred in a sample of ten textbooks commonly used in high school algebra classes.

Students in Mayer's (1982) study each read eight story problems for two minutes each. They were directed to read and paraphrase each problem, but not to solve it. After studying the problems, they wrote down what they recalled from each problem. Students who recalled all of the relevant information were said to have recalled the problem. Mayer determined the proportion of students recalling problems of each of the sixteen types and correlated this with the frequency of occurrence of each problem type in textbooks. He found a moderately strong relationship of .66.

These findings can be interpreted in the following way. Students develop organized knowledge for the most frequently occurring story problem types in their textbooks. When asked to study new problems, they try to

Table 9.14. The proportions of students judging each segment in the word problem to be relevant. "Q first" means that the problem question occurred before the problem statements. "Pass 1" and "pass 2," respectively, refer to the first and second readings of the problem. (From Robinson and Hayes, 1978.)

	Q FIRST		Q LAST	
	PASS 1	PASS 2	PASS 1	PASS 2
1. Problem-relevant items with a 6 m.p.h. tailwind) back against the same headwind) ratio of speed w/t against wind is 9:8)	.93	.92	.84	.89
2. Space items plane must dust rectangular tobacco field) .5 miles wide) .6 miles long) per .001 sq. mile) 44 ft. wide strip) plane flies length of field)	.65	.65	.93	.45

3. Weight items
 2000#   60# per hour)
  250#   80# per hour)
 with a density)
  200#)
	.77	.65	.93	.48

Categories 2. and 3. combined	.82 (Pass 1)		.56 (Pass 2)	

4. Irrelevant/other items
 a crop-dusting plane)
 of Rotenone dusting compound)
 of high test fuel)
 a pilot)
 highly skilled in low-altitude flying)
 a duster-machinery operator)
 the pilot's younger brother)
 the compound must be spread)
  between 6 A.M. and 9 A.M.)
  when there is sufficient light and)
  before dew has evaporated to as-)
  sure adherence of compound)
 the compound must be spread uni-)
  formly despite varying speed)
	.20	.14	.35	.11

match the new problems with their prior knowledge of story problems. If they find a match, it is easier to encode a problem because the relevant aspects of the problem can be focused and elaborated on. This leads to better recall for problems that match students' cognitive structures.

Mayer (1982) also looked at recall of different propositions that occurred across problem types. In particular, story problems contain many of what Mayer calls "assignment" propositions and some of what he calls "relation" propositions. Assignment propositions assign a numerical value to some vari-

Table 9.15. Two of the problems students studied and recalled. (From Mayer, 1982.)

1

A truck leaves Los Angeles en route to San Francisco at 1 P.M. A second truck leaves San Francisco at 2 P.M. en route to Los Angeles going along the same route. Assume the two cities are 465 miles apart and that the trucks meet at 6 P.M. If the second truck travels 15 m.p.h. faster than the first truck, how fast does each truck go?

2

On a ferry trip, the fare for each adult was 50 cents and for each child was 25 cents. The number of passengers was 30 and the total paid was $12.25. How many adults and how many children were there?

---

able. For example, in the first problem shown in Table 9.15, the proposition that the first truck started at 1 P.M. is an assignment proposition, assigning the value of 1 P.M. to the variable of when the first truck started. Relation propositions describe a numerical relationship between two variables. For example, in that same problem, that the second truck travels 15 mph faster than the first truck is a relation proposition. Mayer (1981) found that assignment propositions made up 61 percent of the propositions in a sample of 1100 story problems in algebra textbooks, whereas relation propositions made up only 11 percent. Because of differential frequency of exposure, students are more likely to develop knowledge structures for assignment propositions than for relation propositions, and therefore they should recall assignment propositions better than relation propositions. This result was in fact obtained. Students forgot 29 percent of all relation propositions, but they forgot only 9 percent of all assignment propositions. Heller and Greeno (1978) have found that elementary school children also have trouble with relationship propositions in story problems.

In the Mayer (1982) study, students' knowledge organization affected the *amount* of information they recalled. In addition, knowledge structures may affect the *organization* of what is recalled. Usually, the way information is organized at encoding determines how it will be organized during a recall attempt, and knowledge structures appear to guide the organization of new information at encoding.

Adelson (1981) examined the differences in organization of recall in expert and novice computer programmers. Expert programmers were teaching assistants for a beginning course in Polymorphic Programming Language (PPL); novices were students who had just completed this beginning course.

Adelson presented sixteen lines of PPL code (shown in Table 9.16) to her subjects. Five, five, and six of these lines came from each of three programs designed, respectively, to sort items in a list, to randomly order a list (method 1), and to randomly order a list (method 2). The last two programs performed the same function (randomly ordering a list), but they did so by using two different procedures. The first and last program performed different functions (sorting versus randomly ordering), but they used similar procedures.

Another way to think of the sixteen lines of program code is as if they were sixteen sentences coming from three different stories, one story about a farmer who makes a million dollars by hard work, a second about a lazy mountain climber who reaches the top of a mountain by getting a helicopter ride three-fourths of the way to the top, and a third about a mountain climber who reaches the top of a mountain through hard work. The sentences from the second and third story share a topic (mountain climbing), just as the lines of code from the second and third programs share a function (randomly ordering items). The first and third stories differ in

Table 9.16. The lines of code presented (randomly) to students. Here the lines of code are grouped according to their membership in one of three programs. (From Adelson, 1981.)

STIMULUS MATERIALS LABELED ACCORDING TO EACH ITEM'S PROGRAM MEMBERSHIP

1	2	PROGRAM 1
1	[1.0]	[x]$sort.within(sorting.list)ij, temp.sort
2	[1.1]	[x]for i< −1:length(sorting.list) dothru %3
3	[1.2]	[x]for j< −i:length (sorting.list) dothru %3
4	[1.3]	[x]if sorting.list[i]>sorting.list[j] then,
		temp.sort< −sorting.list[j];
		sorting.list[j]< −sorting.list[i];
		sorting.list[i]< −temp.sort
5	[1.4]	[x]return sorting.list

		PROGRAM 2
6	[2.0]	[x]$random.to.new(old.list)new.list,n,random.place
7	[2.1]	[x]new.list< −make(tuple,length(old.list),null),n< −0
8	[2.2]	[x]loop:n < −n+1; if n=length(old.list)+1 then return new.list
9	[2.3]	[x]random.place< −int(length(old.list)*random(0))+1
10	[2.4]	[x]if old.list[random.place]#null then
		new.list[n]< −old.list[random.place];
		old.list[random.place]< −null;
		goto loop else goto %3

		PROGRAM 3
11	[3.0]	[x]$random.within(random.list);c,d,random.test,temp.within
12	[3.1]	[x]for c< − 1 :length(random.list) dothru %4
13	[3.2]	[x]for d< − 1 :length(random.list) dothru %4
14	[3.3]	[x]random.test < −int(2*random(0))+1
15	[3.4]	[x]if random.text= 1 then temp.within < −random.list[d];
		random.list[d] < −random.list[c];
		random.list[c] < −temp.within
16	[3.5]	[x]return random.list

Note—Column 1 indicates the number of each item. The first number in Column 2 indicates the program in which the item occurs; the second number indicates its position within the program.

topic, but share a procedure for meeting a goal (hard work), just as the first and third programs differ in function, but share a procedure for meeting their goals.

Table 9.16 shows the sixteen lines of PPL code grouped according to program membership. Table 9.17 shows an alternative way to group these lines, which is according to their syntax. For example, the lines in the middle of Table 9.17, labeled I, are condi-

tional (IF) statements, which carry out some procedure only when certain preconditions are met. The three lines below the I lines, labeled A, are assignment statements that assign values to variables. This grouping of program statements is analogous to grouping sentences from stories according to their function—for example, grouping all topic sentences together and all descriptive sentences together.

Table 9.17. The lines of code randomly presented to students. Here the lines are organized according to their syntactical category. (From Adelson, 1981.)

STIMULUS MATERIALS LABELED ACCORDING TO EACH ITEM'S SYNTACTIC CATEGORY

1	2	FUNCTION NAME OR "HEADER" (H)
1	H	[x]$sort.within(sorting.list); i,j,temp.sort
6	H	[x]$random.to.new(old.list/new.list,n,random.place
11	H	[x]$random.within(random.list); c,d,random.test,temp.within

		ITERATION OR "FOR" STATEMENTS (F)
2	F	[x]for i< −1:length(sorting.list) dothru %3
3	F	[x]for j< −1:length(sorting.list) dothru %3
12	F	[x]for c< −1:lenght(random.list) dothru %4
13	F	[x]for d< −1:length(random.list) do thru %4

		CONDITIONAL OR "IF" STATEMENTS (I)
4	I	[x]if sorting.list[i]>sorting.list[j]then; temp.sort< −sorting.list[j]; sorting.list[j]< −sorting.list[i]; sorting.list[i]< −temp.sort
8	I	[x]loop:n< −n+1; if n=length(old.list)+1 then return new.list
10	I	[x]if old.list[random.place] #null then; new.list[n]< −old.list[random.place]; old.list[random.place]< −null,goto loop else goto %3
15	I	[x]if random.text=1 then temp.within< −random.list[d]; random.list[d]< −random.list[c]; random.list[c]< −temp.within

		ASSIGNMENT STATEMENTS (A)
7	A	[x]new.list< −make(tuple,length(old.list),null); n< −0
9	A	[x]random.place< −int(length(old.list)*random(0))+1
14	A	[x]random.test< −int(2*random(0))+1

		RETURN STATEMENTS (R)
5	R	[x]return sorting.list
16	R	[x]return random.list

Column 1 indicates the item's number; Column 2 indicates the item's syntactic category.

The lines of code from all three programs were pooled and presented to subjects randomly. Subjects studied each line of code for twenty seconds, and, after all lines had been seen, took eight minutes to recall as much as they could. This procedure was repeated nine times, using a different random presentation order each time.

Adelson (1981) examined the recall data to see which lines followed which other lines (how subjects organized their recall). Figures 9.8 and 9.9 show the organization of recall for experts and novices, respectively. (The pictures in those figures are produced by the statistical techniques of hierarchical clustering and multidimensional scaling.) The experts

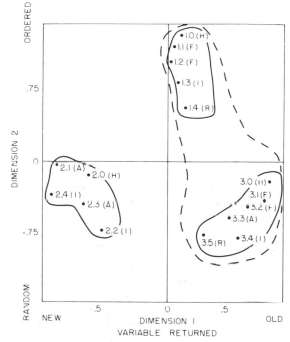

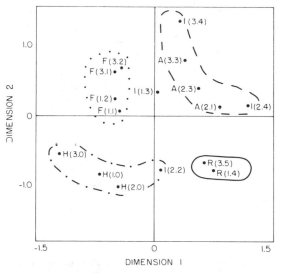

Figure 9.8. The organization of recall of lines of program code by experts. The solid lines indicate one level of grouping (by program), and the dotted lines indicate a second level of grouping (by procedure used in the program). (From Adelson, 1981.)

in the lower right quadrant for the novice's recall. One is from the third program and one from the first. Both, however, are return (R) statements. That is, they both come from the same syntactical category in the PPL language. Similarly, the three lines in the lower left quadrant are from three different programs, but they are all headers (H). Thus, novices appear to organize their recall of program code according to syntactical category of the code rather than its membership in a program or its procedural quality.

The novices' method of organization was not as effective as the experts'. The novices recalled fewer lines of code overall (about ten) than did the experts (about thirteen). The novices' method may be less effective because it is not as hierarchical as the experts'. The experts had two layers of organization: the procedures used by the programs and the programs themselves. The novices had only

clearly recall the lines from each program together. For example, all the items numbered 2 are from the second program, and these are grouped together in recall as indicated by the solid line surrounding them. In addition, every expert subject recalled all the lines from programs 1 and 3 before recalling those from program 2, as is signified by the dashed line that groups these two sets. This suggests that experts noted the similar procedure used in programs 1 and 3, and this then influenced their encoding and retrieval processes.

The lines that novices grouped together in recall tended to be from the same syntactical category rather than from the same program or procedural category. For example, look at the two lines of code that are circled

Figure 9.9. The organization of recall of lines of program code by novices. The letters indicate syntactical categories, and the numbers indicate program membership. In general, the lines that are grouped together are from a common syntactical category. (From Adelson, 1981.)

one layer of organization: the syntactical category to which the statement belonged.

Summary. People who are more and less competent in a given domain of mathematical content appear to differ in their knowledge organization. That is, they differ in the patterns of relationships they see among concepts. Those who are more competent on achievement and problem-solving tests also seem to structure relationships among concepts in a way similar to the structure of these concepts in textbooks. These cognitive structures appear to mediate attention, encoding, and retrieval, and therefore affect the quality of problem solving.

There are some striking similarities between the research in mathematics on cognitive structure and the research in reading comprehension on text structure. Just as the mathematics research shows that capable math students have greater knowledge of mathematical structures (Silver, 1981; Geeslin and Shavelson, 1975a), so the reading research shows that capable readers have greater knowledge of text structures (B. Meyer, Brandt, and Bluth, 1980). Just as the math research shows that students who use structural knowledge to guide their encoding and retrieval also recall more (Adelson, 1981), so too the reading research shows that students who use text structure to guide them recall more (Meyer, Brandt, and Bluth, 1980). Thus, it appears that cognitive structures are an important part of understanding across skill areas.

Estimation

Another important aspect of competence in mathematics is estimation. Skill in estimation is an important part of self-monitoring in mathematics. A good estimator can approach many mathematics problems from two directions: estimation and precise calculation.

When the solutions arrived at by these two procedures are similar, the problem can be considered to be solved. However, if the estimated and calculated solutions differ by a great deal, something is probably wrong with the solution, and another solution should be sought. Poor estimators do not have the ability to check their solutions in this way and therefore are less likely than good estimators to alter their behavior adaptively.

Recent studies of estimation have begun to identify some of the strategies used by good estimators (Reys, Rybolt, Bestgen, and Wyatt, 1982; Siegel, Goldsmith, and Madson, 1982). Reys et al. interviewed fifty-nine good estimators in grades 7–12 to determine their strategies. Three common strategies were *reformulation, translation,* and *compensation.* In reformulation, numbers are rounded off to make them more manageable (e.g., 87,236 might be rounded by 87,000). In translation the structure of the problem is changed from the structure suggested in the problem statement. For example, to estimate the answer to the addition problem:

$$504$$
$$492$$
$$+487$$

a good estimator will translate this into a multiplication problem and say, "500 times 3 is 1500. . . . The answer will be about 1500." Finally, in compensation, good estimators compensate for one adjustment by making an equal and opposite adjustment. For example, in the just-mentioned addition problem, someone using compensation might say, "The answer will be 500 times 3 . . . about 1500 . . . and a little below 1500 because I added more than I subtracted in rounding each number to 500."

Strategies are procedures stimulated by mental goals. Like other procedures, they are teachable. As more is learned about successful strategies, more will be known about what to teach students who do not seem to have discovered these strategies on their own. Thus, as we come to understand estimation strategies better, we will be better equipped to teach them.

INSTRUCTION

Although there are many implications for instruction in this chapter, one of the most important is that a decision about what to teach depends very much on what the child has in his or her head. Is there a misconception? Is there a failure to integrate a set of skills? Is there a lack of prerequisite skills? Is there a superficial knowledge of structure? Is there a familiar structure to which learning of a new abstract structure can be tied? Is there an effective self-monitoring strategy?

Once the cognitive goal of instruction has been precisely defined, learning often proceeds smoothly. An example of this is in teaching counting procedures for addition to nursery school children. Recall from the beginning of this chapter that Groen and Parkman (1972) identified five counting procedures called COUNT BOTH, COUNT FROM FIRST, COUNT FROM SECOND, COUNT FROM MINIMUM, and COUNT FROM MAXIMUM. These are good examples of precise cognitive descriptions that could serve as goals of instruction. Groen and Resnick (1977) selected COUNT BOTH and COUNT FROM MAXIMUM as their goals for instruction with ten nursery school children. Although they hoped that some students would discover COUNT FROM MAXIMUM, they did not teach this procedure directly.

Instruction proceeded in fifteen- to twenty-five-minute sessions spread out over several weeks of school. The children selected knew how to count but did not know how to add. There were three phases of instruction. During the first phase children were given blocks to use for counting and a series of cards with problems of the form $m + n =$ _____ on them. Each child was directed to (1) read m, (2) count out m blocks, (3) read n, (4) count out n blocks, (5) merge the sets of m and n blocks, and (6) count out the result.

The second phase of instruction involved having the child solve problems of the form $m + n =$ _____ using the blocks, but without being cued in each of the steps in the procedure (unless necessary). This phase was continued until the child consistently used the COUNT BOTH procedure without prompting.

Finally, the researchers asked each child to solve problems without using blocks. Also, in this phase, children indicated their responses on a keyboard that recorded their reaction times. This was done so that the procedure being used by each child could be determined by fitting his or her reaction time data to the predicted form of the data for each of the five procedures. Groen and Resnick (1977) thought that during this final phase the children would be motivated to invent a procedure that was more efficient than COUNT BOTH, because they no longer had the blocks to rely on.

The results showed that the children used COUNT BOTH consistently after an average of eight sessions. Also, half of the children changed to COUNT FROM MAXIMUM during the final phase of instruction, in which they solved problems without using blocks. This was done without any explicit instruction in how to perform COUNT FROM MAXIMUM.

This experiment in instruction demonstrates two important learning conditions—modeling and motivating. The researchers directed children to create a concrete model of COUNT BOTH by using blocks. This resulted in a 100 percent success rate. Then they attempted to motivate children to invent a more efficient procedure by making COUNT BOTH more burdensome. This was enough to cause half the children to discover COUNT FROM MAXIMUM. Probably the other half would have learned the more efficient procedure if the researchers had modeled its use.

A CONCLUDING EXAMPLE

Here is a word problem that was given recently to a large national sample of seventeen-year-olds in the National Assessment of Educational Progress (as reported in Mayer, 1982):

> Lemonade costs 95 cents for one 56-ounce bottle. At the school fair, Bob sold cups holding 8 ounces for 20 cents each. How much money did the school make on each bottle?

Of these students 71 percent failed this problem. Yet this type of problem comes up often in personal money-management situations. Some students who fail such problems in test situations may succeed at them in their personal lives, but it is probable that many who fail in test situations also fail to solve such problems in everyday situations.

How can teachers improve students' mathematics skills? In this chapter I have suggested that computation skills, a knowledge of the conceptual structure of mathematics, and estimation skill each have a role to play in mathematics competence. Other competencies, such as general problem-solving skill, understanding of individual concepts, and mental imagery are probably also important.

My purpose in this chapter was to discuss most, but not all, of the important aspects of mathematical competence. In so doing, I hoped to exemplify the notion that it is important to determine the differences in cognitive representations and processes between skilled and less skilled individuals as a way of understanding what should be taught.

ADDITIONAL READING

Anderson, J. R., ed. (1981). *Cognitive skills and their acquisition.* Hillsdale, N.J.: Lawrence Erlbaum Associates.

Carpenter, T. P., J. M. Moser, and T. A. Romberg, eds. (1982). *Addition and subtraction: A cognitive perspective.* Hillsdale, N.J.: Lawrence Erlbaum Associates.

Greeno, J. G. (1976). Understanding and procedural knowledge in mathematics instruction. *Educational Psychologist,* 12, 262–83.

Mayer, R. E., J. Larkin, and J. Kadane (1983). A cognitive analysis of mathematical problem solving ability. In R. J. Sternberg (ed.), *Advances in the psychology of human intelligence,* vol. 2. (pp. 231–73). Hillsdale, N.J.: Lawrence Erlbaum Associates.

Resnick, L. B. and W. W. Ford (1981). *The psychology of mathematics for instruction.* Hillsdale, N.J.: Lawrence Erlbaum Associates.

Riley, M. S., J. G. Greeno, and J. I. Heller (1983). Development of children's problem-solving ability in arithmetic. In H. P. Ginsberg (ed.), *The development of mathematical thinking* (pp. 153–96). New York: Academic Press.

Shavelson, R. J. (1981). Teaching mathematics: Contributions of cognitive research. *Educational Psychologist* 16, 23–44.

SOLUTIONS TO WORD PROBLEMS

9.1. x = # of hens; y = # of rabbits

$$x + y = 50, \text{ therefore } x = 50 - y.$$
$$2x + 4y = 140$$

$2(50 - y) + 4y = 140$	(substitution)
$100 - 2y + 4y = 140$	(multiply by 2)
$100 + 2y = 140$	(collect terms)
$2y = 40$	(transpose)
$y = 20$	(divide by 2)
$x = 30$	(substitute 20 for y in $x = 50 - y$)

9.2. number of hens = $6(4) + 2(3) =$
   $24 + 6 = 30$

number of rabbits = 5(6) + 3(4) =
30 + 12 = 42

9.3. x = number of dimes; y = number of quarters

$$x + y = 20, \text{ therefore } x = 20 - y.$$

$$10x + 25y = 410$$
$$10(20 - y) + 25y = 410 \quad \text{(substitution)}$$
$$200 - 10y + 25y = 410 \quad \text{(multiply by 10)}$$
$$200 + 15y = 410 \quad \text{(collect terms)}$$
$$15y = 210 \quad \text{(transpose)}$$
$$y = 14 \quad \text{(divide by 15)}$$
$$x = 6 \quad \text{(substitute 14 for } y \text{ in } x = 20 - y)$$

Chapter

10

Science

SUMMARY

1. The goals of science instruction usually include acquiring organized knowledge of different branches of science, problem-solving procedures for specific branches of science, and general reasoning procedures.

2. Individuals differ in their organization of knowledge about science both as a function of age and as a function of direct instruction.

3. Skill in domain-specific problem solving in science is related to possession of prerequisite skills, organization of relevant declarative knowledge, and quality of problem-solving processes.

4. Humans have difficulty with certain inductive and deductive reasoning tasks.

5. Since one important part of science is the acquisition of organized declarative knowledge, instruction that encourages organization facilitates learning in science.

Science is the study of phenomena through reliable and valid observation, and the generation of theories to account for what is observed. Science is thus both process and product. Its processes include observation and inductive and deductive reasoning. Its immediate products are the several branches of physical, biological, and social science. At a greater distance, its products include technological developments.

As a society becomes more technological, it is increasingly important for its citizens to understand both the processes and products of science. Without such understanding, people cannot make the choices they need to make about such issues as pollution control, weapons development, nuclear waste management, and health care.

In this chapter we will see what is known about the psychological processes involved in performing the tasks of science. Such information should interest science teachers, of course. But it should also interest others as

an analog to other subject matter areas. For example, an early section of this chapter describes changes in the propositional network that result from instruction in science. Surely analogous changes occur in teaching declarative knowledge in any subject.

COMPONENTS OF SCIENCE INSTRUCTION

Most science instruction is directed at one of three general goals: acquiring organized knowledge of a particular branch of science, improving the ability to solve problems in a specific domain of science, and improving general reasoning skills. Table 10.1 shows test questions that emphasize one or another of these goals. The first question tests knowledge of the higher-order group to which the element xenon belongs and thus taps knowledge organization. The second question emphasizes the ability to use a specific principle to solve a problem. A person who under-

---

Table 10.1. Sample science questions that emphasize knowledge organization (1), domain-specific problem solving (2), and general reasoning skills (3).

1. Xenon is a member of _____.

   a. the metals   b. the halogens

2. Using what you know about the relationship of supply, demand, and price, tell which of the following tables is more plausible.

   a.
Year	Supply	Demand	Price
1964	4.5 million bushels	.05 bushels/capita	$.20/lb.
1965	5.5 million bushels	.05 bushels/capita	$.15/lb.
1966	3.5 million bushels	.05 bushels/capita	$.25/lb.

   b.
Year	Supply	Demand	Price
1964	4.5 million bushels	.05 bushels/capita	$.20/lb.
1965	5.5 million bushels	.05 bushels/capita	$.25/lb.
1966	3.5 million bushels	.05 bushels/capita	$.15/lb.

3. A scientist proposes the following theory to explain why "fidgets" (a type of swimming worm) always turn left in their swimming:

   Fidgets turn left due to a gene for left-turning.

   The scientist then deduces that if he removes the suspected gene and the fidgets no longer turn left, that his theory is proved.

   Do you agree or disagree with his conclusion? Why or why not?

stands the law of supply and demand should be able to answer this question. The final question is intended to test for general reasoning skills. The fact that the question is about a nonsense domain makes it clear that the skill being tested is thought to be a general one.

Most of this chapter will contain descriptions of what is known from an information-processing perspective about performance in each of these three areas.

ORGANIZED KNOWLEDGE

Knowledge Differences between Children and Adults

When I was a primary school teacher in West Africa, I was surprised to find that my students believed that the harmless variety of chameleon in the area was poisonous. Similarly, adults are often surprised at the "misconceptions" (from the adult's point of view) that children have about various natural phenomena. Very young children, for example, believe that the earth is flat, and, although older children believe that the earth is a sphere, they also think that all people live on the top of this sphere (Nussbaum, 1979; Sneider and Pulos, 1983).

One concept that has been studied developmentally in great detail is that of *alive*. Siegler and Richards (1983) asked both children and adults a variety of questions that revealed their knowledge of "aliveness." For example, they asked them to name some things that were alive, to evaluate whether something (e.g., a car or a tree) was alive or not, and to name the attributes they thought distinguished living from nonliving things. From the answers to these questions they developed a model of the propositional networks for *alive* possessed by typical children and adults.

Figures 10.1 and 10.2 show the network representations for four-year-olds and adults, respectively. The solid lines indicate "strong" links, and the dashed lines indicate "weak" links. Strong links were to attributes that clearly differentiated between alive and not alive, whereas weak links were to attributes that somewhat less reliably differentiated alive and not alive. Both the four-year-olds and adults have strong propositions representing the ideas that animals are moving things, noisy things, things with eyes, growing things, and reproducing things, and that they are alive. Similarly, both have strong propositions for the ideas that plants are growing things, reproducing things, and things with roots. However, only the adults have a proposition for the idea that plants are alive. Also, the adults have stronger propositions than the children for the ideas that reproducing things are alive and growing things are alive. Finally, the adults have a proposition to represent the idea that moving things are alive in the sense of being lively as distinct from having biological life.

When asked whether a tree is alive, a person can answer this question by retrieving the proposition directly . . . ([trees are alive]), by retrieving some other propositions (e.g., [plants are alive] and [trees are plants]) and drawing an inference ([therefore trees are alive]), or by determining the amount of overlap between the attributes of living things and the attributes of trees. If there is substantial overlap, it is concluded that trees are alive.

Siegler and Richards (1983) found that four-year-olds were much less likely to say that a tree is alive than were adults, and we can see why this is so. First, they have not stored the fact that trees are alive. Second, they do not have all the other facts needed to draw an inference that trees are alive; specifically, they have not stored the fact that plants are alive. Finally, trees have only one of five of the attributes associated with living

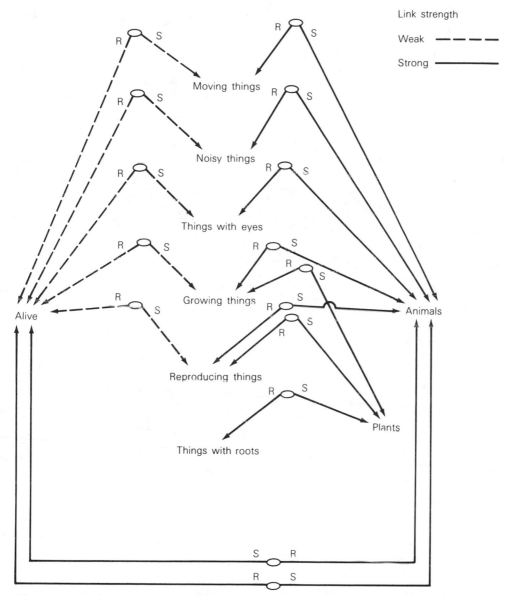

Figure 10.1. A hypothetical propositional network for a four-year-old's concept of *alive*. R = Relation, S = Subject. (Adapted from Siegler and Richards, 1983.)

things—they grow. (Of course, they also reproduce, but this is probably not known to four-year-olds). Because there is little overlap for the four-year-old between the attributes

of living things and the attributes of trees, they conclude that trees are *not* alive.

In contrast, adults can deduce that trees are alive from the proposition that plants are

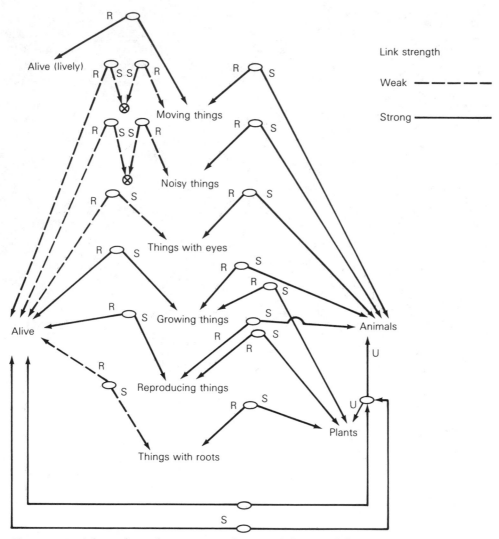

Figure 10.2. A hypothetical propositional network for an adult's concept of *alive*. (Adapted from Siegler and Richards, 1983.)

alive. Also, for them there is more overlap between attributes of living things and attributes of trees. Besides knowing, as young children do, that trees grow, adults are likely to know that trees reproduce and that they have roots. Thus trees have three attributes in common with aliveness. Furthermore, two of these attributes are stored as strong propositions, which means they are more likely to be activated than are weak propositions dur-

ing attribute comparison. Thus adults' propositional networks are much more likely to lead them to conclude that trees are alive.

Knowledge Changes Following Instruction

One can imagine that the change from the four-year-old to the adult conception of living things could occur even in individuals who never take a biology class. Such nonschool activities as tending a garden or caring for pets could lead parents to instruct children about the nature of living things. Some science knowledge, however, is more likely to develop as a function of formal instruction. Champagne, Klopfer, Desena, and Squires (1981), Manelis and Yehovich (1984), and Shavelson (1972) have documented knowledge changes that result from instruction, respectively, in geology, experimental psychology, and physics.

Champagne et al. (1981) worked with thirty eighth graders to study changes in knowledge about geology. Before instruction, the students were shown thirteen geology concept labels written on cards ("granite," "igneous," "lava," "limestone," "magma," "marble," "metamorphic," "pumice," "rock," "sediment," "sedimentary," "shale," and "slate"). They were given a large piece of paper and asked to arrange the terms on the paper in a way that showed how they went together. These diagrams were then used to draw inferences about the student's knowledge structures before instruction.

Figure 10.3 shows the preinstruction knowledge structure for one student in the study. This student was more advanced than some others in the study; he already knew that metamorphic, igneous, and sedimentary were different kinds of rock and had ideas about what were examples of each kind. However, he had no knowledge of the dynamics of rock formation.

After pretesting, the students received four weeks of instruction on types of rocks and how they are formed. Following this, they were again asked to arrange the thirteen geology concepts on a large sheet of paper and indicate the relationships between concepts. Figure 10.4 shows the postinstruction structure produced by the student whose preinstruction structure was shown in Figure 10.3. Notice that to the preinstruction structure has been added new knowledge about how igneous rock forms metamorphic rock and metamorphic rock forms sedimentary rock. Also, there has been a good amount of rearrangement of examples of each kind of rock. For instance, before instruction this student classified granite as a metamorphic rock, whereas after instruction he classified it as igneous.

Thus, people's declarative knowledge about scientific concepts seems to change over time, sometimes without formal instruction and sometimes as a direct result of instruction. The possession of accurate, well-organized science knowledge is important for a variety of reasons. For one, people who have such knowledge will be better able to

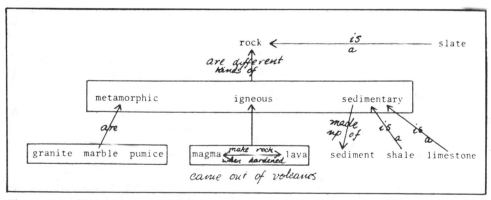

Figure 10.3. Preinstruction knowledge organization for geology knowledge. (From Champagne, Klopfer, Desena, and Squires, 1981.)

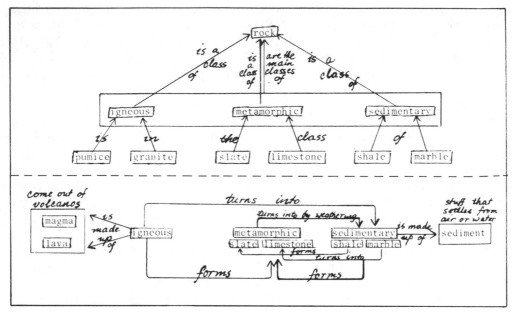

Figure 10.4. Postinstruction knowledge organization for geology knowledge. (From Champagne, Klopfer, Desena, and Squires, 1981.)

keep up with knowledge advancement through reading or watching popular science programs on television because they have more and better-organized prior knowledge to which they can attach the new knowledge. Also, as we have already seen in Chapters 6 and 9, knowledge structure appears to affect the success of problem solving.

Although it may seem obvious that people's knowledge of science changes with instruction, the exact nature of these changes is not so obvious. The work that has just been described is quite specific about the nature of change. Because of this specificity the assumptions made about knowledge structure can further be tested experimentally so that they can be refuted, upheld, or refined. Specificity about the nature of knowledge change is helpful for practitioners as well. It helps teachers know exactly what knowledge their students have and lack. For example, an elementary school teacher, familiar with the results of the Siegler and Richards (1983) study

of the *alive* concept, might try to think of dramatic ways to demonstrate that plants reproduce in order to show children another attribute that plants and living things have in common.

DOMAIN–SPECIFIC PROBLEM–SOLVING

Several characteristics appear to distinguish between skilled and less skilled individuals in science problem-solving tasks. These include possession of prerequisite procedural knowledge, organization of declarative knowledge, problem representation, and problem-solving processes.

Possession of Prerequisite Procedural Knowledge

Recall from Chapter 9 that successful mastery of prerequisites was crucial for success in solving linear algebra problems (R. M. Gagné and N. E. Paradise, 1961). The same phenomenon has also been demonstrated for chemistry.

A common type of problem in introductory chemistry classes is predicting whether or not, when two chemicals are mixed together, a precipitate (solid matter) will form. The answer depends on whether or not the solution is saturated. Once the saturation point is reached, a precipitate will form because a given product can no longer be dissolved.

A task analysis of the prerequisites needed to solve such problems is shown in Figure 10.5. Prerequisites were determined in the same way as for the linear algebra problems (see p. 237). Inspection of this analysis shows that several mathematics skills are needed (skills IIa and IIb and their prerequi-

sites) in addition to several skills specific to chemistry (skill IIc and its prerequisite). Overall the analysis reveals that many skills are thought to be prerequisite to successful performance.

Okey and Gagné (1970) had high school students work through an instructional program designed to teach the prerequisite skills as well as the final skill of predicting whether or not a mixture would form a precipitate. This instruction took place during science class and lasted for about a week. They then tested the students on several new prediction problems as well as on their mastery of each prerequisite skill. Figure 10.6 shows what they found out about the relationship between the number of prerequisite skills mastered and successful problem-solving ("criterion test") performance. In general, as

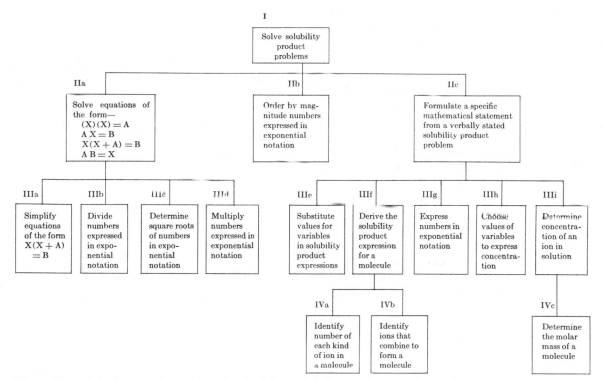

Figure 10.5. A task analysis of the task of solving solubility product problems. (From Okey and Gagné, 1970.)

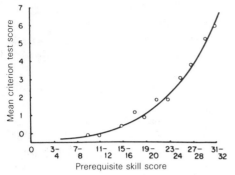

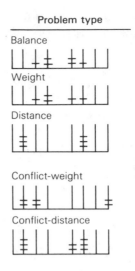

Problem type

Figure 10.6. Relationship between knowledge of prerequisite skills and problem-solving performance. (From Okey and Gagné, 1970.)

knowledge of prerequisite procedures increased, so did performance on the criterion test. Thus, successful problem-solving is associated with knowledge of prerequisite procedures.

Siegler (1976) has demonstrated the same notion with elementary school children solving balance beam problems. Figure 10.7 shows the apparatus used by Siegler, consisting of a balance beam with four pegs placed at equal intervals in each arm. Metal washers could be placed on these pegs, and the arms could move up or down or stay level depending on the arrangement of washers. The experimenter placed washers in various positions while holding the beam steady. He then asked the child to predict what would happen when he released the beam: would the left arm go up or down or would the beam not move at all?

The experimenter presented each child with six problem types, shown in Figure 10.8. In the *balance* problems, equal numbers of

Figure 10.8. The types of problem used to study children's knowledge of factors that influence balance. (Adapted from Siegler, 1976.)

washers were put at equal distances from the fulcrum on each arm, so that the arms should balance. In the *weight* problems, only the weight (number of washers) varied, so that the prediction as to which arm would dip down could be made solely on the basis of weight. Similarly, in the *distance* problems, only the distance of the washers from the fulcrum varied, so the correct answer could be determined solely on the basis of distance. The final three problem types varied both the number of washers and their distance from the fulcrum. In the *conflict-weight* problems, weight was a stronger factor than distance, whereas in the *conflict-distance* problems, distance was the stronger factor. Finally, in *conflict-balance* problems, the factors of weight and distance were equal, and the beam would balance.

Table 10.2 shows the percentage correct

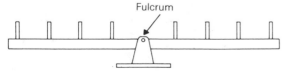

Figure 10.7. The balance beam used in Siegler's experiments. (Adapted from Siegler, 1976.)

Table 10.2. Percentage correct for different problem types as a function of age. (Adapted from Siegler, 1976.)

PROBLEM TYPE	AGE			
	5–6	9–11	13–14	16–17
Balance	94	99	99	100
Weight	88	98	98	98
Distance	9	78	81	95
Conflict-weight	86	74	53	51
Conflict-distance	11	32	48	50
Conflict-balance	7	17	26	40

for different problem types as a function of age. Here all age groups get almost all balance problems correct. Also, the youngest children (5–6) do not do too badly on weight problems and actually do better than older children on conflict-weight problems. For the remaining problem types, there are sizable increases in success rate across the age groups. The most surprising result is the excellent performance of the five- and six-year-olds on the difficult conflict-weight problems.

Siegler (1976) reasoned that the youngest age group was getting the conflict-weight problems correct not because they were carefully comparing both weight and distance, but rather because they were ignoring distance. The fact that these children did poorly (only 9 percent correct) on the distance problems supports this explanation. Siegler further suggested that one prerequisite to performing competently across all problem types was adequate representation of both weight and distance dimensions. In the terms used in this book, the younger children did not have a pattern-recognition production for the variable of distance.

To test this hypothesis Siegler (1976) placed one balance beam in front of his subjects and one in front of himself. He then placed washers on various pegs on his beam and asked the children to match this on their balance beams. If children are attending to weight only, they will correctly match the numbers of washers but not the exact pegs on which these washers are put, whereas if they are attending to both weight and distance, they will correctly match both the numbers of washers and the exact pegs used by the experimenter. The data showed that five-year-olds were 51 percent accurate for number of washers but only 16 percent correct for peg placement. By contrast, eight-year-olds were 73 percent and 56 percent correct, respectively, for number of washers and peg placement. These data confirmed the hypothesis that the five-year-olds were not attending to distance.

If representation of distance is a prerequisite to good performance on balance beam problems, then training children to attend to this dimension should lead to better overall performance. Siegler (1976) trained some five-year-olds to encode distance by using the task in which the children matched on their balance beams what the experimenter had put on his beam. Now, however, the experimenter modeled the process of carefully counting the number of pegs out from the fulcrum. Also, after the child placed her washers, the experimenter gave feedback. Following several training trials, the five-year-olds showed representation of distance 51 percent of the time (compared to 16 percent with no training). They also improved on their ability to predict what way the balance beam would tilt, especially for problems in which distance was crucial.

The Okey and Gagné (1970) study demonstrated that successful problem solvers possessed more prerequisite procedural knowledge. The Siegler (1976) studies also demonstrated this. In addition, Siegler went on to demonstrate a causal connection between prerequisite procedures and problem-solving performance by showing that a group trained on a prerequisite improves its problem-solving ability.

To demonstrate causality one must manipulate, rather than just observe, differences. Training studies manipulate differences by training one group on the cognitive variable that is thought to be causally related to the task of interest and comparing this group's performance to that of an untrained control group. Alternatively, the trained group's preinstruction performance can be compared with its postinstruction performance. (Campbell and Stanley, 1966, discuss the advantages and disadvantages of various designs for training studies). In either case, if improved performance on the task of interest is observed due to training, one can conclude that the variable that was trained is causally related to the task of interest.

In general, for the studies that compare skilled and less skilled individuals (or experts and novices) one needs to remember that causality has not been proved. In order to confirm the causal conclusions that it is tempting to draw from these studies, training studies are needed. We are at a point now where training studies that are specifically designed to validate models of expertise would be quite valuable.

The Organization and Content of Declarative Knowledge

In Chapter 6 you were introduced to the notion that experts not only have *more* knowledge than novices, but they also have *better organized* knowledge. The example given in that chapter was of expert and novice cardiologists. The expert cardiologists acted as if they possessed a hierarchical network of knowledge about symptoms of congenital heart disease. A major division in the hierarchy was between diseases with and without a systolic heart murmur. Further down in the hierarchy, within the set of diseases in which there was no blueness under the skin, there were three subtypes of problems, each

associated with a different pattern of symptoms. The novice medical students, by contrast, seemed to associate symptoms with particular diseases but had no overall structure to their knowledge.

As in medicine differences in the organization of knowledge by experts and novices have been observed in physics. Chi, Feltovich, and Glaser (1981) gave Ph.D. physicists (experts) and students who had had one course in physics (novices) the same twenty category labels for describing physics problems. These labels had been generated by experts and novices when asked to classify problems. For example, "block on incline" was a typical label generated by a novice, and "Newton's second law" was a typical label generated by an expert. Subjects were asked to tell all they could about problems of the type signaled by the label and how these problems might be solved. From the responses, the experimenters inferred a declarative knowledge network that reflected the ideas described by each subject. In addition, if a subject mentioned the conditions under which a given principle should apply, then a box signifying procedural knowledge was added to the declarative knowledge structure. Only the experts mentioned conditions for application.

Figures 10.9 and 10.10 show the memory structures derived for the label "inclined plane" for one novice and one expert, respectively. As you can see, many of the nodes in the novice's structure are descriptive (e.g., "pulley," "angle of incline"). Other nodes are attributes associated with these concrete entities (e.g., mass and height are attributes that one associates with blocks). Finally, one node is for a higher-order principle (conservation of energy) but this principle is *subordinate* in the novice's memory structure.

The expert's memory structure contains more fundamental principles (conservation of energy and Newton's force laws) than does

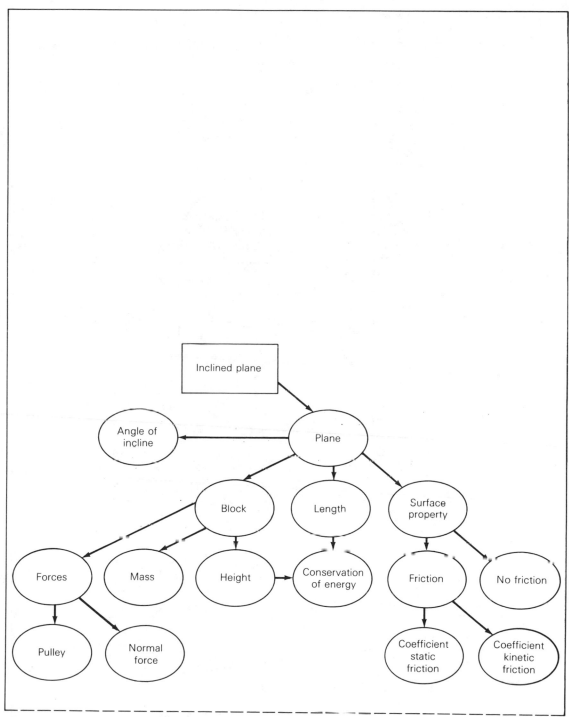

Figure 10.9. A novice's memory structure surrounding *inclined plane.* (From Chi, Feltovich, and Glaser, 1981.)

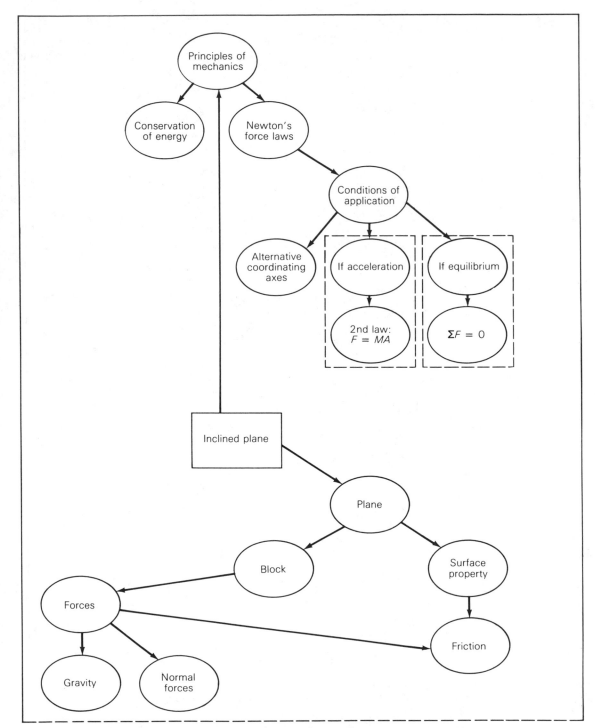

Figure 10.10. An expert's memory structure surrounding *inclined plane*. (From Chi, Feltovich, and Glaser, 1981.)

the novice's. Also, these principles are not subordinate to more superficial nodes. Finally, the expert's structure contains procedural knowledge for applying Newton's force laws. Thus, novices and experts differ in the content and organization of declarative knowledge, and only experts exhibit procedural knowledge.

Bromage and Mayer (1981) have also found a difference in memory content between good and poor problem solvers. The domain that they studied was the operation of 35mm cameras. They had college students (who were not familiar with 35mm cameras) read a passage that described (1) how to operate a 35mm camera to achieve various results, and (2) the basic principles that explained why the camera worked the way it did. They then had students recall what they had read and solve some hypothetical problems in camera use. For example, one problem asked the students to describe in writing the adjustments of the camera that would be made to "take a picture of a pole vaulter on a cloudy day."

Students' recall protocols were scored for content. The types of content that Bromage and Mayer (1981) were interested in were called "variables," "descriptive relationships," and "explanatory relationships." Variables were all the things that could be changed on a camera, such as f-stop and shutter speed. Descriptive relationships were empirical summaries of relationships among variables (e.g., "If the f-stop is changed you can compensate by changing shutter speed"). Finally, explanatory relationships were descriptions of the underlying causes or effects of changing some variable ("If the f-stop is changed, there will be a smaller or larger hole for letting light into the camera"). Each student's protocol was scored for the number of variables mentioned and the numbers of descriptive and explanatory relationships given.

The students were divided into low, intermediate, and high problem solvers according to their scores on the problem-solving test. Then the recall data for these three groups were examined. Table 10.3 shows the average recall of variables, descriptive relationships (called d-relations), and explanatory relationships (called e-relations) for each group. The average amount of variables and descriptive relationships recalled did not differ significantly across groups, but the high problem solvers recalled more explanatory relationships than did either the intermediate or low groups. In fact, the high group recalled about twice as many explanatory relationships as did the other groups.

Thus good problem-solvers have more access to explanatory principles and to the conditions for applying these principles than do poor problem solvers. Whether or not these knowledge differences *cause* the problem-solving differences is not known. (Recall what was said in a previous section about nonmanipulative experiments). Nonetheless, there is good reason to suppose that knowledge differences play an important role in

Table 10.3. Amount of recall of different types of content from a passage about cameras and problem-solving performance. (Adapted from Bromage and Mayer, 1981.)

PROBLEM-SOLVING ABILITY	RECALL TEST			PROBLEM-SOLVING TEST
	VARIABLES	D-RELATIONS	E-RELATIONS	
Low	9.0	11.0	2.1	6.5
Intermediate	11.1	13.3	2.7	10.5
High	11.0	11.4	5.3	15.0

domain-specific problem solving. One of the current limitations in artificial intelligence work is a lack of good ways to give a computer easily accessible domain-specific knowledge so that it can become a good domain-specific problem solver.

A basic assumption of current information-processing theory is that knowledge representations and processing strategies are highly interactive. The knowledge one activates creates the conditions for a particular strategy to apply, and the result of applying this procedure is a different knowledge state, which then sets up the conditions for another procedure, and so on. Thus, within the information-processing framework, the question is not *whether* knowledge influences problem-solving, but rather *how* it exerts its influence. This is a major question that cognitive psychologists are currently addressing, and its answer will have importance for instruction. A promising beginning in thinking about this question can be found in Reif and Heller (1982).

Problem Representation

We may begin to get a feel for how knowledge and processing interact by looking at the ways experts and novices solve problems. The problem-solving process starts with the solver forming a mental representation of the problem in working memory. And it turns out that experts and novices differ a great deal in their problem representations.

Physical Sciences. One technique for studying problem representation is to ask people to categorize problems. Their categories can then be used to infer what aspects of the problem they represent mentally. Chi, Feltovich, and Glaser (1981) gave expert and novice physicists the same set of physics problems to sort in any way they wanted. The experts were Ph.D. physicists and the novices were taking their first course in physics.

Figures 10.11 and 10.12 show typical sorting for some of the problems by novices and experts, respectively. Notice that the problems grouped by the novices had very similar diagrams. For example, problems 10(11) and 11(39), which were grouped together by novices, both have a rotating disc. Problems 7(23) and 7(35), which were also grouped together by novices, both have an inclined plane. Problems grouped together by experts did not necessarily have similar diagrams. Instead, they shared a solution principle. For example, problems 6(21) and 7(35) in Figure 10.12 are both solved by using the conservation of energy principle, and problems 5(39) and 12(23) are both solved by using Newton's second law. These results suggest that novices represent more superficial aspects of a problem than do experts.

The novices' and experts' explanations for their groups further corroborates the notion that novices are representing more superficial aspects of the problem than are experts. For example, novices stated that problems 7(23) and 7(35) go together because they both have inclined planes. Experts claimed that they put 6(21) and 7(35) together because they both involved the principle of conservation of energy.

These results are quite similar to those obtained by Silver (1981) for sixth-grade arithmetic word problems (described in Chapter 9). Recall that in Silver's study the good problem solvers classified problems according to the solution principle, whereas the poor problem solvers classified them according to their story line (e.g., farmer stories). Thus, the quality of problem representation appears to be important across problem-solving domains. Another domain in which it appears to be important is social science.

Social Sciences. Voss, Tyler, and Yengo (1983) find problem-representation differences between experts and novices in the social sciences like those found for physics.

Problem 10 (11).

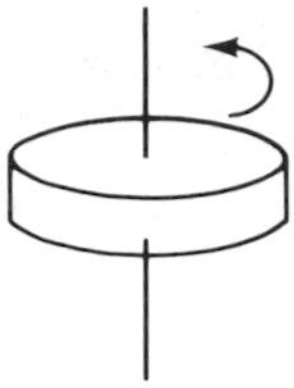

Novice 2: "*Angular* velocity, *momentum*, circular things"
Novice 3: "*Rotational* kinematics, *angular* speeds, *angular* velocities"
Novice 6: "Problems that have something *rotating; angular* speed"

Problem 11 (39)

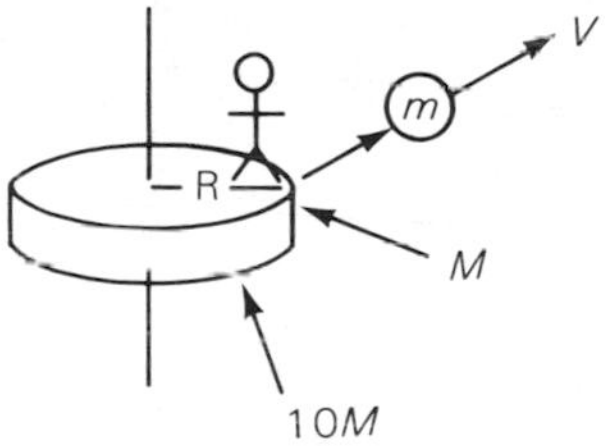

Problem 7 (23)

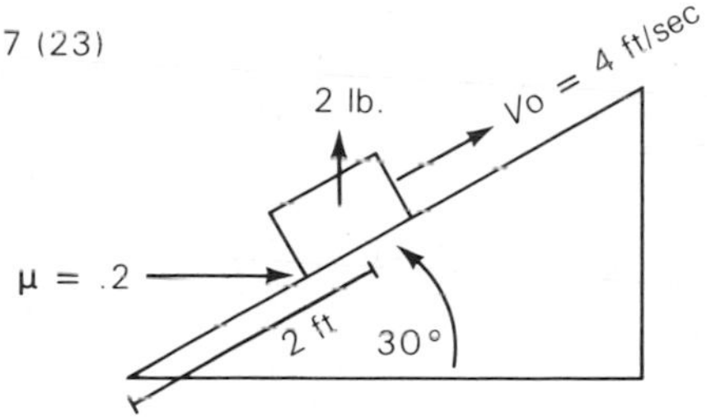

Novice 1: "These deal with blocks on an *inclined plane*"
Novice 5: "*Inclined plane* problems, coefficient of *friction*"
Novice 6: "Blocks on *inclined planes* with angles"

Problem 7 (35)

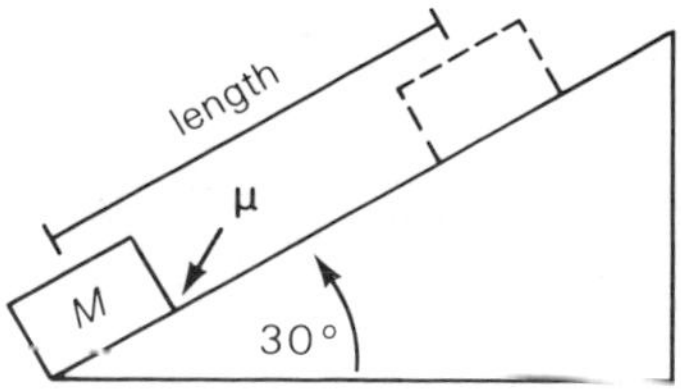

Figure 10.11. Two pairs of problems grouped together by novice physics students and their explanations for the grouping (From Chi, Feltovich, and Glaser, 1981.)

| Diagrams Depicted from Problems Categorized by Experts within the Same Groups | Experts' Explanations for Their Similarity Groupings |

Problem 6 (21)

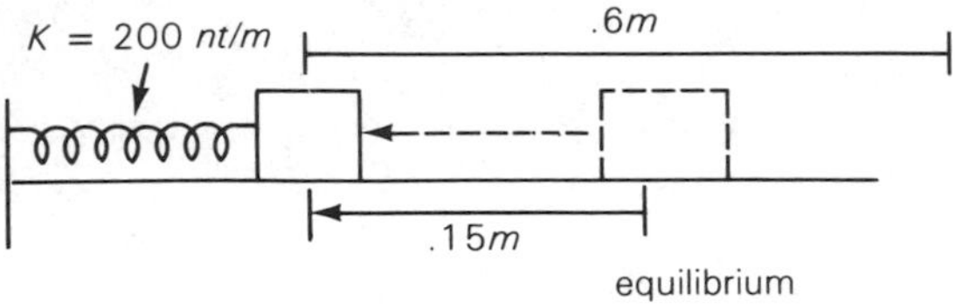

$K = 200\ nt/m$

.6m

.15m

equilibrium

Expert 2: *"Conservation of Energy"*
Expert 3: *"Work-Energy Theorem. They are all straight-forward problems."*
Expert 4: *"These can be done from energy considerations. Either you should know the Principle of Conservation of Energy, or work is lost somewhere."*

Problem 7 (35)

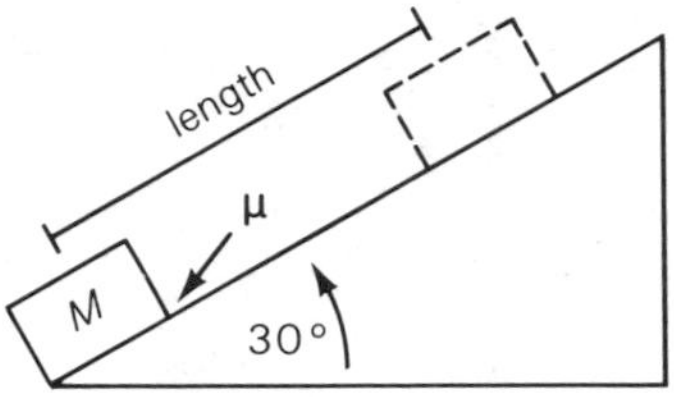

length

μ

M

30°

Problem 5 (39)

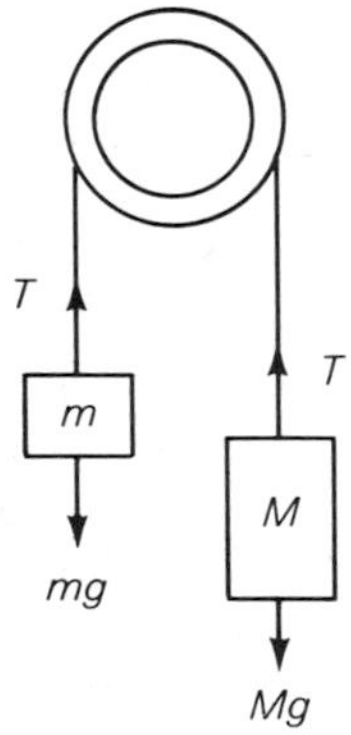

T

T

m

M

mg

Mg

Expert 2: *"These can be solved by Newton's Second Law"*
Expert 3: *"F = ma; Newton's Second Law"*
Expert 4: *"Largely use F = ma; Newton's Second Law"*

Problem 12 (23)

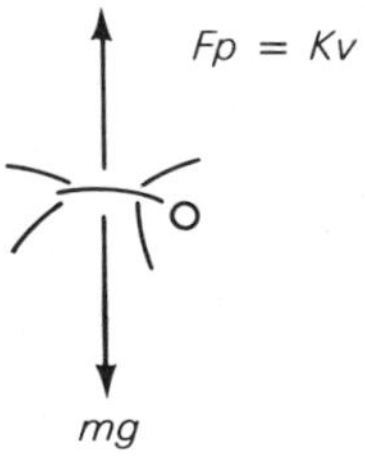

$Fp = Kv$

O

mg

Figure 10.12. Two pairs of problems grouped together by expert physicists and their explanations for why they grouped them. (From Chi, Feltovich, and Glaser, 1981.)

These researchers compared thinking-aloud protocols of political scientists whose specialty was Soviet politics and college students taking a Soviet political science course. The problem given to all these individuals was:

Assume you are head of the Soviet Ministry of Agriculture and assume crop productivity has been low over the past several years. You now have the responsibility of increasing crop production. How would you go about doing this?

In comparing the protocols of the Soviet experts and the students, Voss et al. found that 24 percent of the experts' protocol statements were devoted to defining the problem, whereas almost none of the students' statements had to do with problem definition. What the experts did during problem definition was specify constraints within which they thought the problem had to be solved. For example, Soviet ideology was a constraint, as was the fact that very little of Soviet land is arable. The students failed to define the problem further, but began immediately to give a string of possible solutions.

Although there are of course great differences between problems confronted in different domains, it is interesting that similarities in the problem-solving behavior of experts and novices can be detected across domains. In political science the experts clearly represented the problem at a deeper level than did the novices, and in this sense they are similar to experts in physics problem solving.

Problem-Solution Paths

Experts and novices differ not only in how they represent problems, but also in how they solve them.

Physics. Recall from Chapter 6 that, in solving novel problems, a great deal of searching is involved. Various strategies are used to limit search to relevant areas of memory. One of the most powerful of these is means-ends analysis, in which one defines one's goal and then retrieves from memory known ways of reaching that goal. Solving familiar problems does not involve much search. Rather, the solver acts fairly automatically, recognizing a familiar set of conditions and carrying out the associated actions.

Larkin and her colleagues (Larkin, 1981; Larkin, McDermott, Simon, and Simon, 1980b) have found that novice problem solvers in physics behave as people in general do when confronted with novel problems whereas, experts behave as people in general do when confronted with familiar problems. That is, novices engage in a lot of searching while trying to find a solution. Many of them, in fact, use means-ends analysis. For example, they first determine the goal of the problem and then try to come up with rules that get them closer to the goal.

As an example of this means-ends procedure consider the physics problem shown in Figure 10.13. Even if you have never had a physics course, read through the problem. Do not worry about the content, but pay attention to the form. The form of the problem is similar to that of problems in many other domains: it has to do with variables and relationships among variables. The goal in this problem is to find the block's speed (v) when it reaches the bottom of the plane. The givens are the angle of the plane from the horizontal (θ), the length of the plane (l), the mass of the block (m), and the coefficient of friction between the block and the plane (μ).

Larkin et al. (1980b) had expert and novice physicists think aloud while solving this problem. From the protocols they extracted the principles each subject used and the order of use. Table 10.4 shows these data for one expert and one novice. Notice that every

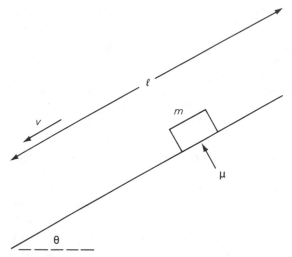

Figure 10.13. A physics problem used to study problem-solution paths. (Adapted from Larkin, McDermott, Simon, and Simon, 1980*b*.)

The known principle for force is then used to determine the unknown value for acceleration (*a*) and *a* is then used to determine the unknown value for time (*t*). Finally, velocity is determined from the known values for *a* and *t*. Clearly, this is a "working-forward" solution path: it starts with some of the givens in the problem and uses these to generate more information that is needed to determine the unknown velocity.

By contrast, the novice uses a working-backward solution path. He starts by retrieving a formula that contains the desired unknown (*v*). Then he sees that there are other unknowns in this formula, so it cannot be used to solve for *v*. He thus retrieves another formula containing the unknown *v*. This formula also contains another unknown, but this time, instead of abandoning the formula, he sets a subgoal to find the other unknown (*a*). He (incorrectly) thinks that *a* is a function only of normal force (*N*). Since *N* is also unknown, he sets the subgoal of finding *N*. At this point, the novice stops in his attempts to solve the problem.

step taken by the expert contributes information needed for the solution. The first and second steps determine the two force components that add together to make force (*F*).

Table 10.4. Solution paths for an expert and novice solving the physics problem shown in Figure 10.13. (Constructed from information in Larkin, McDermott, Simon, and Simon, 1980*b*.)

AN EXPERT'S SOLUTION PATH		
STEP	PRINCIPLE APPLIED	QUANTITY COMPUTED
1	$Fg'' = mg \sin \theta$	Finds gravitational force (Fg'')
2	$f = \mu N$	Finds frictional force (f)
3	$F = Fg'' + f = ma$	Finds acceleration (a)
4	$x = v_0 + 1/2 \, (at^2)$	Finds time (t) by substituting the known value l for x
5	$v = v_0 + at$	Finds velocity (v)

A NOVICE'S SOLUTION PATH		
STEP	PRINCIPLE APPLIED	GOAL
1	$v = v_0 + at$	Tries to solve for velocity
2	$v^2 - v_0^2 = 2ax$	Tries to solve for velocity
3	$a(N)$	Tries to solve for acceleration (a), thinking (incorrectly) that a is solely a function of normal force (N)
4	$f = N$	Tries to solve for N

The important aspect of the novice's protocol is its working-backward character. He starts by identifying the goal (v), then finds a formula that contains v, then works backward through a series of subgoals to try to solve this formula. The novice's order of applying principles is almost exactly opposite to the order used by the expert. For example,

Table 10.5. An expert's thinking-aloud protocol while solving the Soviet agriculture problem. (Adapted from Voss, Tyler, and Yengo, 1983.)

I think that as minister of agriculture, one has to start out with the realization that there are certain kinds of special agriculture constraints within which you are going to work. The first one, the most obvious one, is that by almost every count only 10 percent of the land in the Soviet Union is arable. This is normally what is called the Blackland in the Ukraine and surrounding areas. And secondly, even in that arable 10 percent of the total land surface, you still have climate for instance, problems over which you have no direct control. Okay, so that is sort of the overall parameter in which we are working.

Now we have traditionally in the Soviet Union used three kinds of policies to increase agricultural production. Of course, agricultural production has been our "Achilles' heel" and something that we have inherited from the time the czars freed the serfs. Even before then, the agricultural production was low because historically the aristocracy had no need to fend for itself, as it turned to the czar for its support and hence never, like the English aristocracy for instance, introduced modern methods of fertilization, never went to enclosures or consolidations of lands, never experimented with crop rotation. That was passed on to the peasants and throughout the period when the peasant had been freed to do what he willed with the land, he's responding with the old, rather inefficient ways.

At any rate, we have had three different ways by which we have tried to increase agricultural production. The first one might be labeled exhortation. The Soviet approach to agricultural production is to mount campaigns continually to call for more effort on the part of the peasants and agricultural workers and put more effort into their labor activities for agricultural production. Those things are mounted periodically, quite frankly, I think that they are a waste of time and energy and they really, as minister of agriculture I must say, that they really do nothing more than give the party a sense of false importance because it's normally incumbent upon the party to develop these ideological indoctrination campaigns and the notion of mind over matter in this case hasn't paid off and it leaves the party with the belief that ideological, and if you'll excuse the term, spiritual policies can overcome objective limitations. So, I wouldn't emphasize very much exhortation.

It seems to me that the second way that we traditionally go about trying to increase agricultural production is through constant reorganization. That leads to confusion, that leads to mismanagement and that has forced a mind set upon the peasant agricultural worker of sort of laying back and waiting because this too will also pass. We've gone through collectives, state farms, and machine tractor stations, the latest attempt at reorganization is through the development of what are called agroindustrialist complexes, which has knocked down, by the way, the number of collectives from about 250,000 to 30,000 in the last five years, in which the former collective farmer becomes a wage earner.

So, I think we're going to have to tend, and I'm going to talk a minute, we have to tend to the nature of agricultural production. I want to say one thing, and I have to recognize that this is clear as day, and that is, that in all of these cases more or less except for stringent ideological periods we've always allowed the private crop to exist even though we take it to be a much more primitive, less historically progressive form of agricultural production. We must realize that in terms of some of our food staples, even until today, roughly 40 percent of the food staples are grown on the private plots.

The third thing that we've done and this is where I'd like to start off in terms of turning around agricultural production, the third thing we've done is we've tried to mechanize, and I want to use that in the broad sense because it is not the word I want, we have tried to mechanize industrial production. Not just mechanize it but also introduce scientific advances in Soviet production.

Table 10.6. A novice's thinking-aloud protocol while solving the Soviet agriculture problem. (Adapted from Voss, Tyler, and Yengo, 1983.)

Old-fashioned methods of farming. So maybe what needs to be done is to introduce newer methods of farming and obviously the people probably need to be educated on how to use these new methods, especially if they introduce new machinery. I remember reading somewhere that on the land that the people own themselves, that crop production is much higher than it was on the state plots. Perhaps if the people could be allocated more benefits from the state land, rather than giving it all to the state, crop production might increase. Maybe the organization of how the crops are planted and harvested is not adequate. Perhaps that should be changed. What kind of system they use to plant the crops, if people from a certain town have to go out to a state plot and plant at a certain time. Maybe if it has to be worked around their own little private ground, perhaps they are planting and harvesting at the wrong times. It seems that just education in general may be a problem, like updating of methods.

[What about their machinery?] I think they would need new machinery. When I think of the machinery they have, they probably have old rusting harvester machinery. And if they got it, they'd probably import their new machinery, and they'd have to educate the people on how to use it, or there would probably be only a handful of people could use it, and if something should break, I doubt there would be very many people who would know how to repair, so maybe something on that line maybe if their machinery is broken down. Maybe soil fertilization methods and maybe their horticulture isn't very good. Maybe the people have been planting crops on this land year in and year out and they never fertilized land and its just really arid and not fertile.

[What about climate?] I'm not sure about their climate. I know its very wintery and pretty dry, a short summer. Maybe they're not planting the right crops for the climate. Maybe they're trying to grow the wrong types of plants. Maybe they should study the climate more and what types of crops grow better in that type of climate. They're probably not growing pineapples. Maybe their irrigation is bad. If it's dry maybe they have no irrigation system and the crops all just dry up and wither away, but maybe to have an efficient irrigation system, they would need better engineering. Maybe they don't have that.

That's about it. [Can you think of anything else?] The government is probably very much involved in crop production anyway, but maybe they would really study the problem of why crop production is lower, if they would get more people involved at the lower level where its happening rather than have like a bureaucratic overlook of the thing and maybe have a few foreman-type people supervise them. The people who are doing the planting and who are deciding what needs to be planted and who are tending the crops—maybe people don't tend the crops, if it is state land. Maybe they're tending their own crops on their own land. Maybe weeds are overcoming them. Maybe there's a way to get the people more incentive. I think that's probably important. If they don't have any incentive, they're not going to take care of the crops very well, if they have to give them all away and have old machinery and no irrigation and dry land and that's about all I can think of.

---

the first principle used by the novice is the last one used by the expert.

Working backward is a powerful strategy for a novice because it limits the search of memory to areas that have relevance to the goal. If one is lost in a forest, one is better off determining the direction (N, S, E, or W) of one's goal and limiting one's search for a path to this direction than wandering around at random. The difference between novices and experts is that experts are not lost; they know a path that leads to the goal and follow it.

Social Sciences. The solution paths of experts and novices in social science are not well characterized as "working forward" and "working backward." Problems in social science are typically ill-defined, in that experts may disagree on the best solution (Voss, Tyler, and Yengo, 1983). Clearly, this was not the case for physics: any expert physicist can agree on the correct answer to the problem shown in Figure 10.13. Perhaps because of this difference in problem types, the solution processes for social science look different from those for physics. (Of course, some physics problems are ill defined, but not the ones typically confronted by students.)

An expert's solution to the Soviet agriculture problem is shown in Table 10.5. The expert starts out by adding constraints to the problem, such as the small amount of arable land available in Russia. He then discusses what has been done in the past to solve this problem—exhortation and reorganization—and states why these attempts have failed. Finally, he proposes a solution—mechanization and technological advancement—that is good within the constraints identified.

A novice's solution is shown in Table 10.6. The novice's entire protocol is devoted to generating solutions. Even in the first paragraph, for example, the novice proposes mechanization, more incentive, reorganization, and education as four possible solutions. This generation of solutions continues throughout the protocol.

Voss et al. (1983) found two major quantitative differences in the protocols of experts and novices. First, the experts backed up any given claim with an average of 8.8 arguments, whereas the novices used only 2.3 arguments. Second, the experts followed a given line of reasoning for an average of 7.1 ideas, whereas the novices produced only 2.6 ideas in a given chain of thought.

Summary

In this section we have seen that skilled and less skilled problem solvers represent problems differently and then proceed to solve them differently. We have also seen that they differ in the procedural and declarative knowledge they possess relevant to the domain in which they are solving problems. It seems obvious that these knowledge differences in some way influence the differences in problem representation and problem solution-paths. However, exactly what "in some way" means must await further research.

In the meantime, it is already clear from cognitive psychological research that domain-specific knowledge is tremendously important for successful domain-specific problem solving. This conclusion suggests that science curricula that emphasize general process skills *to the exclusion* of specific knowledge and skills will not result in a population that has a reasonable level of scientific literacy. This is not to say that the teaching of general reasoning skills should have no place in science curricula. Rather, it should be balanced with the teaching of more specific declarative and procedural knowledge.

GENERAL REASONING SKILLS

General reasoning skills can be broken down into two subcategories, inductive and deductive. Inductive reasoning processes are used to reach conclusions that are *probably* correct, whereas deductive processes are used to reach conclusions that are *necessarily* correct. For example, I reason inductively from the knowledge that my spouse has bicycled to work for the past year to the prediction that he will again bicycle to work tomorrow. On the other hand, I reason deductively from the knowledge that all plants are living things, and that cacti are plants, to the conclusion that cacti are living things.

People seem to have difficulty with certain inductive and deductive reasoning skills, and cognitive psychologists have been exploring the exact nature of these difficulties. Perhaps as we come to understand the difficulties in reasoning, we will be better able to teach students to avoid these difficulties.

Inductive Reasoning: Estimating Probabilities

One area in which people make large errors is in estimating the likelihood of certain events or classifications, and probability estimation underlies a great deal of everyday decision making. For example, a traveler buys a new car for a trip across the country when she determines that the probability is low that the old car will make it without a breakdown. A parent of an infant decides to quit work for a year to take care of the infant because he believes that the child's chances of optimal development are much lower without his care. In June a consumer decides to wait until August to buy a sofa because the probability of a sale on sofas in August is higher than for a sale in June. A teacher decides to punish a student for not doing her homework, even though the student says that she didn't do it because her grandmother died. Since the student has already had two grandmothers "die" this year, the teacher thinks that the probability that the student is lying is quite high.

Although probability estimation underlies decision making, people are not always good at it. For example, Hammerton (1973) had people estimate the probability that a disease was present in a person with a positive test result. Specifically, he told his subjects that (1) a disease (called "psylicrapitis") will cause a positive test result 90 percent of the time, (2) for people who do not have this disease, the test will come out positive one percent of the time, and (3) one percent of the population gets psylicrapitis. He then told the subjects that Mr. Smith has received a positive test result and asked them to estimate the probability that he has the disease. What would you respond? If you are like the ma-

jority of subjects in Hammerton's study, your answer would be in the neighborhood of 85 percent.

The correct answer to this question is actually 48 percent! This is because the frequency of the disease in the population is so low (1 percent), that even though there is only a one percent chance of a positive test result if one does not have the disease, one is about as likely to get this false positive result as to get a true positive result. If, on the other hand, psylicrapitis struck 15 percent of the population, there is a much greater probability that the positive test result is caused by the psylicrapitis. The mathematics behind these statements, which are based on Bayes's Theorem, can be found in the Appendix at the end of this chapter.

Another example of inaccurate probability estimation comes from Kahneman and Tversky (1973). They gave subjects (college students) descriptions of individuals such as the following:

> Jack is a 45-year-old man. He is married and has four children. He is generally conservative, careful, and ambitious. He shows no interest in political and social issues and spends most of his free time on his many hobbies, which include home carpentry, sailing, and mathematical puzzles. (p. 241)

For each description, they asked subjects to give the probability that the individual being described was an engineer. Also, the subjects were told that the description was drawn at random from a sample of 100 descriptions. For half the subjects the experimenter said that seventy of the descriptions were of lawyers and thirty were of engineers; for the other half the experimenter said the reverse (seventy were of engineers and thirty of lawyers).

It is more probable that the above description is of an engineer if 70 percent of the pool of descriptions are of engineers than if only

30 percent of the pool are engineers (see the Appendix for a proof). However, subjects in both groups estimated the probability that Jack was an engineer to be about the same.

In short, people do not seem to take *base rates* into account when estimating probabilities (although they do in some situations—see Kassin, 1979). This might not be surprising if the base rates are not known, but base rates were given in both the Hammerton (1973) and the Kahneman and Tversky (1973) studies. Instead of base rates people use what Tversky and Kahneman (1974) call a "representativeness" heuristic. This heuristic only uses information on how representative a given observation is for a given category. A positive result on a test for a disease is representative of that disease, and conservatism and enjoyment of math puzzles are representative of engineers.

Why do people ignore useful information when it is provided? Perhaps most people simply do not understand all of the factors that contribute to probabilities. If so, then as science and math courses begin to include more about probability theory (and in particular about Bayes's Theorem) perhaps people's ability to estimate probabilities will improve. Indeed, there is some evidence that statistical training reduces the tendency to make errors in estimating probabilities (cf. Nisbett, Krantz, Jepson, and Kunta, 1983; Tversky and Kahneman, 1983).

Another possibility is that people do understand the importance of baserate information for estimating probabilities, but that the computations are too complex to perform mentally. Carroll and Siegler (1977) tested this hypothesis by telling subjects that 70 percent of a population had occupation *A* and 30 percent had occupation *B*. The subjects were then asked to predict the occupation of ten people sampled at random from this population. These subjects were more accurate in their predictions (seven have occupation *A*

and three have occupation *B*) than subjects for whom the proportions were 75 percent and 25 percent. One can easily translate 70 and 30 percent into seven and three people but not 75 percent and 25 percent. Thus the ease of computation may be one factor determining how people use information about base rates.

There is still much to be learned about this fascinating aspect of human reasoning. For example, we do not know if experts in an area make the same grievous mistakes in probability estimation as do nonexperts. There is some evidence that they do not. For example, Shavelson, Cadwell, and Izu (1977) found that expert teachers were accurate in assessing students' abilities and adjusting their assessments on the basis of additional information. Also, although it is known that sometimes statistical training improves reasoning about probabilities and sometimes it does not, the reason for this difference is not known.

Deductive Reasoning

Besides having difficulty with inductive reasoning, people also have difficulty with certain forms of deductive reasoning. For example, try the following problem:

$$E \quad K \quad 4 \quad 7$$

For each of the above cards, a letter appears on one side and a number appears on the other. What cards would you have to turn over to decide whether the following rule is true?

If a card has a vowel on one side, then

it has an even number on the other

side.

If you answered that you would have to turn over the *E* and the 4 cards, you were like

55 percent of the subjects in two studies performed by Wason (1968). If you said only the E card, you were like 24 percent of the subjects. If you said the E and 7 cards must be turned over, which is the correct answer, you were like only 7 percent of the subjects in Wason's studies. The 4 card does not need to be turned over because it does not matter if a vowel is on the other side. However, the 7 card does need to be turned over because if a vowel is on the other side, it would invalidate the rule.

When problems in deduction involve familiar domains, subjects are much less likely to make errors. For example, Johnson-Laird, Legrenzi, and Legrenzi (1972) presented subjects with a problem that was formally equivalent to Wason's. The problem, presented to British students, is shown in Figure 10.14. The students were told to pretend that they were mail sorters in a post office. They were to catch any sealed letters that did not have enough postage. The correct amount of postage for a sealed letter was 50 pence. That is, they were to ensure that "if letter is sealed, then it has a 50 pence stamp on it," which is formally equivalent to the rule, "if vowel, then even number."

The subjects were shown the five letters displayed in Figure 10.14. They were asked to specify which must be turned over in order to make sure the rule had not been violated. This time, 88 percent of the subjects were correct in saying that the sealed letter and the letter with the 40 pence stamp on it should be turned over.

Just why familiarity with the content of a problem decreases the probability of deductive reasoning errors is not known. One speculation is that familiarity allows one to verify in different ways a deductive conclusion that one is not certain about. For example, one may have a hunch in the E K 4 7 problem that it is not necessary to turn over the 4, but one may turn it over anyway because one is uncertain. In the post-office problem, one's deductive hunch that the 50-pence letter does not need to be turned over can be supported with thoughts such as "What difference does it make if someone puts a 50 pence stamp on an unsealed envelope? They're wasting money, since all they need is 40 pence, but they aren't breaking the law."

The fact that people improve in their reasoning skills when situations are familiar is encouraging because it suggests that for everyday problems people will not make serious errors. Still, the fact that grievous errors are made in novel situations is important, because these situations make the most demands on our reasoning abilities. Thus, it is important to teach people to avoid errors in induction and deduction. There is some evidence that brief training programs can dramatically reduce errors on deductive reasoning tasks (Simpson and Johnson, 1966;

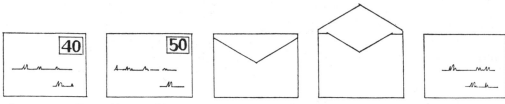

Figure 10.14. Post-office problem stimuli. (From Johnson-Laird, Legrenzi, and Legrenzi, 1972.)

Wason, 1969). However, whether the benefits of training are maintained or transferred is not known.

INSTRUCTIONAL DESIGN

In Chapters 7, 8, and 9 we examined the three "basic skills" of reading, writing, and mathematics. In this chapter we have considered a "subject matter" area. Now we are in a position to ask whether or not cognitive distinctions can be made between basic skills and subject matter domains.

Although both basic skills and subject matter areas are represented declaratively and procedurally in typical students' minds, the relative amounts of procedural and declarative knowledge seem to differ somewhat. For basic skills we hope that much knowledge has become proceduralized and, indeed, composed so that it can apply quickly and automatically. This is because basic skills are frequently used in a wide variety of everyday tasks and job tasks. On the other hand, we hope that a rich declarative knowledge structure is developed for subject matter areas. We also hope that rudimentary procedures are practiced and represented, but it would be unrealistic to hope that many procedures become composed, except for someone seeking advanced training in that subject. It has been estimated that it takes ten to fifteen years to become an expert in the sense of having many composed procedures. If this is true, then we would have to have much greater life spans than we do in order to become expert in even a few areas of knowledge.

If subject matter knowledge, in either declarative or rudimentarily procedural form, is stored in a way that can be accessed, it will be activated when problems in daily living require it. If a declarative representation of a procedure is activated, then people's general interpretive procedures can translate this representation so that the appropriate actions can take place.

Because of this difference between subject matter and basic skill areas, the examples I will give of science instruction emphasize a mixture of declarative and procedural knowledge. I have given many examples that emphasize procedural knowledge in previous chapters, so this is a good opportunity to give examples with a mixed emphasis on procedural and declarative knowledge.

Teaching Students to Read Scientific Texts

Recall from Chapter 4 that the important conditions for acquiring declarative knowledge are organization and elaboration. Therefore, to help students learn new science information, a teacher should do things that encourage organization and elaboration. Since, at least in high school and college, much of a student's initial contact with new information comes from texts, it should be useful to teach students how to organize this information. In a dissertation study supervised by Mayer, Cook (1983) designed some instructional materials for junior college chemistry students to achieve just this goal.

Cook (1983) has identified five types of structure commonly used in scientific texts. In her training program, she focused on three of these types: enumeration, generalization, and sequence. (The other two are classification and compare/contrast.) Enumeration structures give a topic, some subtopics, and several facts related to each subtopic (as in Table 10.7). A generalization structure gives a concept or principle and supporting evidence or examples (as in Table 10.8). Finally, a sequence structure describes a series of events (as in Table 10.9).

Students in Cook's (1983) training group were first taught to detect these text structures and then to use a different strategy for

Table 10.7. Passage with an enumeration structure in which there are several subtopics and several facts related to each subtopic. (From McElroy and Swanson, 1968.)

DNA is unique in three respects. First, it is a very large molecule, having a certain outward uniformity in size, rigidity and shape. Despite this uniformity, however, it has infinite internal variety. Its varied nature gives it the complexity required for information-carrying purposes. One can, indeed, think of the molecule as if it had a chemical alphabet somehow grouped into words which the cell can understand and to which it can respond.

The second characteristic of DNA is its capacity to make copies of itself almost endlessly, and with remarkable exactness. The biologist or chemist would say that such a molecule can replicate, or make a carbon copy of itself, time and again with a very small margin of error.

The third characteristic is its ability to transmit information to other parts of the cell. Depending upon the information transmitted, the behavior of the cell reflects this direction. As we shall see, other molecules play the role of messenger, so that DNA exercises its control of the cell in an indirect manner.

reading each type. For enumeration passages they learned to identify the subtopics and then organize the facts associated with each subtopic. For generalization passages they learned to identify the main idea, to define each word in it and to explain how the supporting evidence relates back to it. For sequence passages they learned to identify each step in the sequence and then organize details around each step.

To conduct her study, Cook (1983) assigned students in a remedial chemistry course to a strategy training group or a control group. The week of training for the strategy training group was integrated into their regular work for the chemistry course for that week. The assigned reading for the week was a textbook chapter on the electrical properties of atoms. The control group read the textbook in their normal fashion, whereas the strategy training group read using the new strategies they were learning. For them, the chapter was divided into nine sections, three each representing enumeration, generalization, and sequence structures.

At the beginning of the week, the strategy training group attended a special lecture designed to motivate them to adopt different

Table 10.8. Passage with a generalization structure in which a concept or principle is defined and then evidence or examples are given to illustrate the general rule. (From Cook, 1983.)

The human body has an amazing capacity to speed up or slow down physiological processes when changes occur in internal states. This ability is defined as homeostasis. The most sophisticated system in our body which carries on homeostasis is the endocrine system. This is a series of glands in our body which produce hormones. The endocrine system operates on a principle similar to a home heating unit. A thermostat detects the need for heat, turns on the furnace when the temperature is too low, and then turns off the furnace when the temperature is again normal.

One example is the hormone vassopressin, which causes the capillaries to constrict. When the body suffers severe bleeding due to an injury, the amount of this hormone is drastically increased. This helps to slow down blood flow by closing off small blood vessels. Thus, blood flow to the injured area is reduced. The antidiuretic hormone, ADH, helps the body conserve water by directing the kidneys to reabsorb water. A normal amount of ADH tells the kidneys to reabsorb all but about one liter of water daily. However, when the body becomes dehydrated from water loss due to perspiration during hot weather, more ADH is released telling the kidneys to reabsorb more water than usual to make up for that lost.

Table 10.9. Passage with a sequence structure in which an ordered set of events is described. (From Cook, 1983.)

ULTRACENTRIFUGATION

The principle behind this is simple. First, a suspension of whole cells in a sugar solution is placed in an ordinary kitchen blender. The solution is mixed in the blender. This causes the cell membrane to break down, and the cell parts are set free in the sugar solution. Then, the mixture is placed in a test tube and the tube spun rapidly for a short time. The most dense parts of the cell, such as the nucleus, are thrown farthest away from the center. They settle in the bottom of the test tube. After these parts are removed, the solution can be spun again at higher speeds. Then the next most dense parts can be removed. Eventually, most of the major parts of the cell can be separated and studied.

---

reading strategies for different text structures and to teach them to identify the three structures. The motivation was achieved by asking students to state sentences that might occur in two passages: one entitled "Lunch at a Restaurant" and one entitled "The Substantia Nigra." The students were able to generate a complete story for "Lunch at a Restaurant," but virtually nothing for "The Substantia Nigra." This demonstration was used to point out the difference in familiarity between text on everyday topics and scientific text. The lecturer then stated that scientific text did have predictable structures that could be used to help readers organize unfamiliar information and therefore improve learning. Furthermore, they would be learning how to identify and use such structures.

The second part of the lecture was devoted to getting the students to distinguish among enumeration, generalization, and sequence passages. This was done by describing the distinguishing criteria for each type of passage and giving an example of each. The examples were segments taken from the students' reading assignment for the previous week. Finally, the steps in each reading strategy (shown in Tables 10.10, 10.11, and 10.12) were demonstrated using the sample passages. At the end of the lecture the students received a folder containing copies of the reading strategies.

Throughout the week these students came in, at times convenient to them, to do their chemistry reading under supervision. They were directed to identify the type of structure used in the chapter segment on which they were working and then to use the reading strategy associated with that structure. That is, they were to write down their findings for each of the steps in the strategy. When a student completed a segment, he or

Table 10.10. The steps in the reading strategy associated with enumeration passages. (From Cook, 1983.)

Enumeration

Step 1: What is the general topic?

Step 2: Identify the subtopics
    A.
    B.
    C.
    D.
    -
    -
    -

Step 3: Organize and list the details within each subtopic (Do one subtopic at a time, use your own words)
    A.
    B.
    C.
    D.
    -
    -
    -

Table 10.11. The steps in the reading strategy associated with generalization passages. (From Cook, 1983.)

Generalization

Step 1:   Identify the generalization (main idea)

                List and define key words in the generalization
                       Word   Definition

                Restate the generalization in your own words

Step 2:   What kind of support is there for the generalization? Does it use examples,
                illustrations? Does it extend or clarify the generalization?

                       Supporting Evidence   Relation to Generalization

Table 10.12. The steps in the reading strategy associated with sequence passages. (From Cook, 1983.)

Sequence

Step 1:   Identify the topic of the passage.

Step 2:   Take each step, name it, and then outline the details within each:
                  Step 1
                  Step 2
                  Step 3
                  Step 4
                  -
                  -
                  -

Step 3:   Discuss (briefly) what is different from one step to the next.
                  Step 1 to 2
                  Step 2 to 3
                  Step 3 to 4
                  -
                  -
                  -

she brought what had been written to the instructor for evaluation. The instructor pointed out any errors and asked the student to correct them. When a student turned in an error-free worksheet, the instructor gave him or her an oral examination over the points covered by the worksheet. Students were not permitted to look at their notes or text during this test.

The purpose of the training program was to enable students to learn more from unfamiliar scientific passages by organizing the information better. To evaluate the success of the program, students in both the strategy training and control groups took pre- and posttests. These tests consisted of reading unfamiliar science passages, one each with enumeration, generalization, and sequence structures. After reading, the students used free recall for information contained in the passages and answered twelve questions over each passage. Eight questions were on information directly stated in the passage, and the other four required the application of text information to novel situations. The highest possible score on the twelve questions across the three passages was 96 points.

Figure 10.15 shows the pre- and posttest results for the twelve questions as a function of training. As you can see, the strategy training group's posttest scores improved by about 20 points over their pretest scores but the control group's scores did not improve at all.

Students' recall protocols were scored for the number of idea units correctly recalled at high and low levels in the conceptual structure of the text. Figure 10.16 shows the results of this analysis. Following training, the strategy training group became better at recalling information high in the conceptual structure of passages. This suggests that they did learn to organize the passage information better.

Overall, the results of this study are quite

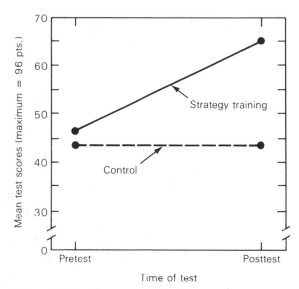

Figure 10.15. Mean correct test scores for strategy training and control groups at pretest and posttest. (Adapted from Cook, 1983.)

promising. They suggest that students can be taught to identify passage organization and then use this organization to structure the propositions that they store in long-term memory. B. J. Bartlett (1978) has obtained similar results.

It is interesting to think about the cognitive objectives of Cook's training program. I see her objectives as being a set of three pattern-recognition and three action-sequence productions, shown in Table 10.13. Recall that to teach pattern-recognition procedures, one must engage the learner's generalization and discrimination processes. In the Cook study, this was done by describing the patterns associated with enumeration, generalization, and sequence structures, which should have called students' attention to the crucial attributes for these structures. Then the students practiced identifying each pattern three times and received feedback on their accuracy. During practice they should have been forming the pattern-recognition productions shown in Table 10.13.

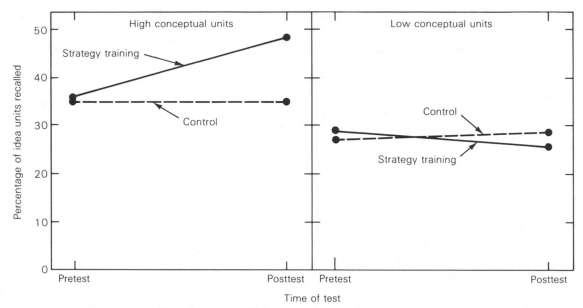

Figure 10.16. Percentage of idea units recalled (high and low) by strategy training and control groups at pre- and posttests. (Adapted from Cook, 1983.)

To teach action sequence procedures it is important to give students cues to the correct sequence while they are proceduralizing their knowledge. The cues in the Cook (1983) study were the worksheets that described the three reading strategies. For action sequences to become composed, practice and feedback are needed. In the Cook study there were three practice and feedback trials for each strategy. Thus, Cook provided the instructional support needed for teaching pattern-recognition and action-sequence procedures.

Instruction to Facilitate Transfer of Problem-Solving Skill

Much research over the past decade points to the notion that meaningfulness in the learning of rules influences the amount of transfer of these rules to new situations. Meaningfulness depends on the amount and quality of prior knowledge that an individual associates with the new rules. One type of prior knowl-edge that seems to be especially useful for transfer is an analogy. Royer and Cable (1976), Mayer (1975), and West and Kellett (1981) have all demonstrated the beneficial effects of analogy on transfer in several math and science domains.

Beeson (1981) has also demonstrated the beneficial effects of analogy on transfer. The rules studied by Beeson were those used to determine the resistance or current in electrical circuits. The task of determining resistance in circuits is analyzed in Figure 10.17. Beeson developed an instructional program to teach students the prerequisite skills and the final skill shown in the analysis. The program included practice and feedback on each skill.

Beeson (1981) had tenth-grade students work through this learning program. A subgroup of the students first read a three-page description of an analogy between electricity in circuits and water in pipes, one page of which is shown in Table 10.14.

Table 10.13. Pattern-recognition and action-sequence productions for organizing information from technical passages.

		PATTERN-RECOGNITION
Enumeration	IF	MAIN IDEA states that there are *N* ELEMENTS
	And	*N* > 1
	THEN	Classify as ENUMERATION PASSAGE.
Generalization	IF	MAIN IDEA states RULE
	And	RULE applies to more than one case
	THEN	Classify as GENERALIZATION PASSAGE.
Sequence	IF	PASSAGE describes ACTIONS or EVENTS
	And	ACTIONS/EVENTS are in order
	THEN	Classify as SEQUENCE PASSAGE.
		ACTION SEQUENCES
Enumeration	IF	PASSAGE is ENUMERATION
	THEN	Identify SUBTOPICS,
	And	list DETAILS within each SUBTOPIC under subtopic HEADING.
Generalization	IF	PASSAGE is GENERALIZATION
	THEN	Identify MAIN IDEA
	And	list KEY WORDS in MAIN IDEA
	And	paraphrase MAIN IDEA
	And	list SUPPORTING EVIDENCE for MAIN IDEA
	And	state RELATIONSHIP between SUPPORTING EVIDENCE and MAIN IDEA.
Sequence	IF	PASSAGE is SEQUENCE
	THEN	Identify TOPIC
	And	list each STEP
	And	name each STEP
	And	give DETAILS of each STEP
	And	state DIFFERENCE between each pair of STEPS.

After the students had completed the instructional program, they took a test that included near, intermediate, and far transfer problems. The results showed that the students who had read the analogy before instruction were better on transfer problems (especially far transfer) than were the students who had not read the analogy.

Although many studies have demonstrated the utility of including analogies in instruction about rules, the mechanisms underlying their effect on transfer are not known. One possibility is that on transfer problems, students represent the problem declaratively in working memory and then some part of the representation activates the familiar side of the analogy. This familiar part can then be used to retrieve or reconstruct the new rules. Another possibility is that presenting an analogy during learning causes the learner to induce more abstract conditions for rule application. More abstract conditions would allow the rule to apply to a broader set of future situations.

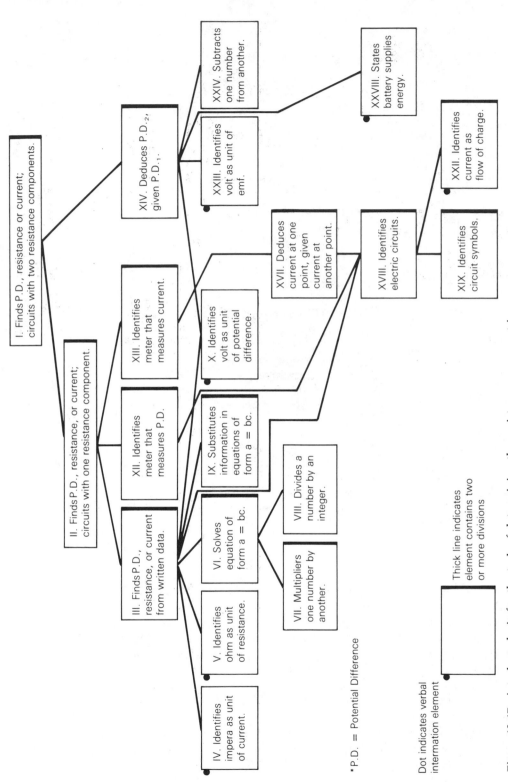

Figure 10.17. A task analysis for the task of determining the resistance or current in electrical circuits. (From Beeson, 1981.)

Table 10.14. Part of the analogy used in Beeson's (1981) study.

ELECTRIC CIRCUITS

In an *electric circuit* electric charges move around the circuit. The battery supplies the energy to keep the charges moving. This movement of electric charges is called an electric current.

Here is a diagram of an electric circuit and the corresponding water circuit. We use simple symbols to stand for the parts of the electric circuit.

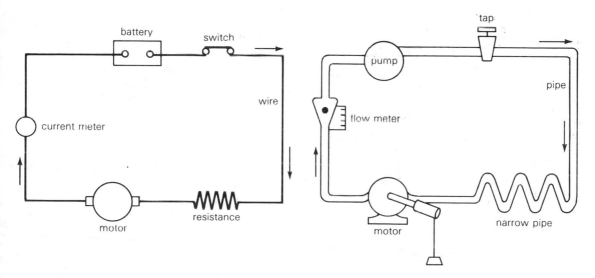

Diagram 2. An electric circuit, and the corresponding water circuit.

We can see that certain parts of the electric circuit correspond to parts of the water circuit, as follows:

ELECTRIC CIRCUIT		WATER CIRCUIT
battery	corresponds to	pump
connecting wires	"	pipes
switch	"	tap
motor	"	motor
resistance	"	narrow pipe
electric current	"	flow of water
current meter	"	flow meter

In the electric circuit we can measure the *current* in the circuit. We could also measure the *potential difference* across parts of the circuit (compare with pressure differences in a water circuit).

In both electric circuits and water circuits we could also work out the *resistance to flow* that a particular appliance caused.

WHAT WE KNOW
AND DON'T KNOW

A major theme of this chapter has been the relationship between organized knowledge and problem-solving. There is ample evidence that skilled problem solvers operate from a different knowledge base than do less skilled problem solvers. They have more knowledge of causal principles, and their knowledge is more likely to be organized around these causal principles. Furthermore, they have more prerequisite procedural knowledge and better knowledge of the conditions of application for various rules. It is consistent with the assumptions of information-processing theories that these knowledge differences account, in large part, for the observed problem-solving differences.

Nonetheless, since few training studies have been done to determine whether or not teaching these types of knowledge improves problem-solving ability, the causal relationship between domain-specific knowledge and problem-solving remains unproven. One type of research that would be beneficial over the coming years is training research designed to validate specific cognitive models. Training research is tremendously expensive, and it requires a major commitment on the part of school personnel, but the benefits from such studies at this point in the development of cognitive models of school tasks seem tremendous.

An important task for cognitive psychologists is to develop more specific theories of how domain-specific knowledge and general reasoning skills affect problem-solving behavior. Voss, Tyler, and Yengo (1983) found in their study of political science problem solving that a majority of Ph.D. chemists who were given the Soviet agriculture problem behaved like the student novices. However, one chemist's protocol looked more like an expert's even though he lacked domain-specific

knowledge of Soviet politics and economics. Voss et al. suggest that this chemist used some general reasoning strategies that he had acquired during his scientific training. If this is the case, why didn't the other chemists also use such strategies? This is just one example of the complex questions that lie ahead for cognitive research in scientific problem solving.

ADDITIONAL READINGS

Champagne, A. B., and L. E. Klopfer (1981). Problem solving as outcome in science teaching: Insights from 60 years of experience. *School Science and Mathematics* 81, 3–8.

Falmagne, R. C. (1975). *Reasoning: Representation and process.* Hillsdale, N.J.: Lawrence Erlbaum Associates.

Gelman, R. (1969). Conservation acquisition: A problem of learning to attend to relevant attributes. *Journal of Experimental Child Psychology* 7, 167–87.

Gilhooly, K. J. (1982). *Thinking: Directed, undirected, and creative.* London: Academic Press.

Gorodetsky, M. and R. Hoz (1980). Use of concept profile analysis to identify difficulties in solving science problems. *Science Education* 64, 671–78.

Gunstone, R. F., A. B. Champagne, and L. E. Klopfer (1981). Instruction for understanding: A case study. *The Australian Science Teachers Journal* 27, 27–32.

APPENDIX

The exact probability can be computed by using Bayes's Theorem which is:

$$P(H/E) = \frac{P(H)\,P(E/H)}{P(H)\,P(E/H) + P(\bar{H})\,P(E/\bar{H})}$$

where:

$P(H/E)$ = the probability that a given hypothesized cause (H) is observed given a particular event (E).

$P(H)$ = the probability that a given hypothesized cause occurs (the "base rate" for a cause).

$P(E/H)$ = the probability that a given event (E) is observed given a particular cause (H).

$P(\overline{H})$ = the probability that other causes occur.

$P(E/\overline{H})$ = the probability that a given event (E) is observed given causes other than H.

Applied to the situation in which the base rate for psylicrapitis is 1 in 100 (i.e., 1 percent), we get:

$P(H)$ = .01 (the base rate for psylicrapitis)

$P(E/H)$ = .90 (the probability for a positive test result given that one has psylicrapitis)

$P(\overline{H})$ = .99 (the base rate for not having psylicrapitis)

$P(E/\overline{H})$ = .01 (the probability for a positive test result given no psylicrapitis)

So,

$$P(H/E) = \frac{(.01)(.90)}{(.01)(.90) + (.99)(.01)} = .48$$

So, when the base rate of psylicrapitis is only one in one hundred, the chances that a positive test result is caused by psylicrapitis are only about 1 in 2.

When the base rate of psylicrapitis is 15 in 100, the terms in the Bayesian formula are:

$P(H)$ = .15

$P(E/H)$ = .90

$P(\overline{H})$ = .85

$P(E/\overline{H})$ = .01

and:

$$P(H/E) = \frac{(.15)(.90)}{(.15)(.90) + (.85)(.01)} = .94$$

Thus, when the base rate of psylicrapitis is 15 in 100, the chances that a positive test result is caused by psylicrapitis are 94 in 100.

Again, Bayes's Theorem can be used to work out the "engineer" problem. Specifically, when 70 percent of the descriptions are of engineers, then:

$P(H)$ = .70 (the base rate for engineers)

$P(E/H)$ = .90 (the probability that this type of description is observed given that the person is an engineer)

$P(\overline{H})$ = .30 (the base rate for nonengineers)

$P(E/\overline{H})$ = .10 (the probability that this type of description is observed given that the person is not an engineer)

and

$$P(H/E) = \frac{(.70)(.90)}{(.70)(.90) + (.30)(.10)} = .95$$

Thus, the probability that the person is an engineer, given this type of description (e.g., socially uninvolved, likes mathematical puzzles, conservative) is .95.

When 30 percent of the descriptions are of engineers, then the terms change to:

$P(H)$ = .30

$P(E/H)$ = .90

$P(\overline{H})$ = .70

$P(E/\overline{H})$ = .10

and

$$P(H/E) = \frac{(.30)(.90)}{(.30)(.90) + (.70)(.10)} = .79$$

Thus, when only 30 percent of the population are engineers, even though the description is highly representative of engineers, there is a reduced probability that the person is, in fact, an engineer. The chances are now only about 8 in 10 that the individual is an engineer.

SECTION

IV

Classroom Processes

Chapter

11

Motivation

SUMMARY

1. Motivation is that which gives direction and intensity to behavior.

2. A behavioristic view of motivation emphasizes the role of external events in determining the direction and intensity of behavior. A cognitive view of motivation does not deny the importance of external events but also assigns importance to internal events.

3. Some internal events that have been shown to influence motivation are conceptual conflict, causal attributions, expectations for success, and memories of other people's behavior.

4. Conceptual conflict can be created by surprising, novel, incongruous, or uncertain information.

5. People attribute their successes and failures to luck, effort, ability, or task difficulty, and their attributions affect their persistence.

6. Students can be encouraged to attribute success to effort by giving them individual goals, stating effort attributions, and avoiding displays of sympathy for failure.

7. People learn behavioral directions by observing others and then recalling what others did in a given situation.

8. There is growing evidence that the informational aspect of feedback is more important for motivation than is the pleasure aspect.

Motivation is that which gives direction and intensity to behavior. It is of utmost concern to teachers because the lack of it seems to be a major obstacle to learning. Some students seem to be bored, others anxious, and still others hostile. Yet these same students, outside the classroom, often seem enthusiastic, calm, and friendly. Why are many students unmotivated in the classroom and yet tremendously motivated in out-of-school pursuits?

The focus in this book is on the cognitive aspects of school learning, and this is the intent in this chapter as well. However, a leading opposing view has been a behavioristic one. Thus, to clearly distinguish the two views I will first present a traditional behavioristic view and then contrast it with a cognitive approach to motivation. In the behavioristic model a central theorem is that organisms respond in ways that have been reinforced in the past. Thorndike (1898) first stated this principle, calling it "the law of effect." Later Skinner studied reinforcement extensively and elaborated the view (1938). He described the response patterns that occur under different schedules of reinforcement (e.g., intermittent versus continuous) and also the idea of shaping a response by reinforcing successive approximations to the desired behavior. These ideas form the core of a behavioristic view of motivation.

How can these ideas explain the fact that some students seem motivated for out-of-school pursuits and unmotivated for schoolwork? The explanation is that such students are experiencing reinforcement for out-of-school activities and not for in-school activities. One does not need to look hard to see that videogames or athletics allow more opportunities for success for some students than do classroom assignments or projects.

Although the behavioristic view provides a partial answer to the mysteries of motivation, it is far from complete. A major problem with this view is its failure to explain the wide range of student motivation under apparently similar reinforcement contingencies (both past and present). For example, why will two students of roughly equivalent competence and reinforcement histories behave differently in math class—one patient and persistent in solving homework problems and the other giving up quite quickly? Or, why would two students, again with roughly equal competence and reinforcement histories, choose tasks that vary a great deal in difficulty?

The behavioristic view is incomplete because behaviorists deal only with observable stimuli and observable responses. They do not speculate about what thoughts and emotions might mediate between these observables. By contrast, cognitivists propose that thought influences the direction and intensity of behavior. In recent years there has been a renewed interest in a cognitive view of motivation (cf. Weiner, 1972) and it is clear that this view is adding precision to the purely behavioristic models.

BEHAVIORISTIC VERSUS COGNITIVE VIEWS OF MOTIVATION

Figure 11.1 shows the behavioristic view of motivation and a more elaborate cognitive view. The elements of the behavioristic view are an initiating external stimulus (S), a response (R), and a reinforcer (Reinf). What occurs between the S and the R is not discussed.

The first element in both the behavioristic and cognitive views is an initiating stimulus—some event that sets in motion a sequence of responses. However, there are differences in what is meant by "initiating stimulus" in the two views. In the behavioristic view the initiating stimulus is an occurrence in the environment that has been associated with reinforcement following a particular response. For example, a first-grade teacher flicks the light switch to get order in the classroom. The light's flicking is associated with praise for the children if they come to order. In the cognitive view the initiating stimulus is a goal. A goal may be suggested by a teacher ("Do problems 1–10 for your homework tonight"), or it may be a self-generated goal ("I'd like to know more about how cars run"). Thus the initiating stimulus in the cognitive view may come either from the environment or from the learner's own thoughts. It functions not so much as a cue for reinforcement opportunity but as a representation of a problem.

In the behavioristic view the initiating stimulus directly causes the response, whereas in the cognitive view it activates a variety of internal events, which in turn result in a response. Some types of internal event that seem to play an important role in motivation include (1) conflicting thoughts or uncertainty, (2) causal attributions for what led one to succeed in reaching the goal of in-

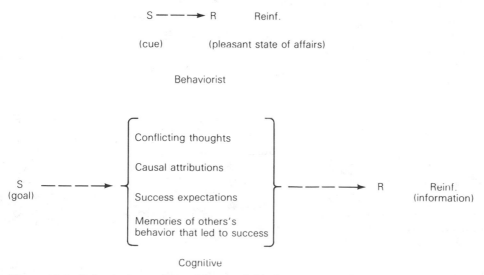

Figure 11.1. Behaviorist and cognitive models of motivation. S = initiating stimulus, R = response, and Reinf. = reinforcer.

terest in the past, (3) emotions, (4) expectations that one can succeed in reaching the goal in the future, and (5) memories of what others did before reaching the goal. Probably other types of internal event contribute to motivation, but those just listed have a good empirical foundation. In the rest of this chapter, I will discuss the role that each of these internal events plays in motivation.

UNCERTAINTY AND CURIOSITY

Uncertainty is produced when we experience something novel, surprising, incongruous, or complex (Berlyne, 1960). It results in a heightened state of arousal in the central nervous system. For example, when a child goes to school expecting to see the regular fourth-grade teacher, and instead finds a substitute teacher this produces uncertainty about what the teacher is like and what will be expected of the child. If we were to measure the child's physiological responses on discovering the substitute teacher, we might observe an increased heart rate, shallow breathing, or pupil dilation, which are signs of increased nervous system arousal. This moderately aroused state in the face of uncertainty is what Berlyne (1960) calls curiosity.

Curiosity leads to exploratory behavior directed at reducing uncertainty. For example, the fourth grader might spend a good deal of time looking at the substitute teacher or listening to what he or she said to other students. Another form of exploration would be to ask the new teacher questions such as "Do we have to have science today?" As one gathers information through exploration, one's arousal level is reduced. According to this theory, reduction in arousal is reinforcing. According to Berlyne, it is reinforcing in much the same way as food is reinforcing to a hungry individual. That is, both hunger and curiosity are seen as having innate physiological bases. Since the reduction of uncertainty should have survival value, it is not

surprising that such reduction is innately reinforcing.

Berlyne (1960) distinguishes between *perceptual* and *epistemic* curiosity. Perceptual curiosity is caused by novel, incongruous, surprising, or complex sensory stimuli. For example, a sudden loud noise causes people to orient in the direction of the noise in order to get more information about it. Epistemic curiosity is caused by "discrepant thoughts, beliefs, or attitudes" (that is, by internal stimuli). Although both perceptual and epistemic curiosity may play a role in classroom learning, epistemic curiosity is the form most clearly related to cognition. Berlyne assumes that discrepant thoughts lead to increased arousal and that the increased arousal leads to exploratory behavior directed at resolving the discrepancy and thus reducing arousal.

One example of curiosity in elementary school children comes from a study done by Berlyne and Frommer (1966). These researchers read stories to kindergarten, third-, and fifth-grade children and then invited the children to ask questions about the stories. The stories varied in novelty or uncertainty of outcome. Two that differed in novelty were an Aesop's fable called "The Fox and the Raven" (low novelty) and the same fable using a tayra and an auk in place of the fox and the raven (high novelty). Two stories that differed in uncertainty were about a little boy who had to make a decision. In the low-uncertainty story there were two possible outcomes, one of which was presented as the likely one. In the high-uncertainty story, there were three possible outcomes, all of which were presented as equally likely. The children in this study asked more questions about the high-novelty and high-uncertainty stories than about the low-novelty and low-uncertainty stories.

According to Berlyne's theory the novel and uncertain stories produced more conceptual conflict. For example, in the novel version of the Aesop's fable, children may have tried to compare a tayra to a more familiar animal, and this comparison would lead to conflicting thoughts. A child may think some aspects of the tayra make it seem like a wolf and others make it seem more like a cow. Asking questions should lead to information that would favor one of these thoughts over the other and thus reduce conflict.

The interesting proposal in Berlyne's theory is that thoughts affect the direction and intensity of behavior; that is, they affect motivation. Piaget (1967; 1980) also postulates an important role for cognitive conflict (disequilibrium) in motivation. Both Berlyne and Piaget argue that the resolution of conceptual ambiguity is adaptive for the species.

What techniques can a teacher use to create cognitive conflict? Setting up debates on political issues in social science classes should create uncertainty about what position is the best. In science, demonstrating an experiment that gives unexpected results produces conceptual conflict and motivates students to understand why the results were different from those expected. In English literature one might create uncertainty by having different students propose interpretations of symbolic stories, thus raising questions about which interpretation is best. This should motivate students to defend their interpretations with specific details and examples.

Entire methods of instruction capitalize on the motivation inherent in conceptual conflict. One of these is "Inquiry Teaching" in science (Suchman, 1962). In this method students are asked questions rather than given answers. Another method, called "socratic teaching," involves countering students' claims with discrepant information and hence motivating the students to resolve the discrepancy. R. C. Anderson and G. W. Faust (1974) and Collins and Stevens (1982) provide examples of socratic teaching.

Any teacher who has tried one of these techniques is aware of the powerful effect they can have. They also require a great deal of preparation and planning to anticipate what types of response students will give and how one should respond. Other techniques can be used with somewhat less planning. One is simply posing questions rather than always making statements; it should increase curiosity because the student will experience uncertainty about the answer.

Optimal Level of Arousal

There is a fundamental relationship between arousal and performance that seems to hold not only for humans but for other animals as well. The relationship (called the "Yerkes-Dodson law") is shown in Figure 11.2. This figure shows a curvilinear relationship between arousal and performance, such that, starting from a very low level of arousal and going to a moderate level, performance increases. Then any further increases in arousal cause performance decrements. Thus there is an optimum level of arousal.

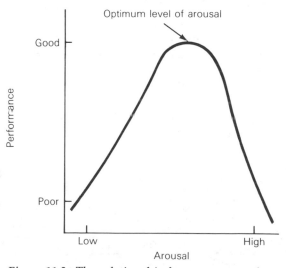

Figure 11.2. The relationship between arousal and performance (Yerkes-Dodson law, 1908). A low level of arousal produces poor performance, as does a very high level. However, a moderate level of arousal produces good performance.

This law has implications for epistemic curiosity, in that it suggests conditions under which a teacher's attempts to induce curiosity might not work. Specifically, the attempts would not work if they generated too much arousal. This might happen, for example, with a student who was very anxious (aroused) about performance in front of a group. A question that produced conceptual conflict would increase this student's arousal level to a nonproductive point. Another situation in which curiosity-inducing procedures might not work is when they produce too little arousal. A student who already knows the explanation for a counterintuitive experimental result would not experience conceptual conflict after seeing the experiment and would therefore not be aroused. Thus curiosity-producing techniques will be effective only when they generate an optimal arousal level.

The Value of Curiosity

Despite the problem of determining optimal arousal levels, curiosity seems to be an important type of motivation to encourage. It is a type that is intrinsic to knowledge, and thus it is cheap and always available. It is also a motivation that learners can use throughout their lives as they acquire new knowledge. Finally, it appears to play a significant role in the lives of inventors, scientists, artists, and other creative individuals (cf. Barron, 1963; Roe, 1960).

CAUSAL ATTRIBUTIONS AND SUCCESS EXPECTATIONS

Besides uncertainty, some other types of thought influence motivation: causal attributions and success expectations. *Causal attributions* (within achievement situations) are the explanations people give for why they or others achieved success or failed to achieve it. *Success expectations* are people's subjective estimates of their chances of succeeding at a given task. Both of these classes of thought have been studied by Weiner (1979, 1980) as he has developed a theory of motivation called *attribution theory*.

Attribution theory, like curiosity theory, gives thought a central role in motivation. However, unlike curiosity theory (in which the important dimension is the *amount* of uncertainty produced by various thoughts, independent of their content), in attribution theory the *content* of thoughts is important. Only thoughts that have to do with causal attributions and success expectations are relevant.

Following Heider (1958), Weiner (1979) postulates that within achievement situations people tend to attribute their failure or success to one of four broad classes of cause: their ability, their luck, their effort, or the difficulty of the task. These attributions in turn determine people's feelings about themselves, their predictions of success, and the probability that they will try harder or less hard at the task in the future. For example, if a person attributes her failure to something that she can control (e.g., effort) then she will feel guilt, will predict that she can succeed in the future if she exerts more effort, and, in fact, will exert more effort in the future. On the other hand, when someone attributes his failure to low ability, he will feel depressed, he will predict that he will fail again, and he will use less effort in the future. Thus, attributions are said to affect (1) expectations of success, (2) emotional (affective) reactions, and (3) persistence at achievement-related tasks. I will illustrate each of these links with experimental evidence.

Attributions and Success Expectations

Weiner, Nierenberg, and Goldstein (1976) gave students up to five (or no) consecutive success experiences on a block-design task. This task involves arranging, in a limited time period, several blocks to match a pattern presented by the experimenter (like a picture puzzle). This task is useful when the experimenter wishes to control the success rate of the subject: by watching the subject and saying that time is up before he or she is done, the experimenter produces a failure situation. (Of course, in all such experiments, subjects are carefully debriefed following the experiment.)

In the Weiner et al. (1976) study, after each trial on which success feedback was given, students were asked five questions. First, they were asked to indicate how many of the next ten designs, which were similar to designs already done, they felt they would complete successfully. This question measured success expectations. Second, they were asked four questions that determined their success attribution—to luck, task ease, high ability, or effort. The findings revealed that expectancy for success was higher for people who attributed success to either task ease or high ability than for people who attributed success to luck or effort. Task ease and ability are usually considered to be stable characteristics of a situation, whereas luck and effort are usually considered unstable. It makes sense that people who thought their success was due to a stable characteristic would be more confident of future success, because they believe the characteristic will exist in the future.

In many situations people perceive effort to be an unstable characteristic, and hence when they attribute their success to effort they do not, as the Weiner et al. study showed, raise their success expectations. This is unfortunate, since it does not lead to increased effort. If people perceived their effort as a *stable* characteristic, then they should raise their expectations for future success and should also keep putting forth effort.

A study by Rosenbaum (1972; as reported in Weiner, 1980) suggests that when people perceive effort to be stable they are

likely to raise their expectations for future success. Rosenbaum gave groups of subjects a story about a boss and his subordinate working together on a project. The success of the project was evaluated, and a causal attribution for the outcome was given. Half of the groups were told that the project succeeded and half were told that the project failed. Crossed with this outcome information was the attributional statement. For half the groups the success or failure was attributed to an unstable cause (ability or effort), and for the other half the outcome was attributed to a stable cause. For example, a success outcome might be attributed to the subordinate's character as a hard worker (stable effort) or to the subordinate's unusual effort on this occasion (unstable effort). Or, success might be attributed to the subordinate's consistent ability to produce high-quality products (stable ability), or to a sudden increase in ability to produce (unstable ability).

A randomly selected set of subjects read each version of the story and then rated how probable they thought it was that the boss and subordinate would succeed on future projects. The results are shown in Figure 11.3. As you can see, what was crucial to the differentiation of expectancy was not whether ability or effort was seen as the cause, but whether the cause was seen to be stable. When either effort or ability were thought to be stable, whatever outcome had already occurred was predicted for the future.

This experiment suggests ways of both encouraging students to attribute their success to effort and increasing their expectancy of success. If this is one's goal, it seems that after a student exerts effort and experiences success, it would be better to say to that student, "You are a hardworking person" than to say, "You really tried hard that time." That is, it may be better to encourage students to see their effort-making propensity as a stable trait because this will lead them to have a higher hope of future success. Since expec-

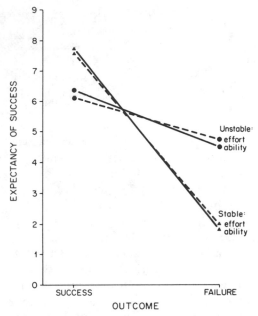

Figure 11.3. Expectancy of future success as a function of type of outcome and stability of outcome. (From Rosenbaum, 1972, p. 83, as reported in Weiner, 1980.)

tancy of success causes people to persist longer (James and Rotter, 1958), encouraging students to see their effort-making as a stable trait should increase their persistence.

Attributions and Affective Reactions

Attributions are related not only to expectancy of success, but also to affective reactions. One study that demonstrated this idea was conducted by Weiner, Russell, and Lerman (1979). They had subjects retrospect about times when they had succeeded on an exam because of ability, unusual effort, usual effort, help from others, luck, or personality factors. Then they asked the subjects to list three emotions they experienced in that situation. The percentages of respondents listing various emotions for different attributions are shown in Table 11.1.

Happiness was experienced fairly uniformly independent of the perceived cause of success. However, other emotions were correlated with particular attributions. For example, pride was more strongly associated with attributions to ability than with attributions to unusual effort, help, or luck. Satisfaction and relief were associated with unusual effort. For failure outcomes, (not shown in Table 11.1), attributions to low ability were associated with resignation and incompetence, and lack of effort was associated with the feeling of guilt.

Attributions and Effort

We have seen that different attributions precede different levels of success expectation and are correlated with different types of affect. Attribution theory also claims that attributions affect the amount of effort people exert. If people attribute their past failures to lack of effort, they are likely to try harder, whereas if they attribute their failure to lack of ability, they are likely to give up. Similarly, if people attribute a failure to bad luck, they are likely to keep trying because things could change, but if they attribute failure to task difficulty, they are likely to give up when they do not think task difficulty will change.

Meyer (1970; as reported in Weiner, 1980) demonstrated these ideas in a study involving digit-symbol substitution. He created failure by telling subjects their time was up before they had completed the task. He then attributed subjects' failures to bad luck, low ability, task difficulty, lack of effort, or both low ability and task difficulty. After this, the subjects performed on another trial, and the difference in performance speed between trials was measured. Normally one would expect greater speed in trial 2 simply because of practice, but as Figure 11.4 reveals, the increase in speed varied a great deal as a function of attributions. Subjects who heard their

Table 11.1. Emotions reported as being experienced following different attributions for success. (From Weiner, Russell, and Lerman, 1979.)

	PERCENTAGE OF EMOTIONAL RECOLLECTION AS A FUNCTION OF THE CAUSAL ATTRIBUTION FOR SUCCESS					
AFFECT	ABILITY	UNSTABLE EFFORT	STABLE EFFORT	PERSONALITY	OTHERS	LUCK
Competence	30[a]	12	20	19	5	2
Confidence	20	19	18	19	14	4
Contentment	4	4	12[a]	0	7	2
Excitement	3	9	8	11	16[a]	6
Gratitude	9	1	4	8	43[a]	14
Guilt	1	3	0	3	2	18[a]
Happiness	44	43	43	38	46	48
Pride	39[a]	28	39	43[a]	21	8
Relief	4	28[a]	16	11	13	26[a]
Satisfaction	19	24[a]	16	14	9	0
Surprise	7	16[a]	4	14	4	52[a]
Thankfulness	0	1	0	0	18[a]	4

[a]$p < .01$.

failure attributed to bad luck or lack of effort increased their speed more than did those who heard their failure attributed to low ability, task difficulty, or both.

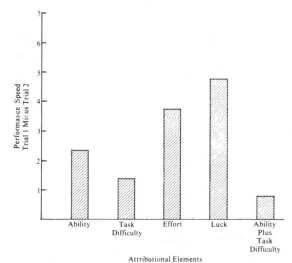

Figure 11.4. Amount of speed up in performance (in seconds) from Trial 1 to Trial 2 as a function of attribution for prior failures. (Adapted from Meyer, 1970, as reported in Weiner, 1980.)

Interaction of Thought, Feeling, and Behavior

Attributions have been shown to influence expectations for success, to be correlated with affective responses, and to influence effort. A question that is receiving attention currently, and one that will probably continue to receive attention for quite a while, is Just how do the cognitive, emotional, and behavioral consequences of attributions interact? Do thoughts cause feelings, which cause actions, or do thoughts concomitantly cause actions and feelings, or are they all quite interactive (see Figure 11.5)? Recently two theoretical positions have been forwarded on the interaction of affect and cognition (Bower, 1981; Zajonc, 1980), and a symposium has been devoted to this topic (Clarke and Fiske, 1982). However, the answer is not clear yet.

On the more specific question of how cognition, affect, and behavior interact within achievement settings, Weiner's (1980) position is shown in Figure 11.6. In his view, the outcome of a task (success or failure) may lead a person to try to infer the cause of the suc-

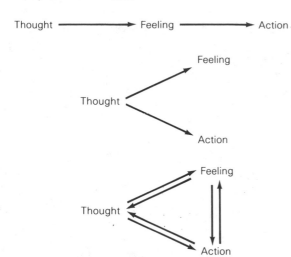

Thought ⟶ Feeling ⟶ Action

Thought → Feeling
Thought → Action

Thought ⇄ Feeling
Thought ⇄ Action
Feeling ⇅ Action

Figure 11.5. Some possible pathways of influence among thought, feeling, and action.

cess or failure. These attributions then lead to feelings such as pride or guilt and further thoughts about the future chances of success. Both feelings and expectations then influence behavior. One example of how this sequence might operate in the classroom is when a student who thinks she has low ability in math experiences success on her first algebra test. She might infer (since success could not be due to her ability) that it was due to an easy test, and hence she would experience relief (see Table 11.1). She would increase her expectation for future success, because the difficulty level of tests is a stable aspect of the situation. (It is stable because teachers are per-

Figure 11.6. The flow of causation of Weiner's attributional model of achievement behavior. (Adapted from Weiner, 1980, p. 388.)

Stimulus Task outcome → Attribution for success or failure → Affect → Action
Attribution for success or failure → Expectancy for success or failure → Action

ceived to maintain a consistent level of difficulty across their tests.) The attribution of success to task ease would not lead to much increase in effort, since effort is not seen to be a cause of success.

Now suppose that this student does well on a second test and meanwhile finds that half the class flunked. This information might cause her to change her attribution of success from task ease to effort or ability. Then she would experience feelings of competence and pride, and think that if she keeps trying she may continue to succeed. The result would be that she would continue to exert effort. Alternatively, she might do well on the second test and find out that everyone got an A. She would not feel proud and would begin to think her chances of success even without exerting much effort were good. In this situation there would be neither emotional nor cognitive reasons to exert much effort, and she would stop trying.

The most depressing cycle that one can think of, using Weiner's (1980) model, is that in which a student attributes failure to lack of ability. This leads to depression and resignation and predictions of more failure. Resignation leads to lack of effort, as does the thought that failure is a certain outcome. Most teachers have had students who show signs of possessing this negative motivation cycle. These students do not try hard and believe (whether they are willing to admit it or not) that they are not capable of academic success. There is evidence that children of lower socioeconomic status are more likely to be victims of this cycle (Falbo, 1973; Raviv, Bar-Tal, Raviv, and Bar-Tal, 1980).

Attribution Training Programs

Can students who attribute their failure to low ability learn to change their attributions? Specifically, can they learn to attribute failure to lack of effort and success to adequate effort? If so, their affective reactions to failure should change from resignation to guilt, and guilt should lead to action rather than inaction. Furthermore, their thoughts about future success would change from "I can't succeed; I'm too dumb" to "If I try hard, I might succeed," which should also encourage action.

Several studies suggest that students can learn to change their attributions and that changes in attributions are paralleled by changes in persistence (Andrews and Debus, 1978; Chapin and Dyck, 1976; Dweck, 1975). Andrews and Debus (1978), for example, identified forty-two sixth-grade boys who were below average in attributing their failures to lack of effort. They then had two-thirds of these pupils perform a block-design task. The trainer controlled the success or failure outcome by giving time limits that were either very liberal or too strict. The pupils were allowed to experience success on half of the trials.

After each trial the student indicated what he attributed his success or failure to—luck, task difficulty, effort, or ability. Whenever the pupil attributed success to effort or failure to lack of effort, the trainer reinforced that attribution by saying such things as "That's good!" or "Very Good!" or "OK!" If the pupil attributed success or failure to something other than effort, the trainer simply said, "Here's your next design," and did not look directly at the pupil. The pupils were trained until they made effort attributions 80 percent of the time or for sixty trials, whichever came first.

After training, the pupils performed on two other tasks and were asked to give their attributions for success and failure on these (another block-design task and an anagrams task). They also performed a third (insolvable) task, and their persistence (amount of time spent trying to solve this task) was measured. The third of the boys who did not re-

ceive training (control group) also performed on these three tasks. The pupils who received attribution training were much more likely than the control group pupils to attribute both success and failure to effort and to persist at an insolvable task. Furthermore, another test given a week later showed the same results.

A strict behaviorist would say these results were due to establishing a history of partial reinforcement in the training group and not in the control group. That is, for the training group the 50 percent success rate became a cue that success would be forthcoming, and so they persisted. Chapin and Dyck (1976), however, independently varied partial reinforcement and attribution training and found that, although partial reinforcement had a positive effect on persistence, attribution training caused more persistence than did partial reinforcement alone. Thus there is good evidence that causal attributions mediate motivation.

Because these training studies directly manipulate attributions, they provide strong evidence for the causal role of attributions in motivation. Most studies of attributions simply observe attributions and effort and determine the correlation between them. As has been stated previously, correlations can be used to suggest causal relationships, but experimental manipulation is needed to verify that the suggested factor does play a causal role.

It is worth noting that in the Andrews and Debus (1978) study, the trainer asked the pupil to make the attribution and then selectively reinforced effort attributions. In the Chapin and Dyck (1976) and Dweck (1975) studies, however, the trainer made the attribution for the pupil (e.g., "You must have really tried hard"). Either procedure appears to work.

Teachers who attempt to change student attributions must be both careful and patient. Care is needed to select tasks at which the student can succeed with effort. Following the behavioristic principle of shaping, it may be better to start with tasks that require only a small (but perceptible) amount of effort and then, as the student shows a greater willingness to exert effort, increase the amount needed for success. If the teacher selects tasks that require no effort and then attributes the student's success to effort, the teacher will lose credibility.

Patience is needed because people seem to cling to their self-concepts, whatever they are (see Ames, Ames, and Garrison, 1977). Thus people with low ability self-concepts do not seem willing to give them up. For example, suppose that a teacher arranges for a student who believes he has low ability to succeed at a task after some effort. To the student, this success is a surprising event and surprising events tend to be attributed to unstable causes such as luck or task ease (Simon and Feather, 1973; Valle and Frieze, 1976). It seems to take many trials for a student with a low self-concept to accept the teacher's attribution of success to effort. In fact, a teacher may patiently spend an entire year in trying to change a student's attributions without seeing any change. The teachers who have the student the following year, however, will reap the rewards of the former teacher's patience.

Classroom Goals and Attributions

There is growing evidence that competitive goals cause children to be more ability-focused in their causal attributions whereas individualistic goals cause them to be more effort-focused (for a review see C. Ames, 1984a). One study that demonstrates this relationship was done by C. Ames (1984b). In this study, fifth and sixth graders were asked to trace two sets of line-drawn puzzles. Half of the children were told to try to be the winner (competitive goal) and half were told to try to solve as many puzzles as they could and to try to solve more puzzles on the second set (individualized goal).

After performing on the second set of puzzles, children were asked about their attributions for success or failure and about instructions they had given themselves. The results revealed that children given the individualized goal selected more effort-related attributions than did children given the competitive goal. Conversely, children given the competitive goal selected more ability-related attributions than did children given the individualized goal. The children given the individualized goal also gave themselves more facilitative instructions such as "I will work carefully," "I will take my time," or "I will make a plan." That is, they seemed to think about the details of strategies that would help them reach their goals.

Thus, teachers may be able to encourage both effort attributions and facilitative self-instructions by focusing students on individual goals and self-improvement. A major obstacle to doing this is that it requires a good deal of planning, organization, and management to individualize instruction effectively. However, the rewards in terms of student motivation may be worth it. M. Wang and her colleagues have demonstrated one way of managing the task of individualization, by teaching students to take more and more responsibility for goal-setting and planning of instructional sequences (Wang, 1974).

Teacher Behavior and Attributions

One very powerful constellation of cues about student ability comes from the teacher. Some teachers treat high- and low-ability students quite differently. For example, they ask high-ability students more challenging questions and follow up on these students' answers, but they give low-ability students more help and praise for mediocre work. If students in fact perceive this differential treatment, they may use it to infer ability differences. The work of R. S. Weinstein and others (reviewed by R. S. Weinstein, 1983) suggests that children do perceive such differential treatment.

In one study (Weinstein, Marshall, Brattesani, and Middlestadt, 1982), fourth-through sixth-grade children were questioned about how their teachers would treat hypothetical high- and low-ability children. Some teachers were not perceived to give much differential treatment, but those who were perceived to give differential treatment were said to give high achieving students more opportunities and choices and higher expectations, and to give low achievers more negative feedback, more directions, and more work and rule statements.

Besides differential teacher behavior towards students (praise, types of assignments, etc.) another cue for attributions is differential teacher affect. Graham and Weiner (in press) have shown that children as young as six years old can distinguish between teacher pity and teacher anger. Furthermore they infer from a teacher's pity that the student being pitied could not control the outcome (was of low ability) whereas they infer from a teacher's anger that the student could control the outcome (didn't try hard).

Graham (1982; reported in Graham and Weiner, in press) conducted an experiment with sixth-grade children in which the children were given four trials on a novel puzzle task. After each trial they received failure feedback. The "teacher" accompanied the failure feedback with both verbal and nonverbal affective cues. For the sympathy group, the teacher said, "I feel sorry for you," and for the angry group she said, "I'm angry with you." A control group did not receive any cues about the teacher's emotions.

After receiving these different affective cues for five trials, the students were asked to state why they thought they were doing

poorly at the task and to predict their chances for success in the future. Figures 11.7 and 11.8 show the results for attributions and predictions, respectively. The children who received anger cues were most likely to attribute their failure to lack of effort, and the children who received sympathy cues were most likely to attribute their failure to lack of ability (Figure 11.7). The children who received anger cues maintained a higher level of expectation for success than did the children who received sympathy cues. This is especially evident on the fifth trial (Figure 11.8). Since other studies have shown that a very low expectation of success leads to a lessening of effort, it is likely that the children who received sympathy would decrease their effort over trials.

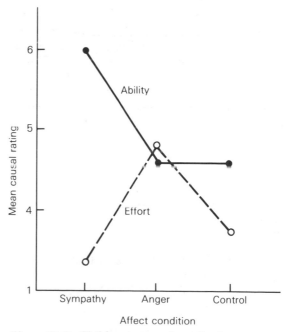

Figure 11.7. Children's causal attributions as a function of the teacher's affect. (From Graham and Weiner, in press.)

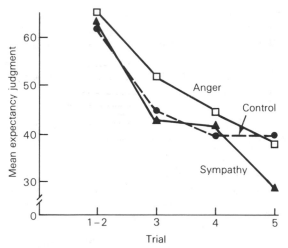

Figure 11.8. Children's changes in success expectations given different teacher affect following the childrens' failures. (From Graham and Weiner, in press.)

Summary

Students' thoughts about the causes of success and failure influence their motivation. In particular, if students think that their failures are due to lack of effort and their successes are due to effort, and if they see themselves as hardworking, they will persist longer in achievement situations. Teachers can play a role in encouraging such effort-related attributions by calling attention (when appropriate) to success due to effort, by emphasizing individual improvement rather than competition, and by being aware of the effect of their own behavior and emotions on students' perceptions of ability.

MEMORIES OF HOW OTHERS ACHIEVED SUCCESS: OBSERVATIONAL LEARNING

Besides the influence on motivation of conflicting thoughts and of attributions, thought influences motivation in another way. This is through retrieved thoughts about prior events that an individual has observed. Specifically, people sometimes choose a particular course of action because they remember that this choice brought positive results for some other person. This process is called "observational learning" and is described in Bandura's social learning theory (Bandura, 1977).

Figure 11.9 shows a typical sequence of events in observational learning. First, someone other than the learner (*M* for Model) responds in a particular way (*R*). While *M* is responding the learner (*O* for observer) is paying attention and creating propositions that describe what is happening. The model's response is followed by something that the observer considers to be rewarding. Some time later, when the observer is in the same situation as the model, he or she will recall the model's response and the pleasant consequence. This recollection will lead *O* to infer that if she makes the same response, she too will receive reinforcement.

In the sequence of events shown in Figure 11.9, the observer chose to do something (raise her hand) that had resulted in reinforcement to someone else in the past. This form of observational learning is called *vicarious reinforcement*. In another form of observational learning, the observer may choose to *not* do something because it was observed in the past to be followed by negative consequences to someone else. This process is called *vicarious punishment*. Studies of aggression, for example, have shown that children are less likely to engage in aggressive behaviors if they have observed another being punished for aggression (Rosenkrans and Hartup, 1967).

People often imitate models even when they do not observe the model receiving reinforcement (Harris, 1970). This seems to be especially true when the model is respected or someone with whom the observer identifies. One example of this type of observational learning is given in a study by Lippett, Polansky, and Rosen (1952). These researchers observed the frequency with which chil-

Figure 11.9. An example of observational learning. O = Observer, M = Model.

dren imitated the actions of other children at a summer camp. They found that a few boys who had a lot of power were the most frequently imitated. Imitation occurred whether or not the observed action was seen to be directly reinforced. Apparently, people believe that the behaviors of respected others are likely to receive reinforcement, and this belief is enough to lead them to imitate their behaviors.

Instructional Implications of Observational Learning

What are the implications of observational learning for classroom motivation? One is that students learn from the behavior of their teachers. In the classroom they may choose to work at problems longer if they have first observed their teacher take time with a difficult sample problem, persisting until it is solved. Too, if a teacher tells his students about out-of-school activities that he pursues (e.g., ''Last night, I read in the newspaper that . . .''), then they may be inclined to imitate these activities. Of course, the tendency for students to learn from teachers' behaviors depends on how well liked and respected the teacher is. Thus, it is important for teachers to do things, particularly at the beginning of the year, to create an atmosphere of warmth and mutual respect.

Another implication is that other students can serve as models of desirable classroom behavior. Teachers can call students' attention to the successful behavior of a classmate. For example, a teacher might have a session in which students discussed how they had come up with their ideas for a composition they had just completed. One student might report that she tried writing down her free associations first and that she thought this had helped her find a focus. Hearing this, other students might try it for the next composition.

As high school teachers know, for many adolescents the most imitated person in the classroom is neither the teacher nor the academically most successful student; it is the most popular student. If this student is not motivated to do schoolwork, many other students will imitate his or her lack of motivation. Thus, it behooves teachers of adolescents to determine early in the year which students are most popular and then seek to get them academically involved. Once they show positive academic motivation, the rest of the class is likely to as well.

In conclusion, students observe the extent to which teachers, parents, and friends persist in learning and problem solving, and they observe the positive or negative consequences of such persistence. They also observe others' learning strategies and whether or not such strategies benefited those others. Finally, they observe the activities respected others choose as careers and as recreation. Later, when they must decide whether or not to persist, the decision will be influenced by memories of these observations. When they must decide what learning strategy to use, the decision will be influenced by memories of effective strategies. And when they must decide what elective to take or whether or not to go to college, the decision will be influenced by their observation of the consequences of others' choices. Memories of the behavior of others, then, play an important role in human motivation.

THE REINFORCER

In Figure 11.1, you saw a contrast between a behavioristic and a cognitive view of motivation. So far in this chapter the two models have been contrasted in terms of how the initiating stimulus is conceptualized (either as a cue or as a goal) and in terms of the role played by mediating thoughts and affect (either the role is excluded from consideration or it is given a prominent place). Now let us turn to the final element in both types of models—the reinforcer.

Strictly speaking, for behaviorists a reinforcer is anything that increases the probability of the response it follows. However, many practitioners with a behaviorist bent consider a reinforcer to be something that brings about pleasant feelings. Praise is reinforcing because it makes people "feel good," avoidance of pain is reinforcing because of a feeling of relief, and candy is reinforcing because it tastes good. Indeed, Thorndike (1913), who first described the "law of effect," explained that it worked because it brought about a satisfying state of affairs. Thus, many people hold the theory that reinforcers work because they *are pleasing*.

An alternative conception of reinforcers is that they work because they *provide information*. This view is consistent with the information-processing framework presented throughout this book. In this view, people tend to repeat a behavior that has previously led to a positive state of affairs, because they have formed a *rule* that such behavior has desirable consequences. The important aspect of the consequence is thus its informativeness, not its pleasantness.

Is it the pleasure aspect or informational aspect of reinforcers that accounts for increases in responding? This has been a difficult question to answer because no one could think of a way to vary the pleasure and informational aspects of reinforcement independently. Nonetheless, it is an important question because it bears on the role of feedback in learning. If feedback works because it provides a satisfying state of affairs, then teachers should avoid critical feedback, because it will make an individual feel badly. However, if feedback works because it provides information, then teachers should use critical feedback if it is specific and therefore informative.

Recently, researchers have become clever about separating the pleasure and informational aspects of feedback (Estes, 1972; Guthrie, 1971; Surber and Anderson, 1975). In Estes's (1972) experiment, subjects were asked to pretend that they were traffic-control workers for an airline. They were seated in front of computer terminals on which they viewed a set of arrows that indicated an airplane (see Figure 11.10). Their job was to choose a command (one of two keys) to give the pilot. If they chose the correct command,

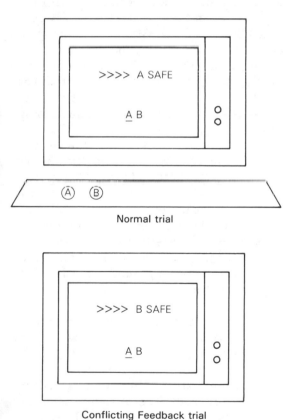

Normal trial

Conflicting Feedback trial

Figure 11.10. Displays for normal and conflicting feedback trials in the Estes (1972) experiment. On a normal trial the "pilot" received the message sent. On a conflicting feedback trial the pilot received a different message from the one sent. (Adapted from Estes, 1972.)

[handwritten note at top of page: But they could have experienced unpleasantness instead knowing that if the noise wasn't there they would have caused the plane to crash, feeling bad because of it.]

the word SAFE appeared on the screen, indicating that the plane had avoided a collision. If they chose the wrong command, the word FAIL appeared on the screen indicating a collision. The subject had to learn which key of the pair communicated the correct information, because on later trials (following some trials for other pairs of keys) he or she would see again this same pair of keys from which to choose.

In a normal situation a SAFE trial produced a display such as that shown at the top of Figure 11.10. At the bottom of the screen are shown the choices of two keys (A or B). The line under the A indicates that A was selected by the subject. At the top of the screen are the arrows, depicting the airplane, a letter stating what message (A or B) was received by the pilot, and the result (in this case SAFE). Thus, in the normal situation the message sent by the subject was the message received by the pilot.

On some trials, however, the pilot received a different message from the one sent by the subject. These were called "conflicting feedback" trials. An example of one such trial is shown at the bottom of Figure 11.10. In this example the subject selected A, but the pilot received B. Subjects had been warned that sometimes there was noise in the radio communication between ground control and the airplane, so that sometimes the pilot would receive a different message than the one sent. In this example the pilot was SAFE only because he received the message *not* selected by the subject.

Thus, on conflicting feedback trials the pleasure and information aspects of feedback were uncorrelated. The pleasure the subject received because the pilot avoided a collision should lead to an increase in responding the *same* way (e.g., an increase in selecting A in the example at the bottom of Figure 11.10). However, the information the subject received told her that the key *not* selected (B in this example) is actually the key that leads to a safe outcome most of the time. Thus the information aspect of feedback should lead to an increase in selecting the nonselected key in the future.

What did subjects actually do following conflicting feedback trials? On the average there was a *decrease* in responding with the previously selected key following such trials. This was in contrast to the increase in responding with the previously selected key following normal trials. In other words, subjects did not respond in the manner that led to a pleasant outcome most recently; rather they responded in a manner that they *expected* would lead to a pleasant outcome in the future, based on information received during feedback.

Thus, although in most reinforcement situations behavioristic and cognitive views lead to the same predictions, under some, predictions differ. When they do, the cognitive framework accounts for the data better. People appear to be seekers of information more than seekers of immediate pleasure. This orientation is adaptive for our species, because it leads us to explore new environments and ultimately to learn to exist in new environments. If we had sought pleasure at the expense of information for the past 4 million years, it is doubtful that we would have survived as a species.

CONCLUSIONS AND DIRECTIONS FOR FUTURE RESEARCH

The theme of this chapter has been that internal events play an important role in motivation. This has been demonstrated for conflicting thoughts, attributions, predictions of success, and memories for what others did to achieve a goal. The effects of thought on motivation help explain why similar reinforcement histories do not necessarily lead to similar levels of motivation in two people. One needs to know how a person interprets his or her successes and failures and what he or she recalls about the successes and failures of others to make more accurate predictions about the effects of reinforcement on that person. Now that it is clear that thought influences action, we can increase our understanding of the specific ways in which thought exerts its influence on action. Also of interest is how (and whether) affect and thought interact in determining action. These are complex questions, the answers to which will surely increase our understanding of motivation.

ADDITIONAL READINGS

Bandura, A. (1977). *Social learning theory.* Englewood Cliffs, N.J.: Prentice-Hall.

Clarke, M. S. and S. T. Fiske (1982). *Affect and cognition: The seventeenth annual Carnegie Symposium on Cognition.* Hillsdale, N.J.: Lawrence Erlbaum Associates.

Covington, M. V. and R. G. Berry (1976). *Self-worth and school learning.* New York: Holt, Rinehart and Winston.

Kulhavy, R. W. (1977). Feedback in written instruction. *Review of Educational Research 47*, 211–32.

Weiner, B. (1980). *Human motivation.* New York: Holt, Rinehart and Winston.

Zimbardo, P. G., ed. (1969). *The cognitive control of motivation.* Glenview, Ill.: Scott, Foresman.

Chapter

12

Strategies for Effective Teaching and Learning

SUMMARY

1. Strategies for effective teaching include those directed at keeping students engaged with instructional materials (*management strategies*) and those directed at facilitating learning in other ways (*instructional strategies*).

2. Effective teachers appear to be well organized from the very first day of school. They set up rules, spend time having students practice appropriate behavior, and criticize inappropriate behavior.

3. Effective teachers review prerequisite knowledge, give clear directions and presentations, relate content to student interests, and give students opportunities to respond and get feedback.

4. During instruction, experienced teachers attend more to student performance relative to the goal of instruction than do inexperienced teachers.

5. Attempts to train teachers to use strategies used by expert teachers have been successful.

6. Strategies for successful learning include *attention* strategies and *encoding* strategies.

7. More successful learners are better at choosing the most important parts of an instructional stimulus to attend to.

8. More successful learners are more likely to use elaboration and organization as strategies for learning new declarative knowledge.

9. Students can be taught to use successful learning strategies, although how much these strategies transfer to new situations is not known.

In recent years there has been a great deal of criticism of American public education. For example, a 1983 article in *The New York Times* stated, "Reading-test results disclosed in 1981 by the National Assessment of Educational Progress showed a decline in inferential reasoning of students in both junior and senior high school. In 1979 results of the National Assessment mathematics tests showed that problem-solving ability had declined during the 1970's" (Maerhoff, 1983). The causes of the decline in students' competencies are no doubt many and complex. Some fix most of the blame on the schools, whereas others assign the blame to unmotivated students.

Besides verbal criticism of education, a more action-oriented criticism has begun to appear—students' lawsuits against the schools for failing to educate them. In several states students must now pass a test of minimum competency in order to receive a high school diploma. Some students who have failed these tests have sued their school district. The legal argument in such cases revolves around whether teachers or students are more to blame for failures to learn.

In this chapter no attempt is made to resolve the moral and legal issues of assigning responsibility. Rather, it is assumed that teachers and students share the responsibility for learning. In this chapter we will thus ask, first, what teachers can do to improve their teaching, and second, what students can do to improve their learning.

TEACHING STRATEGIES

Teaching is a complex problem-solving activity, the goal of which is to facilitate student learning. The "teacher" may be a designer of instructional software, a writer of textbooks, a producer of educational videotapes, an industrial trainer, or a classroom instructor. Each of these people has a goal of increasing student learning.

Of these teacher roles, that of classroom instructor is probably the most difficult, because it involves the attempt to reach many goals with limited resources. A typical classroom teacher has twenty-five to thirty-five individuals to teach in a limited time period. Since each student has a different configuration of prior declarative and procedural knowledge and different motivational tendencies, each should be given different learning goals. In pursuit of this ideal a few school systems have changed to individualized instruction. However, for many teachers, individualized instruction is not feasible. In such cases the problem of classroom teaching becomes one of *optimizing* the learning of individuals rather than *maximizing* it. In this chapter we will see how successful teachers solve the problem of optimizing instruction.

Some people believe that teachers do not make a difference in school learning. However, several studies have shown that teachers do make a difference. Chall and Feldmann (1966), for example, found that in reading achievement the curriculum materials used were not as important as the teacher. Inman (1977) estimated that 25 percent of the variance in student achievement is accounted for by the teacher's actions, and found that for children of low socioeconomic status the importance of teachers increased. What, then, do effective teachers do that less effective teachers do not do? That is, what are the strategies involved in teaching?

One set of strategies has to do with *management*. These are strategies needed to bring students into contact with instructional material and *keep them in contact with it* for a good deal of time. Obviously, if students are not even paying attention, if the class is chaotic, or if it is quiet but the students are daydreaming, then no learning can take place. Beyond this minimal contact produced by management strategies, a teacher needs *instructional strategies* to facilitate learning from the instructional material. Studies have shown that more and less effective teachers differ in their management and instruction strategies.

Management Strategies

Differences between effective and ineffective classroom managers have been studied at both the middle school (Moskowitz and Hayman, 1976) and elementary school levels (Emmer, 1982; Emmer, Evertson, and Anderson, 1980; Evertson and Anderson, 1978), with similar results.

Management During the First Few Weeks. Emmer, Evertson, and Anderson (1980) studied fourteen third-grade teachers, seven of whom were effective managers and seven of whom were ineffective. The students in effective and ineffective managers' classes did not differ at the beginning of the year on aptitude or achievement test scores. However, throughout the school year the students in the effective managers' classrooms showed more on-task behavior and, by the end of the year, they showed greater achievement gains than did the students in the ineffective managers' classrooms. The researchers were particularly interested in how these effective and ineffective teachers differed during the first few weeks of class, so they made extensive observations at this time. Since they did not know at the time of observation which teachers would fall into the effective and ineffective manager categories, their observations were unbiased.

The results showed that effective and ineffective managers differed. The typical effective teacher started out the first day by greeting students, giving them assignments, and informing the class about such things as where to put their personal belongings and rules about going to the bathroom and water fountain. If a parent or school administrator tried to interrupt, the effective teacher resisted these attempts and refused to leave the classroom on this crucial first day. The typical ineffective teacher (who was often a beginning teacher) started the first day in a less organized fashion. He or she did not have rules for going to the bathroom or drinking fountain or for lining up. No name tags were handed out, and the children were not given activities to work on while waiting for other students, so they wandered about most of the time. If a parent or administrator called on the teacher, the teacher left the room and the children were left unsupervised.

Besides acting more organized on the first

day of school, the effective teachers were persistent in teaching classroom rules during the first few weeks of school. Routines, such as lining up to sharpen pencils, were rehearsed, and their rationale was explained. Any transgressions were stopped quickly with a reminder to the transgressor about the rule. The initial "seatwork" done by students was relatively easy so that students could learn the routines for doing seatwork without being confused by difficult material at the same time. Ineffective teachers, on the other hand, did not teach rules to their students, or if they did, the rules were taught ineffectively. One ineffective teacher gave a rule that was too vague for children to follow: "Be in the right place at the right time." Another teacher did not follow up on enforcing a stated rule. She told the children that one bell ring meant for them to stop talking and two bell rings meant for them to pay attention, but when the students did not immediately follow these rules, she abandoned them. The effective teachers seemed to have an implicit or explicit understanding that rules about classroom behavior, just like rules about addition and subtraction, were skills to be learned through the use of practice and feedback. The ineffective teachers seemed to lack this insight.

Table 12.1 shows other ways in which the effective and ineffective managers differed during the first three weeks of instruction. The scores ranged from 1, which indicated

that the teacher exhibited very little of this characteristic, to 7, which indicated a high frequency. One interesting observation is how the effective managers dealt with disruptive behavior (item 5). Some textbooks advise teachers to "ignore disruptive behavior and praise correct behavior." Yet the effective managers were more likely to stop quickly when disruptive behavior occurred and do something about it, whereas the *less* effective managers were more likely to ignore the disruptive behavior (item 6). The idea of ignoring disruptive behavior may be based on the idea that pleasure is the most important aspect of reinforcement. That is, one should not criticize students for being disruptive because criticism is unpleasant. However, if one thinks of the information aspect of reinforcement, as was discussed in Chapter 11, then calling attention (in a constructive manner) to unacceptable behavior is highly informative. Like any other matched nonexample, it helps students make discriminations.

One of the most interesting findings of the Emmer et al. (1980) study was the extent to which behavior during the first few weeks of class determined the discipline and achievement in the class for the whole year. This finding supports what many experienced teachers know about the importance of "getting things off to a good start." This is not to say that a class that gets off to a bad start can never be turned around. However,

Table 12.1. Differences between effective and ineffective classroom managers. (Adapted from Emmer, Evertson, and Anderson, 1980.)

VARIABLE	MORE EFFECTIVE MANAGERS	LESS EFFECTIVE MANAGERS
1. Variety of rewards	4.3	3.1
2. Signals appropriate behavior	5.4	3.8
3. Eye contact	6.1	4.9
4. States desired attitudes	5.5	3.9
5. Stops it disruptive behavior	4.9	3.5
6. Ignores disruptive behavior	2.9	3.6

starting school in an organized manner and teaching classroom procedures early seems to help a great deal in keeping students "on task."

Homework. In middle school, if not before, students start to receive homework assignments. The collection and correction of homework are tasks that can be managed more and less effectively. Leinhardt (1983) observed expert and novice math teachers' homework-checking behavior and found large differences between them. A typical expert started class by calling the roll. Students responded yes if they had done their homework and no if they had not. The students who responded no put their names on the blackboard. This procedure gave the teacher information about how many people had done their homework and who had not. The information would not be forgotten, because it was on the board, and it was obtained efficiently, since while a student wrote his or her name on the board, the teacher continued the roll call.

After the roll call the teacher asked for choral answers to each homework problem. When the chorus weakened, the teacher tagged the problem as being difficult. The students marked their own problems, after all answers had been given, and the teacher tallied how many students got each problem correct by calling out each number and asking students to raise a hand if they got that problem right. This tally gave the teacher a summary of how the class was doing and of which problems were difficult. The summary was used in adapting the day's lesson if students had not done well on their homework. The entire homework-checking procedure took about two minutes.

In contrast to the expert, one typical novice teacher took six minutes to check homework. She started out by asking the group, "Who doesn't have their homework?" Some students responded by holding up their pa-

pers, others walked up to the teacher to tell her that they either did or did not have their homework, and still others called out that they did not have it. The teacher then marked down who had and had not completed homework. Unlike the expert teacher, the novice did not end up with a visible tally of those who had not completed homework. Next the novice teacher asked the slowest child in the class to give the answers to problems 1–10. The child answered very slowly because she was unprepared and was trying to do the problems (unsuccessfully) on the spot. The students checked their work but the teacher did not collect a tally at the end, so she did not know how many children had missed each problem.

The difference between the expert and the novice here seems to be that the expert had a smooth action sequence that the novice lacked. The novice was on the way to acquiring such a sequence, but some of the steps in the sequence (such as calling on the slowest student) disrupted the flow. With experience, the novice is likely to develop a better strategy.

Summary. In summary, expert teachers differ from inexpert teachers on several management strategies. They are more organized on the first day of school, and they spend enough time teaching students the norms for their classrooms. They have efficient methods of checking homework, such as having students check their own work, getting a summary of how well the class did, and then using this summary to adjust the lesson plan.

Instructional Strategies

What strategies, in addition to management strategies, do effective teachers have that ineffective teachers appear to lack? This question has also been studied at both elementary and middle school levels, with some fairly consistent findings emerging from the data

(Emmer, Evertson, and Anderson, 1980; Evertson, Emmer, and Brophy, 1980; Good and Grouws, 1979; Housner and Griffey, 1983).

Clarity. Table 12.2 shows some additional findings from the Emmer et al. (1980) study that was described in the previous section. At the end of the year the most and least effective teachers were identified using pupil achievement tests. As you can see in Table 12.2, the more effective teachers differed from less effective ones in several ways. They communicated objectives, directions, and content (items 1, 5, and 6) more clearly. They also seemed to adapt their instruction to the students' interests, skill levels, and attention spans (items 10, 9, and 8). Finally, they explained to students *why* they were learning particular material (item 7). The ineffective teachers gave vague directions for seatwork, failed to give a rationale for such work, and failed to check to see that the children understood directions. Thus, being clear and monitoring students appear to be important instructional strategies.

Feedback. Students' questions, comments, and responses are crucial to learning, for both procedural and declarative knowledge. This is because they provide a means for teachers to give informative feedback (Kulhavy, 1977). For learning declarative knowledge, feedback should enhance the organization of information or stimulate students to elaborate on the information. For learning pattern-recognition procedures, feedback should help students distinguish examples from nonexamples. And, for learning action sequence procedures, feedback should remind the student of the steps in the procedure.

Do more and less effective teachers differ on how they respond to students? The answer is yes, although investigators have not yet looked at whether teachers give different feedback for the different types of knowledge just mentioned. Nonetheless, their results are suggestive. Evertson, Emmer, and Brophy (1980), for example, found several differences between more and less effective middle-school math teachers on the feedback they gave to student responses. Table 12.3 shows some of their findings.

The first two items in Table 12.3 indicate that the more effective teachers asked more questions than did the less effective teachers. By asking questions they were initiating opportunities for students to obtain feedback and increasing the probability that students would learn accurately. Item 4 shows that effective teachers were far more likely than in-

Table 12.2. Teacher variables of more and less effective classroom managers during first weeks of school. (Adapted from Emmer, Evertson, and Anderson, 1980.)

TEACHER BEHAVIOR	MORE EFFECTIVE MANAGERS	LESS EFFECTIVE MANAGERS
1. Describes objectives clearly	5.1	3.1
2. Uses a variety of materials	5.6	3.7
3. Materials are ready	6.2	4.4
4. Materials support instruction	6.0	4.3
5. Clear directions	5.2	3.8
6. Clear presentation	5.8	4.1
7. Provides/seeks rationale or analysis	4.9	3.4
8. Attention spans considered in lesson design	5.2	2.8
9. High degree of pupil success	5.5	3.9
10. Content related to pupil interests	5.2	3.6
11. Reasonable work standards	5.8	4.6

Table 12.3. Differences in management of feedback by more and less effective teachers. Numbers indicate the average frequency in a fifty-minute period. (Adapted from Evertson, Emmer, and Brophy, 1980.)

VARIABLE	MORE EFFECTIVE	LESS EFFECTIVE
1. Process questions	5.91	1.29
2. Product questions	17.42	6.95
3. Correct answer praised by teacher	4.26	.32
4. New question after correct answer	2.93	.25
5. Correct answer integrated into discussion	3.25	.60
6. Correct answer — no feedback	.38	.06
7. Wrong answer — teacher criticizes	.01	.01
8. Wrong answer — new teacher question	.41	.07
9. Wrong answer — process feedback	.28	.09
10. Wrong answer — teacher gives answer	.72	.27
11. Student-initiated comments given feedback	1.00	.28

effective teachers to follow up a correct answer with another question to the same student, thereby rewarding that student and encouraging him or her to think further. For wrong answers the differences between effective and ineffective teachers are not very large, but the effective teachers did ask another question of the same student or give process feedback more often. (In process feedback the teacher identifies what step in the process produced the wrong answer, rather than just saying that the answer was wrong.) Finally, effective teachers were four times as likely as ineffective teachers to follow up with feedback when students initiated comments (item 11). Thus, although we cannot tell from these data whether teachers adjusted feedback for different types of knowledge, we can tell that the effective teachers gave students more opportunities to get feedback and were more likely to be clear and specific in the feedback they gave. Clear and specific feedback is important for any type of knowledge.

Review of Prerequisite Knowledge. In Chapter 9 we saw how important a student's ability to recall prerequisite skills was for acquiring more complex skills. Effective math teachers appear to be aware of the importance of recalling prerequisites. Evertson et al. (1980) found that their more effective teachers spent significantly more time than less effective teachers reviewing whole-number operations and fractions before teaching decimals, percentages, and algebra topics. This finding held up even when all the items relevant to whole-number operations and fractions were eliminated from the achievement test used to judge effectiveness. Thus, effective teachers seem to know when reviews are needed.

Summary. In summary, effective teachers have several instructional strategies that ineffective teachers appear to lack. These include giving clear directions and explanations, monitoring seatwork and homework, giving ample opportunity for students to receive feedback, and reviewing prerequisite knowledge.

The Dynamics of Instruction

Effective teachers not only have better management and instruction strategies than do ineffective teachers, but these strategies appear to be better organized and better timed.

Many of them are performed automatically. The smooth nature of an experienced teacher's strategies has been described in some recent studies (Fogarty, Wang, and Creek, 1983; Housner and Griffey, 1983).

Housner and Griffey (1983) asked sixteen physical education teachers to teach soccer and basketball dribbling skills to groups of four eight-year-old children. Eight of the teachers were experienced, having spent five or more years as elementary PE teachers. The other eight were training to be elementary school PE teachers and so were inexperienced as teachers.

The teachers were given sixty minutes to plan their lessons. They were told that they were to teach two lessons—one on soccer and one on basketball dribbling skills—and that if they wanted more information, they must ask for it. They were told to think aloud while planning, and their protocols were tape recorded. After the planning session the teach-

ers were videotaped while teaching their lessons. They then viewed the videotape with the researchers and reported what cues they were attending to while teaching and what decisions they were making.

Planning. During planning, the experienced teachers asked an average of 6.5 questions of the researchers and the inexperienced teachers asked 4.5. Both groups asked about the number of students they would be teaching, their ages, sex, and ability, and about what equipment was available and the amount of time they would have to teach. However, the experienced teachers asked more questions about the students' prior experience with soccer and basketball dribbling. This result suggests that the experienced teachers planned to teach differently depending on the skill level of their students.

Table 12.4 shows the types of decision

Table 12.4. Decisions made by experienced and inexperienced teachers during planning. The numbers are percentages of the total number of decisions of a particular class: activity or instructional. (Adapted from Housner and Griffey, 1983.)

	EXPERIENCED	INEXPERIENCED
ACTIVITY DECISIONS		
Structure	42.6%	54.5
Procedures	24.6	28.0
Formations	4.9	1.5
Time	9.0	6.8
Adaptations	18.9	9.1
INSTRUCTIONAL DECISIONS		
Management	13.4%	4.8
Assess/feedback	22.8	15.9
Demonstrate	7.9	7.9
Transitions	5.5	6.4
Focus attention	18.9	19.1
Equipment use	7.9	7.9
Verbal instruction	19.7	34.9
Time	3.9	3.2

made by experienced and inexperienced teachers during their planning sessions. Activity decisions were related to what activities the students would engage in (*structure*), the rules for this activity (*procedures*), its spatial arrangement (*formation*), the amount of time, and plans for any adaptations if the students could not do the activity. Instructional decisions included plans for setting rules and motivating students (*management*), observing students and giving feedback, demonstrating a motor skill, moving students from one activity to another (*transitions*), focusing students' attention on specific aspects of a motor skill, giving verbal explanations or directions, and allocating time.

As you can see, the percentage of thinking-aloud statements related to some of these decisions was different for the two groups. The four types of decisions for which experienced and inexperienced teachers differed significantly were *adaptations, management, assess/feedback,* and *verbal instructions.* In the first three categories the experienced teachers made more decisions. That is, they planned ahead more for contingencies, for establishing rules and motivation, and for assessing students and giving them feedback. In verbal instructions the inexperienced teachers made more decisions, suggesting that they relied more on verbal instructions than did the experienced teachers.

Interactive Decision-Making. While watching videotapes of their teaching, the teachers reported what cues they heeded during instruction. Table 12.5 shows these results. The experienced teachers were more likely than the inexperienced teachers to heed the students' performance and their own mood and feelings. The inexperienced teachers were more likely than the experienced teachers to heed the students' interests, verbalizations, and moods. Thus the experienced teachers paid attention to the most informative aspect of the students' behavior—their dribbling performance—whereas the inexperienced teachers paid attention to the more salient, but somewhat less informative, aspect of the students' behavior—their apparent interest. Certainly student interest is important over the long run, but it can fluctuate from minute to minute. Also, what develops interest over the long run is success. Therefore, the experienced teachers' focus on student performance was well founded. This difference between expert and novice teachers is reminiscent of the differences between expert and novice physics problem solvers and expert and novice medical diagnosticians. That is, the novices attend to an aspect of the problem (student interest) that may not be particularly relevant to solving the problem.

Table 12.6 shows the percentage of time that a heeded cue resulted in teachers' chang-

Table 12.5. Types of cues heeded by experienced and inexperienced teachers. (Adapted from Housner and Griffey, 1983.)

CUES	EXPERIENCED	INEXPERIENCED
Student performance	30.1%	19.0
Student involvement	27.4	22.6
Student interest	11.8	27.3
Student verbalizations/requests	3.2	7.7
Student mood/feelings	3.2	6.5
Teacher's mood/feelings	5.3	1.7
Other	19.0	15.2

Table 12.6. The percentage of time that a given type of cue resulted in a change of teaching plans during instruction. (Adapted from Housner and Griffey, 1983.)

	EXPERIENCED	INEXPERIENCED
STUDENT BEHAVIOR CUES		
Performance	35.7%	28.1
Involvement	33.3	23.6
Interest	54.5	30.4
Verbalization/request	33.3	76.9
Mood/feeling	50.0	27.2
Interactions	40.0	0.0
Other	44.4	33.3
TEACHER/CONTEXT CUES		
Instructional behavior	20.0%	50.0
Mood/feeling	10.0	33.3
Time	54.5	35.7
Equipment/facility	40.0	0.0
Average percentage of cues that resulted in a change in teaching	37.6%	32.1

ing their lessons from what they had originally planned. The experienced teachers made changes based on observing cues more often than did inexperienced teachers. This result is similar to a result obtained by Peterson and Clark (1978) for teaching social studies. They found that effective teachers seemed to have more alternatives available when something "went wrong." Less effective teachers were aware that something was wrong but were either less willing or less able to make changes.

Table 12.6 also shows that the inexperienced teachers were far more likely to make changes based on student verbalizations and requests (76.9 percent) than were experienced teachers (33.3 percent). One gets the impression that the students were controlling the inexperienced teachers rather than vice versa. (Of course, there are situations in which teachers should make changes based on student verbalizations, but teaching drib-

bling is probably not one of them.) The experienced teachers more frequently made changes based on cues from the students' performance.

The experienced teachers act as if they have procedural knowledge that is activated by student performance of the motor skills being learned. Table 12.7 shows, in informal production system terms, some of this knowledge. Production 1 applies when students are not quite getting the skill, and its action is that the teacher demonstrates the skill. Production 2 applies when some students are not quite getting the skill but others appear to have it. Its action is that the teacher asks a skilled student for a demonstration rather than demonstrating it him- or herself. Production 3 applies under more drastic conditions, when the students are not even close to performing correctly. Under those conditions the teacher backs up and has the students work on a component skill.

Table 12.7. Some procedural knowledge available to experienced teachers that can be activated by poor performance on the part of the students.

P_1	IF	Students are not quite getting skill
	THEN	Stop activity
		And demonstrate skill.
P_2	IF	Some students are getting skill
		And others are not
	THEN	Stop activity
		And have a proficient student demonstrate skill.
P_3	IF	Students are performing very poorly
	THEN	Stop activity
		And select a component skill
		And demonstrate component skill
		And have students practice component skill.

In contrast to the experienced teachers, the inexperienced teachers act as if they are using some procedural knowledge that is relevant to many social situations but is not relevant to teaching. For example, they act as if they have the productions shown in Table 12.8. Production 1 embodies the social norm that when people make requests, one tries to comply. Production 2 embodies the norm that when others talk, it is polite to listen. What inexperienced teachers need to learn is to discriminate general social situations from teaching situations. That is, they need to develop specialized productions for teaching, such as the one shown in Table 12.9. When all its conditions are met, this specialized production overrides the more general production, $P1$, shown in Table 12.8.

Table 12.8. Some procedural knowledge about social behavior. This knowledge is available to inexperienced teachers and is applied inappropriately in instructional settings.

P_1	IF	Person makes request
	THEN	Try to comply with request.
P_2	IF	Other person talks
	THEN	Pay attention
		Ask followup questions.

Teaching Strategies to Teachers

So far we have seen that classroom teaching involves optimizing the learning of all students in the class. This difficult problem is solved partially through good management strategies and partially through good instructional strategies. Effective teachers have many smooth action sequences that are conditioned on student performance. Because of this knowledge, they can plan for various contingencies and adapt when contingencies arise.

Can less effective teachers learn to use the strategies employed by more effective teachers? Several studies have attempted to train teachers in the use of effective strategies (Ev-

Table 12.9. A production that is specific to instructional contexts and that inexperienced teachers need to learn.

IF	Student makes a request
	And student's safety and health are not at stake
	And request is irrelevant to instruction.
THEN	Ignore request
	Or ask student to make the request later
	Or explain to student that request is irrelevant.

ertson, Emmer, Sanford, and Clements, 1983; Good and Grouws, 1979).

Good et al. (1977) developed a descriptive list of strategies that have been shown to distinguish more from less effective fourth-grade mathematics teachers. Using this list as a starting point, they developed a forty-five page training manual that was intended to teach teachers to use these strategies. Table 12.10 shows some of the key instructional and management strategies that were described and explained in the manual. These included (1) having a daily review, (2) developing new material meaningfully and responsively, (3) supervising seatwork efficiently, (4) assigning homework, and (5) having periodic reviews over more content than was covered in daily reviews.

Good and Grouws (1979) attempted to train twenty fourth-grade teachers (volunteers) from schools serving low-socioeconomic-status students, to use these strategies. Another twenty teachers served as a control group. The teachers in the training group heard a ninety-minute explanation of research on teaching strategies. They were then given the forty-five page teaching manual and were told to read it and begin implementing its ideas in their classrooms. Two weeks later there was another ninety-minute session with the teachers in the training group. During this session the experimenters responded to teachers' questions about specific strategies and gave suggestions for overcoming difficulties in implementing the strategies.

After this session each teacher was observed six times over the next two and a half months. The observers recorded incidences of the targeted strategies. The teachers in the control group were also observed six times during the same period. These observations allowed the experimenters to determine whether or not the teachers in the training group actually implemented the strategies about which they had read. To measure

Table 12.10. Instructional and management strategies that teachers were trained to use. (From Good and Grouws, 1979.)

Daily review (first 8 minutes except Mondays)
  a. review the concepts and skills associated with the homework
  b. collect and deal with homework assignments
  c. ask several mental computation exercises
Development (about 20 minutes)
  a. briefly focus on prerequisite skills and concepts
  b. focus on meaning and promoting student understanding by using lively explanations, demonstrations, process explanations, illustrations, etc.
  c. assess student comprehension
    1. using process/product questions (active interaction)
    2. using controlled practice
  d. repeat and elaborate on the meaning portion as necessary
Seatwork (about 15 minutes)
  a. provide uninterrupted successful practice
  b. momentum — keep the ball rolling — get everyone involved, then sustain involvement
  c. alerting — let students know their work will be checked at end of period
  d. accountability — check the students' work
Homework assignment
  a. assign on a regular basis at the end of each math class except Fridays
  b. should involve about 15 minutes of work to be done at home
  c. should include one or two review problems
Special reviews
  a. weekly review/maintenance
    1. conduct during the first 20 minutes each Monday
    2. focus on skills and concepts covered during the previous week
  b. monthly review/maintenance
    1. conduct every fourth Monday
    2. focus on skills and concepts covered since the last monthly review

teaching effectiveness, students of both the training- and control-group teachers took a standardized mathematics achievement test before and after the training program.

Table 12.11 shows the percentage of time

Table 12.11. The percentage of time that trained and control group teachers used the targeted skills. An asterisk indicates a significant difference. (Adapted from Good and Grouws, 1979.)

VARIABLE	TRAINED	CONTROL
1. Did the teacher conduct review?	91%*	62%
2. Did development take place within review?	51%*	37%
3. Did the teacher check homework?	79%*	20%
4. Did the teacher work on mental computation?	69%*	6%
5. Did the teacher summarize previous day's materials?	28%	25%
6. There was a slow transition from review.	7%	4%
7. Did the teacher spend at least 5 minutes on development?	45%	51%
8. Were the students held accountable for controlled practice during the development phase?	33%	20%
9. Did the teacher use demonstrations during presentation?	45%	46%
10. Did the teacher conduct seatwork?	80%*	56%
11. Did the teacher actively engage students in seatwork (first 1½ minutes)?	71%*	43%
12. Was the teacher available to provide immediate help to students during seatwork (next 5 minutes)?	68%*	47%
13. Were students held accountable for seatwork at the end of seatwork phase?	59%*	31%
14. Did seatwork directions take longer than 1 minute?	18%	23%
15. Did the teacher make homework assignments?	66%*	13%

that the trained and control teachers showed each targeted strategy. For most of the targeted behaviors, the trained teachers showed a higher frequency than did the control teachers. Some of the largest differences were in conducting reviews, checking homework, working on mental computation, and assigning homework. However, there were some targeted strategies that the trained teachers did not exhibit more frequently than controls. These included summarizing the previous day's materials, spending at least five minutes on development, and using demonstrations during presentations. Nonetheless, the overall picture shows a rather successful implementation of the strategies.

Did the use of the strategies affect student achievement? Yes, it had a substantial effect. Students in the trained teachers' classes had an average percentile gain of 31 from the pre- to the posttest, whereas the control group students had an average percentile gain of 19. Furthermore, several of the strategies correlated significantly with student achievement. Specifically, conducting a review ($r = .37$), checking homework ($r = .54$), working on mental computation ($r = .48$), holding students accountable for seatwork ($r = .35$), and giving homework assignments ($r = .49$) each correlated significantly with student achievement. Thus, the strategies used strongly affected student performance.

The results of this study are remarkable both because the training was easy and because the gains observed were dramatic. Since the teachers were volunteers, results might be less dramatic for teachers who had less freedom to decide whether or not to take the training. Even so, many teachers are eager to improve, and it appears that this training is effective for motivated teachers.

LEARNING STRATEGIES

Not too long ago, the common wisdom was that some students are slow learners and some are fast learners and that, furthermore, not much could be done about learning speed. Now, however, as psychologists and educational researchers come to understand the processes that account for slower and faster learning, there is a hope that at least some of these processes will be teachable.

If one assumes that learning is a knowledge domain just as physics and medicine and Soviet politics are, then by analogy to what is known for these latter domains, skilled learners should have more and better-organized knowledge of learning processes than do less skilled learners. Some support for this hypothesis comes from the many studies of metacognitive awareness, which show developmental increases in the amount that people know about their own cognitive processes (cf. Brown and DeLoache, 1978; Flavell, 1979).

The elements of effective learning include (1) strategies for selectively attending to the most informative aspects of an instructional stimulus, (2) strategies for effective encoding of new material so that it will be easily retrieved later on, (3) knowing the conditions under which a given strategy is effective, and (4) monitoring the effectiveness of one's strategies. A description of what is known about each of these elements follows.

Strategies for Selective Attention

Knowledge of Learning Goals. One important set of learning strategies includes those which guide attention to relevant material. Expectations for test content seem to influence what parts of the instructional material are heeded. For example, Rothkopf and Billington (1979) found that high school and college students spent more time reading and

had more eye fixations for parts of text over which they expected questions than they did for other parts.

Reynolds (1979) obtained similar results. He had college students read, on a computer screen, a twenty-seven-page expository passage. The time to read each screenful of material was recorded. Students periodically saw questions about material just read. For some students the questions were all about proper names, whereas for others they were all about technical terms. In addition, students performed a secondary task requiring them to press the space bar whenever they heard a tone. Their response latencies for this secondary task were recorded.

The results showed that students who read questions about proper names spent more time reading parts of text that contained proper names. Moreover, they reacted more slowly to the secondary task while they were reading about proper names, and, finally, they performed better on a posttest for proper names than did the other students. On the other hand, students who had inserted questions over technical terms spent more time reading parts of text that contained technical terms. Moreover, they reacted more slowly to the secondary task if they were reading about technical terms, and they performed better on a posttest of technical terms than did the other students. The results, then, support the notion that students' expectations about test items affect their distribution of attention and their intensity of concentration.

Individual Differences in Selective Attention to Content. There is a developmental trend in the extent to which learners use attention-focusing strategies effectively. As we would expect, younger students are poorer than older ones at focusing on important and/or unlearned parts of new material. This was demonstrated in a study by Brown and Smiley (1978) in which fifth graders, seventh graders, and college students were given two stories to learn for gist recall. The students were allowed to take notes or underline while they studied. After a study period for each story they wrote down what they could remember. Then they were given five more minutes to study with the suggestion that they might wish to take notes or underline. Finally they were asked to recall the story again.

Figure 12.1 shows the proportion of idea units recalled for the different age groups as a function of the importance level of the idea unit (1 = unimportant, 4 = main idea). The amount recalled both before and after the extra study time is shown. The seventh graders and college students improved their recall of important idea units when given extra time to study, but the fifth graders, in general, did not. However, a subgroup of fifth graders did improve when given extra study time. This subgroup consisted of fifth graders who had spontaneously underlined important idea units during their first study period.

These results strongly suggest that improved recall following extra study time was

due to paying attention to the important idea units during the extra time. Obviously a necessary precondition for paying attention to important idea units is being able to recognize such units. As was seen in Chapter 7, fifth graders are not very good at differentiating among ideas varying in importance. This, then, may be why many fifth graders cannot focus on important idea units during extra study time.

Besides age-correlated differences in attention-focusing strategies, skill-correlated differences have also been observed. Thorndyke and Stasz (1980) compared the attention-focusing strategies of adults who were faster or slower at learning information in maps such as the one shown in Figure 12.2. For each map the subjects were given six two-minute study trials, each of which was followed by a test. Subjects were asked to think aloud while studying. For the test the subjects were given a blank piece of paper and a pencil and asked to reproduce the map they had studied. Their drawings were scored for the number of elements (e.g., buildings, streets, railroads) and the number of correct relationships among elements (e.g., Park Drive is shown south of Green Street).

The thinking-aloud protocols revealed two major categories of selective-attention strategy. One, called *partitioning*, involved dividing the map into smaller units (e.g., the southeast quadrant) and focusing only on this smaller unit until it was mastered. The other major category was *sampling*, which referred to ways of changing focus. One could move one's focus randomly over the map (*random sampling*), move it to an adjacent element (*stochastic sampling*), move it according to some rule, such as "learn all of the towns first" (*systematic sampling*), or move it to unlearned elements (*memory directed sampling*). Did efficient learners, who had learned 90 percent of the map by the sixth trial, use different selective attention strategies than the less effi-

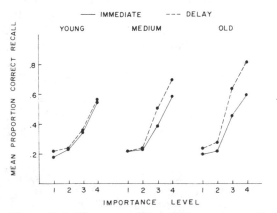

Figure 12.1. The proportion of idea units recalled as a function of importance level, 1 = unimportant, 4 = very important), and also as a function of whether the subjects were given extra study time (delay). (From Brown and Smiley, 1978.)

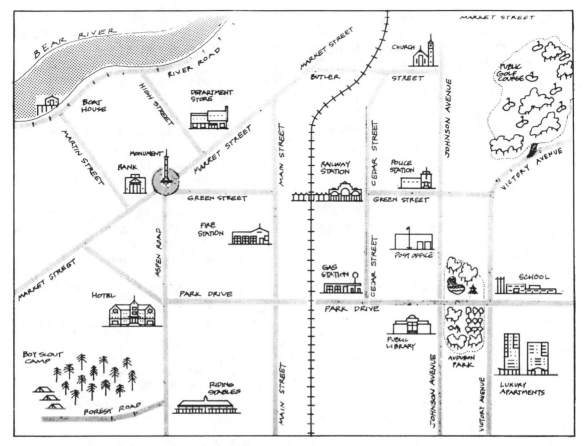

Figure 12.2. One of the maps used to study map learning strategies. (From Thorndyke and Stasz, 1980.)

cient learners, who had learned on the average only 58 percent of the map by the sixth trial? What would you predict?

Table 12.12 shows the results for frequency of strategy use per protocol. The faster learners used partitioning an average of 2.33 times per protocol whereas the slower learners used this strategy 1.50 times. Though the difference between these two numbers was not significant, it is in the direction that you probably predicted, with the faster learners being more likely to partition.

Within the possible sampling strategies, the faster learners were significantly more

Table 12.12. The frequency of use of various selective attention strategies by faster and slower map learners. An asterisk signifies a significant difference between the two groups. (Adapted from Thorndyke and Stasz, 1980.)

STRATEGY	FASTER LEARNERS	SLOWER LEARNERS
Partitioning	2.33	1.50
Random sampling	0.00*	1.10
Stochastic sampling	1.33	1.00
Systematic sampling	2.17*	.90
Memory-directed sampling	10.17*	6.20

likely to use systematic sampling and memory-directed sampling. The slower learners were more likely to use random sampling. Clearly, the faster learners are better at directing attention to relevant (unlearned) parts of the map. The random sampling by the slower subjects is likely to lead them to attend to already-learned elements. The results as a whole, then, show that faster learners have better selective-attention strategies.

An interesting aspect of Thorndyke and Stasz's (1980) study reflects on the assumption that learning is a domain of knowledge in its own right. Three of Thorndyke and Stasz's subjects were adults whose jobs involved the use of maps, whereas five were college undergraduates with no special expertise in map reading. If a great deal of knowledge of maps is important for learning map elements, then one would predict that the three map users would be the faster learners. However, the recall of two of the three people who used maps on the job put them in the *slower* learner category. By contrast, the recall of three of the five college students put them in the *faster* learner category. Although these findings are for only a small number of subjects, they are what one would predict if one assumed that college students are more expert at learning than are adults who are not attending school. Of course it is probably true that some rudimentary knowledge of maps was used by all the subjects in this study. For example, the decision to study streets before buildings calls on knowledge of which symbols represent streets and buildings. However, beyond this rudimentary knowledge, the expertise that appeared to be important was expertise in learning, not in map reading.

These speculations focus on an important research area, which is the interaction of strategies with other forms of knowledge. We need to know more about how both declarative and procedural knowledge in a domain affect the selection of learning strategies. That is, are some learning strategies better for people with little knowledge of the domain about which they are learning and other strategies better for people who possess a great deal of relevant knowledge?

Individual Differences in Selective Attention to Feedback. In the acquisition of procedural knowledge, attention to feedback when one has made a mistake plays a crucial role in learning. Therefore, one might expect that more effective students are more likely to heed feedback when they make a mistake than less effective students. E. Gagné and J. Anzelc (1984) observed high school students' attentiveness to feedback in a FORTRAN class. The correlation between attention to feedback after making a mistake and achievement in FORTRAN was .83. By contrast, the correlation between attention to feedback following correct responses and achievement was only .34. Thus, successful students appear to pay particularly close attention to feedback when they have made a mistake.

Encoding Strategies

Elaboration. Besides having more effective strategies for selective attention, better learners also have more effective strategies for encoding new information. We have already seen evidence of this from the A. Y. Wang (1983) and Stein et al. (1982) studies reported in Chapter 4. You will recall that both of these studies, Wang with college students and Stein et al. with fifth graders, showed that better learners produced more effective elaborations for remembering new material. Specifically, better learners generated elaborations that connected a likely retrieval cue to that which was to be retrieved.

Besides generating better elaborations, better students are simply more likely to elaborate. In a study reported in Chapter 7, Weinstein (1978) showed that successful college students frequently reported use of elaboration study techniques, whereas less successful college students reported using rote rehearsal.

Several other investigators have found a pattern similar to the one found by Weinstein (Moss, 1982; Ribich, 1977; Schmeck and Grove, 1979; Spring, 1983). Schmeck and Grove (1979) gave 790 college students a questionnaire called "Inventory of Learning Processes." The items on this questionnaire measure four distinguishable scales, called deep processing, elaborative processing, methodical study, and fact retention. The questions measuring *deep processing* included "I can usually state the underlying message of films and readings" and "I read critically." Thus deep processing appears to produce excellent understanding of a message on its own terms. *Elaborative processing* was measured by items like "New concepts usually make me think of similar concepts" and "I learn new words or ideas by visualizing a situation in which they could occur." Thus elaborative processing appears to produce understanding of relationships between the new information and already known information. Both deep and elaborative processing are included in what is called elaboration in this book. *Me-*

thodical study was measured by such items as "I have regular weekly review periods" and "I carefully complete all course assignments." Finally, *fact retention* was measured by such items as "I do well on examinations requiring factual information" and "I do well on tests requiring definition." Unlike the other three scales, the fact retention scale appears to measure a product rather than a process.

Table 12.13 shows what Schmeck and Grove (1979) found for high versus low GPA students on each of the four scales. Although the high and low GPA students did not differ on the methodical study scale, they did differ on all of the other scales. Specifically, the high GPA students scored higher on both deep and elaborative processing, and also on fact retention. Quite possibly, high GPA students do well on fact retention because they use both deep and elaborative processing strategies.

A straightforward interpretation of these results is that the deep and elaborative processing scales reflect study strategies used by high-GPA students and these strategies explain why they do better in school. However, other interpretations of these data are possible. Perhaps the most obvious alternative is that high-GPA students are brighter than low-GPA students and brighter students tend

Table 12.13. Differences between high- and low-GPA students on four scales of learning processes. An asterisk signifies a significant difference. (Adapted from Schmeck and Grove, 1979.)

SCALE	TOTAL POSSIBLE ON SCALE	AVERAGE SCORE LOW GPA	AVERAGE SCORE HIGH GPA
Deep processing	18	10.40	12.58*
Methodical study	23	10.15	10.57
Fact retention	7	4.26	5.11*
Elaborative processing	14	9.80	10.53*

to process information more deeply. That is, there may be no causal relationship between learning strategies reported and GPA. However, Ribich (1977) found an association between the deep processing scale and the ability to organize information from a lecture, even when intelligence was statistically controlled.

So far in this section we have looked at studies that suggest that good learners generate more and better elaborations than do poor learners. If we assume that declarative knowledge weighs more heavily in the determination of GPA then does procedural knowledge, then these findings make sense, because elaboration is an effective way to create many retrieval pathways for propositions stored in long-term memory.

Organization Strategies. The other process that leads to effective encoding of declarative knowledge is organization. Spring (1983) has found that successful college students are more likely to organize information than are less successful college students. Also, Thorndyke and Stasz (1980), in their study of map learning, found that good learners were more likely to use organization strategies. For example, they clustered items (e.g., north–south streets) and noted how many elements were in a given group. They then rehearsed this group of elements together. Also, good learners encoded spatial relationships among elements, thus imposing a spatial organization on what they were learning. For example, one good learner noted that Victory Avenue is "below the golf course" and "parallel to Johnson."

Another type of organization strategy is summarizing. Summarizing organizes material by indicating the superordinate-subordinate relationships in a set of information. Brown and Day (1983) have analyzed summarization into a set of five rules and have

examined the frequency with which each is used by various populations of students.

The rules, in order of increasing difficulty, are called *delete trivia, delete redundancies, substitute a superordinate, select the main idea,* and *invent the main idea.* In deleting trivia, as the name implies, one does not include material of lesser importance in a summary. Deleting redundancies refers to not including information in a summary if it has already been included, albeit in a slightly different form. Substituting a superordinate refers either to replacing a list (e.g., "pansies, daffodils, roses") with a category label ("flowers") or to replacing a sequence of actions (e.g., "Sally turned off the alarm clock, stretched, and rolled out of bed") with a more general action ("Sally got up").

The next most difficult rule to use is selecting the main idea, which refers to choosing a topic sentence for a paragraph. This rule is more difficult because it can involve non-sequential processing of sentences, whereas the three previous rules can be applied to each sentence in a text sequentially. Finally, the invent-the-main-idea rule is used when a paragraph lacks an explicitly stated main idea. In this case, the learner must read the paragraph and *construct* a proposition that represents the main idea.

To study the proportion of time that students apply these rules (when appropriate), Brown and Day (1983) had several groups of learners read and summarize, in sixty words or less, two short expository passages. The summaries were scored for the use of the five rules under appropriate conditions. The groups studied were fifth, seventh, and tenth graders, freshmen at a four-year university, freshmen at a two-year junior college, and graduate students in English ("experts").

The results showed that all groups used the two deletion rules, rules about 90 percent or more of the times that they were appropriate. For the more complicated rules, however, age-related differences were observed. Table 12.14 shows some of these differences. For superordination and selection, the seventh graders were slightly better than the fifth graders and somewhat worse than tenth graders and four-year college students, but the last two groups did not differ from each other. For the invention rule, however, the tenth graders did not perform as well as the four-year college students.

Not shown in this table is the interesting finding that the junior college students' performance was between the seventh and tenth graders for these three rules. Thus, although there are age differences in the ability to organize declarative knowledge by summarizing, there is also a wide range of differences in this ability within the same age level.

Study Techniques and Encoding Strategies. The previous section described differences in encoding strategies associated with differences of either age or academic learning skill. The results are consistent with the idea that more able students do better because they organize and elaborate new material more, thus making it more accessible and transferable later on. To improve the learning of less able students, it would be convenient if they could simply be told to engage in certain study techniques that might stimulate organization and elaboration.

Several studies have been conducted to see if simply suggesting a study technique would improve learning (for a review, see T. H. Anderson and B. B. Armbruster, 1984). Some researchers have told one group of subjects to summarize the material being studied and have then compared the recall performance of this group with another group that was not told to summarize (e.g., Bretzing and Kulhavy, 1979; Stordahl and Christensen, 1956). Some researchers have told one group of subjects to outline or map the material being studied and have then compared the recall performance of this group with that of an equivalent group that was not told to outline or map (e.g., Armbruster and Anderson, 1980; Todd and Kesslar, 1971). The results of these studies are mixed, with some finding a beneficial effect for the prescribed technique and others not.

The explanation for the mixed results suggested by Anderson and Armbruster (1984) is that sometimes these techniques do not stimulate "deep processing" (here called elaboration and organization) and when they do not, no beneficial effect is obtained. For example, at worst, a summary can be a random selection of sentences that are copied verbatim from the study materials. Or, an

Table 12.14. Age-related differences in use of summarization rules. Data are reported as the proportion of time the rule was used when it would have been appropriate. (Adapted from Brown and Day, 1983.)

	SUPERORDINATION	SELECTION	INVENTION
5th	.26	.28	.14
7th	.31	.33	.23
10th	.54	.52	.38
4-year college	.55	.53	.46

outline can be a verbatim copy of sentences written in an outline format. Obviously, in these situations students are not elaborating on or organizing material, and so there is no reason to expect improved learning (Glover, Plake, Roberts, Zimmer, and Palmere, 1981).

Apparently it is important for students to learn not an observable behavior (a study technique) but rather a cognitive process. This process may then be implemented by using one of *a variety of techniques*. In a later section of this chapter a program that trains students to use elaboration will be described.

Knowledge of When to Use a Given Strategy

We have just seen that there are many strategies for learning new material. One can generate summaries for new information, or one can think of applications for new information. One can focus on important elements, unlearned elements, or elements from a common category. Given so many choices, how can learners select an appropriate strategy?

One of the most important factors in strategy selection is the learner's knowledge of the criterion task—that is, her or his knowledge of what the test will be like or what future use there is for the material being learned. Many studies have shown that students do better on test items if they expect that type of item than if they do not know what to expect (for a review see T. H. Anderson and B. B. Armbruster, 1984). Knowledge of the criterion task can be communicated by statements about whether the test will be multiple-choice or essay (G. Meyer, 1936), by questions embedded in textbook material (R. C. Anderson and Biddle, 1975), or by statements of objectives (E. D. Gagné and Rothkopf, 1975). No matter how this knowledge is communicated, it appears to induce learners to select more effective study strategies, since students given such knowl-

edge perform better than do uninformed students.

In one study in this area, E. D. Gagné, Bing, and Bing (1977) trained high school students to discriminate two types of criterion task—completion and sorting. The completion task always involved being given a name of some entity and being asked to fill in blanks with several attribute values for that entity (for example, "The shape of the fruit Tarran is _____"). The sorting task involved being given the names of several members of a group and being asked to state the value of a given attribute for each group member (e.g., "Give the shape of each of the following fruits: Tarran_____, Nebon_____, Parfis _____"). Subjects in this study learned to distinguish these two types of criterion tasks.

After this discrimination training, all of the subjects were given a ten-page passage to read and study. The passage consisted of a description of three imaginary planets, which were discussed in sequence. Half of the subjects expected a sorting test and half expected a completion test.

In order to see how expectation influenced organization strategies, the experimenters gave all subjects a free-recall test following reading. The recall protocols were scored for organization. The protocol of a subject who recalled facts about each planet together (e.g., size, shape, color, inhabitants) before moving on to another planet was classified as having a *topic* organization. That for a subject recalling attribute values for two or more planets in a sequence (e.g., the color of Planet *A* followed by the color of Planet *B*) was scored as having an *attribute* organization.

The results showed that subjects who expected a completion test had an attribute organization only 4 percent of the time, whereas subjects expecting a sorting test had an attribute organization 59 percent of the time. Thus criterion task expectations appeared to influence the choice of organizational strategy. It is useful to organize by attributes for the sorting test, because that test requires discriminating the attribute values for various elements.

The selection of an appropriate learning strategy is important because it can determine the effectiveness of an entire study session: if one selects poor strategies, the session will not be effective. Despite this, we know relatively little about strategy selection beyond the fact that it is influenced by knowledge of the criterion task. Specifically, we do not know what distinctions students make among criterion tasks, and then what strategies follow from making these distinctions. A student with an implicit understanding of differences between criterion tasks that measure procedural versus declarative knowledge should be able to select elaboration and organization for tasks emphasizing declarative knowledge, practice and feedback for tasks emphasizing procedural knowledge, or both sets of strategies for tasks requiring both types of knowledge. Whether some students actually have such implicit knowledge is not known.

Another unknown in this area is the developmental sequence for acquiring knowledge about criterion tasks. The majority of studies have used high school and college students, and these subjects clearly do distinguish among tasks. It is not known, however, whether elementary and middle school children make similar distinctions.

Monitoring the Effectiveness of Learning Strategies

One way that learners may find out when a given strategy is appropriate is through monitoring the effects of strategies selected and then correlating success or failure with task conditions. In other words, monitoring sets up the necessary conditions for generalization and discrimination.

In their study of map learning, Thorndyke and Stasz (1980) noted that all of their subjects would stop during study and give themselves tests to see whether they could recall certain map elements. Thus, all of their subjects were monitoring their learning. However, the faster learners were more efficient at monitoring: 81.5 percent of their monitoring was targeted on unlearned elements, whereas only 61.5 percent of the slow learners' monitoring was so targeted. Also, whereas the fast learners were nearly perfect (97 percent) in deciding correctly whether an element needed further study, the slower learners had an accuracy rate of only 82 percent. Finally, when fast learners identified an unlearned element, they immediately studied it about 95 percent of the time. The slow learners immediately studied unlearned elements that they had discovered through monitoring only 75 percent of the time. In short, the fast learners knew where to look for learning deficits, could assess deficits, and were more likely to correct a deficit immediately.

Another study of monitoring shows a developmental trend for this skill. Brown, Smiley, and Lawton (1978) gave four age groups of students two Japanese folk tales to read. The groups were fifth graders, seventh/eighth graders, eleventh/twelfth graders, and college students. After reading, half of the subjects in each age group were asked to write down what they could remember from the story. All subjects were given a list of idea units in each story and were asked either to select the twelve most important idea units or to select the twelve they would most like to have available to them if they were asked to remember the story.

Figures 12.3 and 12.4 show the results of this study. "Naive" and "experienced" subjects were those who had not or had received

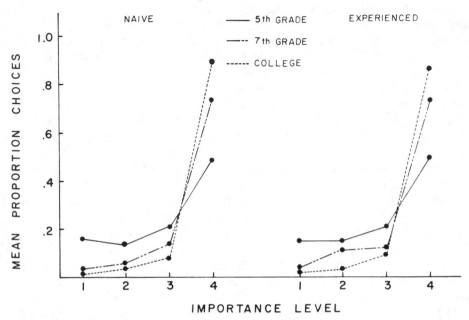

Figure 12.3. The distribution of idea units selected as most important as a function of actual importance. (From Brown, Smiley, and Lawton, 1978.)

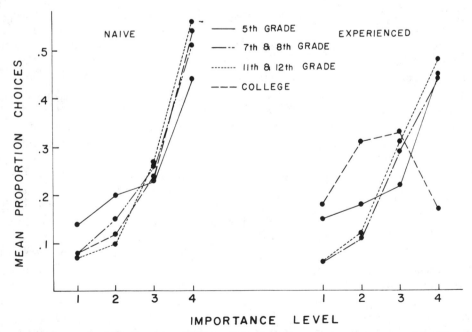

Figure 12.4. The distribution of idea units selected as retrieval cues as a function of importance, experience, and age. (From Brown, Smiley, and Lawton, 1978.)

a recall test, respectively. As you can see in Figure 12.3, all age groups, when asked to select the most important units, selected a majority of units from those that independent raters had identified as being most important. The fifth graders, however, showed less discrimination among importance levels than did the older students. These findings are consistent with other findings reported in Chapter 7 and earlier in this chapter.

In Figure 12.4 notice that the "experienced" college students favored idea units of *moderate* levels of importance. All other groups favored *high*-importance units as retrieval cues. Apparently, the college students have learned from their experience in recalling the stories that they can recall the most important ideas without cues. Therefore, it would be more useful to have less important idea units available during a recall test. Since other studies (Brown and Smiley, 1978) have shown that all of these age groups recall a high proportion of the main ideas from these stories, it would have been just as appropriate for the younger groups to select moderately important ideas for retrieval cues. The fact that they did not suggests that they are not as effective at monitoring their study strategies as are college level students.

Teaching Strategies to Learners

So far in this section on learning strategies, we have seen that successful learners are better than unsuccessful learners at focusing their attention, at elaborating and organizing, and at monitoring their study strategies. These differences lead to the question of whether learning strategies can be taught, and if so, how they should be taught.

In training people to use strategies the emphasis is usually on teaching the action sequence part of the strategy. Students are told the steps in the strategy and are given practice and feedback in following these steps. Unfortunately, not much time is devoted to

teaching pattern recognition. That is, students are not taught to recognize *when* a given action sequence is most likely to be effective. The result of this neglect is that people learn various study techniques so that they can perform them when directed to, but they rarely use them spontaneously.

The training program described here (E. D. Gagné, Weidemann, Bell, and Anders, in press) was designed to teach both the pattern-recognition and the action sequence parts of an elaboration strategy. The program was tried out on some seventh graders during regular school time for fifty minutes a day over ten days.

Cognitive Objectives. Table 12.15 shows the main cognitive objectives of this instructional program, formulated in production-system language. Notice that the condition sides of the productions contain various statements of mental goals (e.g., "If goal is to remember what I am reading"). Mental goals are the hallmark of strategies. Because strategies are procedures directed at achieving one's mental goals, a necessary condition for strategy application is the recognition of a given goal. The action side of the productions describes

Table 12.15. Cognitive objectives for the strategy of elaboration.

IF My goal is to be able to remember target *A*
  And I understand target *A*
THEN Generate elaborations to target *A*.

IF My goal is to generate elaborations to target *A*
THEN Compare target *A* to something else
  Or create an image of target *A*
  Or think of an example of target *A*
  Or think of a superordinate for target *A*.

IF My goal is to retrieve target *A*
  And I cannot
THEN Think of an elaboration generated while studying target *A*.

the mental actions that can be used to elaborate on information. Thus, the main goal of instruction was for the learners to acquire elaboration strategies. This involves not only learning elaboration skills such as comparing and contrasting, but also learning *when* it is appropriate to use these skills.

Overview of the Methods and Materials of Instruction. During the first seven days of instruction, the following sequence typically occurred: (1) The teacher gave a brief explanation of a new idea and wrote important points on the board. (2) Students responded to examples of this new idea in their workbooks while the teacher circulated to provide individual feedback. (3) One or two students told their answers to the whole class, and the teacher gave them public feedback so that all students could evaluate the correctness of their responses. This cycle was repeated for as many new ideas as could be "covered" in a given class period.

The last three days of instruction did not involve the introduction of new ideas but were devoted to practice and feedback on all of the steps involved in the elaboration strategy. During these three days students worked on various practice passages at their own speed. Occasionally, a contest between boys and girls was used to keep motivation high during practice.

The sequence of lesson topics for the ten-day period is shown in Table 12.16. This table also shows the four days of practice given to the control group.

Promoting Generalization. A central idea in developing elaboration strategy is that of elaboration. An elaboration is the product of elaborative processing. It is a thought that is generated by the learner relevant to the target instructional material. To teach this idea, many and varied examples of elaborations were provided throughout instruction. In particular, the examples varied on the type of elaboration (e.g., comparison, image, detail) and on the subject matter. Most of these examples were generated by the learners themselves. Table 12.17 lists some of the materials to which students generated elaborations. During feedback some students read their elaborations out loud and the teacher explicitly commented on how different students' elaborations varied. Thus, generalization of the idea of elaborations was promoted by providing examples that varied widely on irrelevant attributes.

Table 12.16. The sequence of lesson topics for elaboration strategy training and for the control group. (Adapted from E. D. Gagné et al., 1984.)

TOPIC		
TRAINED	CONTROL	DAY(S)
What is an elaboration?		1
Why use elaborations?		2
Good elaborations generate much information		3,4
Good elaborations organize information		5,6
Good elaborations add to main ideas	Practice Session 1	7
When to elaborate		8
What to do when trying to recall	Practice Session 2	8
Practice in deciding whether to elaborate, elaborating,	Practice Session 3	9
and recalling elaborations	Practice Session 4	10

Table 12.17. The variety of textual materials for which students practiced elaboration.

Passages from students' math text

Passages from students' history text

Passages from students' science text

Passages from students' literature text

A shopping list

Directions for the Heimlich manuever

A Superman story

An expository passage on the history of the telephone

Eleven sentences

Two one-paragraph passages

Promoting Discrimination. There was a risk that the students might overgeneralize the idea of an elaboration to some things that were not elaborations. To reduce this risk the students were asked to identify examples of elaborations when these were mixed with matched nonexamples. The workbook exercise requiring this discrimination is shown in Table 12.18. Numbers 2, 5, and 6 are elaborations because they are thoughts that are (1) generated by the learner, and (2) related to instruction. Number 3 is not an elaboration because, although it is a thought that is generated by the learner, it is not related to instruction. Number 4 is not an elaboration because, although it is a thought that is related to instruction, it is not generated by the learner. Thus, these nonexamples each have a different crucial attribute missing. This focused the student's attention on each crucial attribute in turn and hence promoted discrimination.

Promoting Proceduralization and Composition. The elaboration strategy involved several steps and hence was an action sequence. Figure 12.5 shows a flow chart of these steps. Step 1 was to ask oneself, "Do I want to remember this material?" If the answer was no,

Table 12.18. An exercise requiring students to discriminate between elaborations and nonelaborations. The students learned that elaborations must be *self*-generated. (From E. D. Gagné et al., 1984.)

Here are six examples of things that are elaborations and things that are not elaborations. Read each example. In the blank of the left of each example, write E if you think that the example is an elaboration. If you think the example is not an elaboration, write NE in the blank.

E = Elaboration

NE = Not an Elaboration

1. __NE__ A student reads "Columbus discovered America in 1492" and decides she wants to remember it. She repeats in her head, "Columbus discovered America in 1492."

2. __E__ John reads "Columbus was a Spaniard. He sailed to America in 1492." He wants to remember this information, so he thinks, "Columbus most likely sailed West to America because the shortest way to get to America from Spain is to go West."

3. __NE__ Jack reads "Columbus discovered America in 1492. Columbus was a Spaniard." He thinks "I wonder what's for lunch?"

4. __NE__ Susan hears her arithmetic teacher say, "To divide fractions, invert the divisor and multiply." Then the teachers says, "Remember the divisor is what you divide by."

5. __E__ Sally hears her arithmetic teacher say, "To divide fractions, invert the divisor and multiply," and thinks "That's another rule for working with fractions. In the multiplication of fractions, you *don't* invert the divisor, you must multiply."

6. __E__ A student hears his science teacher say, "Molecules are farther apart in gases than in liquids, so gases are lighter." The student thinks "That is like loosely woven cloth is lighter than tightly woven cloth of the same material."

there was no need to elaborate and the strategy was not used. If the answer was yes, then the next step was to ask oneself if one understood the material. If the answer was no, then

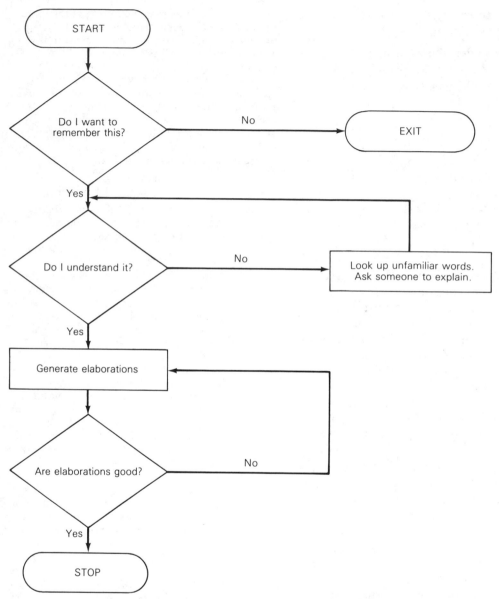

Figure 12.5. The steps in the action sequence for using an elaboration strategy.

it would be difficult to elaborate because elaboration assumes a basic understanding. So the elaboration strategy would be abandoned until some other strategy, such as using a dictionary, led to an improved understanding. Once the material was understood, elaborations were generated.

The goal of instruction was for students to use this sequence for any new reading event. Practice in the first step (recognizing that one wanted to remember something) was given early in instruction. (A sample workbook exercise for this is shown in Table 12.19.) It was assumed that the students were already well practiced in step 2 (recognizing whether or not they understood something), so this step was not practiced in isolation during the ten-day instructional period. Practice in the third step (generating elaborations) was provided on several days of instruction. On the eighth day the three steps were explicitly brought together. After the sequence of steps was described to the students, several practice passages were given over the next few days. At first students were encouraged to refer to their diagram of the sequence as they practiced. Then they were given question cues after reading a passage (e.g., "Do I want to remember this?," "Do I understand it?," "Write down elaborations"). Finally, they were directed to use the elaboration strategy with no cues provided. This sequence of events was selected to encourage first the changing of knowledge from declarative to procedural form (proceduralization) and then the creation of larger procedures from smaller ones (composition).

Was Instruction Effective? This method of teaching an elaboration strategy was compared to a "control" method in which the same practice materials were used and readers were asked questions that caused them to generate elaborations. However, the control group received no instructions in when, why, or how to use elaborations. Thus, the two methods were equated on practice, but there was no attempt in the "control" method to teach the underlying procedural knowledge.

Students taught by both methods were given a posttest in which they studied new material that they expected to be tested on later, but they were not prompted to use the elaboration strategy. Immediately after a study period students were asked what they did to study. Students in the group given instruction in the elaboration strategy were much more likely to use this strategy than were students given instruction with the control method. Table 12.20 shows the frequencies of students reporting the use of elaboration in each group. In addition, the students in the trained group recalled significantly more than did the students in the control groups.

Thus it appears that many students learned the elaboration strategy from this instructional program and furthermore, that elaboration enhanced recall. The program was carefully designed to support generalization, discrimination, proceduralization, and composition processes. From this study one cannot say whether one of these processes was more important than another, as they were not systematically varied. However, an information-processing view of procedural learning would suggest that all of these pro-

Table 12.19. A workbook exercise to teach discrimination of when one does and does not want to remember something.

For each of the following goals decide whether you should think of elaborations or not. Write *E* if you should think of elaborations and *NE* if you should not think of elaborations.

NE   Goal 1: Remember your answer to a math problem the teacher is asking about long enough to raise your hand and say it.

E   Goal 2: Remember the rule for dividing fractions so that you can divide fractions when you're 30 years old!

NE   Goal 3: Read a space odyssey book for fun. Don't care to remember it.

E   Goal 4: Understand the main ideas about how a computer works. Don't know whether you want to remember it or not.

E   Goal 5: Remember some information about early humans so that you can use that information in a high school history class.

Table 12.20. Frequencies of students in the trained and control groups who reported using elaborations while studying on the posttest.

	USE ELABORATIONS	DO NOT USE ELABORATIONS
Trained	8	3
Control	6	12

cesses are important for adequate strategy acquisition.

SUMMARY AND CONCLUSIONS

In this chapter we have explored what is known about strategies for effective teaching and effective learning and we have seen some preliminary demonstrations of successful training of these strategies. An important issue for future research is how to train strategies so that they transfer. We do not know, for example, whether or not the students in the Gagné et al. (in press) study continued to use their new strategies in their regular school work.

The issue of transfer is central for educational research, since formal schooling rests on the assumption that learning in one context will transfer to other contexts. Many of the research questions raised in this book seem to be relevant to the topic of transfer. For example, how procedural and declarative knowledge interact is related to how transfer occurs, since declarative knowledge may mediate the transfer of procedural knowledge. Similarly, how strategic knowledge is supported by other forms of knowledge is relevant to transfer, since strategies may transfer only when there is enough support from other types of knowledge. The conceptual and methodological tools are now available to tackle some of these questions, and the information we gain from the answers will be extremely useful.

ADDITIONAL READINGS

Teaching

Clark, C. M., and P. L. Peterson (1985). Teachers' thought processes. In M. C. Wittrock (ed.), *Handbook of research on teaching* (3rd ed.). New York: MacMillan.

Emmer, E. T., C. M. Evertson, J. P. Sanford, B. J. Clements, and M. E. Worsham, (1984). *Classroom management for secondary schools*. Englewood Cliffs, N.J.: Prentice-Hall.

Evertson, C. M., E. T. Emmer, B. S. Clements, J. P. Sanford, and M. E. Worsham (1984). *Classroom management for elementary teachers.* Englewood Cliffs, N.J.: Prentice-Hall.

Good, T. L. (1979). Teacher effectiveness in the elementary school. *Journal of Teacher Education* 30, 52–64.

Shavelson, R. J., and P. Stern (1981). Research on teacher's pedagogical thoughts, judgments, decisions, and behavior. *Review of Educational Research* 51, 455–98.

Winne, P. H., and R. W. Marx (1982). Students' and teachers' views of thinking processes for classroom learning. *Elementary School Journal* 82, 493–518.

Learning

Brown, A. L., J. D. Bransford, R. A Ferrara, and J. C. Campione (1983). Learning, remembering, and understanding. In J. H. Flavell and E. M. Markman (eds.), *Carmichael's Manual of Child Psychology* (vol 1). New York: John Wiley and Sons.

Curtis, M. E., and R. Glaser (1981). Changing conceptions of intelligence. *Review of Research in Education* 9, 111–48. Washington, D.C.: American Educational Research Association.

Glaser, R. and J. Pellegrino (1982). Improving the skills of learning. In D. K. Detterman and R. J. Sternberg (eds.), *How and how much can intelligence be increased.* Norwood, N.J.: Ablex.

O'Neil, H. G., Jr., and C. D. Spielberger, eds. (1979). *Cognitive and affective learning strategies.* New York: Academic Press.

Weinstein, C. E. (1982). Learning strategies: The metacurriculum in community college teaching. *Journal of Developmental and Remedial Education* 5, 6–7, 10.

References

Adelson, B. (1981). Problem-solving and the development of abstract categories in programming languages. *Memory and Cognition* 9, 422–33.

Akin, O. (1981). *Models of architectural knowledge.* London: Pion.

Ames, C. (1984a). Competitive, cooperative, and individualistic goal structures: A motivational analysis. In R. Ames and C. Ames (eds.), *Research on motivation in education: Student motivation* (Vol. 1, pp. 177–207). New York: Academic Press.

——. (1984b). Achievement attributions and self-instructions under competitive and individualistic goal structures. *Journal of Educational Psychology* 76, 478–87.

Ames, R., C. Ames, and W. Garrison (1977). Children's causal ascriptions for positive and negative interpersonal outcomes. *Psychological Reports* 41, 595–602.

Anderson, J. R. (1976). *Language, memory, and thought.* Hillsdale, N.J.: Lawrence Erlbaum Associates.

——. (1980a). *Cognitive psychology and its implications.* San Francisco: W. H. Freeman.

——. (1980b). Concepts, propositions, and schemata: What are the cognitive units? In J. H. Flowers (ed.), *Nebraska Symposium on Moti-*

vation (Vol. 28, pp. 121–62). Lincoln, Neb.: University of Nebraska Press.

———, ed. (1981). *Cognitive skills and their acquisition*. Hillsdale, N.J.: Lawrence Erlbaum Associates.

———. (1982). Acquisition of cognitive skill. *Psychological Review* 89, 369–406.

———. (1983a). *The architecture of cognition*. Cambridge, Mass.: Harvard University Press.

———. (1983b). A spreading activation theory of memory. *Journal of Verbal Learning and Verbal Behavior* 22, 261–95.

Anderson, J. R., and G. H. Bower (1973). *Human associative memory*. Washington, D.C.: Winston.

Anderson, J. R., P. J. Kline, and C. M. Beasley, Jr. (1980). Complex learning processes. In R. E. Snow, P-A Federico, W. E. Montague (eds.), *Aptitude, learning, and instruction* (Vol. 2, pp. 199–235). Hillsdale, N.J.: Lawrence Erlbaum Associates.

Anderson, J. R., P. J. Kline, and C. H. Lewis (1977). A production system model of language processing. In M. A. Just and P. A. Carpenter (eds.), *Cognitive processes in comprehension* (pp. 271–311). Hillsdale, N.J.: Lawrence Erlbaum Associates.

Anderson, J. R., and L. M. Reder (1979). An elaborative processing explanation of depth of processing. In L. S. Cermak and F. I. M. Craik (eds.), *Levels of processing in human memory* (pp. 385–403). Hillsdale, N.J.: Lawrence Erlbaum Associates.

Anderson, R. C., and W. B. Biddle (1975). On asking people questions about what they are reading. In G. H. Bower (ed.), *Psychology of learning and motivation* (Vol. 9, pp. 90–132). New York: Academic Press.

Anderson, R. C., and G. W. Faust (1974). *Educational psychology: The science of instruction and learning*. New York: Dodd Mead.

Anderson, T. H. (1979). Study skills and learning strategies. In H. F. O'Neil, Jr. and C. D. Spielberger (eds.) *Cognitive and affective learning strategies* (pp. 77–97). New York: Academic Press.

Anderson, T. H., and B. B. Armbruster (1984). Studying. In P. D. Pearson (ed.), *Handbook of research in reading* (3rd ed.). New York: Longman.

Andrews, G. R., and R. L. Debus (1978). Persistence and causal perception of failure: Modifying cognitive attributions. *Journal of Educational Psychology* 70, 154–66.

Applebee, A. N. (1982). Writing and learning in school settings. In M. Nystrand (ed.), *What writers know: The language, process, and structure of written discourse* (pp. 365–81). New York: Academic Press.

Applebee, A. N., R. Durst, and G. Newell (1984). The demands of school writing. In A. N. Applebee (ed.) *Contexts for learning to write* (pp. 55–77). Norwood, N.J.: Ablex.

Armbruster, B. B., and T. H. Anderson (1980). *Effect of mapping on the free recall of expository text*. Urbana, Ill.: Center for the Study of Reading (Tech. Rep. No. 160).

Atwell, M. (1981). *The evolution of text: The interrelationship of reading and writing in the composing process*. Paper presented at the annual meeting of the National Council of Teachers of English, Boston, Mass.

Ausubel, D. P. (1968). *Educational psychology: A cognitive view*. New York: Holt, Rinehart and Winston.

Badian, N. A. (1977). Auditory-visual integration, auditory memory, and reading in retarded and adequate readers. *Journal of Learning Disabilities* 10, 108–14.

Baker, L., and A. L. Brown (1984). Metacognitive skills and reading. In D. Pearson (ed.), *Handbook of Reading Research* (pp. 353–94). Newark, Del.: International Reading Association.

Bandura, A. (1977). *Social learning theory*. Englewood Cliffs, N.J.: Prentice-Hall.

Barron, F. (1963). The needs for order and disorder as motives in creative activity. In C. W. Taylor and F. Barron (eds.), *Scientific creativity: Its recognition and development* (pp. 153–60). New York: John Wiley and Sons.

Bartlett, B. J. (1978). *Top-level structure as an organizational strategy for recall of classroom text*. Unpublished doctoral dissertation, Arizona State University, Tempe.

Bartlett, E. J. (1982). Learning to revise: Some component processes. In M. Nystrand (ed.), *What writers know: The language, process, and structure of written discourse* (pp. 345–63). New York: Academic Press.

Bartlett, F. C. (1932). *Remembering*. Cambridge, England: Cambridge University Press.

Beeson, G. W. (1981). Influence of knowledge context on the learning of intellectual skills. *American Educational Research Journal* 18, 363–79.

Bell, M. S. (1980). *The relationship between a metaphor and its context: Effects on comprehension of the metaphor and the context*. Unpublished masters thesis, University of Georgia, Athens.

Bereiter, C. (1980). Development in writing. In L. W. Gregg and E. R. Steinberg (eds.), *Cognitive processes in writing* (pp. 73–93). Hillsdale, N.J.: Lawrence Erlbaum Associates.

Bereiter, C., and M. Scardamalia (1981). *Information processing demand of text composition*. Paper presented at the Deutsches Institut fur Fernstudien au der Universitat Tubingen, Tubingen, Germany.

Berlyne, D. E. (1960). *Conflict, arousal, and curiosity*. New York: McGraw-Hill.

Berlyne, D. E., and F. D. Frommer (1966). Some determinants of the incidence and content of children's questions. *Child Development* 37, 177–89.

Birnbaum, J. C. (1982). The reading and composing behaviors of selected fourth- and seventh-grade students. *Research in the Teaching of English* 16, 241–60.

Bloom, B. S. (1976). *Human characteristics and school learning*. New York: McGraw-Hill.

Boring, E. G. (1950). *A history of experimental psychology*, (2nd ed.). New York: Appleton-Century-Crofts.

Bousfield, W. A. (1953). The occurrence of clustering in recall of randomly arranged associates. *Journal of General Psychology* 49, 229–40.

Bower, G. H. (1981). Mood and memory. *American Psychologist* 36, 129–148.

Bower, G. H., J. B. Black, and T. J. Turner (1979). Scripts in memory for text. *Cognitive Psychology* 11, 177–220.

Bower, G. H., and E. R. Hilgard (1981). Information-processing theories of behavior. In G. H. Bower and E. R. Hilgard *Theories of learning*

(5th ed., pp. 353–415). Englewood Cliffs, N.J.: Prentice-Hall.

Bransford, J. D. (1979). *Human cognition: Learning, understanding and remembering*. Belmont, Calif.: Wadsworth.

Bretzing, B. B., and R. W. Kulhavy (1979). Note-taking and depth of processing. *Contemporary Educational Psychology* 4, 145–53.

Bridwell, L. S. (1980). Revising strategies in twelfth grade students' transactional writing. *Research in the Teaching of English* 14, 197–222.

Britton, B. K., B. J. Meyer, M. H. Hodge, and S. M. Glynn (1980). Effects of the organization of text on memory: Tests of retrieval and response criterion hypotheses. *Journal of Experimental Psychology: Human Learning and Memory* 6, 620–29.

Britton, B. K., A. Piha, J. Davis, and E. Wehausen (1978). Reading and cognitive capacity usage: Adjunct question effects. *Memory and Cognition* 6, 266–73.

Britton, J., T. Burgess, N. Martin, A. McLeod, and H. Rosen (1975). *The development of writing abilities (11–18)*. London: Macmillan.

Bromage, B. K., and R. E. Mayer (1981). Relationship between what is remembered and creative problem-solving performance in science learning. *Journal of Educational Psychology* 73, 451–61.

Brown, A. L. (1978). Knowing when, where, and how to remember: A problem of metacognition. In R. Glaser (ed.), *Advances in instructional psychology* (pp. 77–165). Hillsdale, N.J.: Lawrence Erlbaum Associates.

Brown, A. L., J. D. Bransford, R. A. Ferrara, and J. C. Campione (1983). Learning, remembering, and understanding. In J. H. Flavell and E. M. Markman (eds.), *Carmichael's manual of child psychology* (Vol. 1). New York: John Wiley and Sons.

Brown, A. L., and J. D. Day (1983). *Macrorules for summarizing text: The development of expertise* (Tech. Rep. No. 270). Champaign, Ill.: Center for the Study of Reading.

Brown, A. L., and J. S. DeLoache (1978). Skills, plans, and self-regulation. In R. S. Siegler (ed.), *Children's thinking. What develops?* (pp. 3–35). Hillsdale, N.J.: Lawrence Erlbaum Associates.

Brown, A. L., and S. S. Smiley (1977). Rating the importance of structural units of prose passages: A problem of metacognitive development. *Child Development* 48, 1–8.

——. (1978). The development of strategies for studying texts. *Child Development* 49, 1076–88.

Brown, A. L., S. S. Smiley, and S. Q. C. Lawton (1978). The effects of experience on selection of suitable retrieval cues for studying text. *Child Development* 49, 829–35.

Brown, J. S., and R. Burton (1978). Diagnostic models for procedural bugs in basic mathematical skills. *Cognitive Science* 2, 155–92.

Brown, R. (1981). National assessments of writing ability. In C. H. Frederiksen and J. F. Dominic (eds.), *Writing: The nature, development, and teaching of written communication* (pp. 31–38). Hillsdale, N.J.: Lawrence Erlbaum Associates.

Bruner, J. S., J. J. Goodnow, and G. A. Austin (1956). *A study of thinking.* New York: John Wiley and Sons.

Burtis, P. J., C. Bereiter, M. Scardamalia, and J. Tetroe (1983). The development of planning in writing. In B. M. Kroll and G. Wells (eds.), *Explorations in the development of writing* (pp. 153–74). Chicester, England: John Wiley and Sons.

Calfee, R. C., P. Lindamood, and C. Lindamood (1973). Acoustic-phonetic skills and reading—kindergarten through twelfth grade. *Journal of Educational Psychology* 64, 293–98.

Campbell, D. T., and J. C. Stanley (1966). *Experimental and quasi-experimental designs for research.* Chicago: Rand McNally.

Carpenter, P. A. and M. A. Just (1975). Sentence comprehension: A psycholinguistic processing model of verification. *Psychological Review* 82, 45–73.

——. (1981). Cognitive processes in reading: Models based on reader's eye fixations. In A. M. Lesgold and C. A. Perfetti (eds.), *Interactive processes in reading,* (177–213). Hillsdale, N.J.: Lawrence Erlbaum Associates.

Carpenter, T. P., J. M. Moser, and T. A. Romberg eds. (1982). *Addition and subtraction: A cognitive perspective.* Hillsdale, N.J.: Lawrence Erlbaum Associates.

Carroll, J. B. (1964). *Language and thought.* Englewood Cliffs, N.J.: Prentice-Hall, 1964.

Carroll, J. S., and R. S. Siegler (1977). Strategies for the use of base rate information. *Organizational Behavior and Human Performance* 19, 392–402.

Carver, R. P., and J. V. Hoffman (1981). The effect of practice through repeated reading on gain in reading ability using a computer-based instructional system. *Reading Research Quarterly* 16, 374–90.

Case, R. (1972). Validation of a neo-Piagetian mental capacity construct. *Journal of Experimental Child Psychology* 14, 287–302.

——. (1978). Intellectual development from birth to adulthood: A neo-Piagetian interpretation. In R. S. Siegler (ed.), *Children's thinking: What develops?* (pp. 37–71). Hillsdale, N.J.: Lawrence Erlbaum Associates.

Cermak, L. S., and F. I. M. Craik, eds. (1979). *Levels of processing in human memory.* Hillsdale, N.J.: Lawrence Erlbaum Associates.

Chall, J., and S. Feldman (1966). First grade reading: An analysis of the interactions of professed methods, teacher implementation and child background. *Reading Teacher* 19, 569–75.

Champagne, A. B., and L. E. Klopfer (1981). Problem solving as outcome in science teaching: Insights from 60 years of experience. *School Science and Mathematics* 81, 3–8.

Champagne, A. B., L. E. Klopfer, A. T. Desena, and D. A. Squires (1981). Structural representations of students' knowledge before and after science instruction. *Journal of Research in Science Teaching* 18, 97–111.

Chapin, M., and D. G. Dyck (1976). Persistence in children's reading behavior as a function of N length and attribution retraining. *Journal of Abnormal Psychology* 85, 511–15.

Chase, W. G. (1978). Elementary information processes. In W. K. Estes (ed.), *Handbook of learning and cognitive processes* (Vol. 3, pp. 19–90). Hillsdale, N.J.: Lawrence Erlbaum Associates.

Chase, W. G., and H. A. Simon (1973a). The mind's eye in chess. In W. G. Chase (ed.), *Visual information processing* (pp. 215–78). New York: Academic Press.

———. (1973b). Perception in chess. *Cognitive Psychology* 4, 55–81.

Chi, M. T. H. (1978). Knowledge structures and memory development. In R. S. Siegler (ed.), *Children's thinking: What develops?* (pp. 73–96). Hillsdale, N.J.: Lawrence Erlbaum Associates.

Chi, M. T. H., P. J. Feltovich, and R. Glaser (1981). Categorization and representation of physics problems by experts and novices. *Cognitive Science*, 5, 121–52.

Chi, M. T. H., R. Glaser, and E. Rees (1982). Expertise in problem solving. In R. S. Sternberg (ed.), *Advances in the psychology of human intelligence* (Vol. 1). Hillsdale, N.J.: Lawrence Erlbaum Associates.

Chomsky, N. (1959). Verbal behavior (a review). *Language* 35, 26–58.

Clark, C. M., and P. L. Peterson (1985). Teachers' thought processes. In M. C. Wittrock (ed.), *Handbook of research on teaching* (3rd ed.). New York: Macmillan.

Clark, H. H., and W. G. Chase (1972). On the process of comparing sentences against pictures. *Cognitive Psychology* 3, 472–517.

Clarke, M. S., and S. T. Fiske (1982). *Affect and cognition: The seventeenth annual Carnegie Symposium on Cognition*. Hillsdale, N.J.: Lawrence Erlbaum Associates.

Cohen, E., and M. Scardamalia (1983, April). *The effects of instructional intervention in the revision of essays by grade six children*. Paper presented at the annual meeting of the American Educational Research Association, Montreal.

Collins, A. M., and M. R. Quillian (1969). Retrieval time from semantic memory. *Journal of Verbal Learning and Verbal Behavior* 8, 240–47.

Collins, A. M., and A. L. Stevens (1982). Goals and strategies of inquiry teachers. In R. Glaser (ed.), *Advances in instructional psychology* (Vol. 2). Hillsdale, N.J.: Lawrence Erlbaum Associates.

Collins, J. L., and M. M. Williamson (1981). Spoken language and semantic abbreviation in writing. *Research in the Teaching of English* 15, 23–35.

Cook, L. K. (1983). *Instructional effects of text structure-based reading strategies on the comprehension of scientific prose*. Unpublished doctoral dissertation, University of California, Santa Barbara.

Cooper, L. A., and A. N. Shepard (1973). Chronometric studies of the rotation of mental images. In W. G. Chase (ed.), *Visual information processing* (pp. 95–176). New York: Academic Press, 1973.

Covington, M. V., and R. G. Beery (1976). *Self-worth and school learning*. New York: Holt, Rinehart and Winston.

Covington, M. V., and R. S. Crutchfield (1965). Facilitation of creative problem solving. *Programmed Instruction* 4, 3–5, 10.

Covington, M. V., R. S. Crutchfield, and L. B. Davies (1966). *The productive thinking program*. Berkeley, Calif.: Brazelton.

Crutchfield, R. S. (1966). Creative thinking in children: Its teaching and testing. In H. Brim, R. S. Crutchfield, and W. Holtzman (eds.), *Intelligence: Perspective 1965* (pp. 33–64). New York: Harcourt, Brace and World.

Curtis, M. E. (1980). Development of components of reading skill. *Journal of Educational Psychology* 72, 656–69.

Curtis, M. E., J. M. Collins, D. H. Gitomer, and R. Glaser (1983, April). *Word knowledge influences on comprehension*. Paper presented at the annual meeting of the American Educational Research Association, Montreal.

Curtis, M. E., and R. Glaser (1981). Changing conceptions of intelligence. *Review of research in education* (Vol. 9, pp. 111–48). Washington, D.C.: American Educational Research Association.

Czepiel, J., and E. Esty (1980). Mathematics in the newspaper. *Mathematics Teacher* 73, 582–86.

Daneman, M., and P. A. Carpenter (1980). Individual differences in working memory and reading. *Journal of Verbal Learning and Verbal Behavior* 19, 450–66.

Diehl, W. A., and L. Mikulecky (1980). The nature of reading at work. *Journal of Reading*, 24, 221–27.

Donders, F. C. (1969). On the speed of mental processes. *Acta Psychologica* 30, 412–31. (Translated by W. G. Koster from the original in *Onderzoekingen gedaan in het Physiologisch Laboratorium der Utrechtsche Hoogeschool*, 1868, *Tweede reeks* II, 92–120).

Duke, D. (1975). The student centered conference and the writing process. *English Journal* 64, 44–47.

Dweck, C. S. (1975). The role of expectations and attributions in the alleviation of learned helplessness. *Journal of Personality and Social Psychology* 31, 674–85.

Egan, D. E. (1983). Retrospective reports reveal differences in people's reasoning. *Bell System Technical Journal* 62, 1675–97.

Egan, D. E., and D. D. Grimes-Farrow (1982). Differences in mental representations spontaneously adopted for reasoning. *Memory and Cognition* 10, 297–307.

Egan, D. E., and B. J. Schwartz (1979). Chunking in recall of symbolic drawings. *Memory and Cognition* 7, 149–58.

Ehri, L. C. (1982, September). *Learning to read and spell*. Paper presented at the American Psychological Association annual meeting, Washington, D.C.

Ehri, L. C., and L. C. Wilce (1983). Development of word identification speed in skilled and less skilled beginning readers. *Journal of Educational Psychology* 75, 3–18.

Elstein, A. S., L. Shulman, and S. A. Sprafka (1978). *Medical problem solving*. Cambridge, Mass.: Harvard University Press.

Emmer, E. T. (1982). *Management strategies in elementary school classrooms* (Tech. Rep. No. 6052). Austin, Tex.: Research and Development Center for Teacher Education, University of Texas.

Emmer, E. T., C. M. Evertson, and L. M. Anderson (1980). Effective classroom management at the beginning of the school year. *Elementary School Journal* 80, 219–31.

Emmer, E. T., C. M. Evertson, J. P. Sanford, B. S. Clements, and M. E. Worsham (1984). *Classroom management for secondary teachers*. Englewood Cliffs, N.J.: Prentice-Hall.

Ericsson, K. A., and H. A. Simon (1980). Verbal reports as data. *Psychological Review* 87, 215–51.

Estes, W. K. (1972). Reinforcement and human behavior. *American Scientist* 60, 723–29.

———. (1980). Is human memory obsolete? *American Scientist* 68, 62–69.

Evertson, C. M., and L. Anderson (1978). *The classroom organization study: Interim progress report* (Tech. Rep. No. 6002). Austin, Tex.: Research and Development Center for Teacher Education, University of Texas.

Evertson, C. M., E. T. Emmer, and J. E. Brophy (1980). Predictors of effective teaching in junior high mathematics. *Journal for Research in Mathematics Education* 11, 166–78.

Evertson, C. M., E. T. Emmer, B. S. Clements, J. P. Sanford, and M. E. Worsham (1984). *Classroom management for elementary teachers*. Englewood Cliffs, N.J.: Prentice-Hall.

Evertson, C. M., E. T. Emmer, J. P. Sanford, and B. S. Clements (1983). Improving classroom management: An experiment in elementary school classrooms. *Elementary School Journal* 84, 173–88.

Faigley, L., and A. Skinner (1982). *Writer's processes and writer's knowledge: A review of research* (Tech. Rep. No. 6). Austin, Tex.: University of Texas, Writing Program Assessment Project.

Faigley, L., and S. Witte (1981). Analyzing revision. *College Composition and Communication* 32, 400–14.

Falbo, T. (1973). The attributional explanation of academic performance by kindergartners and their teachers [Summary]. *Proceedings of the 81st Annual Convention of the American Psychological Association* 8, 122–23.

Feltovich, P. J. (1981). *Knowledge based components of expertise in medical diagnosis* (Tech. Rep. No. PDS-2). Pittsburgh, Pa.: University of Pittsburgh Learning Research and Development Center.

Feltovich, P. J., P. E. Johnson, J. H. Moller, and D. B. Swanson (1984). LCS: The role and development of medical knowledge in diagnostic expertise. In W. J. Clancey and E. H. Shortliffe (eds.), *Readings in artificial intelligence in medicine: The first decade*. Reading, Mass.: Addison-Wesley.

Fisher, C. W., N. N. Filby, R. S. Marliave, L. S. Cahen, M. M. Dishaw, M. M. Moore, and D. C. Berliner (1978). *Teaching behaviors, academic learning, time and student achievement. Final report of Phase III-B, Beginning Teacher*

Evaluation Study (Tech. Rep. No. V–1). San Francisco: Far West Laboratory for Educational Research and Development.

Flanagan, J. C., ed. (1978). *Perspectives on improving education.* New York: Praeger.

Flavell, J. H. (1979). Metacognition and cognitive monitoring. *American Psychologist* 34, 906–11.

Flower, L., and J. R. Hayes (1981*a*). A cognitive process theory of writing. *College Composition and Communication* 32, 365–87.

———. (1981*b*). The pregnant pause: An inquiry into the nature of planning. *Research in the Teaching of English* 15, 229–43.

Fogarty, J. L., M. C. Wang, and R. Creek (1983). A descriptive study of experienced and novice teachers' interactive instructional thoughts and actions. *Journal of Educational Research* 77, 22–32.

Frase, L. T. (1973). Integration of written text. *Journal of Educational Psychology* 65, 252–61.

———, ed. (1982). Special issue: The psychology of writing. *Educational Psychologist* 17, 129–79.

Frederiksen, C. H., and J. F. Dominic (eds.) (1981). *Writing: Process, development, and communication.* Hillsdale, N.J.: Lawrence Erlbaum Associates.

Frederiksen, J. R. (1981). Sources of process interactions in reading. In A. M. Lesgold and C. A. Perfetti (eds.), *Interactive processes in reading.* Hillsdale, N.J.: Lawrence Erlbaum Associates.

———. (1982). A componential theory of reading skills in their interactions. In R. J. Sternberg (ed.), *Advances in the psychology of human intelligence.* Hillsdale, N.J.: Lawrence Erlbaum Associates.

Frederiksen, J. R., P. A. Weaver, B. M. Warren, J. H. P. Gillotte, A. S. Rosebery, B. Freeman, and L. Goodman (1983). *A componential approach to training reading skills.* (Report No. 5295). Cambridge, Mass.: Bolt Beranek and Newman.

Freedman, S. (1981). Evaluation in the writing conference: An interactive process. In M. Hairston and C. Selfe (eds.), *Selected papers from the 1981 Texas Writing Research Conference* (pp. 65–96). Austin, Tex.: University of Texas.

———. (1982). The student teacher writing conference: Key techniques. *Journal of English Teaching Techniques* 12, 38–45.

Freedman, S., and D. Swanson-Owens (1983, April). *Metacognitive awareness and the writing process.* Paper presented at the annual meeting of the American Educational Research Association, Montreal.

Gagné, E. D. (1978). Long-term retention of information following learning from prose. *Review of Educational Research* 48, 629–65.

Gagné, E. D., and J. Anzelc (1984). Individual differences in strategies for using feedback. University of Texas, Austin, Texas: Unpublished manuscript.

Gagné, E. D., and M. S. Bell (1981). The use of cognitive psychology in the development and evaluation of textbooks. *Educational Psychologist* 16, 83–100.

Gagné, E. D., S. B. Bing, and J. R. Bing (1977). Combined effect of goal organization and test expectations on organization in free recall following learning from text. *Journal of Educational Psychology* 69, 428–31.

Gagné, E. D., and E. Z. Rothkopf (1975). Text organization and learning goals. *Journal of Educational Psychology* 67, 445–50.

Gagné, E. D., C. Weidemann, M. S. Bell, and T. D. Anders (In press). Training thirteen-year-olds to elaborate while studying text. *Journal of Human Learning.*

Gagné, R. M. (1962). The acquisition of knowledge. *Psychological Review* 69, 355–65.

———. (1965). *The conditions of learning.* New York: Holt, Rinehart, and Winston.

———. (1974). *Essentials of learning for instruction.* Hinsdale, Ill.: The Dryden Press.

———. (1977). *The conditions of learning* (3rd ed.). New York: Holt, Rinehart, and Winston.

———. (1980). Learnable aspects of human thinking. In A. E. Lawton (ed.), *The psychology of teaching for thinking and creativity* (pp. 1–27). 1980 Yearbook of the Association for the Education of Teachers in Science Education. Columbus, Ohio: ERIC.

———. (1984). Learning outcomes and their effects. *American Psychologist* 39, 377–85.

Gagné, R. M., and L. J. Briggs (1974). *Principles of*

instructional design. New York: Holt, Rinehart, and Winston.

Gagné, R. M., and N. E. Paradise (1961). Abilities and learning sets in knowledge acquisition. *Psychological Monographs: General and Applied* 75, whole No. 518.

Garner, R., and R. Reis (1981). Monitoring and resolving comprehension obstacles: An investigation of spontaneous text lookbacks among upper-grade good and poor comprehenders. *Reading Research Quarterly* 16, 569–82.

Geeslin, W. E., and R. J. Shavelson (1975a). An exploratory analysis of the representation of a mathematical structure in students' cognitive structures. *American Educational Research Journal* 12, 21–39.

———. (1975b). Comparison of content structure and cognitive structure in high school students learning of probability. *Journal for Research in Mathematics Education* 6, 109–20.

Gelman, R. (1969). Conservation acquisition: A problem of learning to attend to relevant attributes. *Journal of Experimental Child Psychology* 7, 167–87.

Glaser, R., and J. Pelligrino (1982). Improving the skills of learning. In D. K. Detterman and R. J. Sternberg (eds.), *How and how much can intelligence be increased?* (pp. 197–212). Norwood, N.J.: Ablex.

Glass, A. L., K. J. Holyoak, and J. L. Santa (1979). *Cognition*. Reading, Mass.: Addison-Wesley.

Glover, J. A., B. S. Plake, B. Roberts, J. W. Zimmer, and M. Palmere (1981). Distinctiveness of encoding: The effects of paraphrasing and drawing inferences on memory from prose. *Journal of Educational Psychology* 73, 736–44.

Glynn, S. M., B. K. Britton, K. D. Muth, and N. Dogan (1982). Writing and revising persuasive documents. *Journal of Educational Psychology* 74, 557–67.

Glynn, S. M., and F. J. DiVesta (1977). Outline and hierarchical organization as aids for study and retrieval. *Journal of Educational Psychology* 69, 89–95.

Goldberg, R. A., S. Schwartz, and M. Stewart (1977). Individual differences in cognitive processes. *Journal of Educational Psychology* 69, 9–14.

Good, T. L. (1979). Teacher effectiveness in the elementary school. *Journal of Teacher Education* 30, 52–64.

Good, T. L., et al. (1977). *Teaching manual: Missouri mathematics effectiveness project* (Tech. Rep. No. 132). Columbia, Mo.: Center for Research in Social Behavior, University of Missouri.

Good, T. L., and D. A. Grouws (1979). Teaching effects: A process-product study in fourth grade mathematics classrooms. *Journal of Teacher Education* 28, 49–54.

Gorodetsky, M., and R. Hoz (1980). Use of concept profile analysis to identify difficulties in solving science problems. *Science Education* 64, 671–78.

Graham, S. (1982). *Communicated sympathy and anger as determinants of self-perception among black and white children: An attributional analysis.* Unpublished doctoral dissertation. University of California, Los Angeles.

Graham, S., and B. Weiner (in press). Teacher feelings and student thoughts: An attributional approach to affect in the classroom. In R. S. Snow, P-A. Federico, and W. Montague (eds.), *Aptitude, learning, and instruction* (Vol. 3). Hillsdale, N.J.: Lawrence Erlbaum Associates.

Graves, D. (1982). *Children learning to write*. Exeter, N.H.: Heinemann.

Graziano, W. G., L. M. Musser, S. Rosen, and D. Shaffer (1982). The development of fair play standards in same- and mixed-race situations: Three converging studies. *Child Development* 53, 938–47.

Greeno, J. G. (1978a). Natures of problem-solving abilities. In W. K. Estes (ed.), *Handbook of learning and cognitive processes* (Vol. 5, pp. 239–70). Hillsdale, N.J.: Lawrence Erlbaum Associates.

———. (1978b). Understanding and procedural knowledge in mathematics instruction. *Educational Psychologist* 12, 262–83.

———. (1980). Some examples of cognitive task analysis with instructional implications. In R. E. Snow, P-A. Federico, and W. E. Montague (eds.), *Aptitude, learning, and instruction* Vol. 2, pp. 1–29). Hillsdale, N.J.: Lawrence Erlbaum Associates.

Groen, G. J., and J. M. Parkman (1972). A chronometric analysis of simple addition. *Psychological Review* 79, 329–43.

Groen, G., and L. B. Resnick (1977). Can preschool children invent additional algorithms? *Journal of Educational Psychology* 69, 645–52.

Gunstone, R. F., A. B. Champagne, and L. E. Klopfer (1981). Instruction for understanding: A case study. *The Australian Science Teachers Journal* 27, 27–32.

Guthrie, J. T. (1971). Feedback and sentence learning. *Journal of Verbal Learning and Verbal Behavior* 10, 23–28.

Guyer, B. L., and M. P. Friedman (1975). Hemispheric processing and cognitive styles in learning-disabled and normal children. *Child Development* 46, 658–68.

Halliday, M. A. K., and R. Hasan (1976). *Cohesion in English.* London: Longman.

Hammerton, M. A. (1973). A case of radical probability estimation. *Journal of Experimental Psychology* 101, 252–54.

Harris, A. J., and E. R. Sipay (1975). *How to increase reading ability.* New York: McKay.

Harris, M. B. (1970). Reciprocity and generosity: some determinants of sharing in children. *Child Development* 41, 313–28.

Harris, P. L., A. Kruithos, M. M. Terwogt, and T. Visser (1981). Children's detection and awareness of textual anomaly. *Journal of Experimental Child Psychology* 31, 212–30.

Haviland, S. E., and H. H. Clark (1974). What's new? Acquiring new information as a process in comprehension. *Journal of Verbal Learning and Verbal Behavior* 13, 512–21.

Hayes, D. A., and R. J. Tierney (1982). Developing readers' knowledge through analogy. *Reading Research Quarterly* 17, 256–80.

Hayes, J. R. (1981). *The complete problem solver.* Philadelphia: Franklin Institute Press.

Hayes, J. R., and H. A. Simon (1977). Psychological differences among problem isomorphs. In N. Castellon, D. Pisoni, and G. Potts (eds.), *Cognitive theory* (Vol. 2, pp. 21–41). Hillsdale, N.J.: Lawrence Erlbaum Associates.

Hayes-Roth, B., and F. Hayes-Roth (1977). Concept learning and the recognition and classification of exemplars. *Journal of Verbal Learning and Verbal Behavior* 16, 321–38.

Hayes-Roth, B., and P. W. Thorndyke (1979). Integration of knowledge from text. *Journal of Verbal Learning and Verbal Behavior* 18, 91–108.

Healy, M. K. (1981). Purpose in learning to write: An approach to writing in three curriculum areas. In C. H. Frederiksen and J. F. Dominic (eds.), *Writing: Process, development, and communication* (pp. 223–33). Hillsdale, N.J.: Lawrence Erlbaum Associates.

Heider, F. (1958). *The psychology of interpersonal relations.* New York: John Wiley and Sons.

Heller, J. I., and J. G. Greeno (1978). *Semantic processing in arithmetic word problem solving.* Paper presented at the Midwestern Psychological Association Convention, Chicago.

Hill, C. C. (1979). *Problem solving: Learning and teaching (an annotated bibliography).* New York: Nichols.

Hogaboam, T. W., and J. W. Pelligrino (1978). Hunting for individual differences in cognitive processes: Verbal ability and semantic processing of pictures and words. *Memory and Cognition* 6, 189–93.

Holley, C. D., D. F. Dansereau, B. A. McDonald, J. C. Garland, and K. W. Collins (1979). Evaluation of a hierarchical mapping technique as an aid to prose processing. *Contemporary Educational Psychology,* 4, 227–37.

Houlihan, D. M., and H. P. Ginsburg (1981). The addition methods of first- and second-grade children. *Journal for Research in Mathematics Education* 12, 95–106.

Housner, L. D., and D. C. Griffey (1983, April). *Teacher cognition: Differences in planning and interactive decision making between experienced and inexperienced teachers.* Paper presented at the American Educational Research Association annual meeting, Montreal.

Houtz, J. C., J. W. Moore, and J. K. Davis (1972). Effects of different types of positive and negative instances in learning ''nondimensional'' concepts. *Journal of Educational Psychology* 63, 206–11.

Humes, A. (1983). Research on the composing process. *Review of Educational Research* 53, 201–16.

Hunt, E. B., J. Davidson, and M. Lansman (1981). Individual differences in long-term memory access. *Memory and Cognition* 9, 599–608.

Hunt, E. B., C. Lunneborg, and J. Lewis (1975). What does it mean to be high verbal? *Cognitive Psychology* 7, 194–227.

Huss, M. (1970). An international challenge. In D. Braken and S. E. Malmquist (eds.), *Improving reading ability around the world*. Newark, Del.: International Reading Association.

Inman, W. (1977). *Classroom practices and basic skills: Kindergarten and third grade*. Raleigh, N.C.: Division of Research, North Carolina State Department of Public Instruction.

James, W. (1890). *Principles of psychology* (Vol. 1). New York: H. Holt.

James, W., and J. B. Rotter (1958). Partial and 100% reinforcement under chance and skill conditions. *Journal of Experimental Psychology* 55, 397–403.

Johnson-Laird, P. N., P. Legrenzi, and M. S. Legrenzi (1972). Reasoning and a sense of reality. *British Journal of Psychology* 63, 395–400.

Johnson-Laird, P. N., and P. C. Wason, eds. (1977). *Thinking: Readings in cognitive science*. Cambridge, England: Cambridge University Press.

Just, M. A., and P. A. Carpenter, eds. (1977). *Cognitive processes in comprehension*. Hillsdale, N.J.: Lawrence Erlbaum Associates.

——. (1980). A theory of reading: From eye fixations to comprehension. *Psychological Review* 87, 329–54.

Kahneman, D., and A. Tversky (1973). On the psychology of prediction. *Psychological Review* 80, 237–51.

Kassin, S. M. (1979). Consensus information, prediction, and causal attribution: A review of the literature and issues. *Journal of Personality and Social Psychology* 37, 1966–81.

Kemeny, J. G. (1955). Man viewed as machine. *Scientific American* 192, 58–67.

Kerst, S. M., and J. H. Howard, Jr. (1977). Mental comparisons for ordered information on abstract and concrete dimensions. *Memory and Cognition* 5, 227–34.

King, M. L., and V. M. Rentel (1981). Research Update: Conveying meaning in written texts. *Language Arts* 58, 721–28.

Kintsch, W. (1977). On comprehending stories. In M. A. Just and P. A. Carpenter (eds.), *Cognitive processes in comprehension* (pp. 33–62). Hillsdale, N.J.: Lawrence Erlbaum Associates.

——. (1979). On modeling comprehension. *Educational Psychologist* 14, 3–14.

Kintsch, W., and T. A. van Dijk (1978). Toward a model of text comprehension and production. *Psychological Review* 85, 363–94.

Klatzky, Roberta L. (1975). *Human memory: Structures and processes*. San Francisco: W. H. Freeman.

——. (1980). *Human memory: Structures and processes* (2nd ed.). San Francisco: W. H. Freeman.

Klausmeier, H. J., and K. V. Feldman (1975). Effects of a definition and varying numbers of examples and nonexamples on concept attainment. *Journal of Educational Psychology* 67, 174–78.

Koestler, A. (1964). *The act of creation*. New York: Macmillan.

Kosslyn, S. M., T. M. Ball, and B. J. Reiser (1978). Visual images preserve spatial information: Evidence from studies of image scanning. *Journal of Experimental Psychology: Human Perception and Performance* 4, 47–60.

Kroll, B. M., and G. Wells, eds. (1983). *Explorations in the development of writing*. Chicester, England: John Wiley and Sons.

Kulhavy, R. W. (1977). Feedback in written instruction. *Review of Educational Research* 47, 211–32.

Kulhavy, R. W., and I. Swenson (1975). Imagery instructions and the comprehension of text. *British Journal of Educational Psychology* 45, 47–51.

LaBerge, D., and S. J. Samuels (1974). Toward a theory of automatic information processing in reading. *Cognitive Psychology* 6, 293–323.

Landauer, T. K., and D. E. Meyer (1972). Category size and semantic memory retrieval. *Journal of Verbal Learning and Verbal Behavior* 11, 539–49.

Larkin, J. H. (1981). Cognition of learning physics. *American Journal of Physics* 49, 534–41.

Larkin, J. H., J. McDermott, D. P. Simon, and H. A. Simon (1980a). Expert and novice performance in solving physics problems. *Science* 208, 1335–42.

———. (1980b). Models of competence in solving physics problems. *Cognitive Science* 4, 317–45.

Leahey, T. H. (1980). *A history of psychology.* Englewood Cliffs, N.J.: Prentice-Hall.

Leinhardt, G. (1983, April). *Overview of a program of research on teachers' and students' routines, thoughts, and execution of plans.* Paper presented at the annual meeting of the American Educational Research Association, Montreal.

Lesgold, A. M., and C. A. Perfetti (1981). *Interactive processes in reading.* Hillsdale, N.J.: Lawrence Erlbaum Associates.

Levin, J. R., M. Pressley, C. B. McCormick, G. E. Miller, and L. K. Shriberg (1979). Assessing the classroom potential of the keyword method. *Journal of Educational Psychology* 71, 583–94.

Lewis, C. (1981). Skill in algebra. In J. R. Anderson (ed.). *Cognitive skills and their acquisition* (pp. 85–110). Hillsdale, N.J.: Lawrence Erlbaum Associates.

Lewis, C. H. (1978). *Production system models of practice effects.* Unpublished doctoral dissertation, University of Michigan, Ann Arbor.

Linden, M., and M. C. Wittrock (1981). The teaching of reading comprehension according to the model of generative learning. *Reading Research Quarterly* 17, 44–57.

Lippett, R. R., N. Polansky, and S. Rosen (1952). The dynamics power. *Human Relations* 5, 37–64.

Loftus, G. R., and E. F. Loftus (1976). *Human memory: The processing of information.* Hillsdale, N.J.: Lawrence Erlbaum Associates.

Luchins, A. S. (1942). Mechanization in problem solving. *Psychological Monographs* 54, No. 248.

Manelis, L., and F. R. Yehovich (1984). Analysis of expository prose and its relation to learning. *Journal of Structural Learning* 8, 29–44.

Maerhoff, G. I. (1983, January 9). Teaching to think: A new emphasis. *The New York Times*, Section 12, pp. 1, 37.

Mansfield, R. S., T. V. Busse, and E. J. Krepelka (1978). The effectiveness of creativity training. *Review of Educational Research* 48, 517–36.

Markle, S. M. (1975, June). They teach concepts don't they? *Educational Researcher* 4, 3–9.

Markle, S. M., and P. W. Tiemann (1969). *Really understanding concepts.* Champaign, Ill: Stipes.

Markman, E. (1979). Realizing that you don't understand: Elementary school children's awareness of inconsistencies. *Child Development* 50, 643–55.

Marshall, J. D. (1984). Process and product: Case studies of writing in two content areas. In A. N. Applebee (ed.), *Contexts for learning to write* (pp. 149–68). Norwood, N.J.: Ablex.

Mayer, R. E. (1975). Different problem-solving competencies established in learning computer programming with and without meaningful models. *Journal of Educational Psychology* 67, 725–34.

———. (1976). Some conditions of meaningful learning for computer programming: Advance organizers and subject control of frame order. *Journal of Educational Psychology* 68, 143–50.

———. (1980). Elaboration techniques that increase the meaningfulness of technical text: An experimental test of a learning strategy hypothesis. *Journal of Educational Psychology* 72, 770–84.

———. (1981). Frequency norms and structural analysis of algebra story problems into families, categories, and templates. *Instructional Science* 10, 135–75.

———. (1982). Memory for algebra story problems. *Journal of Educational Psychology* 74, 199–216.

———. (1983). *Thinking, problem solving, and cognition.* San Francisco: Freeman.

Mayer, R. E., and B. Bromage (1980). Different recall protocols for technical texts due to advance organizers. *Journal of Educational Psychology* 72, 209–25.

Mayer, R. E., J. Larkin, and J. Kadane (1983). A cognitive analysis of mathematical problem solving ability. In R. J. Sternberg (ed.), *Advances in the psychology of human intelligence* (Vol. 2, pp. 231–73). Hillsdale, N.J.: Lawrence Erlbaum Associates.

McCorduck, P. (1979). *Machines who think.* San Francisco: W. H. Freeman.

McCutchen, D., and C. Perfetti (1982). Coherence and connectedness in the development of discourse production. *Text* 2, 113–39.

Medin, D. L., and M. M. Schaffer (1978). A context theory of classification learning. *Psychological Review* 85, 207–38.

Meudell, P. R. (1971). Retrieval and representation in long-term memory. *Psychonomic Science* 23, 295–96.

Meyer, B. J. F. (1975). *The organization of prose and its effects on memory.* New York: American Elsevier.

——. (1977). The structure of prose: Effects on learning and memory and implications for educational practice. In R. C. Anderson, R. J. Sprio, and W. E. Montague (eds.), *Schooling and the acquisition of knowledge* (pp. 179–200). Hillsdale, N.J.: Lawrence Erlbaum Associates.

Meyer, B. J. F., D. M. Brandt, and G. J. Bluth (1980). Use of top level structure in text: Key for reading comprehension of ninth grade students. *Reading Research Quarterly* 16, 72–103.

Meyer, G. (1936). The effects on recall and recognition of the examination set in classroom situations. *Journal of Educational Psychology* 26, 30–40.

Meyer, W. U. (1970). *Selbstverantwortlichkeit und Leistungsmotivation.* Unpublished doctoral dissertation, Ruhr Universitat, Bochum, Germany.

Miller, G. A. (1956). The magical number seven, plus or minus two: Some limits on our capacity for processing information. *Psychological Review* 63, 81–97.

Minsky, M. A. (1975). A framework for representing knowledge. In P. H. Winston (ed.), *The psychology of computer vision* (pp. 211–80). New York: McGraw-Hill.

Mishkin, M., and H. L. Petri (in press). Memories and habits: Some implications for the analysis of learning and retention. In N. Butters and L. Squire (eds.), *Neuropsychology of memory.* New York: Guilford Press.

Monty, R. A., and J. W. Senders (eds.). (1976). *Eye movements and psychological processes.* Hillsdale, N.J.: Lawrence Erlbaum Associates.

Moore, J. W., W. E. Hauck, and E. D. Gagné (1973). Acquisition, retention, and transfer in an individualized college physics course. *Journal of Educational Psychology* 64, 335–40.

Moran, T. P. (1980). *Compiling cognitive skill* (AIP Memo 150). Palo Alto, Calif.: Xerox.

Moskowitz, G., and J. Hayman (1976). Success strategies of inner city teaching: A year long study. *Journal of Educational Research* 69, 283–89.

Moss, C. (1982). Academic achievement and individual differences in the learning processes of basic skills students in the university. *Applied Psychological Measurement* 6, 291–96.

Murdock, B. B., Jr. (1961). The retention of individual items. *Journal of Experimental Psychology* 62, 618–25.

National Commission on Excellence in Education (1983). *A nation at risk: The imperative for educational reform* (Stock No. 065–000–0017–2). Washington, D.C.: U.S. Government Printing Office.

Neves, D. M., and J. R. Anderson (1981). Knowledge compilation: Mechanisms for the automization of skills. In J. R. Anderson (ed.), *Cognitive skills and their acquisition* (pp. 57–84). Hillsdale, N.J.: Lawrence Erlbaum Associates.

Newell, A. (1973). Production systems: Models of control structures. In W. G. Chase (ed.), *Visual information processing* (pp. 463–526). New York: Academic Press.

Newell, A., and P. S. Rosenbloom (1981). Mechanisms of skill acquisition and the law of practice. In J. R. Anderson (ed.), *Cognitive skills and their acquisition* (pp. 1–55). Hillsdale, N.J.: Lawrence Erlbaum Associates.

Newell, A., and H. A. Simon (1972). *Human problem solving.* Englewood Cliffs, N.J.: Prentice-Hall.

Nisbett, R. E., D. H. Krantz, C. Jepson, and Z. Kunda (1983). The use of statistical heuristics in everyday inductive reasoning. *Psychological Review* 90, 339–63.

Nussbaum, J. (1979). Children's conceptions of the earth as a cosmic body: A cross age study. *Science Education* 63, 83–93.

Nystrand, M., ed. (1982). *What writers know: The language, process, and structure of written discourse.* New York: Academic Press.

Okey, J. R., and R. M. Gagné (1970). Revision of a science topic using evidence of performance on subordinate skills. *Journal of research in science teaching* 7, 321–25.

Olton, R. M., and R. S. Crutchfield (1969). Developing the skills of productive thinking. In P. Mussen, J. Langer, and M. Covington (eds.), *Trends and issues in developmental psychology* (pp. 68–91). New York: Holt, Rinehart and Winston.

O'Neil, H. F., Jr., and C. D. Spielberger, eds. (1979). *Cognitive and affective learning strategies.* New York: Academic Press.

Osborn, A. F. (1963). *Applied imagination* (3rd ed.). New York: Scribner's.

Paivio, A. (1971). *Imagery and verbal processes.* New York: Holt, Rinehart and Winston.

———. (1979). *Imagery and verbal processes.* Hillsdale, N.J.: Lawrence Erlbaum Associates.

Palincsar, A. S., and A. L. Brown (1984). Reciprocal teaching of comprehension-fostering and comprehension-monitoring activities, *Cognition and Instruction*, 1, 117–75.

Parnes, S. J. (1961). Effects of extended effort in creative problem solving. *Journal of Educational Psychology* 52, 117–22.

Parnes, S. J., and A. Meadow (1959). Effects of ''brainstorming'' instructions on creative problem-solving by trained and untrained subjects. *Journal of Educational Psychology* 50, 171–76.

Perfetti, C. A., E. Finger, and T. Hogaboam (1978). Sources of vocalization latency differences between skilled and less skilled young readers. *Journal of Educational Psychology* 70, 730–39.

Perfetti, C. A., and T. Hogaboam (1975). Relationship between single word decoding and reading comprehension skill. *Journal of Educational Psychology* 67, 461–69.

Perfetti, C. A., and A. M. Lesgold (1979). Coding and comprehension in skilled reading and implications for reading instruction. In L. B. Resnick and P. A. Weaver (eds.), *Theory and practice of early reading* (Vol. 1, pp. 57–84). Hillsdale, N.J.: Lawrence Erlbaum Associates.

Perfetti, C. A., and S. F. Roth (1981). Some of the interactive processes in reading and their role in reading skill. In A. M. Lesgold and C. A. Perfetti (eds.), *Interactive processes in reading* (pp. 269–97). Hillsdale, N.J.: Lawrence Erlbaum Associates.

Perl, S. (1979). The composing processes of unskilled college writers. *Research in the Teaching of English* 13, 317–36.

Peterson, P. L., and C. M. Clark (1978). Teachers' reports of their cognitive processes during teaching. *American Educational Research Journal* 15, 555–65.

Pflaum, S. W., H. J. Walberg, M. L. Karegianes, and S. P. Rasher (1980). Reading instruction: A quantitative analysis. *Educational Researcher* 9, 12–18.

Piaget, J. (1967). The mental development of the child. In D. Elkind (ed.), *Six psychological studies.* New York: Random House. (Original work published in 1940).

———. (1980). *Adaptation and intelligence: Organic selection and phenocopy.* Chicago: University of Chicago Press. (Original work published in 1974).

Pianko, S. (1979). A description of the composing processes of college freshmen writers. *Research in the Teaching of English* 13, 5–22.

Polson, P., and R. Jeffries (1978). Problem solving as search and understanding. In R. J. Sternberg (ed.), *Advances in the psychology of human intelligence* (pp. 367–411). Hillsdale, N.J.: Lawrence Erlbaum Associates.

Posner, G. J. (1982). A cognitive science view of curriculum and instruction. *Journal of Curriculum Studies* 14, 343–51.

Raviv, A., D. Bar-Tal, A. Raviv, and Y. Bar-Tal (1980). Causal perceptions of success and failure by advantaged, integrated and disadvantaged pupils. *British Journal of Educational Psychology* 50, 137–46.

Reder, L. M. (1976). *The role of elaboration in the processing of prose.* Unpublished doctoral dissertation, University of Michigan.

———. (1979). The role of elaborations in memory for prose. *Cognitive Psychology*, 11, 221–234.

———. (1982a). Elaborations: When do they help and when do they hurt? *Text* 2, 211–24.

———. (1982b). Plausibility judgments versus fact retrieval. Alternative strategies for sentence verification. *Psychological Review* 89, 250–80.

Reed, S. K. (1972). Pattern recognition and categorization. *Cognitive Psychology* 3, 382–407.

Reed, S. K., G. W. Ernst and R. Banerji (1974). The role of analogy in transfer between similar problem states. *Cognitive Psychology* 6, 436–50.

Reif, F., and J. I. Heller (1982). Knowledge structure and problem-solving in physics. *Educational Psychologist* 17, 102–27.

Reitman, J. S., and H. H. Reuter (1980). Organization revealed by recall orders and confirmed by pauses. *Cognitive Psychology* 12, 554–81.

Reitman, W. (1964). Heuristic decision procedures, open constraints, and the structure of ill defined problems. In M. W. Shelly and G. L. Bryan (eds.), *Human judgments and optimality*, pp. 282–315. New York: John Wiley and Sons.

Resnick, L. B. (1976). Task analysis in instructional design: Some cases from mathematics. In D. Klahr (ed.), *Cognition and instruction* (pp. 51–80). Hillsdale, N.J.: Lawrence Erlbaum Associates.

Resnick, L. B., and W. W. Ford (1981). *The psychology of mathematics for instruction*. Hillsdale, N.J.: Lawrence Erlbaum Associates.

Resnick, L. B., A. W. Siegel, and E. Kresh (1971). Transfer and sequence in learning double classification skills. *Journal of Experimental Child Psychology* 11, 139–49.

Resnick, L. B., and P. A. Weaver, eds. (1979). *Theory and practice of early reading* (Vols. 1–3). Hillsdale, N.J.: Lawrence Erlbaum Associates.

Reynolds, R. E. (1979). *The effect of attention on the learning and recall of important text elements*. Unpublished doctoral dissertation, University of Illinois, Champaign-Urbana.

Reys, R. E., J. F. Rybolt, B. J. Bestgen, and J. W. Wyatt (1982). Processes used by good computational estimators. *Journal for Research in Mathematics Education* 13, 183–201.

Ribich, F. D. (1977). *Memory for a lecture: Effects of an advance organizer and levels of processing on semantic and episodic memory*. Unpublished doctoral dissertation, Southern Illinois University, Carbondale.

Rickards, J. P. (1976). Interaction of position and conceptual level of adjunct questions on immediate and delayed retention of text. *Journal of Educational Psychology* 68, 210–17.

Riley, M. S., J. G. Greeno, and J. I. Heller (1983). Development of children's problem-solving ability in arithmetic. In H. P. Ginsberg (ed.), *The development of mathematical thinking*, (pp. 153–96). New York: Academic Press.

Robinson, C. S., and J. R. Hayes (1978). Making inferences about relevance in understanding problems. In R. Revlin and R. E. Mayer (eds.), *Human reasoning* (pp. 195–206). Washington, D.C.: Winston/Wiley.

Roe, A. (1960). Crucial life experiences in the development of scientists. In E. P. Torrance (ed.), *Talent and education* (pp. 66–77). Minnesota: University of Minnesota Press.

Rohwer, W. D., Jr. (1980) An elaborative conception of learner differences. In R. E. Snow, P. Federico, and W. E. Montague (eds.), *Aptitude, learning, and instruction* (Vol. 2, pp. 23–46). Hillsdale, N.J.: Lawrence Erlbaum Associates.

Rohwer, W. D., Jr., and J. R. Levin (1968). Action, meaning, and stimulus selection in paired-associate learning. *Journal of Verbal Learning and Verbal Behavior* 7, 137–41.

Rose, M. (1980). Rigid rules, inflexible plans, and the stifling of language: A cognitivist analysis of writer's block. *College Composition and Communication* 31, 389–401.

Rosenbaum, R. M. (1972). *A dimensional analysis of the perceived causes of success and failure*. Unpublished doctoral dissertation, University of California, Los Angeles.

Rosenkrans, M. A., and W. W. Hartup (1967). Imitative influences of consistent and inconsistent response consequences to a model of aggressive behavior in children. *Journal of Personality and Social Psychology* 7, 429–34.

Rothkopf, E. Z., and M. J. Billington (1979). Goal-guided learning from text: Inferring a descriptive processing model from inspection times and eye movements. *Journal of Educational Psychology* 71, 310–27.

Rothkopf, E. Z., and E. E. Bisbicos (1967). Selective facilitative effects of interspersed questions on learning from written material. *Journal of Educational Psychology* 58, 56–61.

Royer, J. M. (1980). Theories of transfer. *Educational Psychologist* 14, 53–69.

Royer, J. M., and G. W. Cable (1976). Illustrations, analogies, and facilitative transfer in prose learning. *Journal of Educational Psychology* 68, 205–09.

Rumelhart, D. (1975). Notes on a schema for stories. In D. Bobrow and A. Collins (eds.), *Representation and understanding: Studies in cognitive science* (pp. 211–36). New York: Academic Press.

Rumelhart, D. E., and D. A. Norman (1978). Acretion, tuning, and restructuring: Three modes of learning. In J. W. Cotton and R. L. Klatzky (eds.), *Semantic factors in cognition*, pp. 37–53. Hillsdale, N.J.: Lawrence Erlbaum Associates.

———. (1981). Analogical processes in learning. In J. R. Anderson (ed.), *Cognitive skills and their acquisition*, (pp. 335–59). Hillsdale, N.J.: Lawrence Erlbaum Associates.

Ryle, Gilbert (1949). *The concept of mind*. London: Hutchinson's University Library.

Samuels, S. J. (1979). The method of repeated readings. *The Reading Teacher*, 32, 403–08.

Saunders, H. (1980, January). When are we ever gonna have to use this? *Mathematics Teacher* 73, 7–16.

Scandura, J. M. (1977). *Problem-solving: A structural process approach with instructional implications*. New York: Academic Press.

Scardamalia, M., and C. Bereiter (1983). The development of evaluative, diagnostic, and remedial capabilities in children's composing. In M. Martten (ed.), *The psychology of written language: A developmental approach* (pp. 67–95). London: John Wiley and Sons.

———. (1985). Written composition. In M. C. Wittrock (ed.), *Handbook of research on teaching* (3rd ed.). New York: Macmillan.

Scardamalia, M., C. Bereiter, and H. Goelman (1982). The role of productive factors in writing ability. In M. Nystrand (ed.), *What writers know: The language, process, and structure of written discourse* (pp. 173–210). New York: Academic Press.

Schallert, D. L. (1982). The significance of knowledge: A synthesis of research related to schema theory. In W. Otto and S. White (eds.), *Reading Expository Material*, pp. 13–48. New York: Academic Press.

Schank, R. C. (1982). *Dynamic memory: A theory of reminding and learning in computers and people.* Cambridge, England: Cambridge University Press.

Schmeck, R. R. (1983). Learning styles of college students. In R. F. Dillon and R. R. Schmeck (eds.), *Individual differences in cognition* (Vol. 1, pp. 233–79). New York: Academic Press.

Schmeck, R. R., and E. Grove (1979). Academic achievement and individual differences. *Applied Psychological Measurement* 3, 43–49.

Shannon, C. E. (1962). The mathematical theory of communication. In C. E. Shannon and W. Weaver (eds.), *The mathematical theory of communication* (pp. 3–91). Urbana, Ill.: University of Illinois Press. (Reprinted from *Bell System Technical Journal* 47, 1948.)

Shavelson, R. J. (1972). Some aspects of the correspondence between content structure and cognitive structure in physics instruction. *Journal of Educational Psychology* 63, 225–34.

Shavelson, R. J., J. Cadwell, and T. Izu (1977). Teachers' sensitivity to the reliability of information in making pedagogical decisions. *American Educational Research Journal* 14, 83–97.

Shavelson, R. J., and P. Stern (1981). Research on teachers' pedagogical thoughts, judgments, decisions, and behavior. *Review of Educational Research* 51, 455–98.

Shustack, M. W., and J. R. Anderson (1979). Effects of analogy to prior knowledge on memory for new information. *Journal of Verbal Learning and Verbal Behavior* 18, 565–83.

Siegel, A. W., L. T. Goldsmith, and C. R. Madson (1982). Skill in estimation problems of extent and numerosity. *Journal for Research in Mathematics Education* 13, 211–32.

Siegler, R. S. (1976). Three aspects of cognitive development. *Cognitive Psychology* 8, 481–520.

Siegler, R. S., and D. D. Richards (1983). The development of two concepts. In C. Brainerd (ed.), *Recent advances in cognitive developmental theory* (pp. 51–121). New York: Springer Verlag.

Silberberg, N. E., and M. C. Silberberg (1971).

School achievement and delinquency. *Review of Educational Research* 41, 17–33.

Silver, E. A. (1981). Recall of mathematical problem information: Solving related problems. *Journal for Research in Mathematics Education* 12, 54–64.

Simon, H. A. (1974). How big is a chunk? *Science* 183, 482–88.

———. (1978). Information-processing theory of human problem solving. In W. K. Estes (ed.), *Handbook of learning and cognitive processes* (Vol. 5, pp. 271–95). Hillsdale, N.J.: Lawrence Erlbaum Associates.

Simon, J. G., and N. T. Feather (1973). Causal attributions for success and failure at university examinations. *Journal of Educational Psychology* 64, 46–56.

Simpson, M. E., and D. M. Johnson (1966). Atmosphere and conversion errors in syllogistic reasoning. *Journal of Experimental Psychology* 72, 197–200.

Skinner, B. F. (1938). *Behavior of organisms.* New York: Appleton-Century-Crofts.

Sneider, C., and S. Pulos (1983). Children's cosmographies: Understanding the earth's shape and gravity. *Science Education* 67, 205–21.

Snow, R. E. (1980). Aptitude processes. In R. E. Snow, P-A. Federico, and W. E. Montague (eds.). *Aptitude, learning, and instruction* (Vol. 1, pp. 27–63). Hillsdale, N.J.: Lawrence Erlbaum Associates.

Sperling, G. A. (1960). The information available in brief visual presentation. *Psychological Monographs* 74, Whole No. 498.

Spilich, G. J., G. T. Vesonder, H. L. Chiesi, and J. F. Voss (1979). Text processing of domain-related information for individuals with high and low domain knowledge. *Journal of Verbal Learning and Verbal Behavior* 18, 275–90.

Spiro, R. J. (1977). Remembering information from text: The "State of Schema" approach. In R. C. Anderson, R. J. Spiro, and W. E. Montague (eds.), *Schooling and the acquisition of knowledge* (pp. 137–66). Hillsdale, N.J.: Lawrence Erlbaum Associates.

Spiro, R. J., B. C. Bruce, and W. F. Brewer, eds. (1980). *Theoretical issues in reading comprehension.* Hillsdale, N.J.: Lawrence Erlbaum Associates.

Spring, C. (1983). *Comprehension and study strategies reported by university freshmen who are good and poor readers* (Tech. Rep. No. 12). Davis, Calif.: University of California Basic Skills Research Program.

Stallard, C. K. (1974). An analysis of the writing behavior of good student writers. *Research in the Teaching of English,* 8, 206–18.

Stein, B. S., J. D. Bransford, J. J. Franks, R. A. Owings, N. J. Vye, and W. McGraw (1982). Differences in the precision of self-generated elaborations. *Journal of Experimental Psychology: General* 111, 399–405.

Sternberg, R. J. (1979). Stalking the IQ quark. *Psychology Today* 13, 42–54.

Sternberg, S. (1966). High-speed scanning in human memory. *Science* 153, 652–54.

———. (1969). The discovery of processing stages: Extensions of Donder's method. In W. G. Koster (ed.), *Attention and performance II. Acta Psychologica* 30, 276–315.

Stordahl, K. E., and C. M. Christensen (1956). The effect of study techniques on comprehension and retention. *Journal of Educational Research* 49, 561–70.

Suchman, J. R. (1962). *The elementary school training program in scientific inquiry* (Project #216, Grant #7–11–038). Washington, D.C.: Office of Education.

Suppes, P., M. Jerman, and D. Brian (1968). *Computer-assisted instruction: Stanford's 1965–66 arithmetic program.* New York: Academic Press.

Suppes, P., and M. Morningstar (1972). *Computer-assisted instruction at Stanford, 1966–68: Data, models, and evaluation of arithmetic programs.* New York: Academic Press.

Surber, J. R., and R. C. Anderson (1975). Delay-retention effect in natural classroom settings. *Journal of Educational Psychology* 67, 170–73.

Tait, K., J. R. Hartley and R. C. Anderson (1973). Feedback procedures in computer-assisted arithmetic instruction. *British Journal of Educational Psychology* 13, 161–71.

Taylor, B. M. (1980). Children's memory for expository text after reading. *Reading Research Quarterly* 15, 399–411.

Tennyson, R. D. (1973). Effect of negative instances in concept learning using a verbal-learning task. *Journal of Educational Psychology* 64, 247–60.

Tennyson, R. D., and C. L. Tennyson (1975). Rule acquisition, design strategy variables: Degree of instance divergence, sequence, and instance analysis. *Journal of Educational Psychology* 67, 852–59.

Tennyson, R. D., F. R. Woolley, and M. D. Merrill (1972). Exemplar and nonexemplar variables which produce correct concept classification behavior and specified classification errors. *Journal of Educational Psychology* 63, 144–52.

Thibadeau, R., M. A. Just, and P. A. Carpenter (1982). A model of the time course and content of reading. *Cognitive Science* 6, 157–203.

Thorndike, E. L. (1898). Animal intelligence: An experimental study of the associative processes in animals. *Psychological Review Monographs Supplement* 2 (8–7), 23–31.

———. (1913). *Educational psychology: The psychology of learning* (Vol. 2). New York: Teacher's College.

Thorndike, E. L., and R. S. Woodworth (1901). The influence of improvement in one mental function upon the efficiency of other functions. *Psychological Review* 8, 247–61.

Thorndyke, P. W. (1977). Cognitive structures in comprehension and memory of narrative discourse. *Cognitive Psychology* 9, 77–110.

Thorndyke, P. W., and C. Stasz (1980). Individual differences in procedures for knowledge acquisition from maps. *Cognitive Psychology* 12, 137–75.

Todd, W., and C. C. Kesslar (1971). Influence of response mode, sex, reading ability and level of difficulty on four measures of recall of meaningful written material. *Journal of Educational Psychology* 62, 229–34.

Torrance, E. P. (1972). Can we teach children to think creatively? *Journal of Creative Behavior* 6, 114–43.

———. (1981). Predicting the creativity of elementary school children—and the teacher who "made a difference." *Gifted Child Quarterly* 25, 55–62.

Torshen, K. P. (1977). *The mastery approach to competency-based education.* New York: Academic Press, 1977.

Tulving, E., and W. Donaldson, eds. (1972). *Organization of memory.* New York: Academic Press.

Tuma, D. T., and F. S. Rief, eds. (1980). *Problem solving and education.* Hillsdale, N.J.: Lawrence Erlbaum Associates.

Tversky, A., and D. Kahneman (1974). Judgments under uncertainty: Heuristics and biases. *Science* 85, 1124–31.

———. (1983). Extensional versus intuitive reasoning: The conjunction fallacy in probability judgment. *Psychological Review* 90, 293–315.

Valle, V. A., and I. H. Frieze (1976). Stability of causal attributions as a mediator in changing expectations for success. *Journal of Personality and Social Psychology* 33, 579–87.

Venezky, R. L., and D. Johnson (1973). Development of two letter-sound patterns in grades one through three. *Journal of Educational Psychology* 64, 109–15.

Vinner, S., R. Hershkowitz, and M. Bruckheimer (1981). Some cognitive factors as causes of mistakes in the addition of fractions. *Journal for Research in Mathematics Education* 12, 70–77.

Voss, J. F., S. W. Tyler, and L. A. Yengo (1983). Individual differences in the solving of social science problems. In R. F. Dillon and R. R. Schmeck (eds.), *Individual differences in cognition* (pp. 205–32). New York: Academic Press.

Voss, J. F., G. T. Vesonder, and G. J. Spilich (1980). Text generation and recall by high-knowledge and low-knowledge individuals. *Journal of Verbal Learning and Verbal Behavior* 19, 651–67.

Wang, A. Y. (1983). Individual differences in learning speed. *Journal of Experimental Psychology: Learning, Memory, and Cognition* 9, 300–11.

Wang, M. C. (1974). *The rationale and design of the self-schedule system.* Pittsburgh: University of Pittsburgh, Learning Research and Development Center.

Wanner, H. E. (1968). *On remembering, forgetting, and understanding sentences: A study of the deep structure hypothesis.* Unpublished doctoral dissertation. Cambridge, Mass.: Harvard University.

Wardrop, J. L., W. L. Goodwin, H. J. Klausmeier, R. M. Olton, M. W. Covington, R. S. Crutchfield, and T. Ronday (1969). The development of productive thinking skills in 5th grade children. *Journal of Experimental Education 37*, 67–77.

Wason, P. C. (1968). Reasoning about a rule. *Quarterly Journal of Experimental Psychology 20*, 273–81.

———. (1969). Regression in reasoning? *British Journal of Psychology 60*, 471–80.

Watson, J. B. (1914). *Behavior: An introduction to comparative psychology.* New York: H. Holt.

Weiner, B. (1972). *Theories of motivation: From mechanism to cognition.* Chicago: Markham.

———. (1979). A theory of motivation for some classroom experiences. *Journal of Educational Psychology 71*, 3–25.

———. (1980). *Human motivation.* New York: Holt, Rinehart and Winston.

Weiner, B., R. Nierenberg, and M. Goldstein (1976). Social learning (locus of control) versus attributional (causal stability) interpretations of expectancy of success. *Journal of Personality 44*, 52–68.

Weiner, B., D. Russell, and D. Lerman (1979). The cognition-emotion process in achievement-related contexts. *Journal of Personality and Social Psychology 37*, 1211–20.

Weiner, N. (1948). *Cybernetics: Or, control and communication in the animal and the machine.* Cambridge, Mass.: MIT Press.

Weinstein, C. E. (1978). Elaboration skills as a learning strategy. In H. F. O'Neil, Jr. (ed.), *Learning strategies.* New York: Academic Press.

———. (1982). Learning strategies: The metacurriculum in community college teaching. *Journal of Developmental and Remedial Education 5*, 6–7, 10.

Weinstein, R. S. (1983). Student perceptions of schooling. *Elementary School Journal 83*, 287–312.

Weinstein, R. S., H. H. Marshall, K. A. Brattesani, and S. E. Middlestadt (1982). Student perceptions of differential teacher treatment in open and traditional classrooms. *Journal of Educational Psychology 74*, 678–92.

West, L. T., and N. C. Kellett (1981). The meaningful learning of intellectual skills: An application of Ausubel's subsumption theory to the domain of intellectual skills learning. *Science Education 65*, 205–19.

Williams, M. D. and J. D. Hollan (1981). The process of retrieval from very long-term memory. *Cognitive Science 5*, 87–119.

Winne, P. H., and R. W. Marx (1979). Reconceptualizing research on teaching. *Journal of Educational Psychology 69*, 668–78.

———. (1982). Students' and teachers' views of thinking processes for classroom learning. *Elementary School Journal 82*, 493–518.

Witte, S. P., and L. Faigley (1981). Coherence, cohesion, and writing quality. *College Composition and Communication 32*, 189–204.

Wittrock, M. C. (1974). Learning as a generative process. *Educational Psychologist 11*, 87–95.

Wood, G. (1983). *Cognitive psychology: A skills approach.* Belmont, Calif.: Wadsworth.

Yehovich, F. R., and P. W. Thorndyke (1981). An evaluation of alternative functional models of narrative schemata. *Journal of Verbal Learning and Verbal Behavior 20*, 454–69.

Yerkes, R. M., and J. D. Dodson (1908). The relation of strength of stimulus to rapidity of habit-formation. *Journal of Comparative Neurological Psychology 18*, 459–82.

Yussen, S. R., E. D. Gagné, R. Garguilo, and S. Kunen (1974). The distinction between perceiving and memorizing in elementary school children. *Child Development 45*, 547–51.

Zajonc, R. B. (1980). Feeling and thinking: Preferences need no inferences. *American Psychologist 35*, 151–75.

Zimbardo, P. G., ed. (1969). *The cognitive control of motivation.* Glenview, Ill.: Scott, Foresman.

Subject Index

Author Index